The Liberal Tradition in American Politics

The Liberal Tradition in American Politics

Reassessing the Legacy of American Liberalism

David F. Ericson and
Louisa Bertch Green, Editors

Routledge
New York   London

Published in 1999 by
Routledge
29 West 35th Street
New York, NY 10001

Published in Great Britain by
Routledge
11 New Fetter Lane
London EC4P 4EE

Copyright © 1999 by Routledge
Printed in the United States of America on acid-free paper.

Cataloging information is available from the Library of Congress.

In memory of Joan Greenstone

Contents

Acknowledgments ix

Introduction 1

1 Liberalism and Racism: The Problem of Analyzing Traditions 9
   Rogers M. Smith

2 In Search of Political Development 29
   Karen Orren and Stephen Skowronek

3 The Liberal Tradition in American Politics: A Slow Boat
   to Democracy 43
   Louisa Bertch Green

4 Dew, Fitzhugh, and Proslavery Liberalism 67
   David F. Ericson

5 A "Guiding Principle" of Liberalism in the Thought of Frederick
   Douglass and W. E. B. DuBois 99
   Gayle McKeen

6 Liberal Equality and the Civic Subject: Identity and Citizenship in
   Reconstruction America 115
   Carol Horton

7 Gendered Citizenship: Alternative Narratives of Political
   Incorporation in the United States, 1875–1925 137
   Carol Nackenoff

8 Liberalism, Political Culture, and the Rights of Subordinated
   Groups: Constitutional Theory and Practice at a Crossroads 171
   Ronald Kahn

9 Situated Rationality: A Preface to J. David Greenstone's Reading of
   V. O. Key's *The Responsible Electorate* 199
   Ira Katznelson

Conclusion 211

Notes 215

Contributors 263

Index 265

Acknowledgments

The papers in this volume were prepared for a conference on the liberal tradition in American politics, at the University of Chicago, 23 November 1996. At the suggestion of Benjamin Frankel, the conference was held in memory of J. David Greenstone (1937–1990), who was William M. Benton Distinguished Service Professor in Political Science and the College at the University of Chicago.

The editors would like to express their appreciation to the Division of the Social Sciences and the Department of Political Science at the University of Chicago and to Norman Nie, Professor of Political Science, for their support of the conference. The editors would also like to express their appreciation to the following individuals: Kathy Anderson, John Diggins, Ben Frankel, John Mark Hansen, Charles Lipson, the family of J. David and Joan Greenstone, the participants in the conference whose papers appear in this volume, and Paul Peterson, who chaired the conference.

Introduction

David F. Ericson

Louisa Bertch Green

In 1955, when Louis Hartz published *The Liberal Tradition in America,* he argued that American political development was best understood as the unfolding of a single liberal tradition of ideas.[1] The book established a new paradigm for the understanding of American political development, in contrast to the cyclical view emphasized by Charles Beard and other Progressive historians, who saw American political development as a titanic struggle between alternately victorious democratic and reactionary forces.[2]

Over the last forty years, Hartz's thesis has not gone unchallenged. Indeed, some scholars have argued that another paradigm shift in our understanding of American political development occurred in the 1970s when republican revisionists Bernard Bailyn, Gordon Wood, and J. G. A. Pocock argued that American political development, at least for a time, was best understood as the unfolding of a republican rather than a liberal tradition of ideas.[3] The crux of the difference between republicanism and liberalism, as understood by these historians, was the difference between a politics of virtue and a politics of interests.

In the 1980s J. David Greenstone attempted to bolster Hartz's original thesis against such attacks while at the same time subjecting it to his own deep criticism. Relying on a more nuanced analysis of political language(s), Greenstone argued that American political development was best understood in terms of a dialectic between two types of liberalism. In his final formulation, Greenstone called these two types of liberalism *humanist* and *reform* liberalism, the former emphasizing the individual pursuit of interests and the latter the development of individual human faculties.[4]

More recently, both political scientists and historians have favored a more philosophically synthetic approach, arguing that American political development is best understood not as one tradition of ideas but as multiple traditions of ideas. James Kloppenberg's article "The Virtues of Liberalism: Christianity, Republicanism, and Ethics in Early American

1

Political Discourse," has been highly influential in arguing for a "discursive pluralism" of liberal, republican, and Protestant ideas.[5] Rogers Smith presented a similar argument in "Beyond Tocqueville," and his recent book also promises to exert a strong influence.[6]

The present volume on the liberal tradition in American politics is a contribution to this growing, cross-disciplinary field of research. First, the volume extends the field into new areas of research: African-American thought, proslavery thought, contestations over citizenship during Reconstruction and in the Progressive era, and the cultural dimensions of Supreme Court decision making. Second, it explores the microfoundations of American political development by analyzing the conceptions of rationality and of what is public that are implicit in American political development. Third, it shifts the emphasis in research at least partially from the development of political ideas to the development of political institutions. Fourth and finally, the essays together ask a hitherto unasked question: What does it mean to view American political development through the prism of one or more traditions of ideas and how does that approach advance or, alternatively, impede research? In these ways, we believe the volume accomplishes much of the conceptual work now needed to maintain the field of politics and history on a forward course.

THE ESSAYS

Rogers Smith, "Liberalism and Racism: The Problem of Analyzing Traditions"

In this essay, Smith begins with the observation that "isms" and "traditions" are always the human constructions of either primary actors and/or later interpreters based on evidence of past human words, documents, and deeds. The validity of the constructions varies with the quality of the evidence and its interpretation. The range of such constructions, he notes, is between an explicit tradition, in which participation is self-conscious, and an implicit tradition, which is the construction of scholars looking backward. He cites Hartz's liberal tradition as a scholarly construction in apparent contradiction to racism, which, though it is "not ordinarily treated as an American intellectual and political ideology or tradition," lies somewhere between the implicit and the explicit. Concluding that the scholarly construction of liberalism may yet prove the most useful, he nevertheless calls for its rigorous testing as the dominant explanation in American politics.

Karen Orren and Stephen Skowronek, "In Search of Political Development"

This paper integrates existing approaches to American political development into a common framework, arguing that the focus on liberalism has obscured the task of defining other relevant core concepts such as development itself. Orren and Skowronek survey political, cultural, regime theory, and historical-institutional approaches to American politics before defining development as "the dismantlement or durable displacement of one set of governing arrangements by another set of governing arrangements." They stipulate two phases for development: the wresting of authority from established institutions and the rearrangement of authority among institutions relative to one another. Without both, a change is too fragile to count as development. In this way, Orren and Skowronek seek to explain political development without the necessity of assuming that it is either teleological in nature or guided by a consensual liberal tradition.

Louisa Bertch Green, "The Liberal Tradition in American Politics: A Slow Boat to Democracy"

This essay focuses on parallel observations of her own and other scholars to point out the connections between the slow pace of democratization in the United States (and elsewhere), on one hand, and, on the other, a long-standing absence in the literature of American politics of an analytic concept for what counts as "public." Arguing that the historical liberal emphasis on individual rights and property has pragmatically, but not in principle, overshadowed our vaguer ideas of what is public, Green sets aside the question of whether a policy or interest *should be* public in order to propose an analytic framework for determining the prior question of whether and when a given interest, good, or policy *is* public.

David F. Ericson, "Dew, Fitzhugh, and Proslavery Liberalism"

This paper carves out a position "more consensual even than Hartz himself" by arguing that the proslavery arguments of the antebellum era were not aberrations but rather were based on liberal principles. The first section of the paper canvasses the various proslavery arguments offered by the defenders of racial slavery in the antebellum South, and the second compares Thomas R. Dew's *Review of the Debate in the Virginia Legislature* (1832) to George Fitzhugh's *Cannibals All* (1857). In opposition to Hartz, Smith, Eugene Genovese, and others, Ericson concludes that the primary proslavery arguments were liberal ones. To characterize the arguments of the defenders of slavery as merely "racist" is to dismiss them, not to rebut them. The challenge to liberals is to rebut the defenders of slavery and other forms of inequality on liberal grounds, arguing substantively that liberal principles really oppose, rather than support, such practices.

Gayle McKeen, "A 'Guiding Principle' of Liberalism in the Thought of Frederick Douglass and W. E. B. DuBois"

Focusing on the writings of Frederick Douglass and W. E. B. DuBois, this essay notes that many of the essays in the present volume "point us to views of the liberal tradition in America…as diverse and conflictual." McKeen then takes up "the perhaps unfashionable notion of liberalism as a kind of 'whole'"—not a consensus but a process by which members of a previously excluded group "come to see themselves and to construct their identity as individuals and as citizens." McKeen locates a "guiding principle" in the similar aspirations of both men to create "the best circumstances for all humans to develop their nature and express their diverse qualities" and at the same time enjoy "equal rights and obligations in the creation of those circumstances."

Carol Horton, "Liberal Equality and the Civic Subject: Identity and Citizenship in Reconstruction America"

This paper focuses on the issue of the social construction of the liberal subject, which it frames in partial opposition to Greenstone's bipolarity and Smith's multiple traditions. Horton argues that neither approach is sufficient for a consistent separation of liberalism from ideologies of race, class, and gender. The paper focuses specifically on the contested nature of citizenship during Reconstruction and argues that alternative constructions of the individual citizen—or, more formally, the civic subject—were systematically linked to different definitions of civic equality in this period. Horton finds three positions prominent in the politics of the time: anticaste liberalism, phylogenetic liberalism, and black republicanism. She concludes that the joined analyses of the substance and the subject of competing liberalisms are needed for a fuller picture of their meaning and significance.

Carol Nackenoff, "Gendered Citizenship: Alternative Narratives of Political Incorporation in the United States, 1875–1925"

This essay begins with the claim that understandings of citizenship are historically contingent and also entail unstated assumptions about what renders individuals and groups unfit for citizenship. The essay then examines the Progressive era, a key period during which the prevailing meaning of citizenship in the United States came under sustained attack. Nackenoff interprets this period as one in which Jane Addams and other feminists launched a major challenge to masculinist, autonomy-based understandings of citizenship. Their visions of interdependence and the social ethic helped to redraw public-private boundaries and to redefine both state and citizenship, thus shaping the emerging American welfare state. The impact of their visions, however, was limited by a maternalist "discourse of virtue" that was too closely specified by race and class.

Ronald Kahn, "Liberalism, Political Culture, and the Rights of Subordinated Groups: Constitutional Theory and Practice at a Crossroads"

This essay begins with the observation that defining what constitutes a subordinated group deserving of protection from the courts is far more difficult in the 1990s than it was in the immediately preceding decades. The challenge to the courts is how to define "equal protection" in such a way as to protect the rights of subordinated groups. Kahn considers whether the courts have the constitutional and cultural tools available to meet this challenge. He concludes that they do, but only if the courts and the broader interpretive community reconceptualize the relation between constitutional theory and political culture as part of a theory of "constitutive liberalism." Such a theory would offer a way of defining the rights of subordinated groups superior to the "simplistic" alternatives offered by existing constitutional theories.

Ira Katznelson, "Situated Rationality:
A Preface to J. David Greenstone's
Reading of V. O. Key's
The Responsible Electorate*"*

This essay examines the place of consent and rationality in liberal theory, twentieth-century political science, and American politics. The pivot of Katznelson's inquiry is an unpublished essay Greenstone wrote in 1977 that reevaluates Key's *The Responsible Electorate*. Katznelson endorses Greenstone's, and by implication Key's, argument for a broader notion of rationality than the instrumental notions that prevail in "mainstream" political science. Katznelson views this argument as an important one, not only for contests over "rational voting" but for larger contests over "autonomous agency" within liberal theory. In the end, he proposes "situated rationality" as a potential microfoundation for the study of American politics.

CONTEXT AND OVERVIEW

These papers were prepared for the Conference on American Liberalism, hosted by the Division of the Social Sciences and the Department of Political Science at the University of Chicago, 23 November 1996. For this volume the papers were revised and in some cases rewritten to reflect the discussion and comments in the course of the conference and the subsequent comments of readers of the drafts. The conference was held in memory of J. David Greenstone (1937–1990). Greenstone was William M. Benton Distinguished Service Professor in Political Science and the College at the University of Chicago. He was author of *The Lincoln Persuasion: Remaking American Liberalism* and *Labor in American Politics;* coauthor, with Paul Peterson, of *Race and Authority in Urban Politics;* and editor of *Public Values and Private Power in American Politics.*

For the conference and the essays in this volume, the authors did not take on the problem of defining the terms *tradition* and *liberal*. Rather, in keeping with a philosophical synthesis, the essays form a composite study with historical references. Each author's conception of "liberal" and "tradition" is at least implicit in the essay. Exploring different interpretations and characterizations of tradition was considered more important at this stage than agreeing on definitions. Rogers Smith does take on the concepts of "isms" and "traditions" more explicitly in liberalism and racism; Carol Nackenoff, Gayle McKeen, and Carol Horton at least implicitly support multiple traditions by examining distinct but nonmainstream currents in

American politics; David Ericson makes a case for including antebellum defenders of slavery in the liberal tradition; Ronald Kahn examines judicial decisions, one of the methods by which a liberal society becomes "more liberal," that is, "more generous" in its extension of political rights to groups excluded by one prejudice or another; Ira Katznelson critiques the conceptions of instrumental rationality that have become central not only to liberal theory but to contemporary political science and, according to Kahn, constitutional theory; Louisa Green looks at the slow pace of American democratization, described by Smith more generally and Nackenoff, McKeen, and Horton more specifically, and suggests that the pace has been at least partially the result of not being able to define our narrower traditions and our broader tradition together; and Orren and Skowronek distinguish change from development and suggest that not all steps forward are reversible, a point on which Smith differs. What these studies provide is a great deal of new and new kinds of evidence from which to draw more trenchant generalizations about what political experiences Americans share and do not share and how we can more effectively rationalize our political experiences.

If American history and American politics are coextensive, we can be said to share a tradition in the broadest sense, in the family sense; if we want to say that different experiences and their accompanying intellectual discussions constitute different traditions, then we have plural traditions. With further distinctions available for separating our principles and practices analytically, it will be less important what term we apply to what we are describing: *traditions, currents, strains, varieties,* and so forth. McKeen, for example, has made a case for a "guiding principle" that is characteristic of the African-American cultural experiences of Frederick Douglass and W. E. B. DuBois. The identification of African Americans with this principle shares similarities with Horton's "black republicanism" and with Nackenoff's "discourse of virtue." The experiences they describe are each coherent enough to bear the term *tradition*, though in the largest sense they derive from and are responses to the dominant tradition. Furthermore, there is a strong resemblance among those experiences to Greenstone's reform liberal tradition in its emphasis on the development of the physical and mental faculties of individuals, not only as a way for them individually to gain more independence but as a way for them as a group to learn to demonstrate competences for admission into mainstream politics and society.[7]

If we do not wish to allow into "our tradition" the less attractive aspects—Smith's view, *pace* Ericson's—we can acknowledge that we want different words for the positive and negative aspects, always keeping in mind that positive and negative are from particular points of view at particular times. The question of tradition is much like the question of whether something is art. The answer is a complex matter of both preferences and criteria, in which generally accepted, even professional, criteria may or may not include one's own preferences.

Since the tensions between individual preferences and community well-being are not merely the consequence of one or another theoretic argument but are part of the conditions of social life, how well we integrate them and mediate among them becomes the crucial question in determining the quality of our social life.

Liberalism and Racism: The Problem of Analyzing Traditions

Rogers M. Smith

In the 1950s and early 1960s, Louis Hartz said America was a liberal society.[1] In those same years, Malcolm X said America was a racist society.[2] There was substantial evidence for both claims. More than a generation later, we have yet to achieve any broadly persuasive understanding of whether and how both claims can be true.

In this essay I work toward a view of the character and relationship of liberalism and racism in the United States that builds not only on my discussions of America's multiple traditions but also on the insights of colleagues who employ different frameworks. My conclusion—that it all depends on how we define *liberalism* and *racism*, and that different definitions are defensible for different purposes—seems almost too bland to advertise in advance. I hope, however, that the specifications of the different definitions and aims developed here will usefully illuminate what some of our options are. And fear not: I will provoke disagreement by suggesting that though it's not plainly erroneous to use the term *liberalism* as expansively as many scholars now do, and as I have sometimes done myself, it's not clear what good is accomplished by doing so. Ironically, perhaps, I will endorse using Hartz's definition of liberalism, though not his portrait of American political culture as a whole. By so doing, we can have a definition of *liberalism* that does most of the work Hartz wanted it to do while not being handicapped in our efforts to address other issues as well.

THE DOUBLE CONSTRUCTION OF TRADITIONS

I must begin with the problem of defining "isms" and traditions generally, and liberalism and racism in particular. An introductory anecdote, revealing one source of my past errors: When I was refining the topic of my dissertation, which became the book *Liberalism and American Constitutional Law,* I raised with my supervisor, Judith Shklar, the problem of how to define liberalism. She told me, "Rogers, don't read a hundred books. Lean back, close your eyes, and think what you believe is most fundamental to liberalism, reflecting on all you know about its history and philosophical defenses. Then use that."

I was shocked. Shklar was known above all others for insisting that students *must* read a hundred books, and do so within a week. As many panel participants and job-talk givers knew to their sorrow, she was also a relentless stickler for historical accuracy, especially in the history of political ideas. Her advice seemed startlingly unprofessional and un-Shklarian.

But I took it, eventually deciding that for me, the deepest, most compelling value of liberalism was a concern to enhance the powers for rational, reflective self-governance, personal and political, of all humanity. It was not Shklar's definition of liberalism—too "positive liberty" for her, at least at that time—but she still urged me to use it.

Why? How could it be methodologically correct for a green graduate student to rely on his own definition of a key term such as *liberalism*? Shklar recognized that for my purposes, I didn't really need to find the quintessential definition of liberalism, should there be such a thing. She knew I wanted to argue that what I saw as the deepest problems and aspirations of liberal theory played significant roles in the concrete problems of American constitutional governance. She also knew I wanted ultimately to consider how those specific constitutional and theoretical problems could be better addressed.

In order to do so, I first needed to spell out, not what *liberalism* truly was, but rather what were the beliefs, values, and philosophical and normative difficulties in which I was really interested. With that account in hand, the next task would be to see whether those beliefs, values, and difficulties were as manifest in American constitutional discourse as I thought. But although it was very important for me to provide evidence that the notions I identified were indeed significant factors in the legal realms I was studying, so long as that evidence was there it did not really matter much whether or not I called these notions features of "liberalism." That was just a convenient label for the collection of concepts I was examining, and it was as plausible a label as any. So Shklar thought, and I agreed.

I still stand by most of the resulting analysis. Yet I regret that it was cast so as to imply, as I then unthinkingly believed, that the values and problems I designated as features of liberalism were also the overwhelmingly dominant values and problems of American political thought. That implication now seems to me to be wrong. In one sense, this misleading implication doesn't matter. I was chiefly concerned with those particular problems, and much of the analysis of them holds even if they haven't been as hegemonic as I thought. In another sense, however, the implication does matter. Not only does it suggest a claim I did not mean to defend and now think indefensible, but, more important, it arose because I did not adequately see how much other basic problems in American thought and politics, especially problems of political identity, race, and gender, were crucially interwoven with the issues I was addressing.[3] Still, the definition facilitated some work that was useful, at least to me, and that's not bad.

Indeed, that's what definitions of isms do, or ought to do. The broader point of this story is that isms and traditions are always human creations or constructions, crafted for particular purposes. If they are sufficiently well fabricated, they may help accomplish those purposes; but at the same time, they are likely to be less useful for other goals, just as a hammer is ill suited to serve as tweezers. To understand and evaluate a tradition, like any other human creation, it is helpful to know who made it and why.

Toward that end, we can analytically distinguish two categories of such creators, though these categories are best conceived as two ends of a spectrum rather than as wholly distinct entities. Isms and traditions are constructed both by primary actors and by later interpreters of those actors.

The elements of an ism or a tradition are in the first instance past human words, documents, and deeds—all human constructions. That does not mean they are purely subjective. These constructions are real historical events that, to a considerable degree at least, later scholars can reasonably be said to discover and study, not create themselves. The primary actors who first make a tradition, moreover, always feel themselves to have intellectual and political affiliates of some sort on whose words and deeds they are building and to whom they are speaking and acting, although they may not think of that set of affiliates, past and present, as constituting a tradition. Alasdair MacIntyre suggests in fact that participants in traditions "in good working order" are ordinarily not "aware of them as traditions." The members of a tradition carry on activities and discourses shaped by partly unarticulated, unexamined presuppositions—theological, intellectual, political, social—that they regard as simply the way things are. MacIntyre's claim may be overdrawn, at least in the contemporary world. Many who sincerely espouse particular religious, moral, and political views today are accustomed to presenting themselves as dwelling within and advocating a certain tradition, be it Christian, Platonic, or liberal. MacIntyre also portrays participants in a tradition as conscious that they have "critics and enemies external to the tradition" as well as "internal, interpretive debates" with those they recognize as fellow adherents. Hence the primary actors carrying on a tradition do have some kind of notion of their membership in an ongoing collective endeavor, even if *tradition* is often not their term for that endeavor.[4]

But regardless of how self-conscious participants in a tradition may be of it as a tradition, there can be no intellectual and political tradition without identifiable primary actors engaging in discourses and practices shaped by past and present persons of whom they have some awareness. Hence evidence of who and what primary actors knew as well as what they said and did is always relevant to any claim that a past tradition existed. Unless we can show that some group of people spoke, wrote, and acted in ways we claim to be elements of an ideological tradition, and that they did so with at least some knowledge of each other, then there probably never was any such tradition.

Yet the very fact that participants in a tradition may not conceive of it as such calls our attention to the reality that traditions are often constructed by a second category of persons. The isms we commonly call traditions are frequently constructions made by later interpreters of the thought and actions of others. Today such interpreters are usually professional scholars, such as Louis Hartz or John Pocock, though influential accounts have also come from political journalists, public intellectuals, and even active politicians, figures such as Edmund Burke, Herbert Croly, William F. Buckley, and today perhaps Michael Lind.

The contrast between these two categories of tradition constructors should not be understood as an absolute distinction between those who are the true creators of a tradition and those who merely interpret a tradition created by others. For one thing, the primary participants in a tradition must themselves also regularly make interpretive judgments about which people, beliefs, values, and practices they really feel affiliated with and which are external to them. Furthermore, later constructions of a tradition by scholars or political writers may have considerable influence in shaping how that tradition is perceived and developed by its bearers. Sometimes that contribution to the evolution of a tradition is a goal of writers sympathetic to it, as in the case of the writings of Croly and Lind on liberal nationalism or Michael Sandel on republicanism.[5] But even analysts who conceive of themselves as outside the tradition they study may nonetheless become influential elements in its development. They may be taken up in one way or another by persons who do identify with that tradition and seek to extend it, as arguably occurred with Hartz.

Still, a contrast remains. Primary actors are chiefly concerned to carry on the human ways of thinking, arguing, valuing, and living that constitute the tradition in which they participate, even if they must to some degree interpretively define what those elements are in order to continue them. Later interpreters are chiefly concerned to identify the character and content of the tradition as a tradition, even though they may do so with further ends in view. Hence the interpretive component of their constructions of traditions predominates more than with primary actors, for whom a performance component is central. The main work of later scholars or other interpreters is to decide rather self-consciously what texts, statements, and actions to include as parts of the various traditions they identify, and how to expound the content and relative importance of those elements within the traditions so identified. Even so, such interpreters always make their judgments about what belongs to a tradition and what is most definitive of it with certain problems and purposes in mind. They would not engage in such a rarefied human activity if they did not have concerns prompting them to do so.

It will probably be rather obvious that primary actors in a tradition, who usually conceive of it as at least a fairly close approximation of what is true and good in human life, may well construct it differently from later interpreters, who normally have much more critical distance from it even if they are sympathetic to it. It may be less obvious, but it is equally important to see, that constructions of traditions by later interpreters can also vary quite widely, for good reasons as well as bad. Some analysts are doing essentially the same task more poorly than others. For example, two interpreters might agree that liberalism has been, at core, a set of propositions by certain writers about property rights. One might elaborate this liberalism in ways that plausibly accounted for everything pertinent those writers penned, while the other might ignore large numbers of apparently contradictory passages (including passages that deny that some people can possess those rights). Clearly, the first is doing a better job of interpreting the tradition than the second, at least by one important measure.

More interesting, however, is that some later analysts may interpret an ism or tradition differently than others because they are undertaking quite different but equally defensible tasks. One may be most concerned to explore how far expressive liberties can moderate religious conflicts, instead of how far certain property rights can spur productive market forces. In the course of her inquiry, the first analyst may be led to construct a canon she calls "liberalism" that includes different writers than the property-centered scholar's account and that understands some of the same writers, indeed some of the same passages, in ways that have a different emphasis and content. She will thus probably construct a significantly different understanding or definition of liberalism, which may or may not be generally compatible with the property-oriented one. To be sure, it might help the rest of us if these two writers chose different terms for the canons they construct. Yet *liberalism* may seem the most natural term for the products of both efforts, and we have no reason to assign either one greater title to it. Instead, we just have to pay attention to how they are using the term and why.

We have good reason to be vigilant in that regard because no definition of any ism is likely to be adequate to all purposes. Although there *are* things "out there" to be discovered when we discuss historical ideologies, isms, or traditions, they are never simply in plain, undeniable, and relatively unchang-

ing view, like the Great Wall of China seen from the sky. Even isms that have
had proponents who have actively tried to identify and police their affiliates,
such as Marxism, display far too much diversity and contestation to make
any single definition either wholly authoritative or equally instrumental for
all purposes.

Some isms, moreover, are much more plainly "out there" than others. Let
me suggest that, building on the contrast between the two categories of
constructors of traditions, we can make a further rough-and-ready distinction between a tradition that is openly viewed as such by most of those whom
we might reasonably identify as participants in or bearers of that tradition,
and a tradition that is identified chiefly by scholars or other interpreters looking backward. Such scholars might well discern deep continuities among
political thinkers and actors who may not have consciously recognized
themselves as part of any distinct tradition, even though they had some
awareness of continuities and commonalities amongst themselves. We might
call the first sort of tradition explicit, the second implicit.

The distinction can never be more than approximate. Again, anything we
are likely to label a political tradition, including explicit traditions, will
probably display much historical contestation over its content, so that who
is "in" and who is "out" will have long been disputed even among those who
self-consciously identify themselves as acolytes of that tradition. Conversely,
even in constructing an "implicit" tradition, scholars are not likely to link
together in purely arbitrary fashion people who would utterly deny that they
have anything in common. Credible scholarship builds on connections that
many of the people we place in a tradition either did acknowledge or might
well have acknowledged had the question been raised. Yet it can still be said,
I think, that some traditions are more clearly matters of self-conscious identification by the bearers of those traditions than most, while some traditions
are much more matters of later interpretive construction, usually scholarly
construction, than most. And when a tradition is closer to the latter end of
the spectrum, I submit, we should regard it chiefly as a heuristic device suit-
able for clarifying some issues and not others, rather than as a brute fact of
social experience waiting to be discovered and explained from different
points of view.

LIBERALISM AND RACISM

What, then, of American liberalism and racism? The initial historiographical argument I want to make is that, unlike, say, the rather explicit Thomist
tradition MacIntyre invokes—a tradition he describes as originating in
Aquinas's deliberate construction of a system integrating Aristotelian and
Augustinian traditions—Hartz's "liberal tradition" belongs more on the

implicit, "scholarly construction" end of the spectrum.[6] That fact can be overlooked because *liberalism* is now such a familiar term in academic and political discourse that it can seem to have always been "out there." Racism, in contrast, belongs somewhere in the middle—between explicit and implicit—even though it is now so politically disapproved that we tend not to think of it as a full-fledged ideological ism or tradition at all.

Let us begin with Hartz's liberalism. Far from being conventional wisdom, the construction of a Lockean (or, as Hartz preferred, "Lockian") liberal tradition into which he could plausibly place most American political thought was one of the two most striking arguments of his 1955 book (the other being the "no feudalism" explanation for the pattern he observed).[7] To be sure, much of his argument on both points was anticipated by (more truthfully, derived from) Tocqueville and others. But though Tocqueville saw democratic-republican principles and commitments to individual liberties as pervasive features of American political thought, he did not call them part of a tradition of "liberalism." That was simply not a label he employed. Although the struggles leading up to the revolutions of 1848 may soon have popularized cognate terms in Europe, I believe the term *liberalism* (as opposed to *liberty* or *liberal*) was in fact infrequently used in English-speaking countries until the last half of the nineteenth century. Even then it usually referred to the program of specific political parties—the Liberal Party in England or the Liberal Republican faction in the United States—much more than to any distinct broader tradition in the history of political thought.[8]

In the first decades of the twentieth century, scholars such as L. T. Hobhouse, Harold Laski, and John Dewey began to use the term *liberalism* in something like its current form, that is, as a reference for a connected body of political theorizing and political programs that has roots in Protestantism, carries uncomfortably through Hobbes to Locke, then runs on through continental and Scottish Enlightenment thinkers such as Voltaire and Adam Smith to American revolutionaries such as Jefferson and Madison and nineteenth-century utilitarians such as Bentham and Mill, as well as romantics such as Wilhelm von Humboldt and evolutionary thinkers such as Herbert Spencer. They were portrayed as being united in favor of governments that in practice would allow considerable scope for individual liberties, private "pursuits of happiness," and free-market systems.[9]

But in its early-twentieth-century usages, most writers identified this category of liberalism with policies of considerable laissez-faire. As such, the more left-leaning scholars and political activists who were chiefly popularizing the term often used it critically, though adherents of laissez-faire nonetheless proved willing to embrace the term. Figures such as Hobhouse and Dewey had to reinterpret the term *liberalism* substantially and elaborately before an economically interventionist, redistributive, and eventually racially egalitarian "new liberalism" finally emerged. Still, most saw liberalism as a form of "progressivism," and the latter term remained more common in the United States up through the early New Deal. These efforts to give a new meaning to *liberalism* did, however, prompt more conservative political leaders and writers such as Herbert Hoover to protest that the term should be confined to views stressing not only "political equality, free speech, free assembly, free press, and equality of opportunity" but also traditional forms of "economic freedom." Once this juncture was reached, but only at this juncture, did American national campaigns begin to exhibit the pattern that Hartz's analysis would lead us to regard as the norm. They were contests between candidates who both, at least sometimes, explicitly identified themselves as champions of liberalism, albeit different versions of it.[10]

It was not until the 1920s, at the earliest, that the term *liberalism* began to gain wide currency in American political and governmental discourse. The word was, for example, not used in any federal court opinion to mean anything more than relative liberality or openness until a 1935 Court of Appeals decision, *Strecker v. Kessler*. There the cause of liberalism was contrasted to that of Communism in order to argue that the former was not well served by deportations ordered on ideological grounds.[11] It was not used in a Supreme Court decision until the second flag salute case, *West Virginia Board of Education v. Barnette*, where Justice Felix Frankfurter used it in his dissent to refer to the political tradition of protecting civil liberties, especially religious liberties.[12]

Hence it really was not until, at most, the generation before Hartz, who wrote in the early 1950s, that American scholars, and the educated classes more broadly, generally began to define the "liberal tradition" in the ways we usually do today—as running in its infinite diversity from roots in John Calvin to John Locke to John Marshall to John Stuart Mill to John Dewey, and, in our day, to John Rawls. Until then, few if any Americans in that tradition actually described themselves as bearers of liberalism in this extended intellectual-history sense, though many praised liberty and professed allegiance to at least some of the other figures now placed in the modern canon of liberalism. Nor did books on American political thought use the term.[13] The degree to which eighteenth- and nineteenth-century American political actors and thinkers would have recognized themselves as fellow participants in a tradition properly designated "liberalism" is, at best, a matter of dispute.

Hence, at least in the American context, it seems unwise to act as if the "discovery" dimension of defining liberalism is more central than the "constructive" dimension and to wrangle extensively over what liberalism "really" is or involves. Rather, if we choose to use the term, we should stress how we are defining it and what we hope to accomplish by doing so, as well as why the usage seems historically plausible enough to be justifiable.

I will shortly assess several different scholarly views of liberalism in these ways.

First, a word about racism. Although enormously valuable work has been done on the history of the idea of "race," racism is not ordinarily treated as an American intellectual and political ideology or tradition.[14] The first use of this precise term in an official U.S. government document of which I am aware came in the notorious *Korematsu* decision of 1944, where Justice Frank Murphy in dissent used it to characterize some of the arguments for the Japanese internment camps the Court there upheld. That is certainly its first use by the Supreme Court. The word does not even appear in the fifth edition of *Webster's Collegiate Dictionary*, in use at that time, though *racialism,* defined as "racial prejudice; race hatred," does. Obviously, few Americans would have defined themselves as part of a racist tradition then or earlier, and few would do so since. Scholars, moreover, have not gone far toward constructing such a tradition as a matter of later interpretation.[15]

Yet if *racism* is defined as it is in the 1989 edition of *Webster's Encyclopedic Unabridged Dictionary,* as the "belief that human races" exist and "have distinctive characteristics that determine their respective cultures, usually involving the idea that one's own race is superior and has the right to rule others," there clearly has been a racist tradition in American life, and a rather self-conscious one.[16] Thomas Jefferson defended just these notions in *Notes on the State of Virginia,* though he thought slavery unjustified and favored removing inferior blacks from white America, to engage in self-rule elsewhere if they could achieve it. His arguments for black inferiority were cited by later proslavery politicians from the first Congress onward throughout the antebellum era, and also in a series of scientific works on race (now often dismissed as pseudoscience, but quite respectable and influential in their day). Jefferson was invoked by medical critics of Princeton president Samuel Stanhope Smith's claims in the early national period that racial differences were environmental, then by the founders of the "American school of ethnology" in the antebellum era, Samuel George Morton and Josiah Nott. Nott, in turn, was cited by Darwin in his 1871 book, *The Descent of Man,* which explained racial differences in evolutionary terms. Darwinian and non-Darwinian evolutionary thought was then repeatedly invoked in the U.S. Senate to justify excluding the Chinese and other "inferior races." Eventually it undergirded a series of works "proving" the existence of natural racial hierarchies, such as Madison Grant's *The Passing of the Great Race* (1916) and Carl Campbell Brigham's *Study of American Intelligence* (1923). And the tradition continues: The work of the American school of ethnology, Brigham, and others are cited as reputable antecedents in recent works defending racial inequalities, including Herrnstein and Murray's *The Bell Curve* and J. Philippe Rushton's *Race, Evolution, and Behavior.* Though no scholar has written a book entitled *The Racist Tradition in America* or *The Racist Persuasion,* the material to do so is abundant, as I've tried to show in my own work. Most of its protagonists would probably acknowledge their affiliation with this tradition at least as readily as would those commonly identified as adherents of liberalism.[17]

IMPLICATIONS FOR SCHOLARS

This truncated sketch of American intellectual and political traditions of racial inegalitarianism (read racism) only poses our problem, however. Note that the first great American defender of racial inequality was Jefferson. Virtually all constructions of American liberalism also give Jefferson a highly prominent place (though Michael Lind's is a recent partial exception).[18] Many later figures who endorsed claims that races existed and were highly unequal are also strongly identified with different versions of liberalism, such as Andrew Jackson, Francis Lieber, William Graham Sumner, John W. Burgess, John R. Commons, Woodrow Wilson, and Theodore Roosevelt, to name but a few. What do these undeniable facts mean for whether and how we should construct traditions of liberalism and racism and employ them in analyzing American political culture?

Our choices will depend on what we are trying to do, but some choices nonetheless seem to me to make more sense than others. The reasons for Hartz's choices are familiar. He was overwhelmingly concerned to explain why all socialist alternatives were marginalized and demonized in the McCarthyite 1950s. He defined liberalism in opposition to socialism, as involving, at its core, doctrines of democratic rule constrained by legally protected individual liberties, afforded all human members of a liberal society, that especially stressed market property rights.[19] He thought he could show that the pervasive, unthinking, consensual acceptance of such doctrines formed the major barrier to socialism in the United States.

Note that for this explanation to work, Hartz's definition of liberalism had to remain rather clearly bounded. If liberalism were defined broadly enough to encompass virtually every conceivable political position, it would not be possible to argue that its prevalence worked to limit the nation's political options. It was especially important that liberalism not be defined as including socialism, but as Hartz defined it in 1955 and again in 1964, it also could not include any other position that denied to human beings basic capitalist property rights and economic freedoms.[20]

Hartz's argument worked fairly well when attention centered on white men, as his usually did. But in American history, and even after the end of slavery, most African-American men and most white women did not enjoy the range of basic individual rights, including economic rights, that Hartz's definition of liberalism said they should be afforded if they were viewed as human beings at all, as they clearly were, at least after the Civil War. As I've argued previously, I do not believe Hartz ever succeeded in showing how American racism rested on liberalism as he defined it (and he never addressed sexism at all). Hence I believe that if we define liberalism as he chose to do, we cannot sustain his claims for its overwhelming dominance. We can, however, still discern such liberal positions as elements in American thought, and they remain prevalent enough to help explain why American white men did not consider socialism for themselves more seriously.

J. David Greenstone thought Hartz's account of a liberal consensus could not adequately explain the conflicts Greenstone saw in American political development (though I've suggested he was too hard on Hartz on this point).[21] He did, however, share Hartz's sense that certain important alternatives, especially socialism, were somehow ruled "out of bounds" by the dominant elements of American political thought. Thus he wished to retain Hartz's sense of that specific boundedness in American political thought while leaving room for conflict.

Greenstone's ingenious response was to argue that, due to the impact of Protestant traditions, American liberalism came in two often conflictual forms: "humanist liberalism," which stressed a more negative freedom for people to live freely as they now are, and "reform liberalism," which sought to extend greater liberty to all and to equip them to exercise that liberty, to govern themselves, more ably. This framework does supply explanations for many observed clashes in American history more readily than Hartz's, while preserving his "liberal consensus" explanation for why there has been no socialism.[22]

This framework doesn't, however, capture the presence and role of racism so effectively. Having only the two categories, Greenstone is forced to label those who thought the U.S. government should not attempt to end slavery, but rather should protect and extend it, as advocates of letting the status quo prevail unimpeded, supporters of negative liberty or "humanist liberals." But surely endorsement of slavery and racial hierarchy seems neither humanistic nor protective of the rights and liberties of all (whether negative or positive).[23]

David Ericson has tried to salvage Greenstone's salvage of Hartz by insisting that many of the defenses for slavery represent bows to the widespread acceptance of liberal values. In this he is undoubtedly correct. But that fact does not alter the reality that racist defenses were nonetheless also always present, in Nott, in Thomas Dew, in John C. Calhoun (Nott's chief political ally), and in George Fitzhugh (who criticized Nott, but chiefly for his biblical heresies, not his racially inegalitarian views). Though Ericson claims that liberal arguments formed the "central theme" of proslavery defenses, racism is in fact a *more* persistent theme of the various defenders of slavery (including, on his own evidence, all the ones Ericson discusses) than *any* particular liberal trope, such as property rights or limited government.[24] That persistence of racism must be given at least equal recognition with the frequent reliance on a variety of more liberal claims, a reliance that a multiple-traditions view of American political culture also leads us to expect.

It is also vital to recognize that the problem of American racism cannot be resolved by addressing slavery alone. Jefferson was antislavery, but he thought blacks inferior and favored an all-white America. Later, race-based immigration exclusions, mostly *not* aimed at Africans, and Jim Crow laws proliferated long after the end of slavery. In all these variations, the Hartzian insistence on the pervasiveness of something called "liberalism" still is most plausible when we are looking at why socialism is absent, and least plausible when we ask why racism and sexism are so very present.

In her fine essay "A 'Guiding Principle' of Liberalism in the Thought of Frederick Douglass and W. E. B. DuBois," Gayle McKeen concedes these elements all have to be treated as important constituents of American political culture, while arguing they must nonetheless be seen as part of a larger whole, as Hartz insisted.[25] I do not dispute that they should be seen as part of a political culture that is a larger whole, and I suppose we can still label that whole "liberalism" if we wish—that is, if we redefine "liberalism" as including both antiracist and antisexist *and* racist and sexist strains. Doing so, however, makes *liberalism* distinctly less bounded a term than Hartz meant it to be, and I think it greatly weakens the explanatory power of claims about "liberal consensus." We are, at this point, really defining *liberalism* as synonymous with whatever constitutes American political culture. We just call this whole liberalism because academics since Hartz have made it customary to do so. Our explanation of why there has been no socialism in American political culture, then, becomes *not* that "American political culture is hostile to socialism because liberalism is dominant within American political culture, and liberalism is hostile to socialism," but simply that "American political culture is hostile to socialism because American political culture, the totality of which we call liberalism, is hostile to socialism." Hartz's formulation is verbally preserved, but his explanatory force is lost.

I would prefer instead to call the whole of American political thought and culture just "American political thought" or "culture." I believe we should see Hartz's liberalism as indeed capturing powerful elements within American political culture that can help explain the relative weakness of socialism but that are, in other regards, simply not as dominant as he claimed.

Other scholars, including feminist theorists such as Carole Pateman and students of American political development such as Carol Horton and

Ira Katznelson, wish to preserve Hartz's sense of the fundamental place of liberalism in the United States for different and, to my mind, yet more powerful reasons. Without denying that definitions of liberalism such as Hartz's contain claims for universal human rights that are in profound logical tension with American beliefs in racial and sexual hierarchies, they wish to stress the ways those very liberal tenets are at the same time open to combination with defenses of such hierarchies.

The key claim is that the notions of the individual bearers of rights in liberal doctrines are so abstract and disembodied that they leave unanswered many questions about who is in fact eligible to claim to be rights bearers. As Horton puts it, "liberal discourse" has the "capacity" to "incorporate radically divergent conceptions of the individual subject, as well as his or her fundamental rights of citizenship."[26] All such individuals are supposed to meet certain minimal criteria for rationality and human agency, but what are those criteria? Pateman suggests that liberals necessarily always have "fleshed out" their answers by implicitly making male characteristics, and traditional male privileges, definitive of who is acceptably rational, so that liberal theory is patriarchal at its very heart.[27] Horton advances the more moderate, and to my mind more persuasive, claim that the liberal "bearer of rights" does not logically *have* to be defined in practice by taking men or whites as the implicit standard. But, she insists, liberals do have to provide *some* further criteria to indicate who can and cannot claim to be a full rights bearer. Hence liberalism, a "highly plastic discourse," is inherently open to alliance with racist and sexist views, always in danger of being "fleshed out" by powerful actors in invidious, self-serving, and unjustly inegalitarian ways.[28]

I accept that it is reasonable to construct liberalism as a body of theory or ideology that includes such dangerous openings. Indeed, in *Civic Ideals* I tried to suggest how virtually every American political actor from the founding to the Progressive era offered political visions that intertwined liberal themes with ascriptive notions of identity and status, often by appealing to (unconvincing) alleged differences in rationality.[29] Horton and Katznelson have suggested, somewhat as Ericson does, that these openings are more important to the success of racist and sexist understandings in America than racist or sexist notions taken alone. Katznelson indicates that the role racist and gendered ideologies play in meeting the liberal need for more specific answers about who can bear liberal rights does more to give racism and sexism legitimacy within American political culture than anything else.[30]

Yet on these latter arguments, the abstractness and vagueness of liberal theory about rights bearers means only that it can be allied with racist and sexist views. There is no reason that it has to be. I think those alliances *can* in fact be achieved only by ignoring abundant evidence that nonwhites and women possess rational capacities and potential not substantially different, if at all different, from those of white men. Hence even on the relatively abstract terms of liberal theory, as Hartz defined it, all people have strong claims to be full and equal rights bearers.

At a minimum, I insist there always remains an important tension between the claim that all humans are entitled to certain rights and the claim that some humans are not entitled to those rights, the position of many American racial and sexist ideologies. That tension—I would say contradiction—has often formed the staple of effective protest rhetoric by disempowered groups in America. Our sense of that tension and our understanding of that potential for resistance against racial and sexual hierarchies are both diminished if we treat doctrines that define rights bearers in racist and sexist ways and doctrines that define rights bearers in much more inclusive ways as versions of the same thing, which we label "liberalism."

Furthermore, though I am persuaded that advocates of racial and sexual hierarchies have exploited the openings liberal discourses give them to ally themselves with liberal motifs, I know of no evidence to suggest that such alliances are the key to their success, so that they are riding on the back of liberalism. I think the evidence equally supports the claim that no politicians have prevailed with "pure" liberal positions. Many have ridden the back of racism, and all, I've argued, make *some* concession to the all-too-powerful appeal of illiberal, ascriptive ideologies. Hence I also see no reason to say that multiple elements are present but that the liberal elements are somehow the keys, so that the other elements should be presented as at most adjectival modifiers of a core liberal tradition.

In contrast, I prefer the boundedness of Hartz's definition of liberalism. I would keep it, but give up his too-sweeping claims for an American liberal consensus. Instead, I would like for scholars to use more naturally inclusive terminology for the broader wholes, of which I see his liberalism as but a part. As noted above, I prefer to use "American political thought" as the name for the whole of American political thought, rather than "liberalism." But American political thought did not, of course, begin in America. I suggest, in a modification of Greenstone, that we should view the broadest antecedent intellectual streams from which American political culture derives as Protestant Christianity and Enlightenment rationalism, with Hartz's definition of liberalism as but one version of the latter.

I like the broader term "Enlightenment rationalism" because, though I see racism as contrary to liberalism as Hartz usefully defined it, there can be no doubt that notions of race derive extensively from the efforts of Enlightenment thinkers, including Jefferson, to classify humanity scientifically. Hence Protestantism and Enlightenment rationalism can be seen as the two main antecedent streams out of which emerged the multiple civic traditions I have previously discussed: Hartzian liberalism, modern republicanism, and ascriptive Americanism, that is, conceptions of American identity defined in ascriptive (usually racial, ethnic, and gender) terms.

We now often tend to think of Protestantism and Enlightenment rationalism as fitting together fairly seamlessly and as both militating strongly in the directions of republican self-governance and political liberalism. Those tendencies are part of the legacy of the emphasis on consensus to which Hartz so greatly contributed, and though they are not without truth, they too are misleading. From the outset, the European-descended inhabitants of the British colonies were indeed overwhelmingly Protestant, and among the educated, Enlightenment writings from England, Scotland, and to a lesser degree the continent soon did prove highly influential. But as the career of Jonathan Edwards exemplifies, the philosophical task of joining them was experienced as far from easy. It was, instead, probably the greatest intellectual challenge early American thinkers faced. The many different directions they took defined much of the intellectual and spiritual landscape of the new nation.[31]

Furthermore, as Barry Shain has recently argued, though reform Protestantism provided much of the common vocabulary of civic life in early America and would continue to do so well into the twentieth century, its political implications were far from universally perceived as supportive of republican government or expansive personal liberties. The Puritan vision contemplated thickly communal theocracies, and more latitudinarian Church of England adherents tended also to be loyal subjects of the British monarchy right up to the eve of the Revolution. Many remained so long thereafter, though most of these Loyalists did not remain in the new United States, choosing instead to move to Canada or else return to England. But if devotion to God and king was a natural combination for many American Protestants, it is also true that Protestant anticlericalism provided fertile soil for arguments in favor of individual rights of political as well as spiritual self-governance. Exploiting that potential, Tom Paine argued in "Common Sense" that the Bible showed republicanism, not monarchy, to be the form of government God preferred, and the Declaration of Independence argued famously that men possessed "inalienable" rights "endowed by their Creator." Many revolutionaries agreed that they had a religious mission to create a free but faithful Protestant republic in the New World, a "Christian Sparta," in Sam Adams's words. To some American Protestants, such as Yale president Timothy Dwight, such republics still had to have established state churches, but to others, such as James Madison, both faith and reason urged much fuller religious freedom. Hence Protestantism lent important support to multiple political traditions, initially including monarchism and both more and less liberal forms of republicanism, from the nation's very inception.[32]

The situation was the same in regard to racial slavery and patriarchy, and it would remain so on civil rights issues throughout most of subsequent American history. Protestant Christianity provided much of the language through which slavery was assaulted by Revolutionary-era Quakers and later white and black abolitionists, many of whom also championed women's rights, and it supplied much of the moral energy and the most memorable anthems and rhetorical images of the modern civil rights movement. Yet at the same time, ministers (many trained by Dwight) were the leading antebellum defenders of slavery and patriarchy, allegedly sanctioned by scripture. American churches divided over support or opposition to the South's "peculiar institution" as civil war loomed, and they would go on to provide defenders as well as challengers to the post-Reconstruction Jim Crow system (which also saw a decline in support for equal rights for women). Even in the modern era, Martin Luther King Jr. would write his "Letter from Birmingham Jail" to mainstream religious leaders who had joined to speak out against his civil rights activism, and Southern Baptists in 1998 affirmed support for a subordinate role for women on scriptural grounds. In regard to race and gender, too, American Protestantism, increasingly joined by other religious persuasions, has contributed importantly to multiple political traditions, liberal and illiberal.[33]

The same is true of Enlightenment rationalism. Though the prestige of Enlightenment writings among educated eighteenth-century Americans is undeniable, Enlightenment thinkers in England and Europe long supported constitutional monarchies as ardently as republics. Consequently, Loyalists as well as revolutionaries in the United States could see themselves as enlightened men. The political lessons drawn from Enlightenment rationalist outlooks were always diverse. Moreover, modern republicanism has classical and Renaissance roots, predating the Enlightenment, and these had some independent influence on the new United States. Nonetheless, it is true that after the Revolution only forms of republicanism were tenable in American political discourse (and after 1789 only republican forms of government were constitutional). Most versions of republicanism that Americans advanced from Paine onward clearly expressed Enlightenment rationalist outlooks. But while those facts entitle us to stress the centrality of Enlightenment rationalism for American political culture, they still fall short of supporting strong Hartzian consensus claims. Both liberalism and illiberalism—antislavery, antiracist, and antipatriarchal as well as proslavery, proracist, and propatriarchal beliefs—could be and were articulated in "enlightened" terms. For some American advocates of Enlightenment republicanism, such as Benjamin Rush, both slavery and denials of political rights on the basis of race were unjust, and in time these arguments would be extended to women by figures such as Abraham Lincoln. For others, such as Jefferson, the likelihood of black biological inferiority, in addition to the legacies of slavery, made it advisable to seek to make the United States an all-white republic, and self-governance could only be hampered by the presence of women in the chambers of political power.[34]

Subsequently in nineteenth- and twentieth-century Europe, the cultural stream of Enlightenment rationalism can also be seen as a source of two later illiberal variants, Marxism and Nazi racism. The first of these, Marxism, did not have politically powerful cousins in the United States, as Hartz observed; but the second, Nazism, did in the form of the scientific biological and historical doctrines of white (often "Teutonic") racial superiority discussed above, even though Hartz did not adequately acknowledge their power. Hence together, Protestant and Enlightenment rationalist traditions can plausibly be seen as the main antecedent streams out of which the variety of particular American political traditions have emerged. For me this framework helps us salvage what is strongest in Hartz's arguments while correcting for his main errors and omissions.

If we view the colonists as mostly being shaped by these two broad older traditions, we can see that early American conditions—relative equality among white men, but hierarchical relations between whites and nonwhites and between men and women—were conducive to the spread of both Hartz's liberalism and modern republicanism, justified by certain Enlightenment rationalist and Protestant themes and largely expressed in the institutions structuring relationships among white men. Yet those conditions were also simultaneously conducive to the elaboration of racism and sexism, justified by other Enlightenment rationalist and Protestant themes and largely expressed in the institutions structuring relationships between white men and others. Lacking the struggle against feudalism that occurred in Europe, however, American conditions were far less conducive to the eventual development of socialism, just as Hartz suggested.

Conducive conditions are, nevertheless, not enough to explain outcomes. To grasp how and why early American political actors combined liberal, republican, racist, and sexist ideas and institutions, we must go beyond a Hartzian focus on their initial material and intellectual circumstances and attend to their central political tasks. Those tasks were not, first and foremost, the carrying on of any particular tradition, although many early Americans identified with historical figures who had defended personal liberties and championed republican governments. American leaders were most immediately concerned with using available traditions first to mobilize support for the Revolution, then to build a successful new nation, and finally to maintain and extend it in various ways. As I argued in *Civic Ideals*, those nation-building tasks prompted American leaders to craft civic visions that blended the analytically distinct, indeed in some ways logically contradictory, traditions and conceptions available to them into politically potent combinations. Revolutionaries such as Paine thought it necessary to assure their core constituents both that their economic interests, personal freedoms, and political powers would be enhanced by the creation of a national commercial republic *and* that Americans were a new "chosen people" of the Protestant God whose members did not include the native tribes or the African slaves. Later American political parties composed civic ideologies that combined and transformed these traditional elements in important ways. For example, the Jacksonians stood for political equality among white men and extensive civil liberties but also for slavery, and late-nineteenth-century Republicans stood for property rights and a strong national republic but also for racially and religiously justified imperialism.[35]

Such civic visions were, moreover, usually not only instruments of nation building, but also important ways through which individuals shaped by the conditions, traditions, and history of their society made sense of their world. Hence not only the programs of political parties but the outlooks of individuals can be better grasped through the framework suggested here. People such as Jefferson, an Enlightenment rationalist and deist, and the Gilded Age nativist minister Josiah Strong, a devout but forward-looking Protestant, are both rendered more comprehensible, I think, if we take this view of the nation's intellectual history and political culture. The writings and actions of each man vividly display both liberal and racist beliefs. Neither figure is understandable if we try to see them as pure Hartzian liberals for whom racial and religious restrictions on basic rights are impermissible, but both can be seen as advancing views with identifiable Enlightenment and Protestant roots that were powerfully reinforced by their personal and political circumstances as well as their own choices.[36] Their views have some important themes in common but also some important differences that are not well represented by seeing them as simply minor variations on an endless liberal tune. Their outlooks are better interpreted as distinct combinations of recognizable American traditions, traditions that have undergone some quite fundamental changes over time.

Seeing American political culture as originally shaped by broad Enlightenment rationalist and Protestant streams that have issued in multiple, evolving political traditions, of which Hartz's liberalism is but one, does not involve any denial of the point Horton and Katznelson, among others, stress. It remains true that the bearers of rights lionized in liberal political thought have to be "fleshed out" in America, as elsewhere, in ways that leave openings for racist and sexist definitions of rights bearers. The framework proposed here simply insists that if rights bearers are fleshed out in ways that preclude large categories of the population that are nonetheless recognized as human beings, the result is undeniably not what Hartz called liberalism. And if we confine the term *liberalism* to his usage, if we define liberalism and racism as distinct, we can do greater justice to the complexity and tensions in the outlooks of individual American political figures, and in American political culture as a whole, while still seeing them as parts of identifiable broader wholes and historical streams.

But my suggestions are, I am all too aware, still crafted with certain concerns in view, and are likely not to serve so well in addressing others I do not now have in view. I suspect it will always be thus. And so the broader lesson I want to suggest here is that when we construct an ism or tradition in a certain way, we should always remain conscious that this is a grouping, a "tradition," that we have constructed because it seems helpful to us in solving certain problems and explaining certain patterns of behavior. This tradition is much more likely to neglect or distort some aspects of the beliefs and conduct of the actors we include in it, especially those aspects unrelated to the problems we had foremost in our minds in constructing the tradition, than it is to explain everything about them or the "core" or "essence" of their beliefs and identities. Maybe our construct will prove so penetrating that it does all that, but we should use it with *explicit* recognition that the odds are against it.

Nonetheless, our scholarly construct "liberalism," in its original Hartzian or some neo-Hartzian version, may in the end prove best for explaining damn near everything about American political culture. At a minimum, however, I insist that its usefulness must be rigorously tested. And with a view to fair testing, and thus to really helpful scholarly inquiry, my final point is that we should be careful about foregrounding, and giving most of our attention to, any implicit traditions we may construct as a heuristic for interpreting American political thought. Instead, we should feature what we should most be trying to explain: the ideas and actions of major American political actors and thinkers over time. Those are our "dependent variables," as they were for Hartz and Greenstone, each of whom tried to explain the ideologies of political parties, such as the Jacksonians and Whigs, and individual political figures, such as Jefferson and Lincoln, by applying their different scholarly constructions of the liberal tradition in America. Yet too often we end up focusing endlessly on liberalism and/or republicanism, or sometimes now racism and sexism, in ways that end up eclipsing rather than illuminating what American political writers, politicians, and parties actually thought, said, and did. To be sure, all those efforts were useful in addressing certain problems at certain times. But now, I believe, it is time to move beyond the terminology of the 1950s, 1960s, and 1970s and define categories, as accurately as we can, that will help us move ahead in analyzing concrete political actors and events in ways that can better address the problems of today and as far into tomorrow as we can see.

★

In Search of Political Development

Karen Orren

Stephen Skowronek

A major impetus to the study of American political development (APD) over the last three decades has been debate about the nature and role of American liberalism in the nation's past. Debate has swirled around two general propositions: first, that liberal ideology has dominated American culture and institution building, to the virtual exclusion of competing outlooks; and second, that liberalism's prominence has corresponded to an American politics devoid of imperious government and of severe conflict over ends. On one hand, the effort to determine just how liberal America "is" or "has been" opens lines of inquiry not energetically followed before: the interplay between political stability and political change, the relationship between ideas and institutions, and the frameworks and methods by which these may be best studied. On the other hand, this same focus so tightly entangles empirical and normative interests that certain core concepts—development, for instance—escape clear definition.

The essay below follows on the intuition that there is mileage to be gained by the reverse route, that is, *through* development *to* liberalism, or to nonliberalism, antiliberalism, postliberalism, or any other configuration of ideas and practices that might emerge as a result. We do not pretend the *d*-word carries less ideological baggage than the *l*-word, or that development as a concept has been uncontaminated by the *l*-word. If modernization theory is not enough, there are always "d-for-direction" overtones—of Whiggish fate, Spencerian contempt, free-market triumphalism. But we hold out the hope that some agreement can be reached on political development's own features; that is, on a set of criteria for gauging fundamental change that will allow subsequent characterization—ideological, directional, or whatever—to more securely proceed.

29

To this end, our objective will be to briefly survey some approaches and tools already available, to say something about the connections between analytic tacks and conclusions, and to press for a usably precise definition of development. In a community as free-wheeling as ours has been, there is a felt strain in labeling scholarship as one thing or another and scrutinizing it as such. But because our purpose is to assess the value of different insights for the particular statement we have in mind, we trust friends and colleagues will accept this exercise in a spirit of constructive engagement.

FRUSTRATED DEVELOPMENT: CULTURE, IDEAS, AND THE TIMELESSNESS OF AMERICAN POLITICS

Among the richest portrayals of American politics in recent years are the studies that approach political development by way of political culture. These studies in particular demonstrate what is perhaps a fair observation to make about APD generally, which is that it has flourished curiously at odds with its major premise. Political culture as often as not highlights aspects of change that are elusive and problematic; their treatment conveys a clearer sense of what doesn't change in American politics than what does. If nothing else, the suggestion that American politics does not change in fundamental ways, or that the changes that do occur don't add up to anything worthy of the name "political development," confronts a long tradition of loose talk to the contrary. At least since 1800, when republicans dubbed Jefferson's election a "revolution," more sober commentators of every station have been at pains to describe a different reality beneath the hype. As politicians scramble to speak for "real" change, "fundamental" change, "meaningful" change—with each election a campaign to "break with the past," "to set a new course," to "reinvent America"—political culture recalls the arrested developments, the cycles, and even the reversals to temper such enthusiasm.

The seminal work in the field, Louis Hartz's *The Liberal Tradition in American Politics,* took its point of departure from the polity's most timeless and encompassing characteristics.[1] Hartz argued that American politics failed to develop in any essential meaning of the word because an enduring cultural consensus made Americans incapable of sustaining a choice between the political alternatives routinely regenerated. American politics may be changeable, he allowed, but because the advocates of democracy and the advocates of capital have been unable to resist each other's arguments, change never amounted to more than incremental adaptations of the same basic ideological mix. The balance has shifted this way and that, but the conflicts the nation began with have been neither resolved nor superseded.

Now, so much effort has gone into disproving this theory of liberal consensus that to open with Hartz might seem as misleading as it is tiresome. But Hartz conveyed a basic skepticism about the significance of political change in America, and an ambivalence about the United States as a model of development for others, that subsequent challenges to his argument have only served to deepen. Hartz's critics have taken aim at his interpretation of American political culture without targeting the more general limitations that cultural and ideological perspectives present for investigations into change and development. By continuing the discussion in the same cultural terms in which he cast it, they have managed to rebut crucial evidence without discarding his conclusions.

Especially telling in this regard, because they focus directly on a form of American politics Hartz discounted, are recent reappraisals of the political culture of diverse social movements. By recovering the transformative potential of Radical Republicans and Populists and Progressives, this new history has promoted an understanding of American political culture that is in many respects different from that presented by the consensus school. But if the shallowness of radical practices and nonliberal ideology can no longer be accepted out of hand, the elusive character of their developmental significance remains. As the capacity of American political culture to generate new alternatives "from below" is vindicated, the essential question of development shifts onto culture "above"—lodged in dominant institutions and practices—that absorbs and dissolves programs for change with remarkable consistency.

This revised narrative of political change in America begins boldly, with the bearers of a transformative idea, but concludes all the more paradoxically with adaptations that strengthen established governing arrangements. We have in this way sharpened our appreciation of the New Deal's original radicalism, and how it was tamed;[2] of Progressivism's bright "promise," and how it was "lost";[3] of the Populists' "challenge," and how it was co-opted;[4] of labor's own "vision," and how it was constricted;[5] of zealous Reconstruction, and how it was eviscerated;[6] of pre-Revolution republicanism, and how it was transmuted.[7] There can be no denying the gap between the end results of American politics and its full-blown and authentic opposition. But that is the point. Proceeding from "vision," from "alternative Americas," whatever changes ensue become interesting mainly for the shortfall.[8] The "real" changes, the "meaningful" changes, the "fundamental" changes will be the ones that don't happen, and our incremental adaptations will remain pretty much as Hartz described them.

Likewise, it follows that scholars who have sought to incorporate the existence of oppositional movements and ideas into Hartz-size depictions of American political culture would rely less than he did on consensus; yet they have succeeded in giving us scarcely more to go on. In *American Politics: The*

Promise of Disharmony, Samuel Huntington, for example, emphasized conflict instead of consensus, but a conflict that turns out to be on closer inspection remarkably familiar: recurrent surges of idealism consistently overwhelmed by institutional realities.[9] Whether the problem lies, as Hartz said, in the compatibility of our populist democracy with our Whiggish capitalism or, as Huntington has it, in a creed irreconcilable with the rules of governance, the stock image prevails: a political world spinning around on its initial assumptions. Rather than drive forward new questions and new solutions, this American politics keeps recycling the originals.

J. David Greenstone's *The Lincoln Persuasion* perhaps put the problem of culture and development most directly.[10] Greenstone wrestled with Hartz for no other reason than to establish the proposition that despite its liberal, ideological boundaries American political development is not an oxymoron. Greenstone's reading of Lincoln's skilled exploitation of shared linguistic meanings makes a permanent contribution to APD scholarship by demonstrating how development succeeds with available cultural tools and at the same time remolds them for future use. Yet in the effort to define "the precise relationship" between culture and development, the argument comes to rest on an advance so singular in its character and so subtle in its construction as to better remind us how precious and rare exceptions to Hartz's thesis will be than to illustrate developmental impulses or patterns in American history.

In the meantime, the difficulty of Greenstone's restraint has been compounded by scholars who have followed up on political achievements such as Lincoln's, only to find them abandoned just down the road. Rogers Smith, for instance, has scored both Hartz and Greenstone for restricting their search for conflict in America to cultural tensions within the liberal tradition and, by that strategy, missing the vulnerability of liberal advances to reversal.[11] Smith rejects the claim that American liberalism has been hegemonic, arguing that liberalism has had to contend with other, equally ingrained traditions that recurrently call its guiding assumptions into question. As liberalism in America has never conclusively displaced beliefs supporting patriarchy and racism, its every advance remains, in this view, besieged and vulnerable to reversal.

Smith's new story, of multiple traditions fundamentally at cross-purposes, takes us about as far from Hartz's understanding of American political culture as one can imagine without denying liberal culture altogether. But this should not obscure the incidental effect of bringing us full circle on the treadmill of nondevelopment. The shift from liberalism's hegemony to the tentative status of any liberal or, for that matter, nonliberal change we might think to happen defeats once again any effort to specify America's broader developmental course.

Greenstone opened his intellectual struggle with Hartz with the observation that "the connections between ideas of political culture and political development are intrinsically problematic."[12] This remains his most enduring insight. If it is in the nature of political ideas that they are hardly ever totally realized, it is in the nature of political cultures that they seldom totally disappear. As a consequence, cultural and ideological explanations are better suited to obscuring the case for development than for clarifying it.

F I T S   A N D   S T A R T S :
C H A N G E   B E T W E E N   R E G I M E S

Next to studies of political culture, the most fruitful source of APD scholarship has been works we might collect under the name of regime theory. These studies identify policies that cluster according to features said to be characteristic of a given span of years, and explain how it is that some ideas and interests are organized "into" American politics during that time and others are organized "out." Thus, for instance, Theda Skocpol, in *Protecting Soldiers and Mothers,* has argued that "maternalist forces promoting social policies for mothers and women workers were considerably more effective in U.S. politics during the early 1900s than were paternalist forces that simultaneously worked for the enactment of policies targeted on male wage earners." According to Skocpol, this was due to "the 'fit' between the organizational capacities of the maternalist and paternalist forces, and the opportunities afforded by U.S. political institutions."[13]

Skocpol has elevated "fit" to a central analytic construct for the field. However, the same basic idea is found in virtually all studies that periodize American history as a series of political "orders." Indeed, a major attraction of regime theory for studies of political development is the self-conscious attention to time frames: eras when dominant political ideas, institutional patterns, and policies adhere to certain themes or tendencies that separate them from other such groupings in time by moments of fundamental change. In this sense, the notion of "fit" within periods should be considered of a piece with such paradigms of change as "punctuated equilibrium," "electoral realignment," and "constitutional moments."

In a different essay, we have argued that the separation of political history into periods of order and moments of change entails two analytic moves: one of synthesis, specifying the prevailing ideas and structures into which phenomena fit; and the other of division, establishing the rationale for the temporal boundaries of successive regimes.[14] Thus Skocpol distinguishes welfare policy in three eras: during the late nineteenth century, when welfare policy was dedicated to the pension demands of Civil War veterans; during the early 1900s, when it was receptive to the mobilization of middle-class women; and during the 1930s, when it reflected the interests of labor unions. These eras in turn correspond to regimes organized around patronage-based parties, around reform movements, and around white working-class ethnics.

It will be seen that this imagery of order bounded within periods projects a view of politics in time different from that usually found in studies of culture and ideology. Not only does episodic change replace timeless or recurring themes of American politics, but governmental institutions play a different role. Instead of absorbing or stifling transformative impulses from below, institutions structure those impulses and select among them, albeit in characteristic ways during different periods. In any given regime, institutions provide a mix of "opportunities" and "incentives" favoring some groups over others. In the words of one practitioner of this approach, "policy designs create niches for political entrepreneurs, who may take advantage of these incentives to help 'latent groups' overcome collective action problems."[15] The analysis of "fit" expresses state-society coherence. The regime coheres because its institutions and policies provide access and support to social interests that bolster it against internal opposition and external threats.

Regime theory has a lot to tell us about diverse structures and policies generated over American history. But its posture toward development is almost as ambivalent as that found in studies of political culture. With development cast now as a series of fits and starts, with each period a "new beginning," policies established under one order are ended, fundamentally altered, or simply passed by under the next. In its primary formulation as party systems, the Federalists' nationalizing efforts were swept aside by the Jeffersonians, the Jeffersonians' nationalizing efforts were swept aside by the Jacksonians, the Republicans' nationalizing efforts were swept aside by the "return" of the South, and, prospectively, the New Deal's nationalizing efforts will be swept aside by the "Republican revolution."

Skocpol tells such a story. When the substance of welfare policy in the Progressive era no longer "fit" the aims and assumptions of new political circumstances, maternalist policies lost their support, and the intriguing idea of a maternalist welfare state became another of America's lost alternatives. It is here that regime theories dovetail with cultural versions of nondevelopment, for both highlight the precariousness of political changes and their vulnerabilty to reversal. Insofar as the relationship between episodic cycles of change and sustained directional movements remains unclear, regime theory allows us to embrace evidence of fundamental change in politics while still evading the question of whether American politics develops and in what respects.

Just as cultural "tools" may be expected to have a prominent place in any actual study of political change, so likely will regime "fit." For our purposes, however, the idea of "fit" is valuable for its suggestion of where a sturdier conception of political development might be anchored. If, as it appears, some innovations that "fit" are highly susceptible to political reversal, it may be because filling niches without changing anything of significance in the institutional environment leaves their operations highly unprotected against subsequent changes. Innovations, we shall argue, are fragile and precarious precisely to the extent that they do not remake the structures into which they intrude; innovations may gain security to the extent that they alter the rules actors must follow to conform to the requirements of their own operations. This would create a hypothetical range of the developmental capacities of given changes—with fit at one end and wholesale transformation at the other—and we would turn the search for durable developments toward absence of fit.

Even as a preliminary formulation, this alternative view may seem more rhetorical than real. Ideas of displacement and rearrangement have always been at the heart of regime theory's understanding of change. Still, placing incongruity instead of fit at the center of the analysis of change calls into question the basic temporal idea of one coherent order displacing another and opens up the analysis of change to the contradictions that riddle the organization and operation of the polity at any given time. Not only will many changes not align with prevailing assumptions, but neither will they be convincingly enrolled as fitters-into the regime that follows. The Supreme Court's watershed decision in *Brown v. Board of Education* (1954) may be said to have fit the political regime in which it appeared in only the narrowest of meanings, in the sense that civil rights was already on the liberal agenda; on the other hand, it is difficult to see how *Brown's* thrust fit neatly with the subsequent regime either, given how school integration would move on and off the civil rights agenda, shattering political alliances along the way. Another, less well known counterexample might be the Four Year Act of 1820, which limited the terms of federal officers. It displaced the aristocratic practice of continued public service for reasons disowned by contemporaries and not yet understood by historians. Two decades after it was passed it would flourish in the soil of an entirely new political and administrative regime—although it didn't completely fit there, either—providing legislatively set tenures in a period of presidential ascendancy and prefiguring the Tenure of Office Act of 1866, which would be the opening shot of yet another political "order."

Much as development is rendered vulnerable by fit, it seems to thrive on incongruity, attaching itself to policies that contradict the basic operating logic of the system in which they are placed. And just as the notion of fit presumes a history marked by steep temporal boundaries—order within periods and changes in between them—the notion of incongruity supposes an abrasive and grating history with different orderings in contention. But before we elaborate this view, we need to sketch one more tool of analysis currently on the front shelf.

FEEDBACK LOOPS: LOCK-IN, PATH DEPENDENCE, AND INSTITUTIONAL LEARNING

Historical-institutional work in the field of comparative public policy has elaborated a set of concepts that bring us a bit closer to something that might be called political development. Recently arrayed under the rubric of feedback loops, these studies take their cue from E. E. Schattschneider's famous dictum "Policies produce politics."[16] The insight that public policy is as much a cause of politics as it is the objective of political struggle has inspired a generation of political scientists to "bring the state back in" and to expound on the different ways in which government policy influences subsequent political events. While these historical-institutionalists seldom consciously distinguish the older notion of fit from their newer emphasis on feedback (and frequently employ both in the same analysis), it is the latter notion that accords with the directionality or forward movement inherent in the idea of political development.

A feedback loop is a self-contained dynamic that propels the polity through time: Policy alters politics and, in turn, the new politics created alters policy. Where regime fit implies a history organized into stable orders that are periodically changed by sudden, dramatic, often externally administered shocks, feedback loops are sensitive to cumulative effects and accrued barriers to reversal or dismantling. The idea of "institutional learning," for instance, refers to the capacities of program administrators to process new information from the political environment and make incremental adjustments in operations that keep policies abreast of changes in the political system at large. The idea of "lock-in" refers to design decisions made at a program's origin that render it difficult for politicians to contemplate radical changes later on. Lock-in can be direct, in the manner of sunk costs, such as locating a road in one place rather than another; calculated, such as arranging for broad-scale Social Security funding to raise the political costs of tampering with the program later on; or unintended, such as including women among disadvantaged groups as a barrier to later repeal of affirmative action policies. Another, related concept is "path dependence," by which prior decisions made by similar governments in different countries confronted with the same policy problem will push each off on a different historical course, precluding convergence and exchange of solutions to kindred dilemmas.

These concepts constitute vanguard concepts in current thinking about political development, and it would be premature to evaluate studies that are only now beginning to apply them. But from where we stand, there is reason for caution. In part the reason is circumstantial. To the extent that they originate in the comparative study of welfare states, they take the features of post–World War II liberal regimes as givens. To the extent that they endorse studies of a single county, as in the case of *Soldiers and Mothers,* they reiterate the image of fit within particular historical periods. It remains to be seen whether feedback loops will fulfill what from our point of view is their promise; that is, of withstanding shock-induced turnabouts—voting realignments, technological change, economic crisis, and reorganization—by demonstrating that institutions and institutional leaders can, by virtue of the adjustments prompted by such loops, stay the path and shape subsequent events.

Leading advocates of the path-dependence approach have themselves questioned whether learning is an effective mechanism of change in political institutions.[17] These doubts are enhanced by the possibility of negative learning. In "negative learning," where administrators are shown to grapple with maladjustments, irreparable mistakes, and outright failures, there looms the familiar vista of reversal—in other words, where regime theory left us, with fits and starts, only minus the starts. Policy makers clearly do jettison things over time without on that account being indictable for having entirely caved in to history, and no honest analyis of the subject will fail to provide for this possibility. Still, we join the skeptics in asking what "learning" adds except words. If institutions learn to adjust and learn to eliminate, what analytic purchase on development has been gained?

Put differently, as learning keeps institutions on keel, forward and backward, what emerges is a protracted voyage of fit through time. Having overcome the sporadic starts of regime theory, feedback loops would appear to leave us with no temporal outline at all; history is what happens, albeit with a better appreciation for how, at least within political institutions. Institutions in this telling don't so much intercept or interrupt development as shape it, but the results remain indeterminate. To be sure, this may not be the policy analyst's problem, but it is ours. If we may paraphrase Walter Dean Burnham, adding institution learning's "one damn thing after another" to political culture's "same damn thing over and over" still leaves us dancing around the issue of development, touching on episodes and mechanisms but avoiding any hold on what development is.[18] Until we can say more specifically what kinds of changes constitute our core concept and how any given political change expresses its formative potential, the study of American political development will continue to convey the bootstrapped quality of its theoretical underpinnings.

TWO PHASES OF POLITICAL DEVELOPMENT: DISPLACEMENT AND REARRANGEMENT

We begin with a simple definition: Political development entails the dismantling or durable displacement of one set of governing arrangements by another set of governing arrangements. We do not delude ourselves that we can settle all things (or even anything) finally on the basis of definitions, but we do think that this beginning offers a viable entry into our subject matter. Consider the attributes of any analysis that might be motivated by it.

Most obviously, our definition takes as its starting point the polity already in place, the one that is up and operating. Political development in our terms is first and foremost a historical event, the primary referent for which is a *pre-existing political world.* An alternative formulation current today in rational-choice analysis asks how governing arrangements might be generated from a society empty of political content. The famous liberal fiction of a beginning in which "everywhere was America" suits the origins approach just fine, but we see no point in rooting the study of American political development in a place always understood as a myth. Wherever we begin, things look pretty much like downtown Tokyo. Our objective is not to discover government, or to account for its existence,[19] or even to show its distributive effects,[20] but to register its existence as a site for political reconstruction.

This brings us to a second aspect of our definition. The particular historical events it highlights are those that entail dismantling or displacement. In development, governing arrangements already established are overturned, pushed aside, eliminated, replaced. In a nation uniquely imagined in terms of wilderness, foundings, and frontiers, this arguably gives our analysis special bite. The point, however, goes deeper than the observation that government and politics in America did not begin from scratch. The idea that every developmental change dismantles or displaces some previously existing arrangement presumes *total governance,* that is, a governmental realm that is comprehensive in its assertion of ultimate control over affairs within its jurisdiction. Total governance does not suggest that political control is exercised only by government officials, nor does it preclude unexpected niches, or degrees of social liberty, or unclaimed terrain in the way of new agendas. But governing arrangements are, in our conception, pervasive. Any move to fill in open spaces will quickly encounter claimants to authority already there. Innovations, however narrowly tailored, always intrude upon this broadly conceived polity. Treating them as niche fillers or otherwise in isolation will misconstrue their developmental significance, which consists exactly in how they rearrange the specific historical setting they confront.

The emphasis on displacement in our definition means that changes that concern personnel or rules without evident bearing on adjacent government authority are not development under our definition. However, the contrast between internal, as opposed to external, relationships introduces a third attribute of development, which is *the central role of institutions* in the analysis of development. The positing of institutions and the arrangements they structure as the primary referents of political development—what it is that gets created, dismantled, displaced, rearranged—distinguishes our perspective most sharply from approaches through culture. The difference will be registered, we believe, in the greater traction gained by attending to the upending of established institutional arrangements in the presence of evident ideological and cultural continuity.

Unlike regime theory, which also takes institutions as the basis of political analysis, there is nothing in our understanding of development that implies an overarching coherence across institutions, or extended periods of order separated by moments of fundamental change. It is in fact conducive to the image of multiple orders, which originate in different times, with different purposes, operating simultaneously in the moment at hand. In that the property that makes an institution "political" is its built-in purpose to control other individuals or institutions beside itself, this multiplicity of purposes, controls, and orders means that abrasion and conflict among institutional authorities are likely to be the normal state of political affairs.

Political development, as we understand it, proceeds in a temporal condition of "intercurrence," where relations among political institutions are (at least) as likely to be in tension as in fit and the tension generated is an important source of political conflict and change. That the overall effect is not chaos is explained by the final attribute of our definition, which has it that political development begins and ends with *the arrangement of things:* more or less fixed positions of institutions relative to others—discernible if often internally antagonistic constellations—that are key objects of political change. Rearrangement may take many forms: state building, privatization, nationalization, centralization, decentralization. The questions we ask concern how extensively the institutional environment is rearranged, what new contradictions are introduced, and how these contradictions are exploited by political actors. In the American case, tensions among institutions are preordained by the Constitution, and historical rearrangements of power in the United States—state power relative to national power, for instance, or judicial power relative to legislative power—offer prominent instances of political development as we define it. Our interest here isn't in arguing these specifics but in laying down terms for evaluating them. We can imagine an argument, for example, to the effect that while state power may be less, relative to national power, than it was at the turn of the twentieth century, there has been no real development of federal-system dynamics. State power was not effectively dismantled or displaced, but, consistent with the continuities of political culture, lay in reserve, to be revived by the Rehnquist Court and the Gingrich revolution. As it happens, we disagree; but we believe it is now possible to have a sensible discussion.

P A R S I N G   T H E   P R O B L E M
O F   D E V E L O P M E N T

How does our definition bear on the debates about American liberalism that opened these remarks? In the first place, by separating political development from "what happened," it becomes possible to sort through the numerous false starts, abortive programs, and short-lived panaceas and about-faces that pervade American political history without being derailed by them. Nondevelopment is as important to explain as anything else. By laying down the above criteria for development, we hope to open an avenue of inquiry between "what happened" and development, leading to such questions as why changes that seemed solidly grounded in statutes, and with apparent means for their implementation, nevertheless fell short of the mark, and why changes that on the surface appeared to be minor or fragmentary had developmental impact beyond their supporters' intentions. By providing that development has two phases—the wresting of authority from established institutions and the rearrangement of authority among institutions relative to one another or to society—we seek to distinguish, in Greenstone's words, the transient from the permanent.[21] As we have suggested, we expect that changes that elude either phase, that fit smoothly into the existing institutional order, are likely to be fragile, with little long-range impact.

Second, these remarks bear on the recently promulgated idea that liberalism is but one ideological strand among several in American political development, and that for that reason liberalism is subject to periodic reversals as other positions become dominant.[22] The perception of liberal reversals is closely related to "what happened," but with an attitude. The theory of American liberal oscillationism—historical development toward liberal or constitutional values followed by reconstruction of nonliberal institutions through a different long-standing ideology or impulse—would seem on its face to preempt the charges of overdetermination and winner's history that are perhaps the most common causes for ambivalence about development as a premise for historical inquiry. We believe our definition highlights the flimsiness, in fact the ideological overload, of such ideas. If one accepts as plausible the description of a densely organized political universe operating over time, and development as a process by which innovations impinge on the arrangements of political authority, then it becomes hard to imagine return engagements of old political acts. Ideas may live on and values strongly challenged may well surge back, but these ideas and values must seek institutional expression in a different polity. In the meantime, their meaning and practical effect are likely to have been reshaped by new encounters and contradictions. This is not a question of how exacting a standard one applies to "reversal"; rather, it represents a fundamental understanding of political change as we have described it above.

Let us return in this light to our unassuming example of the Four Year Act of 1820. This once-anomalous statute assaulted the hoary principle of property in office and eventually became a building block in a political and administrative system that was unanticipated when the act was passed. The four-year rule and principle was, in its turn, challenged by the Pendleton Civil Service Act of 1883, which also intruded incongruously on a political regime that did not know what to make of it. In fact civil service was the signature issue of the very class of men gradually displaced by the implementation of the Four Year Act; their stated motive was to reverse course, to "rid our country thoroughly and once and for all of [these] dangerous and noxious counterfeits of statesmen, and thus make room for the genuine article, which we produced in good measure a hundred years ago."[23] But while the Pendleton Act also laid a foundation for a new system, there was never any prospect of reversing course, of recapturing the world the Four Year Act had worked to undermine. The merit-based civil service was carried forward on yet other principles, its supporting institutions producing new institutional conflicts, and its displacement orchestrated by still more "modern" government, predictably to be challenged on that account.

Finally, there are the current efforts to dismantle the welfare state. Notwithstanding the rhetoric about turning back the clock, about reversing principles of entitlement a half century old, "ending welfare as we know it" augurs more than anything else a giant leap into uncharted territory that includes among its prominent features all those arrangements of governance that the system of entitlements over the years has helped alter. These developments have affected a broad spectrum of American society: the authority and functions of the American family, the governance of the American city, the regularization and stabilization of the American economy. The future will be told in the manner and extent to which these developments are displaced and rearranged by the current reform effort. Whatever the outcome, it will not likely be the promised reprise for the nostalgic institutions that have pressed "antiliberal" values forward.

As scholars of APD, our aim is to analyze this situation clearly, without ideological axes to grind and without hesitation at the task.

3

The Liberal Tradition in American Politics: A Slow Boat to Democracy

Louisa Bertch Green

Gregory Peck (answering his ten-year-old son's question, "What is [anti-Semitism]?") concludes: "So you see, some people hate Catholics and some hate Jews."

Dean Stockwell (responding brightly): "And no one hates us, 'cause we're Americans!"

Peck: "Well, no. That's another thing again."

—Gentleman's Agreement, *1947 Hollywood film, directed by Elia Kazan,*
screenplay by Moss Hart

In examining the liberal tradition(s) in America, the essays in the present volume as a whole convey the slow empirical pace of the democratization of American politics, *pace* our national rhetoric.[1] We are, in other words, taking a long time to live up to some of our principles. Predictably, there are differences in these essays and the relevant other literature about what constitutes a tradition and what is liberalism. How one defines *liberal* and *tradition* depends a great deal on whether one defines them narrowly or broadly; on how, that is, one deals with the relationship between and among single individuals and groups of individuals. The slow pace of democratization, I will suggest here, is at least partly owed to an absence in the literature on American politics of an analytic concept of "public" with sufficiently coherent criteria by which to judge substantive claims that something—a policy, interest, good, and so forth—is public. *Liberal* shares with *public* ordinary—and contradictory—usage as both encomium and epithet; *tradition* shares with *public* the burden of both broad and narrow referents.

"TRADITION" AND "LIBERALISM"

When in *The Lincoln Persuasion* J. David Greenstone accepted Louis Hartz's thesis of liberal consensus, he nevertheless sought more adequately to account for the conflicts in American politics and especially for that severest of internal American conflicts.[2] He did so by rejecting Hartz's relegation to aberrant status of the South's arguments leading up to and surrounding the Civil War and by attempting instead to fit those arguments into a different account of the liberal consensus. Greenstone sought, that is, the features of the arguments on both sides that bore family resemblances to liberal arguments. In the end, Greenstone relied on the arguments of the founders (including the southerner Jefferson), of northern political figures, and of the northern defenders of the southern position. It remained for David Ericson, in his essay in this volume, to make a case for the liberal aspects of genuinely southern political positions. Greenstone identified three principles of the founding period—beliefs in individual rights, in property, and in government by consent—as the foundation of an original liberalism. His subsequent delineation of a complex bifurcation of the original liberalism attributed the bipolarity to shifts in the relative emphases of different liberal values and the incorporation of other features, but the two poles nevertheless continued to share beliefs in rights, property, and consent.[3]

In the same year, Rogers Smith took issue with the idea of an American liberal tradition, taking specific exception to the "dominant political analysts'" descriptions of "American political culture as the preeminent example of modern liberal democracy, of *government by popular consent* with *respect for the equal rights of all.*"[4] On the contrary, Smith argued, American politics is not a single tradition but multiple traditions, many of which are not (even) liberal.

Both Greenstone's and Smith's accounts are similar in their suggestions that the accounts of Tocqueville, Hartz, et alia were less wrong than incomplete, though Greenstone took the temporally longer view of liberalism, by beginning with the founders; Smith, the substantively broader view of American politics, by including more variants of American political beliefs, rhetoric, and practices. Greenstone looked at what the variants had in common; Smith, at basic contradictions. In Smith's account, tradition is "not merely a set of attitudes" but comprises more substantive, continuing features of American political life, among which he includes the continuing, and continually defended, practices of excluding "others" from—or at least relegating them to second-class status in—active American politics. For Greenstone, tradition also embodied the more or less permanent, continuing features of political life; hence his search for the core beliefs, the basically unchanging features that remained common to the variants of the liberal tradition in America.[5] The different framing in the two accounts determined in part

what each could include in the tradition(s), and within the two sum-
maries—Greenstone's rights, property, and consent, and Smith's government by popular consent and respect for the equal rights of all[6]—two sets of
relevant distinctions emerge: between individual rights and equal rights,
and between government by consent and democratic government.

<h2 style="text-align:center">Liberal or Egalitarian</h2>

Greenstone did not include equality as one of the *principal* beliefs that characterized early American politics. He noted instead the beliefs in rights,
property, and consent.[7] Smith, on the other hand, despite his conditioning of
the terms, has emphasized the (comparative) egalitarianism in American
politics, an emphasis that arises naturally when the story is allowed to begin
with Tocqueville—after whom it is easier to emphasize American exceptionalism. Smith's case that American politics has not been egalitarian is persuasive on several levels, in part, however, because it follows logically from
the principles as Greenstone stated them. Smith's characterization of the original principles is more hopeful and generous than Greenstone's—rights but
not necessarily *equal* rights, and not quite *all* rights; hope and generosity
hovered in the early rhetoric but had no foot on the ground. Because *individual* rights and *equal* rights are not synonymous, there may be the implication—the promise, even—of equality in the idea of individual rights, but
the conditioning of the content of the tradition remains. For Greenstone, egalitarianism was a central issue, even *the* central issue, in contemporary American politics, and it was of considerable importance in his personal politics
as well.[8] Although he did not conflate his own preference for a democratic liberalism with the historical liberalism, his view of early egalitarianism was also
more hopeful than actual. Smith acknowledged the *comparative* egalitarianism of the United States and Europe as a striking factor.[9] Nevertheless, the
traditions he described are clearly characterized by "inegalitarian ideologies
and conditions" that are indeed more or less permanent features of American politics.[10] They are not, however, perversions of an original purer egalitarianism but are rather genuine relics, persistent nondemocratic strains of
American political history.

As long as one of the best-known lines in American political history
remains "all men are created equal," there will be Americans who assume or
insist on a literalness not unintended by the founders. That even African-
American men shared this particular emphasis can be seen in Gayle McKeen's
citation of W. E. B. DuBois: "The final product of our training must be…a
man. And to make men, we must have ideals." Although Jefferson's document may have made American politics appear comparatively more egalitarian than European politics, America's was still a highly culturally
conditioned egalitarianism even for men. So the history of American politics,

given its official cornerstone, is almost bound to have consisted of redefining, stretching, modifying, even making figurative the word *men*.

For two hundred years and more, then, the primary question has remained: Who is equal, to whom, in the exercise of which rights? The answer changes from time to time as challenges for admission by this and that group are successful or simply as they persist. Looked at this way, our political conflicts can be regarded as having been less battles to define principles than battles to determine which principles take precedence and who decides; who will be included and who excluded from the practice of those principles; who will represent and who will be represented, and according to what rules?

DEMOCRACY: A PROCESS, NOT A THING

Despite the American tradition (invented, perhaps) of equality, democratic participation—more than a button to be worn on the day democracy is declared—is a process to be learned; the ceremony is an officially declared beginning, not the thing itself.[11] Presumably, it is important that our declaration of principle is liberal/democratic, otherwise members of excluded groups could gain no purchase at all on the hill.[12]

Greenstone's attempt in *The Lincoln Persuasion* to locate the sources of conflict in American liberalism was fueled in part by the questions of why and how basically principled men could hold political and philosophical positions that were otherwise indefensible in a societal context, and how they could take liberal but inegalitarian positions—the latter is a question Carol Horton also addresses in her essay in the present volume. A partial answer was that equal rights was not an explicit part of the original contract, and rights were to be determined and exercised by those with demonstrated competences and with the most at stake in terms of property. A usual justification, on the part of the excluders, is that those who are excluded are justly so. If many of us have come to accept, ahistorically if more laudably, that "all men" can mean, even if it did not at the time, "all humans," we still are not rid of those who would yet praise British colonial policies or insist, only partly facetiously (which is at least the beginning of ethical irony), that members of this or that group are not really human because they are black, female, irrational, perverted, heathen, and so forth.[13] The list of possible disqualifying adjectives is long. The most difficult empirical challenge of a "real" democracy for its members, singly and together, is probably to accept genuinely that "all are equal" means "all" and not just those you or I or another may currently consider acceptable or desirable company. Sometimes it is the rhetorical resonance of the claims that counts most in these situations, not the validity of the claims; and sometimes to remain in power, those in power have only to resist being persuaded that their justifications are inadequate—Rogers Smith's traditions.[14] Moreover, some who want equality to be a stated principle may want it as much to keep others from having more than they themselves have as to help others have as much as they themselves have.

If we are to preserve an analytic distinction between the principles, rights, responsibilities, rewards, and so forth that are characteristic of or are espoused by a liberal democratic society, on one hand, and, on the other hand, the individuals and groups to whom at any given time the privileges of participation (in principle and in practice) are formally extended, then we cannot arbitrarily limit our idea of liberalism in history to only its most democratic or public forms. However much we may deplore a history of exclusions, including those of our own time, in the matter of principles liberalism has remained comparatively unchanged except for relative emphases. The point here is not to minimize the differences that are the sources of our conflicts but merely to point out that they are mostly still all in the family. In the sense of participation, the progressive democratization of American politics has been very slow; nor is it likely that all those who will challenge for admittance have yet done so. Moreover, it cannot be assumed that even as these or those groups successfully challenge for admission they will automatically deal generously with the next challengers—the natural conservatism of the newly arrived.[15]

A short but important point Smith makes is the reminder that although we have struggled toward a politics that is more democratic and inclusive, the ground that has been won can also be lost. A coherent, analytic concept of public that is also dynamic (rather than static) can bracket our contradictions: our progress toward substantive rather than merely formal or rhetorical equality of access to all parts of a representative system and our progress on our own and others' behalf in the development of individual and collective competences. The unbalanced insistence on differences—"that's politics"—rather than on the whole is easier without such a concept, and each new battle potentially threatens the outcome of the war.[16] As long as there are battles, the war is not lost even though it is unlikely ever to be won once and for all.

If what is public, even if only formally, is largely a matter of access, then the question "Is such and such policy or interest really public?" is a question about who has access to the current procedures, systems, awards, rewards, distributions, resources, and so forth. So the question in each case is who is allowed—by law or convention—and then who can as well as who does, who does not, and why not. What is public need not be a comfortably or misleadingly amorphous concept; what is public is susceptible to analysis, according to specific criteria, when it is important for a claim to be tested. We can, that is, measure how public, how democratic, this or that policy or interest is.

Finally, a fundamental justification for an analytic concept of "public" is the contention that the continued absence of a more specific, nontrivial, and coherent analytic concept of "public" constitutes, if perversely, its own threat to the rights and liberties of individuals, and it guarantees the continued frustration of some kinds of public goals that are inseparable from the protection of individual rights. Our apparent reluctance to formulate a concept seems to stem from a fear that any positive formulation—the reification, in fact—of what is public would be tantamount to creating some entity that is inimical to private rights. More positively stated, however, the justification holds that a liberal democratic society has demonstrable commitments to large public goals—among them, a continuing dedication to the rights and liberties of all its citizens, which both Greenstone and Smith have advanced—that cannot be reached without a concept of public with analytical capacity. We cannot, at the moment, "get there from here."

THE POLITICAL FORM OF ACCESS: REPRESENTATION

In a democratic polity in which political access is through an institutionalized form of representation that comprises both process (procedures and rules) and substance (outcomes), the system is generally assumed to be public—that is, it is traditionally, ideologically, and normatively accessible to (almost) all citizens.[17] However, where ideally the formally stated intention of the rules of the system can be taken at face value to be its substance, more recently and effectively the question of whether or not representation is substantively public has come to be answered by reference to outcomes. Representation is said to be substantively public if the outcomes of its formal processes reflect some benefit to a significant number but also to a commensurate diversity of its constituency. When outcomes exhibit neither proportional representation of participants nor even patterns of random distribution, especially over time, then the laws, rules, or procedures that led to the outcomes become the focus of critical attention. Noticeably in recent years, for example, when half the formal constituency of a public office or agency is African-American, but only whites have been elected to office *and* whites have had exclusive or disproportionate access to services, goods, and appointments deriving from the office, then those outcomes have come to be accepted as evidence that the procedures themselves are in some way inappropriately exclusionary.[18] Similarly, attention has come to be focused on procedures when, for example, women, members of ethnic groups, or the handicapped meet the glass ceiling—that is, they have not been hired into or promoted above middle management positions in government or corporations. Just as American revolutionaries attacked the concept of virtual representation, so women, African Americans, and other previously unrecognized or excluded groups came to attack the self-interested assumptions that underlie virtual representation.[19]

Token representation, one of the earlier remedies for the lack of diversity in decision-making bodies, first and particularly in public bodies, could be only partially effective. When educational administrations, government agencies, and, to forestall criticism, corporate and other kinds of boards began to include among their members a woman, an African American, or, in the case of colleges and universities, a student, the trend was accompanied by the endlessly repeated joke about hiring or appointing one black woman or one woman student to count in two categories. The immediate effects of tokenism on the outcomes of deliberations, policies, and activities were predictably minimal, given that a single vote among thirty or even ten others could not be decisive.[20] Not surprisingly, the recognition of the limited effectiveness of the votes of token representatives, when it did not elicit a cynical resignation, was followed by demands for more effective numbers of members of different groups and for a more concrete acknowledgment of the pluralism of the American polity that would link expression of opinion with effectively more equitable distribution of benefits (or harms). These demands led in turn to (among other things) the revival of arguments and steps in favor of proportional representation.[21] Even, however, when a token representative is persuasive in effectively marshaling votes, the assumption that *one* can or does represent *others* just by belonging to a general category (women, African Americans, the handicapped) that includes these others remains problematic.

Furthermore, ensuring the formal and informal expression of multiple points of view through public procedures (voting, for example), in decision-making bodies, and in public forums (meetings, the media, and so forth) is only a first step. As postpluralists observed, representative democracies do not solve all problems simply by increasing the number and variety of people who are allowed a say at the bar. The central problem—how to accomplish the authoritative integration of multiple opinions into coherent, compatible, compelling, and agreed-to policies—remains central.[22]

There remain, that is, questions and considerations not only about what constitutes access to deliberations but what constitutes effective access. The connections, for example, between expression of views in public forums and the effects of those views on policy are difficult to draw with certainty, so there is often a question about whether or not freedom of expression in public forums constitutes effective and substantive access to decision making.[23] There are also the additional questions of whose views are being represented—an individual's, a group's, the views of which group(s), and with the consent of the individual or the group, or of a trustee?

Consent: Virtual or Direct?

The distinction between individual rights and equal rights is one of two important differences in emphasis in Smith's and Greenstone's accounts; the other is a distinction between consent to virtual representation and consent by more direct representation.[24]

In the case of American political tradition(s), perhaps not enough is made of the distinction between virtual and direct representation after the American Revolution, nor, therefore, between the implied forms of consent—as if the Revolution had in fact eliminated the virtual representation that was a major target of revolutionary rhetoric. Yet much of the representation after the Revolution was still virtual. Neither women nor most black men were going to vote. Since it is expedient to infer consent in the absence of active or organized dissent—individual grousing does not count—consent does not require direct participation or representation, and consent can be encouraged through persuasion and the provision of visible or tangible benefits, without necessarily making it an explicit issue. Direct participation itself—most simply (too simply—see below), the right to vote—implies consent to majority rule. Majority rule, in turn, can effectively displace much of the "static" or "noise" of minority opinions and preferences. Here and there we all grouse, but we still consent to rules and outcomes we have not individually proposed, endorsed, or voted for, an acquiescence that is partly prudential and efficient.

Organized dissent and organized challenges to outcomes, usually more effective than individual complaints, are themselves one means by which members of excluded groups develop the political competences necessary to achieve and maintain an effective political voice. As a process of individual and group development, organization is probably a necessary if not sufficient condition for transforming individuals from mere recipients (of even the most benevolently inclined representation—liberal in the original sense of "generous"), who are always virtually represented, into more direct participants.[25]

The historically weak emphasis on equality as an issue may rest in part on a conscious or unconscious omission to emphasize this distinction between government by consent, which can be consent to virtual representation, and democratic government, which requires one at least to vote. In the former, consent is latent, assumed; in the latter, it is implied in the acts of participation and rests in part on the assumption—tied to our notions of individual freedoms—that changes can be made through structured participation when there is dissatisfaction.

A N   A N A L Y T I C   C O N C E P T

The focus here, therefore, is not on motivation, nor on civic virtue, nor on government. For everyday understanding, indeed, it is generally sufficient to describe an individual citizen as public-spirited, in order to signify that that person is engaged in good works or holds public office; similarly, it is sufficient for general understanding to describe a program, a law, or an activity as public, to signify that it emanates from a governing institution.

The present focus, rather, is on existing states of affairs—is this or that policy, interest, or good *public?* Much of the relevant literature devoted to demonstrating that this or that public thing should be public, or to claiming that it is or is not public, evades the question of what, specifically, something public would look like.[26] For constructive, critical analysis, ordinary usage and understanding are blunt and clumsy. Furthermore, given, on one hand, the inevitability of a continued scarcity of certain resources and the consequent distributive decisions (which are bound to be exclusionary from some points of view), and, on the other hand, the increasing number of politically organized and active specialized interest groups taking their places on the political stage, the usefulness of criteria for measuring what is and is not public can only increase.

In the face of traditional and consistent republican-liberal emphases on individual rights, private property, and government by consent, the formulation of a concept of public can look like a threat and is likely to be rejected out of hand.[27] That is, along with the strong ideological emphasis on the individual in American politics, there is a marked tendency to forget that the public is made up of individuals, so that the tendency to dismiss individuals collectively considered remains perversely at odds with the tendency to revere the individual.[28]

The real issue, however, is not so much the rights of a single individual as the rights of *each of all* individuals, that is, the generalized rights (not merely the majority's rights) of individuals in the context of other individuals; not my individual rights versus yours collectively, but ours individually and collectively. Hence the necessity for devices such as John Rawls's veil of ignorance to remind us of the potential consequences of universalizing a single, particular view. But even decisions behind a veil benefit from experience rather than merely good intentions. What is public is better conceived of, in other words, not as other-regarding but rather as us-regarding or we-regarding. As theorists, we need not, on principle even should not, exclude ourselves from calculation of a public good or policy or interest. Furthermore, if we intend to be other-regarding, we should also be as accurate as possible in our interpretations of what is best for the other(s). Hence the problem with "public"—despite its intelligibility, acceptability, and settled meanings—is its lack of analytic force or capacity.

Government or Public Service

In the context of American politics, the word *public* commonly calls to mind one or both of two general realms of associations. The first and probably more commonly evoked realm, which relates *public* to processes and institutions of government and to politics more generally, distinguishes implicitly between what is public and what relates to the individual, the social, and the private. A second realm of associations, which relates *public* to the concept of civic virtue or public service—as exemplified, for example, in Plato's discussion in *The Republic*—emphasizes other-regarding rather than self-regarding concerns, putatively putting the interests or the good of the community before those of individuals.[29] Each of these realms comprises a constellation of concepts related to or sharing family resemblances, but they are not distinct or mutually exclusive realms, nor do they exhaust between them the category of possible public things. Furthermore, it is difficult to escape the resemblances among these two constellations of meanings, "the politics of interests and the politics of virtues" of revisionists, and the humanist and reform politics of Greenstone's bipolarity.

Furthermore, in each of its other-regarding and institutional senses, *public* may be given either a positive or a negative spin. The good of the polity, or of the community, for example, may be regarded as a "higher" good; obversely, a policy enacted for the public good (conscription, for example, or income taxes) may be viewed as—indeed, may be—coercive of the individual. Similarly, governmental institutions are viewed alternatively either as protective of the rights of individuals or as invasive of those rights. The distinctions sometimes depend on the substance of the issue at stake, and whether or not the individual(s) concerned agree with a policy. Whether the government is perceived to be helping or interfering (i.e., "preaching" or "meddling," as the parishioner said of the pastor) is less a matter of *whether* than a matter of *with regard to what topic*. Objections to this or that generalized aspect of government—taxes, penalties, regulations—are often the product of inconsistent or self-interested reasoning: not taxes for me but the services that they provide; not regulation of my business but trade policy protection for my products; lower taxes but better schools or roads or garbage collection; and so forth. In other words, dissension may have to do as much with habit and the particular content or substance of policy as with the fact of policy making and governance. It would therefore be all the less advisable merely to accept "the govermental" or "the altruistic" as criteria for what is public.

Moreover, links between institutional government, on one hand, and the exercise of civic virtue and responsibility, on the other, although generally conceded, are often quite tenuous, in fact if not in theory. The two realms generally occasion discussions distinct from those we will be concerned with here. The connection between the two is therefore acknowledged but not discussed. Discussions of civic responsibility—what one should do and should want to do, the burdens of public service, the "decline" of the tradition of public service, and attempts to revive the tradition—merely sketch the range of the discussion.[30] Furthermore, the rational-choice arguments, which have formalized and confirmed much of the commonsense skepticism with which a democratic polity regards its public officials in the exercise of civic virtue, have constrained the expectations that a polity may realistically entertain with regard to the disinterestedness of the services and policies of its public figures.[31] "Cui bono?" remains an abiding question. Moreover, as the rational-choice literature also reminds us, the exercise of power to one's own advantage is often a far stronger and, to the individual, far more compelling consideration than fairness or justice. More important, that literature reminds us, as Machiavelli once did, that the person who wields power determines to a great extent the rules of the game to be played.

In the face of the rational-choice literature, however, a different kind of analytical question appears to go unregarded. "Cui bono?" is pertinent, but it does not help to distinguish, for example, among the following: self-interested acts that (might) have constructive public consequences; self-interested acts that (might) have harmful public consequences; public-regarding acts that (might) have constructive public consequences; and public-regarding acts that (might) have harmful public consequences. To distinguish between self-interested and public-regarding acts is not only a difficult behavioral and motivational distinction for either the actor or an observer to make; such a distinction cannot of itself predict whether constructive or harmful consequences for the self or others will follow from the act.[32]

DEMOCRATIZATION: ACCESS AND OUR CONCEPT OF "PUBLIC"

The substantive elements and the basic story of slow democratization are similar in most of the present accounts, even if the terms—and the praise, blame, and caution—differ. Moreover, there is a relationship between slow democratization and our practical and theoretical lack of an analytical concept of "public"—of a concept not of what we mean by the public *interest*, or the public *good*, or a public *policy*, but of what, beyond a general commendation or derogation, we mean by *public;* how, that is, do we judge the validity of a substantive claim that a policy, a program, a service, an interest, a good is public? What counts as public?

Access

Because assessments of what is or is not public or in the public interest and so forth are routinely based on little more than unexamined assumptions or rules of thumb, the results are predictably too general, partial, specialized, or otherwise inadequate for analysis or comparison. The inadequacies can result from the bluntness of a criterion (e.g., a program is government-supported, or a policy is other-regarding); from the failure to apply a criterion systematically to all relevant features of a situation; from the selective application of a criterion to a single feature of a complex situation or to a too-small class of situations, so that the applications have no carrying power; or from an unnecessary multiplication of criteria, so that the data that are articulated lack the common ground needed for comparative purposes.[33]

One such commonly utilized criterion or measure of what is public is *access*—that is, something is public to the extent to which access to it is generalized, universal, or open—and, although the application of access as a criterion to a situation can result in the analytic deficiencies just noted, it need not.[34] Access shares with other criteria for what is public (such as being government-supported or being altruistic) the advantage of being already widely appealed to. Furthermore, it has this additional advantage (among other advantages) over other criteria: To a marked degree it is amenable to controlled adaptation, articulation, and extension. (Metaphorically speaking, access, like a rubber balloon, is expandable and adaptable, but only within limits; it is not boundaryless.) For those and other reasons, therefore, access is essential to the eventual formulation and application of a concept of "public."

Like other criteria, access can be applied incompletely or too casually, but these deficiencies are relatively easily remedied. Access suits the present needs not only because it is available, intelligible, and adaptable but also because of four other more or less obvious characteristics: (1) Access itself is not a thing or a property of persons or things but rather denotes a relationship between or among persons and things;[35] (2) as a relationship, access is bilateral and implies reciprocity, that is, once access is established from A to B, it exists from B to A as well, although the reciprocity is not necessarily—and usually is not—symmetrical;[36] (3) the notion of access entails the notion of barriers and thus of crossing boundaries, passing through gates, or satisfying conditions; and (4) access has no intrinsic value, that is, its measure comprises both active and passive access, as well as access to both benefit and harm. (In this latter characteristic, access as a measure can also accommodate

John Dewey's idea that what is public is to be measured by the scope of its consequences.[37])

These characteristics of access taken together will make it possible to raise and accommodate the answers to primary analytic questions such as who has access, to whom and/or to what, and under what conditions. Furthermore, open access as a measure of what is public allows a multiplication of the questions that can be asked in a given situation in order further to articulate the analysis—without, however, sacrificing the common bases for comparisons. Also, as we will see shortly, defining access can provide the information necessary for defining accountability.

Reciprocity and Multiple Vectors

The reciprocity and the multiple vectors of access in any situation are obvious features, yet seldom is either measure applied thoroughly, and far less often are both applied in the same analysis. Regardless of how obvious it is that the road that leads from my house to town also leads from town to my house, the reciprocity of the connection (between myself and those who live in town or along the road) is not always taken into account, whether inadvertently or by design. The same is true of many kinds of created or existing access, not only of roads but also of friendships, of telephone and fax lines, computer networks, and so forth (though not, perhaps, of surveillance). Once a connection is established or a relationship exists, access is bilateral or reciprocal, although not, as noted above, necessarily symmetrically so.[38] And where the reciprocities are asymmetrical, they may be effectively balanced—or not. In any event, the relative degrees of reciprocity and the dominant (if any) vectors can usually be determined.

Also, in most situations, we can count on there being more, even many more, than one line of access, more than one route between my house and the same or other points. For complex situations that are being analyzed into private or public terms and that thus usually comprise many more than one avenue of access, therefore, a claim that an organization, an office, a service, or a procedure, for example, is *either* private *or* public usually has to ignore not only the reciprocities but also the multiple vectors.[39] The characterization of the official, position, service, organization, or procedure as public according to the status of one or two of its more prominent features is commonplace; it is usually sufficient for descriptive purposes; it is probably an expedient; but it also may be misleadingly selective, if not positively opportunistic, in the service of particular interests. A complete analysis, therefore, requires the identification and assessment of all relevant and operative lines, directions, and degrees of access.

Accountability

Access can be specified and measured virtually for as many vectors as can be identified as relevant to a situation under consideration. Furthermore, since mutual reciprocity, even where it is asymmetrical, is necessary for establishing at least minimal accountability in a relationship, the conditions of mutual use that define the relative balance and symmetries (the comparative degrees of consent, obligation, and accountability) can be considered to be partly inherent or previously determined (by law, for example) and partly to be negotiated.[40] In turn, part of determining whether something is public or not lies in determining whether the reciprocities are merely formal or are also substantive.[41] A dictatorship is unacceptable to democratic and republican polities, for example, precisely because no (even) formal reciprocity—no obligation, consent, or accountability—exists or is prescribed for the relationship between governor and governed. Fortunately, these reciprocities can be specifed with fair accuracy. Whether or not a complex policy, for example, is public and to what degree, therefore, depends not only on an identification of all the relevant vectors of access but also on a determination of the relative degrees of consent, obligation, and accountability within each vector, and also on an assessment of the balances between and among vectors.

Limitations of Access: *Generality and Best Use*

In a representative democracy, two sets of definitional attributes of *public,* in both its simple and its compound forms, are commonly cited, although not necessarily in conjunction with each other, in assessments of, for example, a government policy. Generality of access is one; the other consists of criteria for best use.[42] What is public thus commonly, and paradoxically, encompasses criteria for both generality, which tend to inclusion, and best use, which tend to exclusion. The first set of attributes appeals to ideals of equality, democratic inclusiveness, open access, universality, neutrality, and so forth; the second appeals to ideals of competence, effectiveness, utility, order, quality, and so forth. Together these two sets of attributes capture the contradiction, endemic to liberal democratic regimes, whose most familiar form is probably *equality versus quality,* following a commonplace tendency to accept that generality leads inevitably to mediocrity and that standards are inherently elitist.

Generality: Inclusion—Boundaries, *Constituency, and Commensurate Diversity*

The equation of what is *public* with open (or generalized, or universal) access virtually never means, of course, that public access is wholly unrestricted or literally universal. The measure is almost always a matter of condition or degree, especially given scarce resources (not enough for everyone) and selective preferences (not everyone wants some of *that*, anyway). It is reasonably clear, for example, that many Americans accept—whether they approve or disapprove—that a federal or state policy establishing public health insurance entails the necessity for setting rules that delimit or even eliminate some choices in the context of the distribution of benefits.[43] *Public* in this sense is understood to mean something like "governed by the same rules of access for everyone," governed by rules, that is, that are "neutral."[44] If the rules are neutral, they apply (have access) to everyone; and everyone has access to the (same) benefits (or harms). What is public, therefore, is not only characterized by generalized or open access but is also related to the institutionalization or, less formally, the traditionalization of rules for access to and distribution of benefits, especially in the face of limited resources.[45] The latter concern is not only with generalization but also with equalization; although some exceptions to equal distribution are sometimes allowed (food stamps, for example), the exceptions are usually the most controversial of issues.

Since, commonly, universal or open access is a *formal* description, it follows that even when the rule says anyone *may,* in the event not everyone *does* or *can.* In slight contrast, generalized access may be conceded, for example, if a large number of persons is granted or utilizes access. The number may be, approximately, a "lot," or it may constitute a simple or a larger majority. When a majority is the measure, however, a bounded group of persons is implied—a constituency, narrowly construed, of those who agree about, who voted for, who supported a candidate or policy, and so forth. More usefully for the present discussion, however, *constituency* can be more broadly construed to include those persons or groups who have an interest—self-conscious or not, real or imagined—in or a stance with regard to, or who will be affected by, an issue, policy, agency, or outcome of some kind.[46]

That is, the constituency (e.g., for the policy, office, or agency, etc.) is made up not only of those who directly support or benefit from the policy (office, agency, etc.) but also those who are affected by the consequences—favorably or unfavorably, actively or passively, directly or indirectly. Again, what is public, as Dewey suggested, is in part determined by the scope of its consequences, which, conceptually, includes the harmful as well as beneficial consequences and the potential and future as well as actual and immediate consequences. This point is especially important to further discussion, because what is public can thereby more accurately be defined according to the scope of its effects rather than only according to the legal standing of the effector. A corporation, for example, suddenly closes a plant that has come to constitute the principal economic support of a community; based on the scope of its consequences, the act may be understood to be not solely the private act of an entity with the legal standing of an individual but also a public act. In this context, then, a narrow constituency—a "lot," or a bare or simple majority—constitutes a particular rather than general interest. Hereafter, constituency is assumed, unless specifically conditioned, to be construed broadly to include all those affected one way or another by whatever is being measured.

Nevertheless, judging how open or generalized (and therefore how public) is access is a matter not only of answering the formal questions of who and how many (a lot), or what percentage (what kind of majority), and who may (by the rules) have access, but also of answering questions of who can (is able to) and who does utilize permissible access under existing rules that are assumed to be both formally (procedurally or administratively) and substantively neutral. In addition, asking who can and who does allows us, in turn, to raise explicitly the questions of who cannot and who does not utilize access that exists or has been formally extended, and why not.

We recognize, in other words, that an analytic measure of what is public must be more than a measure only of numbers or percentages; the measure of what is public is also partly a measure of proportional representation, of commensurate diversity, that derives from comparisons among who may and may not have access and who can and cannot utilize access.[47] Importantly, the broad construction of constituency, defined by the scope of effects, which keeps before us the questions of who benefits and who does not, means that for a policy, for example, to be considered public, some significant degree of commensurability must be demonstrable between the makeup of the policy's broad constituency and the makeup of its narrow constituency (the almost certainly smaller group that benefits in some way from the access granted). In other words, the distinction between broad and narrow constituency leads us to stipulate that what is public be required to demonstrate significant measures of correspondence between who may and who does—to demonstrate, that is, that effective access is substantively representative of (e.g., as diverse as) the corresponding broad constituency.

There are, of course, policies that target specific classes of persons as beneficiaries and that are more or less broadly accepted as legitimate; persons must satisfy specific conditions—the ceiling on income to qualify for food stamps, for example—stipulated in the policy in order to qualify for access. This leads to an additional factor, sometimes overlooked, in analyzing diversity of access: Measures need to be evaluated over time. It is unrealistic to expect an overall balance to be accomplished within each single policy—especially since single policies are sometimes devised in the first place to redress some particular imbalance. In fact, we do this or assume this most of the time. The evaluations implied by the balancing of access over time, and overall, will depend directly on the kinds of rules established and followed for best use. The blunt measure of generalized access as a bare or simple majority,

however, remains generally acceptable as a valid rule or rule of thumb of decision making if, over time, the simple majority that benefits (or suffers) from
access to policy outcomes is not consistently made up of the same particular
individuals or class of individuals.

In summary, it is possible to analyze a situation thoroughly, using access
as the measure, by specifying not only how many (numbers and percentages)
but also what kinds or classes (diversity) of persons have access (via public
procedures to public persons, resources, procedures, services, and so forth);
and by specifying who—individuals, as well as classes of individuals—does
not have or does not utilize access that has been formally extended; and by
extending the examination over time. Commensurate diversity, in other
words, need not be demonstrable of single policies alone but can be demonstrable of clusters of policies over a given time period, provided the makeup
of those benefiting bears a recognizable correspondence to the broad constituency.[48] Similar account can be taken of the harm that is imposed by a policy or policies. Furthermore, as we will see, for the measure to be accurate it
must be applied not only to procedures and outcomes but also to the deliberations over procedures and outcomes as well as to ongoing evaluations.

Generality: Outcomes, Procedures, Deliberations

As the course of politics generally shows, dissatisfaction with the outcomes on
the part of those represented may lead to demands for changes in outcomes,
which may in turn require changes in the formal rules that determine access
to the political game.[49] The formal redefinition of eligible players—for example, by changes in the rules for access—may (or may not) increase the number or variety of players or their effectiveness. Sometimes, when procedural
changes in access—provision for token representation, for example—still do
not lead effectively to representative diversity in outcomes (again as in some
affirmative action measures), then there may follow attempts to mandate the
outcomes (for example, to establish quotas in affirmative action procedures).
At other times, when access, measured by reference to outcomes, is judged to
be restricted, attention may be turned first to adjusting or changing the rules,
then back to evaluating the outcomes, and so on.

Sometimes, however, the attention to outcomes—and to the adjustment
of procedures to affect the outcomes—dominates, drawing attention away
from the question of who has access to the deliberations, who, that is,
makes the decisions about the rules and procedures in the first place (a car-
dinal feature of strategies for gaining and holding power).[50] Following the traditional democratic emphasis on suffrage, Americans normally consider
political participation to consist of voting—choosing among the candidates

who appear on a given ballot—only latterly giving much consideration to how, why, or by whom the candidates are chosen or to recognizing the importance of having a say about which candidates get on the ballot in the first place and the importance of becoming candidates themselves.[51]

Along with universality, then, commensurate diversity of access as a measure can be applied not only to outcomes and procedures but also to the original deliberations over procedures and to subsequent evaluations of outcomes and procedures. However, since those who make the rules (legislators, for example) also frequently govern access to the deliberations, the restriction of access to the procedures and outcomes may be perpetuated, especially by bodies accustomed to meeting in closed sessions (a problem the sunshine laws of the 1970s attempted to address). In this context questions arise, such as "In what sense are closed congressional committee meetings public?"; "In what sense are the deliberations of the Supreme Court public?"; and so forth.[52] And those lead us, after consideration of whether or not, and how, collectives are public, to whether or not and how various kinds of representation are public.

There is some risk of a problem of infinite regress in the question of access to the deliberations over rules. However, if we reasonably concede the continuous changes occurring in whatever situation is under discussion—in the demographics, for example, if in no other aspects—then we expect continuous evaluation, reevaluation, and adjustments (a dynamic concept of public, in other words) to be normal. *This* is what we do, in fact, most of the time, although usually, rhetorically at least, as if we were searching for *the* norm, *the* rule, *the* principle, rather than acknowledging a continuing process.

Exclusion: "Best Use" and Competence

Nevertheless, representation is only partly a matter of reflecting the generality and diversity—the pluralism—of a constituency's access to rule making, procedures, outcomes, and evaluations. The concern with universality and diversity is a concern with inclusiveness: the more inclusive is a political system, the more democratic—the more public—it is said to be. (Democratic ↔ inclusive ↔ public).[53] Measures of the generality of access, however, are relatively easier to accomplish than measures of best use or of competence.

As an abstract process of one acting for many, however, representation is also a matter of "best use," of "doing it well"; of doing it, that is—in the absence of enough for everyone—according to recognized, legitimated, consented-to standards of competence and expertise and other kinds of judgments about best use, even though these are inherently exclusionary.[54]

Outcomes may not be substantively public, for example, if they do not significantly reflect the relevant constituency, and also when requirements are exclusionary in fact, even if not in principle or in expressed intent. Best-use standards can serve as a balancing factor in the context of other considerations, as long as we regard them not as absolute rules to be preserved regardless (which, as such, serve principally to preserve existing power relationships) but rather as provisional rules subject to examination.[55] Once a pattern of the exclusion of members of a specifiable group is verified, then it is possible to direct critical attention to the justifications themselves.

The paradoxical exclusivity of best use is most easily justified in the face of scarce resources, which may include but are not limited to opportunities and money to be allocated, jobs or offices to be held, and goods to be consumed. Best use, however, usually has as much to do with preferences as with cost efficiency, for example. Furthermore, when scarce resources are the case, then rules or at least guidelines for best use are in order.[56] Nevertheless, although rules for best use provide one basis for determining access to and distribution of scarce resources, deciding on the rules themselves is the first-order problem, precisely because of the disagreements that inevitably arise over what kinds of rules and which particular rules will be followed. (Affirmative action policies are a good example, especially now that they are under severe scrutiny.) If cost-efficiency is to be the rule, then possible challenges are "at whose cost?" and "efficient to *whose* ends?" Normally, the answer is to *which* ends, which are viewed as neutral and can be claimed as proper ends for everyone; if desires or preferences are the rule, then the challenge might be *whose* desires or preferences.

Often competence is invoked as the criterion, or one of the criteria, for best use. A claim, for example, that a certain group lacks competences—of natural abilities, training, specific skills, and so forth—may lead to a generalized justification for excluding the members of the group from public office, corporate management positions, educational institutions, social organizations, and other kinds of positions or activities. Such exclusions often rest on established procedural and substantive standards, which are justified by assertions that rules or procedures are in themselves neutral with respect to persons but are necessary qualifications for specific jobs. The claim that procedures and standards are neutral, however, can look astonishingly naive once it is examined.[57] To design procedures that effectively determine outcomes and restrict access is relatively simple, and often much is at stake in terms of tangible benefits and of retaining control of decision making.

The exclusion of women and other groups from certain positions when this is the result of the policies and practices of private companies, for example, has traditionally been defended on grounds that the hiring decisions are the preserve of the company as a private entity. When these grounds became less tenable, often in the climate following one or another of the recurring rights movements, attempts to defend exclusionary practices may be shifted to claims that the outcomes merely reflect the higher levels of competence exhibited by those who were hired or promoted—leaving unspoken but implied the imputation of incompetence to members of the excluded groups.[58]

The exclusion of women, African Americans, the blind, and others who have historically been excluded from employment in certain positions is accomplished by relying on generalizations about incompetence, which nevertheless have begun to yield, even if slowly and incompletely, to articulated challenge. It is sufficient in some cases to show that members of the excluded group are in fact either competent in whatever way is required or can learn the requisite competences. This point is important because it reminds us that, in order to be legitimate, exclusion on the basis of competence must withstand two challenges: First, does the generalization genuinely hold for at least most individual members of a group (assuming the generalization to be germane), and second, is the distinction between *can do* and *can learn to do* being respected?[59]

In retrospect, one of the major accomplishments of affirmative action was to demonstrate the fallacies of generalized attributions of incompetences. Such generalizations, of course, can cut both ways, since individuals who are not (or not yet) competent or expert may claim to have been excluded solely because they belong to the excluded group.[60] The two challenges can be applied here too, however. The test of the legitimacy in both cases lies in examining or establishing the qualifications of individuals. This distinction between competence as potential abilities and expertise as graded levels of developed competences acknowledges the material as well as the motivational requirements for access.[61] It might be a necessary condition for me to want very much to be a ballerina or a brain surgeon in order to succeed, but it is not enough, of course; I must be able to develop and demonstrate the requisite competences. The standards for developed competence are themselves subject to (must bear up under) critical scrutiny and are continually changing, sometimes drastically, sometimes almost imperceptibly.[62] The tricky part at any one time still is to meet the questions about what counts as best and who says so; when is "bad" art, for example, still art, and when is it so bad it ceases to be art and is something else?

Furthermore, the distinction between *can* (or cannot) *do* and *can* (or cannot) *learn to do* leads in turn to the recognition that there are both primary, or direct, and secondary, or indirect, forms of exclusion on the basis of competence: direct exclusion, as, for example, when a group (e.g., women or African Americans) is specifically not permitted to vote, and indirect, as when a group (e.g., women or African Americans) is denied access to the venues of education and training that would qualify them for jobs and offices.[63]

A useful, related distinction can be made between competence and expertise. According to the above distinction, I may not at this moment be

goods, and resources—examples of truly public goods being extremely scarce—decisions follow distributive principles or policies that are, again ideally, both equitable and just, conforming in part but not limited to the strict exigencies of cost-benefit analysis.[67] Here as elsewhere, ideal representation is not only formal and substantive but also adaptive; it is thus dynamic, but it is also stable without being static. Representation so conceived is not an act but a process and, furthermore, an interactive process.[68]

CONCLUSION

As the essays by Smith, Nackenoff, Horton, and McKeen reiterate, American political history is partly a history of ongoing conflicts and tensions over the question of access: Just who is admitted to participation, to rights, to equality? Importantly, again, their challenges have not usually been to principles but to being excluded as players from the practices. Challenges from the other side predictably arouse people to the defense—ideological, scientific, emotional—of their possession of the existing arrangements. And, as Ruby Rich once remarked, "When I am at last invited into the room where the power is, I conclude that the power has already moved elsewhere."[69] In the evolution of American politics, a general progression from "merely" republican to "more" democratic is a fair description of our history, but privilege warring with disadvantage is more probably a condition of human relations than a consequence of any particular form of government. So arguments, traditions even, in favor of the exclusion of this or that group of others are only to be expected.

Since struggles over principles are related to but not the same as those over power, the beliefs in individual rights, property, and consent are not necessarily inconsistent with a conviction that those rights can be framed and granted by means of virtual representatives—who, precisely and sometimes explicitly, tried to say that absolute equality for all, will-they, nill-they, wasn't part of it. On the evidence, after all, American politics has not been impressively egalitarian. If American liberalism is made to rest—as it does not, historically—only on egalitarian principles, American politics is not liberal. Many Americans, of course, in the contemporary vernacular of politics, would say, "Of course it is not and should not be; conservatives are not liberals, and they have a political tradition at least as long and strong"—Smith's point. (Conservatism, unlike liberalism, has no entry in the *International Encyclopedia of the Social Sciences*.) It is in part by eliminating upper-case conservatives and liberals from American political science that we preserve the liberal—not egalitarian—consensus.

Consequently, in our contemporary affirmations of egalitarianism as an American political principle, it is important to keep in mind, first, the original American conditioning of equality and its own comparatively short history and, second, the difference between proclaiming a norm and living up to it, to say nothing of contending with competing norms. Smith's emphasis on the recentness of the term *liberal* is corroborated by Hobhouse's observations, in 1911, that egalitarianism was "*not yet* a requisite of liberalism." A parallel case of the slow development of the term and an even slower democratization emerges from a recent work on two centuries of a Mexican politics and liberalism that also did not include egalitarianism.[70]

Three summary points here: (1) in his formulation of a bipolar liberal tradition in American politics, Greenstone did not rule out the possible existence of other traditions; (2) Smith's, Nackenoff's, McKeen's, and Horton's traditions are nonliberal in the more recent sense of exclusionary; and (3) in delineating a liberal tradition, it is necessary to pay attention to the entire family of features that have been regarded as liberal, rather than binding liberalism to a single feature and disallowing forms that do not bear it.

Greenstone did not directly confront the problem of the "purity" of any one tradition, although he was aware of the problem. One of the logical consequences of a strong belief in individual rights is that we cannot guarantee that each prominent political figure—much less prominent nonpolitical figures and ordinary people—will inherit or imbibe only pure (one or the other pole) or even consistent forms of a tradition. Horace Mann, for example, bore characteristics of and made arguments from both humanist and reform liberal traditions, as well as from other sources.[71] In the conflicts in politics, there are always prominent proponents of different views. One might accuse Greenstone of the careful selection of figures who fit his model, but his choices all were highly influential figures in American politics, and the evidence is that their views were as Greenstone represented them and that they fit the liberal criteria as he outlined them.

By explaining the conflict within the confines of liberalism, Greenstone developed the boundaries of the "game." Looking farther, finding other versions, also over which there may have been conflict, would widen the scope but not in itself invalidate the basic observation. While certain combinations of liberal beliefs are more compatible and may be encountered somewhat more often than other combinations, still different combinations may be expected to exist and be held no less strongly by their claimants. Moreover, there is no guarantee of internal consistency within any one set of beliefs, so that contradictions may well exist not only within liberalism but within different strains of liberalism.

Smith's account of our nonegalitarian traditions underlines the slowness of democratization, a process that is still going on. Not until 1920 in the United States were women allowed to vote; not until the 1950s did we again begin seriously to address the egregious exclusion of African Americans from any meaningful role in American politics or culture, to say nothing of our belated recognition of the rights of Native Americans and of other groups—including the handicapped, the elderly, and so forth—who have consistently been targets of discrimination. Even, however, if most of our politics has been liberal by one definition or another, the pace of democratization has been slow enough scarcely to entitle us to claim exceptionalism, regardless of our own and the world's prevalent myths about American democracy. Yet there is *something* there that we are given to, however long a learning process democratization turns out to be. Though we sometimes forget, American democracy works at least in the sense that, despite serious internal conflicts, we have not been faced with a threat of a takeover of the government, except, facetiously, by a political party duly elected; and recently we have evinced a perhaps intentionally perverse tendency to elect a president and a Congress from different parties. Initially, even the South intended only to secede from, not take over, the federal government. Russell Hardin is correct that democracy cannot handle major issues, only minor ones, in the sense that a democracy cannot avoid conflict by providing the single answer for differences of opinion that matter.[72] But single answers are almost bound to violate the spirit of a political ideology that is built on differences. For the moment at least, despite unresolved conflicts, we continue to differ but to maintain some sense of a framework that keeps us battling in the same arena. That sense, presumably, is our chief referrent for liberalism.

4

Dew, Fitzhugh, and Proslavery Liberalism

David F. Ericson

The question that seems to most perplex scholars of the antebellum period of American history is whether the southern defenders of the institution of racial slavery rejected liberal principles. Did the defenders of slavery attempt to square the institution with the nation's liberal, founding principles? Or did they find it impossible to do so because, as everyone from Garrison abolitionists to frontier statesmen to later scholars could plainly see, slavery was an inherently illiberal institution that could be defended only on the basis of feudal, paternalistic, or ascriptive principles?[1]

One of the reasons the view that the defenders of slavery rejected liberal principles is so attractive is because it provides a ready answer to another perplexing historical question: What caused the Civil War? In this view, an increasingly proslavery, illiberal South could no longer remain united with an increasingly antislavery, liberal North. The nation was a "house divided"; the Civil War was "irrepressible."

In his highly influential *Liberal Tradition in America,* Louis Hartz interpreted the antebellum South as undergoing a "reactionary Enlightenment" in the course of defending its institution of racial slavery.[2] Hartz's interpretation of the proslavery movement raised two major interpretive problems for him: how to account for the Civil War, and how to reassert his broader consensus thesis. He largely yielded the first point to his potential critics.[3] On the second, he argued that the proof of consensus is *not* that it forced the proslavery movement onto liberal grounds. Rather, the proof of consensus is that an illiberal proslavery movement was so completely vanquished, not only militarily but ideologically, in the Civil War.[4]

Following Hartz, Eugene Genovese published in the 1960s two major studies of the antebellum South that interpreted the proslavery movement in a similar manner, as a reactionary movement with strong feudal and paternalistic tendencies. His view, however, was not that consensus prevailed despite this aberration but that the aberration proves consensus did not prevail.[5] Rogers Smith has recently developed this view into a deeper critique of Hartz's consensus thesis. He argues that the proslavery movement was merely one of many movements in American history based on ascriptive principles. As he reiterates in his essay in this volume, his view is that the nation's history has been shaped by the interplay between "multiple traditions" of liberal, republican, and ascriptive principles, not by the unfolding of one, liberal tradition.[6]

In the interim, though, several studies had appeared that interpreted the proslavery movement from a liberal or republican perspective. James Oakes argued that the defenders of slavery had engaged in a concerted effort to defend the institution on the basis of the nation's founding principles of liberty, equality, property, and consent.[7] Kenneth Greenberg did, too, though he defined those principles somewhat differently, as republican rather than liberal ones.[8] Despite the difference in language, the thrust of their scholarship was similar in attempting to demonstrate how the proslavery movement was not fundamentally ascriptive in Smith's terms.[9]

Yet, as emerges most clearly in Smith's case, all these works really argue that the proslavery movement was a mixture of diverse elements: liberal, republican, and ascriptive, among others. The differences between them are, then, differences in emphasis. Various studies argue that one or the other element was "the central theme" of the proslavery movement or, alternatively, that it is best understood as a mixture.

Undeniably, the proslavery movement was a multifaceted one. But that does not mean it is best understood in those terms. Scholars will obviously differ on this methodological point, of whether the proslavery movement or any other social phenomenon is best understood in terms of a central theme. They will also differ according to whether their goal is to understand individual proslavery figures or the movement as a whole.[10]

I believe that the proslavery movement is best understood in terms of a central theme and that the central theme in question was squaring the institution of racial slavery with the nation's liberal, founding principles.[11] This view is, of course, a reassertion of Hartz's consensus thesis in a stronger form than he himself put forth.[12] It assumes that, as J. David Greenstone has shown, we can account for conflict, even civil war, within a consensus framework by positing different forms of liberalism.[13] It also explains why proslavery thought was not completely vanquished in the Civil War but, unfortunately, assumed new forms to justify continued racial oppression.[14]

This study moves beyond previous studies of the proslavery movement, including Hartz's own, in using the consensus view as the key to understanding the movement. The consensus view shores up two major weaknesses in those previous studies by supplying a rationale and a dynamic for proslavery liberalism. The reason proslavery figures offered liberal arguments to defend the institution of racial slavery was because they themselves believed in an American liberal consensus and, therefore, that liberal arguments would have the most resonance with the American public. The way the proslavery movement changed over time was to become more liberal in character, since arguments that appealed to liberal principles encouraged responses in kind, spawning a dialectic of response and counterresponse.[15] Given the merits of the consensus view in understanding the proslavery movement, it is surprising Hartz took the route he did in analyzing the movement.

Hartz probably did so because, as Greenstone again has shown, his understanding of liberalism was unidimensional.[16] For him, liberal principles were antislavery, not proslavery; they could not be both. It is also the case that Hartz viewed the proslavery dilemma as primarily a psychological one. He seemed much more interested in how the defenders of slavery could reconcile their liberal psyches with their defenses of an illiberal institution than in how they did, in fact, defend the institution.[17] For my part, I am less interested in trying to fathom what went on in the hearts and minds of the defenders of slavery than in trying to elucidate the character of their public arguments.[18] I view the proslavery dilemma as primarily a rhetorical one. Proslavery figures did not really question their commitment to slavery, but they did question how they could defend that commitment to a nation that seemed increasingly willing to reject slavery as an illiberal institution. I think they responded to this rhetorical dilemma in the most efficacious way they could: by trying to defend slavery as a liberal institution.

My essay consists of two sections. In the first section, I will canvass the proslavery arguments offered by various defenders of slavery in the antebellum South. I will divide these arguments into three categories: deontological, consequentialist, and contextualist. Deontological proslavery arguments defended slavery as a just institution in itself (or as not an unjust institution); consequentialist proslavery arguments defended slavery as a just institution based on its beneficial social consequences (or on the harmful social consequences of abolishing the institution); and contextualist proslavery arguments defended slavery as part of a family of protective institutions and dependent statuses appropriate to all times and places (or as *not* inappropriate to this time and place). If, as I suppose, the primary proslavery arguments were liberal ones, then liberal arguments should be prominent both within and across categories. In the second section, I will compare a major early proslavery work, Thomas R. Dew's *Review of the Debate in the Virginia Legislature* (1832), to a later one, George Fitzhugh's *Cannibals All, or Slaves Without Masters* (1857), as a way of assessing how the proslavery movement changed over time. If, as I suppose, the movement became more liberal over time, then Fitzhugh's defense of slavery in *Cannibals All* should be more liberal than Dew's defense of slavery in his *Review*.

PROSLAVERY ARGUMENTS

Deontology

On deontological grounds, the defenders of slavery were clearly on the defensive. Both the Protestant and liberal principles they presumed most Americans shared seemed to condemn the institution of racial slavery. On the face of it, the institution did appear to violate such "self-evident truths" as that all men are one before God; that they are endowed by their Creator with inalienable rights to life, liberty, and property in themselves and the fruits of their labors; and that all legitimate forms of government are based on the consent of the governed. Still, the defenders of slavery did not think they were in a hopeless polemical situation in trying to combat the prima facie case against the institution.[19]

One of the strategies commonly used to defend slavery was to offer a biblical argument. Proslavery figures emphasized the fact that the ancient Hebrews were slaveholders and charged by the God of the Old Testament with enslaving other nations. They also noted that the Jesus of the New Testament did not condemn Roman slavery, which, they all agreed, was a far crueler form of slavery than the American form. As their trump card, they cited Paul's "Letter to Philemon," in which the apostle counseled a fugitive slave to return to his master and henceforth dutifully serve him. After presenting a series of such proslavery arguments in his public letters to the British abolitionist Thomas Clarkson, James Henry Hammond concluded that "American slavery is not only not a sin, but especially commanded by God through Moses, and approved by Christ through His Apostles."[20]

Typically, proslavery figures did not rely solely on a biblical defense of the institution.[21] They indiscriminately mixed proslavery arguments of a more religious and a more secular nature. As George McDuffie declared in his widely circulated 1835 gubernatorial message to the South Carolina legislature, "Whether we consult the sacred Scriptures, or the lights of nature and reason, we shall find these truths [to the effect that slavery is the status most conducive to the happiness of the African race] as abundantly apparent, as if written with a sunbeam in the heavens."[22]

With particular reference to the Declaration of Independence, which reflected "the lights of nature and reason" for so many Americans at the time, the defenders of slavery pursued two general strategies to attempt to undercut its antislavery appeal.[23] They either denied that the "self-evident truths" of the Declaration applied to blacks, or they claimed those truths had to be carefully circumscribed in practice.

The first strategy was to except blacks from the Declaration on the grounds that they were not qualified for self-government, in either the individual or collective sense. In his contribution to the prominent proslavery compilation *Cotton Is King*, David Christy insisted neither Thomas Jefferson nor the other signers of the Declaration could "ever have intended to apply its principles to any barbarous or semi-barbarous people, in the sense of admitting them to an equality with themselves in the management of a free government."[24] Yet Christy here, as elsewhere in his essay, is unclear about whether blacks are excepted from the Declaration by an inferior nature or by the "barbarous" environment from which they came.[25] The defenders of slavery generally refused to choose between nature and environment, because to choose nature would have conspicuously displayed a racism that seemed fundamentally illiberal and to choose environment would have suggested that southern whites were, again illiberally, enslaving people they should be educating.[26] As a result, the proslavery literature left ambiguous the nature of the reputed inferiority of black Americans.

The preferred strategy, though, was to attack the Declaration of Independence on more general grounds by broadening the exceptions from its "self-evident truths" beyond racial or ethnic criteria. In opposing a Senate bill to organize Oregon as a free territory, John C. Calhoun rebutted the Declaration's central claim that "all men are created equal" by observing: "All men are not created. According to the Bible, only two—a man and a woman—ever were—and of these one was pronounced subordinate to the other. All others have come into the world by being born, and in no sense...either free or equal." He went on to expose "the most dangerous of all political errors" that is often committed in appealing to the document: the presumption that "those high qualities [of liberty and equality] belonged to man without effort to acquire them, and to all equally alike, regardless of their intellectual and moral condition."[27] The intent of this proslavery strategy, however, was not to reject the Declaration and its underlying liberal principles in toto but to stress how those principles were abstractions that had to be adjusted to existing conditions. When those adjustments were made, proslavery figures were confident liberal principles would call for the continued existence of racial slavery rather than its abolition. In his speech on the Oregon bill, Calhoun did not reject "the cause of liberty" but, to the contrary, contended the campaign "to bestow on all—without regard to their fitness either to acquire or maintain liberty—that unbounded and individual liberty supposed to belong to man in the hypothetical and misnamed state of nature, has done more to retard" that cause "than all other causes combined."[28] Accordingly, proslavery figures favored a circumstantial defense of the institution, arguing that under certain conditions, for certain people, liberal principles actually required slavery. This strategy was preferred precisely because it seemed less racist, and hence more liberal, than the first strategy.

The defenders of slavery also confronted the liberal idea of property rights as the right to oneself and the products of one's labor. Again, the presumption was against the right of one man to hold property rights in another, but proslavery figures had several counterarguments at their disposal. In the first place, they argued that even if it was unjust for one man to hold property rights in another, the fact of the matter was that under southern law men did hold property rights in other men. Southern slaveholders, therefore, committed no injustice in holding men in slavery, especially since they were not responsible for the original injustice of enslaving them.[29] Hammond assured Clarkson that

> [t]he means...by which the African race now in this country have been reduced to slavery, cannot affect us, since they are our property...by inheritance or purchase and prescriptive right. You will say that man cannot hold *property in man*. The answer is, that he can and *actually does* hold property in his fellow all the world over, in a variety of forms, and *has always done so.*[30]

Proslavery figures' second counterargument was that southern slaveholders did not really hold property rights in men but only rights to the products of their labor. In this sense, southern slaveholders were analogous to northern capitalists who held rights to the products of the labor of their employees. Unlike free laborers, slaves did not, of course, receive wages in return, but they did receive food, shelter, and clothing. Proslavery figures argued that slaves actually received a better exchange for their labor than free laborers did, since they were guaranteed subsistence for life and free laborers were guaranteed subsistence only as long as they made a profit for their employers. Albert Bledsoe, in his contribution to *Cotton Is King,* asked rhetorically,

> But may not one man have a right to the labor of another,...and yet that other a right to food and raiment, as well as to other things? May not one have a right to the service of another, without annulling or excluding all the rights of that other?...If it may exist for one period, why not for a longer, and even for life? If the good of both parties and the good of the whole community requires such a relation and such a right to exist, why should it be deemed so unjust, so iniquitous, so monstrous?[31]

This second counterargument was the preferred one because, once again, it seemed the more liberal one insofar as it portrayed slavery in quasi-contractual terms. It had the further advantage of favorably comparing the master-slave relations of the South to the employer-employee relations of the North.[32]

Finally, the institution of racial slavery appeared to violate the liberal idea of consent. As Bledsoe admitted, the institution established "a right to the labor or obedience of another without his consent."[33] Other connotations of consent were, however, more favorable to the proslavery cause. Insofar as the defenders of slavery portrayed the institution as involving an implicit exchange of liberty for, at a minimum, subsistence, they read the slaves' consent back into the relationship. Proslavery figures could proceed further along the same line of argument by positing the slaves' apparent contentment with and lack of resistance to their condition as an indication of their tacit consent to it.[34] Proceeding in another direction, proslavery figures could argue that slavery was based on the consent of the governed: the majority of the citizens of the southern states, who, through their representatives in government, continued to pass laws supporting the institution. In his fiery "Mudsill" speech before the United States Senate, Hammond even went so far as to claim that, given the historical prevalence of the institution, slavery was based on "the common 'consent of mankind,'" which he considered the highest proof of "Nature's law."[35] As with the liberal ideas of liberty, equality, and property, the defenders of slavery depicted the institution as one that was perfectly defensible on grounds of the liberal idea of consent.

Whether the institution of racial slavery was so defensible was, of course, not a question that was ultimately decided by its defenders. Most Americans probably continued to believe that the institution violated the nation's founding principles. Thus it is not surprising that proslavery figures stressed the consequentialist arguments supporting slavery and, even more, the consequentialist arguments opposing its abolition. At least initially, the defenders of slavery gravitated toward the "necessary evil" position. They admitted the institution was evil on deontological grounds but argued that its continued existence was necessary on consequentialist grounds. Jefferson memorably expressed this position in the wake of the Missouri crisis: "We have the wolf by the ears, and we can neither hold him, nor safely let him go. Justice is in one scale, and self-preservation in the other."[36]

Consequentialism

Proslavery consequentialist arguments seemed themselves to divide into "necessary evil" and "positive good" arguments. Necessary-evil (antiabolitionist) consequentialist arguments catalogued the possible harmful social effects of the abolition of slavery; positive-good (proslavery) consequentialist arguments detailed the possible beneficial social effects of the continued existence of the institution. Though the former type of argument probably enjoyed more popular support in both the North and the South, the latter type of argument had the greater potential for forging sectional solidarity in the South and converting moderate southerners into more radical ones on the slavery issue. Proslavery figures faced a strong incentive to offer positive-good consequentialist arguments. Over time, therefore, the proslavery movement tended to become more positive-good in orientation, a tendency that included an increasing reluctance on the part of proslavery figures to even admit the institution was evil on deontological grounds. The necessary-evil and positive-good positions did, nonetheless, merge into one another; every defender of slavery was certain to offer both types of consequentialist arguments.[37]

In analogizing the continued existence of racial slavery to holding a wolf by the ears, Jefferson had, of course, taken a necessary-evil position. Of the continued existence of the institution, he remarked

> that there is not a man on earth who would sacrifice more than I would to relieve us from this heavy reproach, in any *practicable* way. The cession of that kind property, for so it is misnamed, is a bagatelle which would not cost me a second thought, if, in that way, a general emancipation and *expatriation* could be effected; and, gradually, and with due sacrifices, I think it might be.[38]

Most Americans, though, were much less sanguine about the prospects of African colonization. Accordingly, proslavery figures attacked abolition on the assumption that it could only be accomplished through other, more drastic means.[39] They then portrayed the consequences of a general emancipation of the southern slaves in apocalyptic terms. The possibilities included incendiary race wars sparked by embittered freed slaves, a worldwide economic depression prompted by the loss of the millions of dollars southern planters had invested in their slaves and by the supposed inefficiency of free black labor, and recurrent social unrest fueled by the impossibility of constructing a racially egalitarian society in a postemancipation South, which would eventually subvert republican government in the nation as a whole and require a despotic government in its stead.[40] The upshot of these worst-case scenarios was that the slaves would not gain from emancipation and everyone else would lose. In particular, the defenders of slavery argued that emancipation would make southern blacks no more free, and perhaps less so, while making southern whites less free.[41] Here, they appealed to the core liberal argument that institutions should be arranged in such a way as to maximize the liberty of the people who might be affected by those institutions. They claimed this "maximum-liberty" argument justified the continued existence of racial slavery in the South rather than its abolition. With the dire possibilities of abolition in mind, archcolonizationist Henry Clay insisted:

> The liberty of the descendants of Africa in the United States is incompatible with the safety and liberty of the European descendants. Their slavery forms an exception—an exception resulting from a stern and inexorable necessity—to the general liberty in the United States.... Their liberty, if it were possible, could only be established by...subverting the union. And beneath the ruins of the union would be buried, sooner or later, the liberty of both races.[42]

These necessary-evil consequentialist arguments merged into positive-good ones. In many cases, the latter simply stated in positive terms what the former stated in negative terms. Yet the purpose of the positive-good consequentialist arguments was precisely to present the case for the institution of racial slavery more positively and more aggressively—to offer not merely antiabolitionist arguments but also proslavery ones. The defenders of slavery attributed a litany of beneficial consequences to the institution for blacks and whites, the North and the South, the United States and the world. They argued that the southern slaves were happy, contented, and better off than the free laborers of the American North and Western Europe; that the institution was an extremely profitable one for the regional, national, and international economies; and that it provided a stable foundation for republican government in the South by disenfranchising a lower class composed exclusively of blacks and elevating a middle class composed exclusively of whites.[43] Again, the positive-good consequentialist arguments converged on the maximum-liberty argument, this time framed in comparative terms: Slave societies are actually freer than free societies. As McDuffie explained the argument:

> But where the menial offices and dependent employments of society are performed by domestic slaves, a class well defined by their color and entirely separated from the political body, the rights of property are perfectly secure, without the establishment of artificial barriers. In a word, the institution of domestic slavery supersedes the necessity of…a hereditary system of government.[44]

McDuffie capped off this argument with the statement for which his gubernatorial message became famous: "Domestic slavery, therefore, instead of being a political evil, is the corner-stone of our republican edifice."[45]

Proslavery figures also argued that the institution of racial slavery "improved" the African slaves by exposing them to a "superior" culture. The logical conclusion of this argument was that the institution was preparing the slaves for freedom and, as a result, was perfectly defensible on those liberal grounds. Not surprisingly, proslavery figures carefully hedged this conclusion and placed it well into the future. The only way they could escape it, however, was by arguing that the slaves would never be fully prepared for freedom because, as members of an inferior race, they were naturally incapable of governing themselves or anyone else. Not being eager to make this illiberal move, Chancellor Harper, in his contribution to *Cotton Is King,* argued for the continued existence of racial slavery into the indefinite future on grounds that "if in the adorable providence of God, at a time and in a manner which we can neither foresee nor conjecture, they [the slaves] are to be rendered capable of freedom…they would be prepared for it in the best and most effectual, because in the most natural and gradual manner."[46]

The defenders of slavery did seem to occupy a stronger polemical position on consequentialist grounds than they did on deontological grounds. The widely shared belief that a racially egalitarian society was impossible, if not also undesirable, suggested slavery would continue to exist for the foreseeable future in the United States.[47] Still, if we assume that the majority, in both the North and the South, took a relatively moderate necessary-evil stance on the slavery issue because they found the antislavery deontological arguments as compelling as the proslavery consequentialist arguments, then proslavery figures had a strong incentive to turn to a third type of argument to break that impasse. They did increasingly turn to contextualist arguments that linked proslavery sentiments to such consensual American values as union, progress, and the nation's special mission in history. This dynamic toward contextualist arguments reinforced the dynamic toward liberal arguments because most Americans defined union, progress, and the American mission in liberal terms. The union was a union dedicated to liberty; progress was progress toward liberal institutions; and the American mission was a mission to spread the blessings of those institutions to other countries around the world.[48]

Contextualism

As was true of the proslavery deontological arguments, the proslavery contextualist arguments constituted a tactical response to a defensive polemical position. The defenders of slavery found themselves in a position of being compelled to deny the "American exemplar," "human progress," and "house divided" arguments. Somehow they had to discover a way to argue that slavery was not an illiberal institution whose continued presence on American soil undermined the nation's special mission in history and exposed Americans as hypocrites; that slavery was not an anachronistic institution that impeded progress and yet was doomed by the further march of progress; and that slavery did not create a house divided in the United States, which must become all free or all slave, or fall.[49] But, again, the defenders of slavery could adopt a more aggressive strategy here. In their more positive forms, the proslavery contextualist arguments insisted that the end of slavery, not its continued existence, was the greatest threat to union, progress, and the American mission.

Even in their more negative forms, proslavery contextualist arguments could serve as vehicles for proslavery figures to find common ground with southern moderates. In denying the antislavery contextualist arguments, the proslavery contextualist arguments contended that the South was not the illiberal, backward, and parochial region of the country the antislavery contextualist arguments asserted it to be. In their more positive forms, however, proslavery contextualist arguments could help push southern moderates into adopting more radical proslavery positions by associating proslavery sentiments more closely with the liberal, progressive, and nationalistic values they shared with proslavery figures.

Instead of southern slavery holding back the nation's special mission in history, proslavery figures claimed southern slaveholders were the principal carriers of that mission. As McDuffie noted,

> More than a half a century ago, one of the most enlightened statesmen who ever illustrated the parliamentary annals of Great Britain [Edmund Burke]...ascribed the high and indomitable spirit of liberty which distinguished the Southern Colonies, to the existence of domestic slavery.... Since those colonies have become independent States, they have amply sustained the glory of their primitive character.... Impartial history will ratify, that the principles of rational liberty are not less thoroughly understood, and have been more vigilantly, resolutely and effectively defended against all the encroachments of power, by the slave-holding States, than by any other members of the confederacy.[50]

McDuffie thus brushed aside the hostile relationship between the spirits of slavery and liberty that was the premise of the "American-exemplar" argument. He went on to contend that the spirit of abolitionism was the greatest threat to the American exemplar because it would destroy the spirit of liberty in a major portion of the country by destroying the institution upon which that spirit depended. He concluded that he "would as soon open a negotiation for selling the liberty of the State at once, as for making any stipulations for the ultimate emancipation of our slaves."[51]

Similarly, proslavery figures claimed slavery was not retarding progress but rather propelling it. Their response to the human-progress argument was fourfold. First, the institution of slavery has, in general, been a civilizing force in history, removing men from more primitive states of existence by permitting more labor-intensive modes of production. Second, the institution of racial slavery has, in particular, meant progress for the African slaves by bringing them into contact with (allegedly) more advanced civilizations. Third, the institution has meant progress for everyone else by producing a higher standard of living than would have been possible in its absence. Fourth, any stable, progressive society relies on the presence of protective institutions such as slavery for its less fortunate members so that, broadly understood, slavery is not a dying institution but an universal one.[52] From this exalted perspective, Harper could designate the defense of southern slavery "the defense of civilization," and Hammond could declare that the southern slaveholders "stand in the broadest light of the knowledge, civilization and improvement of the age."[53] In placing slavery on the side of progress, the defenders of slavery relegated its abolition to the side of regress. Calhoun, speaking in support of a series of proslavery resolutions he had introduced in the United States Senate, warned:

Experience had shown that the existing relation between them [the two races in the South] secured the peace and happiness of both. Each had improved; the inferior greatly; so much so, that it had attained a degree of civilization never before attained by the black race in any age or country. Under no other relation could they co-exist together. To destroy it was to involve a whole region in slaughter, carnage, and desolation; and, come what will, we must defend and preserve it.[54]

This warning suggests how the defenders of slavery rephrased the house-divided argument. They argued that southern slavery had not created a house divided; northern agitation against the institution had. As Calhoun had predicted in an earlier Senate speech defending a gag rule on abolitionist petitions, "Abolition and the Union cannot co-exist. As the friend of the Union I openly proclaim it,—and the sooner it is known the better."[55] In this way, proslavery figures could present themselves as the true defenders of the union.[56] They argued that the spirit of abolitionism, not the spirit of slavery, was the gravest threat to the union; otherwise, it could endure indefinitely half free and half slave. Concurrently, proslavery figures also denied the house-divided argument. If, as they contended, the North and the South merely arranged their labor relations in different, though equally liberal, ways, then the union was not really a house divided against itself.[57] On the eve of the Civil War, Hammond deplored the fact that but for northern aggressions against southern slavery, the union would have lasted "for untold ages" and the American people would have become "the freest, most prosperous and most powerful people that the world has ever known."[58]

The defenders of slavery sought to expand the proslavery appeal by associating proslavery sentiments more closely with consensual American values. The key to this effort was to rebut the main assumption of the antislavery contexualist arguments: that racial slavery was an illiberal institution. The central dynamic of the proslavery movement was, then, to portray racial slavery as an institution that, all appearances to the contrary, actually maximized the practical liberty of those it affected. This dynamic clearly emerges in the comparison of Dew's and Fitzhugh's major proslavery works.

D E W A N D F I T Z H U G H

The Antiabolitionist Argument

Thomas R. Dew seemed to gleefully accept the role of antiabolitionist. The thrust of his review of the 1831–32 debate in the Virginia legislature over the fate of slavery in the state was negative. He did not so much defend slavery as attack the various emancipation schemes that had been proposed during the debate. Dew's focus in the *Review* seems perfectly consistent with the necessary-evil school of proslavery thought.[59]

Yet Dew actually straddled the necessary-evil and positive-good schools. His necessary-evil attack on abolition was framed by a positive-good defense of slavery. While the central section of the essay details the potential harms of abolition, the first and last sections praise the many benefits of slavery.[60]

Given the timing of his essay, it is not surprising that Dew straddled the two schools of proslavery thought. He was on the cusp of a shift in emphasis from antiabolitionist necessary-evil arguments to proslavery positive-good arguments that had emerged by the 1830s in the South. But Dew's *Review* also indicates the lack of demarcation between the two schools.[61]

Necessary Evil

Reviewing the various emancipation schemes that have been proposed or contemplated in the second section of his essay, Dew rejects each of them on consequentialist grounds. He divides the schemes into two categories: emancipation with removals and emancipation without removals. He initially targets emancipation with removals as the general scheme favored by the state's antislavery legislators. Dew seems to take them at face value. At least for the sake of argument, he considers their plans for colonizing Africa with freed Virginia slaves as bona fide efforts to gradually abolish slavery in the state. Here, Dew assumes that everyone—he, they, and the broader public in Virginia and elsewhere—opposes emancipation without removals.[62]

As a plan of emancipation, Dew insists colonization is totally impractical. To rid Virginia of slavery (and blacks), colonization would have to be carried out on such a grandiose scale that it would be economically unfeasible. It would bankrupt the state, which could never bear the costs of compensating the slaveholders for their slaves and transporting the freed slaves to Africa (pp. 357–66). On the other hand, if colonization were carried out on a scale that was economically feasible, it would never come close to ridding Virginia of slavery (or blacks). It would, at best, merely slow the rate of increase of the state's slave (black) population (pp. 366–79). As a plan of emancipation, colonization would inevitably fall far short of its goal.

Dew next criticizes three variations on colonization that seek to shift the costs from the state of Virginia to individual slaveholders or to the slaves themselves: (1) where the slaveholders voluntarily emancipate their slaves and pay the costs of transporting the freed slaves to Africa (pp. 379–81); (2) where the slaves work to purchase their own freedom and pay their own transportation costs to Africa (pp. 381–84); and (3) where the state compels (without compensation) the slaveholders to emancipate their slaves and pay the costs of transporting the freed slaves to Africa (pp. 384–91).[63] According to Dew, these cost-shifting schemes only seem to make colonization more economically feasible. The insuperable barrier to any plan of emancipation with removals is the $100 million Virginians have invested in their slaves. Dew warns that "Virginia will be a desert" if a serious colonization effort were ever undertaken in the state (p. 384; also p. 380).

Even if hundreds of thousands of slaves could be miraculously freed and transported to Africa without costing anyone anything, Dew would still consider colonization an ill-advised policy. He claims the costs to the freed slaves, in terms of the high mortality rates they would suffer as they adjusted to their new environment (pp. 394–400), and to Virginians, in terms of the large sums of money they would have to contribute to the new colony as it struggled to become self-sufficient (pp. 400–4, 411–12)—would be prohibitive. He also claims any serious colonization effort would not, as his opponents contend, result in the freed slaves "civilizing" Africans but rather in wars of extermination between the two now-separate races (pp. 409–10). From every angle, Dew considers colonization a disastrous policy.

At this point in the essay, Dew turns his attention to the second category of emancipation schemes: emancipation without removals. He insists Virginia's antislavery legislators, if they are really serious about ending slavery in the state, will be compelled to move in this direction because of the utter impracticability of any scheme of emancipation with removals (pp. 420–21). While Dew's critique of emancipation with removals emphasized its unfeasibility, his critique of emancipation without removals emphasizes its undesirability.

According to Dew, the reason everyone opposes emancipation without removals is because everyone agrees it is impossible for people of two different races to live together as equals in peace, harmony, and prosperity (p. 444). He presents this impossibility as a historical truth, confirmed by the recent experiences of other nations, such as Haiti (pp. 440–41) and Guatemala (pp. 445–46), with emancipation without removals. Nor, he contends, is the American North a counterexample because of its paucity of blacks (p. 446); beside, as he points out, free blacks do not exactly live as equals to whites there (p. 436). Considering Virginia's large black population, Dew anticipates a dramatic increase in black-on-white violence in the state if emancipation does not include a physical separation of the two races.

> But one limited massacre is recorded in Virginia history; let her liberate her slaves, and every year you would hear of insurrections and plots, and every day would perhaps record a murder; the melancholy tale of Southampton would not alone blacken the page of our history. (p. 444)[64]

Dew sees the slaves' lack of preparedness for freedom as the source of the other undesirable consequences of emancipation without removals (pp. 437, 442). He believes blacks would not prosper as free laborers because they fancy that freedom means freedom from work (pp. 428–30). The freed slaves would become a drain on society, as has occurred in the American North and Latin America (pp. 422–24). Especially given how free black labor would depress free white labor to its own inefficient level (p. 443), Dew believes emancipation without removals could not fail to cause a general famine in Virginia (p. 433). The freed slaves would also injure society (as well as themselves) through high rates of lawlessness (pp. 433–35), drunkeness (p. 439), and indebtedness (p. 440). Dew is "almost certain" that emancipation without removals would "bring down ruin and degradation both on the whites and the blacks" (p. 446; also p. 451).

Even viewing emancipation without removals solely from a black perspective, Dew thinks it is an undesirable policy. He claims the freed slaves "would still be virtually slaves; talent, habit, and wealth, would make the white the master still, and the emancipation would only have the tendency to deprive" them of the "sympathies and kind feelings" of southern whites (p. 437). He predicts Virginia would have to impose a compulsory labor system, "more intolerable" than slavery, on the freed slaves in order to prevent a general famine (pp. 441–42).[65] And he suggests blacks will never be truly free and equal to whites in the United States since they will always face the same racial prejudices they currently face in slavery (pp. 435–36, 447–48). In part because the promise of freedom would remain unfulfilled, Dew insists blacks are happier now as slaves than they would be as free persons (pp. 437, 442).[66] He asks, rhetorically, why "the happiest of the human race are constantly invited to sigh for such freedom, and to sacrifice all their happiness in the vain wish" (p. 442). He also laments the fact that emancipation would prematurely stop the process of improvement blacks are undergoing in slavery (pp. 429, 443). As Dew interprets the historical record, it confirms that "[l]iberty has been the heaviest curse to the slave, when given too soon" (p. 437).

Dew's own racial prejudices facilely place blacks in the category of people unprepared to meet the requirements of self-government, but it is important to note how those requirements are liberal ones. They include a proper definition of "rational liberty," as industriousness and not idleness or licentiousness. They also include certain behavioral components: productive labor and an ability to govern oneself without falling prey to the temptations of crime, alcohol, or debt. In arguing that the black slaves do not meet these requirements, Dew, in effect, is arguing that a liberal society cannot afford to emancipate them because it would mean no more freedom for them and less freedom for everyone else.[67]

After Dew has finished attacking these various emancipation schemes, his readers must have wondered if he thought the time would ever come when the slaves would be prepared for freedom. Later in the essay, he does propose his own emancipation scheme. His plan is to transform Virginia into a more economically progressive state by crisscrossing it with internal improvements (pp. 477–81). His hope is that this policy would make the state more attractive to free labor, thereby decreasing its dependence on slave labor and the proportion of blacks in its population to the point where the state's slave-holders would no longer feel any need to keep slaves nor any danger in free-ing them. Dew expects that "in due time the abolitionists will find this most lucrative system working to their heart's content, increasing the prosperity of Virginia, and diminishing the evils of slavery, without those impoverishing effects which all other schemes must necessarily have" (p. 479).[68]

Beside the fact that Dew's plan of emancipation is open to many of the same objections he has himself leveled against other such plans, his plan places the end of slavery in Virginia in a future so indeterminate that it seems gratituous for him even to offer it as a plan of emancipation.[69] Appropriately, Dew, in the penultimate paragraph of his essay, claims he has now proven "by reasoning almost as conclusive as the demonstrations of the mathe-matician…that the time for emancipation has not yet arrived, and perhaps it never will" (p. 489).

If Dew adhered to the necessary-evil school on southern slavery, he adhered to the necessary-evil school that believed the institution might always be necessary. He provides no dynamics for preparing the slaves for freedom, despite his insistence that they need to be so prepared. He, indeed, strongly implies that they will never be ready to be free persons because, as members of an inferior race, they are naturally unsuited to that status (pp. 421–22, 428–30, 433, 449–50).[70] Dew's necessary-evil defense of slavery merges into a positive-good defense of the institution. The more positive aspects of his defense of slavery clearly emerge in the first and third sections of the essay.

Positive Good

Dew most explicitly presents a positive-good ideology in the third and final section of his essay. There, he parries five objections to the "injustice and evils of slavery": (1) "Slavery is wrong, in the *abstract* at least, and contrary to spirit of Christianity" (pp. 451–54); (2) "the moral effects of slavery are of the most deleterions [sic] and hurtful kind" (pp. 454–61); (3) "slavery is unfa-vorable to a republican spirit" (pp. 461–62); (4) "insecurity of the whites, arising from plots, insurrections, &c., among the blacks" (pp. 462–82); and (5) "slave labor is unproductive, and the distressed condition of Virginia and the whole South is owing to this cause" (pp. 482–89).

In answering the first objection, Dew develops a biblical defense of slav-ery. This defense pivots on the claim that Judeo-Christian principles may in the abstract condemn the institution, but in practice they actually justify it.

Dew's initial response to the objection is that "any question must be determined by its circumstances, and if, as really is the case, we cannot get rid of slavery without producing a greater injury to both the masters and slaves, there is no rule of conscience or revealed law of God which can condemn us" (p. 451). He has already argued the point that abolishing slavery in Virginia would produce a greater injury to both the masters and slaves than the continued existence of the institution would. He has also already argued the point that the British government, not the people of Virginia, was responsible for the original injustice of introducing slavery into the state, a point he repeats here (p. 451).[71] He then admits the truth of the objection but with a serious qualification.

> With regard to the assertion that slavery is against the spirit of Christianity, we are ready to admit the general assertion, but deny most positively, that there is any thing in the Old or New Testament, which would go to show that slavery, when once introduced, ought at all events to be abrogated, or that the master commits any offence in holding slaves. (p. 451)

At this point Dew observes how the ancient Hebrews were themselves slaveholders, and justified in the Old Testament for being so (pp. 451–52). He also observes how the New Testament justifies slaveholding. Even though Jesus "was born in the Roman world—a world in which the most galling slavery existed, a thousand times more cruel than the slavery in our own country…he no where encourages insurrection; he no where fosters discontent; but exhorts *always* to implicit obedience and fidelity" (p. 452). Dew concludes his biblical defense of slavery by quoting the scriptural exhortations to servants to obey their masters, which prove "slavery in the Roman world was no where charged as a fault or crime upon the holder" (p. 453). By this point, Dew's admission of the truth of this first objection seems to be an admission without any substance.

Dew's reply to the second objection is in a more strictly consequentialist vein. He takes this objection from Jefferson's *Notes on the State of Virginia,* citing the passage that describes how the children of slaveholders learn to act like petty tyrants by watching how their fathers treat their slaves (pp. 454–55).[72] Dew claims the children of most slaveholders learn, on the contrary, the most elevated moral sentiments by watching how their fathers treat their slaves. "Instead of being reared a selfish contracted being, with nought but self to look to," the child of the typical slaveholder "acquires a more exalted benevolence, a greater generosity and elevation of soul, and embraces for the sphere of his generous actions a much wider field" (p. 455). Not surprisingly, then, the slaveholding population of the South has generally been characterized not by despotic habits but by "humane and virtuous" ones, as shown by the remarkable record it has amassed for disinterested statesmanship in the national councils (pp. 455–56).[73]

In rebutting the third objection, Dew's attention shifts from the beneficial effects of slavery on those most intimately involved in the institution to its beneficial effects on the broader public. He first cites the ancient Greek and Roman republics as counterexamples to the claim that slavery undermines republicanism (p. 461). He goes on to suggest that slave societies are, as a rule, freer than free societies.[74] For evidence, he quotes Burke to the effect that southerners were more zealous partisans of liberty at the time of the American Revolution than northerners were. He concurs with Burke's reasoning that southerners entertained "a higher and more stubborn" spirit of liberty than northerners did, because they regarded freedom as "a kind of rank and privilege" in comparison to their slaves (p. 461).[75] He adds that in the South the institution of racial slavery has had a leveling effect on whites, making them more equal to each other than in the North, by reserving all menial employments for blacks (pp. 461–62). Dew views "this spirit of equality" as "the generator and preserver of the genuine spirit of liberty" (p. 462).[76]

Dew's response to the fourth objection continues to portray southern slave society as superior to northern free society. He counters the claim that slavery fosters a psychology of fear among southern whites by pointing out that their fears of racial violence would only increase with emancipation (without removals) (p. 462). He also denies the premise of the objection. He contends southern fears of racial violence are not great now, nor should they be, given how infrequently slave revolts have occurred in the South in the past (p. 471).[77] He acknowledges those fears have increased recently due to the Nat Turner rebellion, but he expects that increase to be a temporary aberration (p. 481). He insists the South "enjoys as much or more conscious security, than any other people on the face of the globe," more so than the North and other free societies whose lower classes are not safely tucked away in slavery (pp. 481–82; also pp. 465–66).

In answer to the last objection, Dew claims the real cause of the depressed economic conditions in Virginia and the rest of the South is the unjust policies of the federal government, not slavery (pp. 486–87).[78] He argues that slave labor, while generally inferior to free labor, is the superior form of labor under southern conditions of a predominantly African-American workforce, a semitropical climate, and large-scale crop production (pp. 483–85).[79] Under these conditions, Dew believes slavery significantly boosts regional economic performance.

In this final section of his *Review*, Dew sculpts a positive-good ideology for the antebellum South. He links its institution of racial slavery to such widely shared values as Christian charity, public service, political equality, collective security, economic prosperity, and, above all, the definitive liberal value of personal liberty. In the first section of the essay, Dew states the case for slavery as a positive good on an even grander scale. He chronicles "its effects on the progress of civilization" (pp. 294–324), the "advantages which have resulted to the world from the institution of slavery" (pp. 324–36), and the positive "influence of slavery on the condition of the female sex" (pp.

336–42). In this section, he attempts to align slavery with progress. Central to this effort is a consideration of possible Judeo-Christian and liberal justifications of the institution.

This section contains Dew's first discussion of the Hebraic institution of slavery. Dew uncovers two justifications of the institution. One, it was a substitute for killing captives of war: during their conquest of Canaan, the ancient Hebrews at least partially departed from the then-prevailing practice of killing captives of war by enslaving some of them instead (pp. 306–7). Two, it was a substitute for starvation: the Hebrews, along with other ancient peoples, sold themselves into slavery as a way of paying off their debts or in other cases of extreme poverty (pp. 317–18).[80] Under the circumstances, the institution appears to have been a pragmatic exchange of liberty for life, justified by Judeo-Christian principles on those grounds, and less barbaric than the alternative.

Viewed from a liberal perspective, the nature of slavery seems similar. Dew cites a number of natural-law theorists, including John Locke, on the justice of enslaving captives of war, at least under certain circumstances (pp. 308–10).[81] He goes on to consider William Blackstone's rebuttal of this "just war" justification of slavery. Blackstone had argued that since conquering armies are under no necessity to kill their captives, enslaving them instead is unjust. Dew finds Blackstone's reasoning fallacious because he wrongly assumed slavery exists "in its pure, unmitigated form, 'whereby an unlimited power is given to the master over the life and fortune of the slave,'" when, in reality, the institution never exists in that form (p. 310). To the degree that it is a genuine, and legally regulated, exchange of liberty for life, Dew thinks liberal principles do justify enslaving captives of war and justify the captives in accepting the implicit bargain.

For Dew, liberal and Judeo-Christian principles also coincide in justifying slavery in cases where people sell themselves into slavery in order to preserve their lives. He again criticizes Blackstone for failing to recognize that slavery, in its existing, "impure" forms, is sometimes a good bargain for the slave (p. 321). It is a good bargain on liberal grounds because, according to Dew, the slave receives more than subsistence in exchange. Dew insists that "[i]n most parts of the world" the slave is not only guaranteed "nourishment and subsistence" but "carefully protected in life, limb, and even in a moderate share of liberty, by the policy of the laws" (p. 321). Dew, therefore, is not content to place the slave's bargain solely on the basis of trading liberty for life. In terms of the liberal goals of life, happiness, and liberty, he believes many people around the world would be better off as slaves than they are currently as free persons. His example is a Chinese laborer who lives on the brink of starvation (pp. 321–22). Dew contends this laborer is clearly worse off than a slave, for "he is subjected to all the hardships and degradation of the slave, and derives none of the advantages" (p. 322). When such a laborer sells himself into slavery, Dew believes he is making a good bargain. Dew speculates that more people would sell themselves into slavery if the laws of their countries did not prevent them from doing so. He even contends the supply would exceed the demand. The British capitalist, for one, "could not afford to purchase the operative, and treat him as we do the slave" (p. 322; also p. 319).

Still, his readers might well have asked, what is the relation between these two Judeo-Christian and liberal justifications of slavery and the southern institution of racial slavery? Dew, after all, admits that American laborers, who, unlike Chinese laborers, live in a relatively prosperous and sparsely populated country, do not need to sell themselves into slavery in order to survive (p. 321). Nor does he offer any "just war" justification of southern slavery.[82]

Dew, however, is making a broader point through these two justifications of slavery, one that does apply to southern slavery: that some people do enjoy more practical liberty as slaves than they would as free persons. Dew's racial prejudices, again, facilely place blacks in this category. But his point is not strictly a racial one. Rather, his argument is that all societies are structured around different statuses; that the precise status that leads to the most practical liberty for any one person depends on the capacities of that person and the conditions of the society in which he or she lives; and that the abstract distinction between the status of free persons and slaves confounds the more finely tuned analysis necessary to determine how much practical liberty people actually enjoy in any particular status. On the basis of such an analysis, Dew argues not only that the southern institution of racial slavery is a relatively benevolent one but that the status of slave and statuses analogous to it are extremely prevalent ones. He finds that, "looking to the whole world, we may, even now, with confidence assert, that slaves, or those whose condition is infinitely worse, form by far the largest portion of the human race" (p. 296).[83]

After establishing a universal basis for the institution, Dew moves to tighten the linkage between slavery and progress. He opens this discussion by claiming that "slavery has been, perhaps, the principal means for impelling forward the civilization of mankind. Without its agency, society must have remained sunk into that deplorable state of barbarism and wretchedness which characterized the inhabitants of the Western World, when first discovered by Columbus" (p. 325). He initially stresses the way slavery has made wars more humane because historically, as he has argued previously, it was instituted as a substitute for killing captives of war (pp. 325–26). Once instituted, though, it instigated further progress by elevating men from the hunting stage of civilization to the agricultural stage (pp. 326–29). Dew contends this advance has clearly been evident among the southern slaves. He, indeed, contends "there is not, in the annals of history, an instance of such able to perform some task, but I still may be able to learn to do it. The point is that although I may demonstrate an aptitude or competence for certain kinds of tasks, some of those tasks require performers with immediate (already developed) expertise—those of a brain surgeon, a concert pianist, or the ubiquitous rocket scientist, for example. Here, following Brian Barry, there are criteria for being one and standards for being a good one.[64]

There is also an additional, related distinction between competence as abilities and competence as means: the distinction between the idea of "exclusionary" that inheres in developing competences into expertise to meet requirements and, for example, Robert Goodin's idea of "exclusionary" as it inheres in positional goods.[65] The development of a competence into an expertise, unlike the exclusion of some kinds of consumption or possession, is not restricted by limited availability of goods but by the particular capacities of the individual. Nevertheless, the average person's opportunities for either acquiring a seventeenth-century Dutch still life or becoming a principal dancer for the New York City Ballet are probably equally limited, in the one case by lack of competence in the sense of means and in the other case by lack of competence in the sense of trained or trainable abilities. It is not unusual for these two kinds of competences to be conflated—sometimes intentionally, sometimes conveniently. Members of Parliament in England in the seventeenth century, for example, were able to assert convincingly that the capacity to make or hold a fortune and the capacity to govern were virtually equivalent, arguing by extension that governing in their own interests added up to governing in the public interest. The validity of the argument, as far as it goes, is often compelling in the immediate circumstances.[66]

Judgments about best use are exclusionary, in part simply because decisions are necessary. Some basis is therefore also necessary for the authoritative integration of plural viewpoints into acceptable decision making, and acceptable decision making requires that the rules determining access to deliberating the standards also pass muster. The forms of the deliberations over rules for best use turn out to be at the heart of what is public.

Doing something well includes doing it with expertise and competence and according to standards. Assuming, therefore, willingness and good intentions on the part of a legislative representative, for example, that representative might be expected to be competent in two respects: first, in interpreting the complex and often contradictory or mutually exclusive preferences of a constituency, and second, in acting on the interpretations in the context of other representatives with similar aims (in the legislature, for example). Ideally, the competent aggregation of the complex needs and preferences of one's constituency would be balanced by competence in assigning priorities to issues and making decisions in the context of multiple, competing demands on limited resources, often according to ill-defined or undefined criteria for best use. In other words, given the relative scarcity of offices, rapid improvement in civilization, as that undergone by the negro slaves in our country, since the time they were first brought among us" (p. 334). He claims that slavery has also elevated the status of women by creating a stable family structure (pp. 338–39, 341). According to Dew, the institution has fueled such widespread progress that "even the slave, in the agricultural, is happier than the free man [and woman] in the hunting state" (p. 339; also pp. 337–38).

In this first section of the *Review*, Dew thus dissents from the human-progress argument that characterizes slavery as an regressive institution. Much later, he also dissents from the house-divided argument. In the final paragraph of his essay, Dew notes how the ancient Greek and Roman republics were houses divided against themselves that did stand. He also notes how a tenacious spirit of liberty exists in Poland despite its continuing feudal relations.[84] Dew then draws the parallel to Virginia.

> We must recollect, in fine, that our own country [Virginia] has waded through two dangerous wars—that the thrilling eloquence of the Demosthenes of our land [Patrick Henry] has been heard with rapture, exhorting to death, rather than slavery—that the most liberal principles have even been promulgated and sustained, in our deliberate bodies, and before our judicial tribunals—and the whole has passed by without breaking or tearing asunder the elements of our social fabric. (p. 490)

Here Dew draws together two of his major positive-good arguments: (1) some of the freest societies in history have been slave societies; (2) once we properly situate the status of slave within a more general set of dependent statuses, we recognize its universality. He also reasserts one of the central claims of his defense of slavery: the nation's liberal, founding principles are not antagonistic to the institution.

Yet Dew's main goal is not neutralizing the contextualist human-progress and house-divided arguments but attacking his state's antislavery legislators for failing to realistically assess the probable social consequences of their pet projects. Dew, accordingly, closes his *Review* by reminding them that "the relations of society, generated by the *lapse of ages,* cannot be altered in a *day*" (p. 490). This theme of legislative irresponsibility has been a recurrent one throughout the essay (pp. 288, 293–94, 354–55, 443, 450–51, 482).[85] In particular, Dew accuses his opponents of failing to adjust the nation's liberal, founding principles to existing conditions. In a key passage, he scolds them for "pompously and ostentatiously" proclaiming that "all men are born equal" and "the slave has a natural right to regain his liberty." He retorts that "no set of legislators ever have, or ever can, legislate upon purely abstract principles, entirely independent of circumstances, without the ruin of the body politic" (pp. 354–55). Though Dew straddled the necessary-evil and positive-good schools on southern slavery, his primary arguments remained antiabolitionist consequentialist ones.

By the time of Fitzhugh's *Cannibals All,* published a quarter century after Dew's *Review,* the priorities of the proslavery movement had changed. The immediatist philosophy of the northern abolitionists had replaced the colonizationist philosophy of Virginia's dissident legislators as the principal antislavery vehicle in the United States. While Fitzhugh certainly offers both antiabolitionist and proslavery consequentialist arguments in *Cannibals All,* his focus is elsewhere. As compared to Dew, he develops a more positive-good defense of slavery that does not even admit the institution is wrong on deontological grounds and that much more explicitly defends it on liberal grounds. Given the increased sectional tensions of the 1850s, Fitzhugh's work also betrays a greater contextualist emphasis on how the union (as opposed to Virginia) is, or is not, a house divided.

The Proslavery Argument

In *Cannibals All,* George Fitzhugh developed a two-pronged defense of southern slavery. On the first prong, he defended the institution as part of a broader family of protective institutions, as a universal institution, akin to the institutions of the American North and other parts of the world. On the second prong, he defended the institution as a peculiarly southern institution, as an institution of racial slavery specially fitted for the members of an inferior race. Fitzhugh hoped the first, more liberal prong would carry the second, more racist prong along with it. He, however, could not totally neglect the second prong because the southern institution of racial slavery was the institution he had chosen to defend to the world. Together, the two prongs of his defense of Southern slavery had the advantage of allowing him to appeal to both the liberal and racist sentiments of his audience and of evoking the former as a way of trying to legitimate the latter.[86]

This approach can be confusing, and purposely so. Corresponding to the two prongs of his defense of southern slavery, Fitzhugh uses the terms *slaves, government,* and *slave society* in both narrow and broad senses so that the reader must know which prong Fitzhugh is "on" at any point in the text to follow his argument. *Slaves,* for instance, can refer to slaves per se, or to anyone he sees in a more or less equivalent status—that is, to almost anyone. Similarly, *government* can refer to government per se or to any protective institution, even to public opinion and other, more informal forms of social regulation—that is, to almost anything. Accordingly, *slave society* is the opposite of *free society* either in the sense that it is a society with the specific institution of slavery or in the sense that it is a society with a very imprecise "more of government." Conflating the two prongs can lead to some fairly perverse results: that Fitzhugh favors enslaving the whole working class instead of merely establishing a stronger network of protective institutions for free (white) laborers, or that he favors a substantial increase in governmental powers instead of merely advocating more public responsibility for the "weaker" (white) members of society. All this confusion of language does, however, serve his polemical purposes because it portrays the southern institution of racial slavery as part of a family of institutions few people would reject and obfuscates the way it may differ from those other institutions. By taking his readers' focus off slavery, specifically racial slavery, he can better defend the institution on liberal grounds.[87]

Who Is Really Free?

In *Cannibals All*, Fitzhugh insists on defending slavery as a positive good (p. 199). He even credits his first book with moving the South from a necessary-evil position to a positive-good one (p. 7).[88] What a positive-good defense of slavery means to Fitzhugh is a defense of the institution as a universal one. It is part of a more general set of institutions that promote the benevolent purpose of protecting the "weak" from the "strong." Such institutions are necessary because, according to Fitzhugh's Hobbesian social vision, all people are "cannibals" who strive to live off the labor of others (pp. 16–18, 38–39, 87). He believes all societies have an obligation, and have heretofore fulfilled that obligation, to prevent the most powerful cannibals from devouring their victims, or, less metaphorically stated, to prevent the "strong" from (unduly) exploiting the "weak," by setting up a network of protective institutions (pp. 28, 187, 236).[89]

Fitzhugh considers slavery the most efficient of these protective institutions because it most tightly joins the interests of those in the dominant status ("masters") with the interests of those in the dependent status ("slaves") (pp. 25, 31, 84, 205, 246). He contends feudal serfdom is a closely related institution (pp. 73, 79–80, 107–9, 184–85); but also related, though less closely, are other forms of compulsory labor (pp. 28, 109–10, 187–88, 232–33), families (pp. 28, 80, 187, 235), churches (pp. 99–101), charitable institutions (pp. 28, 109–10, 187–88, 236), and even governments (pp. 65–66, 94, 247, 254–55). Fitzhugh analogizes wives (pp. 80, 99, 187, 235), children (pp. 28, 80, 187, 235), wards (p. 80), apprentices (p. 80), prisoners (p. 80), soldiers (pp. 80, 236), sailors (pp. 80, 236), the poor under the English poor laws (pp. 109–10, 187–88), and imported Chinese laborers in the British colonies (pp. 232–33), as well as the remaining serfs of eastern Europe and central Asia (pp. 79–80, 200). Thus broadly understood, the status of slave is very widespread indeed, and every society seems to be a slave society.

In Fitzhugh's view, contemporary free societies in the American North, Great Britain, and western Europe are unique in attempting to destroy, or at least dilute, all these protective institutions and dependent statuses (pp. 66, 94, 247, 253–54). He cautions that the attempt will not rid these societies of "masters" and "slaves" but only make their interests more antagonistic (pp. 25, 31–32, 34). Free laborers, for example, remain dependent on their capitalist employers, though no longer in a personal manner. They, therefore, are now "slaves without masters" and are only "miscalled" free laborers (pp. 17, 32, 72–73, 78, 221, 258).[90]

Fitzhugh claims that "[s]lavery is the natural and normal condition of society. The situation of the North is abnormal and anomalous" (p. 40). Later, he notes that "[f]ree society is a recent and small experiment" (p. 118; also pp. 72, 102, 106). Unlike slave societies, free societies fail to adequately protect the "weak" from the "strong." They place no legal or moral obligations on "masters" (capitalists) to protect their "slaves" (free laborers) (pp. 15–18, 31–32, 73, 84, 184–85). Neither the interests nor the affections of the capitalist encourage him to protect his employees, in sharp contrast to the master-slave relations of the South (pp. 17, 32, 72–73, 78, 258). In fact, the pecuniary interests of the capitalist encourage him to exploit his employees. "It is the interest of the capitalist…to allow free laborers the least possible portion of the fruits of their own labor; for all capital is created by labor, and the smaller the allowance of the free laborer, the greater the gains of his employer" (p. 25). Public opinion reinforces this message. "That same public opinion which shields and protects the slaves encourages the oppression of free laborers—for it is considered more honorable and praiseworthy…to make good bargains than bad ones" (p. 25). The actual enslavement of the working classes of free societies would be resisted not by the workers but by the capitalists, "for the gain would be all on the laborer's side, and the loss all on that of the capitalist" (p. 223).[91]

For Fitzhugh, though, the comparison between slave society and free society is not only a comparison between a society with the institution of slavery and a society without that specific institution. It is also a more general comparison between a society with strong protective institutions and a society without such institutions. As a result, the choice between the South and the North is a choice not only between slave labor and free labor but also "between more of government and no government" (p. 94; also pp. 65–66, 247, 253–55). Fitzhugh considers this choice unproblematic. He believes the North is a society on the verge of institutional collapse, a society on the road "to no private property, no church, no law, no government" (pp. 253–54). Conversely, he believes those institutions are in good repair in the South, so much so that "Southern institutions are far the best now existing in the world" (p. 246; also pp. 66, 97, 106, 191–92).

As Fitzhugh describes the free North, it is a society rife with crime, violence, vice, poverty, unemployment, and destitution (pp. 65, 231–34, 245, 247, 259)—all because of its relative lack of protective institutions and its underlying laissez-faire philosophy. He notes that many admit the failure of free society but few agree on a cure (pp. 9, 85–106, 191, 209–12, 225–27). Consequently, the North is also a society rife with "isms": "Bloomer's and Women's Right's men, and strong-minded women, and Mormons, and anti-renters, and 'vote myself a farm' men, Millerites, and Spiritual Rappers, and Shakers, and Widow Wakemanites, and Agrarians, and Grahamites, and a thousand other superstitious and infidel Isms" (p. 103; also pp. 9, 93, 96, 228–29, 234). Fitzhugh insists the slave South suffers neither from those social ills nor from these pretended cures (pp. 9, 97, 228-29, 234, 259). He reminds abolitionists, socialists, and other would-be social reformers that it is free society, not slave society, that has failed (p. 106).

Paralleling his attack on free society, Fitzhugh attacks its abolitionist champions. Ironically, he claims the abolitionists are the champions of free society not in thinking free society is healthy but in thinking the remedy for its ills is still less government.[92] He accuses them of desiring to abolish "slavery in every form" (p. 218). Abolishing racial slavery is only their immediate goal, and not their real motive, for "[t]hey would not spend so much time and money for the mere sake of the negro" (p. 253; also p. 201).[93] Eventually, they mean to abolish all protective institutions; "to disregard the natural relations of mankind, and profanely to build up states, like Fourierite Phalansteries, or Mormon and Oneida villages, where religion shall be banished, and in which property, wife and children shall be held somewhat in common" (p. 72; also pp. 85, 98–99, 190, 198, 214). Fitzhugh is convinced all the popular isms of the day share this same goal. He contends "the great movement in society, known under various names, as Communism, Socialism, Abolitionism, Red Republicanism and Black Republicanism, has one common object: the breaking up of all law and government, and the inauguration of anarchy" (p. 194; also p. 254). But rather than achieving a utopia of liberty and equality for all, Fitzhugh predicts they will achieve a dystopia of despotism: "Abolition ultimates in 'Consent Government'; Consent Government in Anarchy...and 'Self-elected Despotism winds up the play'" (p. 244; also pp. 245, 254).

Fitzhugh's strategy here is clear. He seeks to associate attacks on slavery, which few Americans would strongly defend, to attacks on the family and other institutions most Americans would strongly defend. In pursuit of this strategy, he offers a "slippery slope" argument to the effect that abolishing slavery would result in the end of all those other institutions. Fitzhugh's own defense of slavery then becomes a defense of all those other institutions and a seemingly well-intentioned effort to prevent the total collapse of American society. What is not clear is how such a defense of slavery is a liberal one.

In this connection, it is important to note how Fitzhugh argues that protective institutions provide the "weak" with other benefits besides protection. He, accordingly, believes slavery would be a good bargain for the free laborers of free societies because they would gain much beside protection. Slaves are less exploited than free laborers because they retain a greater share of what they produce in the form of food, shelter, and even personal property (pp. 15–18, 31–32, 73, 84, 184–85). Unlike free laborers, they do not live on the brink of starvation (pp. 18, 32, 185, 201, 258). And for this and other reasons, they may actually enjoy more practical liberty than free laborers do (pp. 12–13, 17, 21, 32, 223–24).

A major portion of Fitzhugh's argument on this point involves a comparison of the condition of the British working class before and after the end of serfdom, an institution that he again considers closely related to slavery.[94] According to Fitzhugh, such a comparison shows the condition of the British working class to have deteriorated substantially since its "emancipation" (pp. 12, 73, 107–9, 184–85, 258). He claims British workers enjoyed not only a more secure and comfortable existence as serfs than they do now as free laborers but also a greater degree of freedom.

> [T]he laborers of England are not half so free now as before their pretended emancipation. They have lost all their rights, half their liberty…and live in a state of continued destitution, hunger, and excessive labor, from generation to generation—from infancy to old age. (p. 185; also pp. 12, 21, 73, 78, 107–9)

Following the same line of argument, Fitzhugh also claims British workers, as free laborers, are less free than southern slaves.

> Free laborers have not a thousandth part of the rights and liberties of negro slaves. Indeed, they have not a single liberty, unless it be the right or liberty to die. (p. 19; also pp. 12, 15–16, 32, 185, 222–24)[95]

He goes on to suggest that southern slaves are even freer than British (and American) capitalists.

> But the reader may think that he and other capitalists and employers are freer than negro slaves. Your capital would soon vanish, if you dared indulge in the liberty and abandon of negroes. You hold your wealth and position by the tenure of constant watchfulness, care, and circumspection. You never labor; but you are never free. (p. 19)[96]

Fitzhugh seems to delight in the paradox of suggesting how slaves are really free and free persons are really not. Yet, polemically, the suggestion that slavery is not really slavery was a suggestion he was almost compelled to make by the dynamics of a liberal consensus.[97]

In the end, Fitzhugh wants to defend slavery on the grounds that in a certain sense no one, including the wealthiest capitalist, is *really* free and in a certain sense everyone, including the poorest slave, *is* really free. More precisely, he analyzes the question of who is really free into the following propositions: (1) Everyone in every society is constrained in some way or another; (2) no one in any society is constrained in every way; (3) there are many different ways of gauging how constrained people are; (4) overall, some people are more constrained than others are; (5) a person's legal or social status is not always a very accurate gauge of how constrained he or she is; and (6) the ways people are constrained are, or should be, calculated to increase either their own practical liberty or the aggregate liberty of the members of the society in which they live. This analysis is liberal in character, not only because of the goal it is intended to serve but because of the question it is intended to answer.

Fitzhugh imagines slaves as having traded liberty for security. He, however, imagines them as not having traded away all their liberty and also having gained a certain amount of liberty through the greater security they now enjoy. He, therefore, imagines slaves having made a trade that is of the same genus as the trade classical liberal theorists imagine everyone makes in entering civil society. Alternatively, Fitzhugh contends free societies verge on states of nature, as if the proponents of such societies and their underlying laissez-faire philosophies had not learned the liberal lesson that governments and other protective institutions actually increase the aggregate liberty of the members of a given society.[98] Finally, he insists that slaves are better off than free laborers for having made an "additional" trade of liberty for security.

> Free laborers have less liberty than slaves, are worse paid and provided for, and have no valuable rights. Slaves, with more of actual practical liberty, with ampler allowance, and constant protection, are secure in the enjoyment of all the rights which provide for their physical comfort at all times and under all circumstances. (p. 32)

Racial Slavery

At this and many other points in *Cannibals All*, Fitzhugh seems primed to recommend slavery as the optimal condition for the laboring classes across racial, and sectional, lines. He does not, however, ever actually make that recommendation. Instead, he advocates continued racial slavery in the South and "more of government" in the North. He attributes the impending collapse of free society in the North not to its failure to enslave its working class but to its failure to distance itself from laissez-faire philosophy.

> We must, in all sections, act upon the principle that the world is "too little governed." You of the North need not institute negro slavery, far less reduce white men to the state of negro slavery. But the masses require more of protection, and the masses and philosophers equally require more of control. Leave it to time and circumstances to suggest the necessary legislation; but rely upon it, "Anarchy, plus the street constable" won't answer any longer. (p. 247)[99]

The key chapter in Fitzhugh's "retreat" from white slavery is, not surprisingly, the chapter entitled "Negro Slavery." He opens the chapter by announcing his "new" strategy to "vindicate that institution in the abstract" (p. 199). Such a defense of slavery must include the possibility of white slavery because "[t]o insist on less, is to yield our case, and to give up our religion; for if white slavery be morally wrong, be a violation of natural rights, the Bible cannot be true" in view of the nonracial character of the Hebraic institution of slavery (p. 200).

Fitzhugh then begins his retreat. He acknowledges that "[h]uman and divine authority do seem in the general to concur, in establishing the expediency of having masters and slaves of different races" (p. 200). He contends the Hebraic institution of slavery did not violate this generalization because native-born slaves were treated more like wards and apprentices than slaves. As for the other slaves of Judea and the other nations of antiquity, he notes that in most cases they at least belonged to different nationalities than their masters. He ascribes the present-day animus against racial slavery to the fact that world opinion has latched onto the cruelties of the African slave trade and West Indian slavery (pp. 200–1).[100] Southern slavery, though, has progressed far beyond West Indian slavery, for it has developed into "a benign and protective institution, and our negroes are confessedly better off than any free laboring population in the world" (p. 201).

At this point, Fitzhugh briefly returns to the possibility of white slavery, querying, "How can we contend that white slavery is wrong, whilst all the great body of free laborers are starving; and slaves, white or black, throughout the world, are enjoying comfort?" (p. 201).[101] He soon answers his own query, and finalizes his retreat from white slavery, by invoking racial inequality to justify the wholesale enslavement of the black, as opposed to the white, race. Fitzhugh asserts that

> as a general and abstract question, negro slavery has no other claims over other forms of slavery, except that from inferiority, or rather peculiarity, of race, almost all negroes require masters, whilst only the children, the women, the very weak, poor, and ignorant, &c., among the whites, need some protective and governing relation of this kind. (p. 201)[102]

According to Fitzhugh, the "protective and governing" relation appropriate to "weak" white Americans is not slavery. It is not even the dependent statuses appropriate to many Europeans; it is merely "more of government." Only for most blacks is the best fit slavery. Fitzhugh's defense of the specific southern institution of racial slavery is less abstract or universalistic than it is circumstantial. Whether slave status or some other status is best suited to any one individual depends on the state of the society in which he or she lives as well as on his or her own moral and intellectual development. Fitzhugh's analysis of these different statuses is fairly complex. At least in the American case, though, it concludes on two basic statuses: that of slave for blacks, that of free person for whites.[103]

Because Fitzhugh wants to take his readers' focus off *racial* slavery, he does not engage in much analysis of why he believes blacks are best suited to the status of slave. He does, however, engage in some of that type of analysis, and he moves back and forth between natural and environmental explanations of racial inequality (pp. 18–19, 77, 185, 187, 199–201). In his most extended statement on race in *Cannibals All,* he claims that:

> The blacks in America are both positively and relatively weak. Positively so, because they are too improvident to lay up for the exigencies of sickness, of the seasons, or of old age. Relatively so, because they are wholly unequal to the whites among whom they live, in the war of the wits and free competition, which universal liberty begets, and political economy encourages. (p. 187)

Fitzhugh also claims the enslavement of blacks to whites is helping them ascend the scale of civilization (pp. 29, 79–80, 185, 200). It may then only be the mixing of relatively "weaker" and "stronger" races that temporarily makes slavery a necessary institution in the American South. Yet even as Fitzhugh holds out this "necessary evil" possibility, he never suggests that black Americans will ever attain moral or intellectual equality with white Americans, or that the two races will ever live together as equals in the same society.

In his views on racial inequality, Fitzhugh echoes Dew. His defense of slavery does, however, surpass Dew's in two respects. Only once does he even refer to the possibility of abolishing southern slavery, and he never refers to southern slavery as an evil institution on deontological or any other grounds.[104] His defense of the institution is clearly more positive-good than Dew's.[105]

If Fitzhugh does not follow Dew into the polemics of antiabolitionist consequentialism, he does follow him into the polemics of proslavery consequentialism. Here, Fitzhugh goes beyond Dew in his focus on the benefits of southern slavery for the nonslaveholding whites of the South.[106] These benefits are clearly the benefits of racial, specifically black, slavery, not of slavery per se or, obviously, of white slavery.

Fitzhugh explicitly targets the abolitionist charge that slavery especially disadvantages lower-class whites in the South by subordinating them to an ever-encroaching slavocracy.[107] He argues that, to the contrary, the institution "elevates those whites; for it makes them not the bottom of society, as at the North…but privileged citizens, like Greek and Roman citizens, with a numerous class far beneath them." He goes on to argue that "one white man does not lord it over another" in the South, "for all are equal in privilege, if not in wealth" (p. 220). Fitzhugh later expands this "*Herrenvolk* democracy" argument by claiming slavery allows voting rights to be safely extended to nonpropertied whites in the South, more so than in the North, because the institution unites their interests with those of propertied whites as part of a privileged class (pp. 245–46; also pp. 133, 136). The institution's conservative influence allows the South to support not only a more democratic society than the North but also a more liberal one. Fitzhugh insists "the slaveholding South is the only country on the globe that can safely tolerate" the general extension of such rights as freedom of the press, speech, and religion because it is the only "country" on the globe where the majority can be trusted not to abuse those rights so as to "disturb the peace of society, threaten the security of property, offend public decency, assail religion, and invoke anarchy" (pp. 131, 135).

Accordingly, Fitzhugh's point is *not* that nonslaveholding whites should be enslaved but that they gain greater freedoms from the enslavement of blacks. Of course, any recommendation Fitzhugh might have made for enslaving white Americans would have been politically untenable, and perhaps that is the reason he did not venture to do so.[108] The relevant question, however, is not why he did not actually recommend white slavery but why he constructed such a massive intellectual scaffolding to justify a recommendation he never made.

Fitzhugh's professed reason for this tactic is that the South has to seize the offensive on the slavery issue and thus has to defend its institution of racial slavery as an universal institution, not as a racial and peculiarly southern one. What he gains through this defense of southern slavery is precisely a liberal defense of the institution. By stating his argument in universalistic terms, he shows how slavery is logically one among many types of exchanges of liberty for security, exchanges that are not necessarily racial in character and which, for most people, actually increase their practical liberty. Government is the paradigmatic case of such an exchange. Yet Fitzhugh thinks government is only quantitatively, not qualitatively, different from such exchanges as slavery, serfdom, and marriage. He also gains the important point of showing how slavery is not a dying institution because it belongs to a more general pattern of exchanges of liberty for security, exchanges that are not only endemic to social existence but are highly advantageous to the people who engage in them. Finally, Fitzhugh gains the important point of showing how the union is not a house divided. He suggests that the North and the South merely differ in their general patterns of exchanges of liberty for security; for instance, that they merely arrange their labor relations in different ways (p. 188). He also suggests that to the extent the union is a house divided, it is divided over different philosophies of government, not slavery per se (pp. 106, 254). This conflict is one he is confident will be resolved in the South's favor because "every good citizen" has begun to realize that "'the world is too little governed'" (p. 255; also pp. 6, 52).[109] In his concern to counter the contextualist house-divided argument, Fitzhugh, once again, goes beyond Dew.[110]

In attempting to defend southern slavery, Fitzhugh faced a rhetorical dilemma. On one hand, he had to specifically defend racial slavery in order to defend southern slavery. In developing this more circumstantial, more necessary-evil defense of the institution, he, not surprisingly, used race as a critical determinant of status. On the other hand, he sought to develop a more abstract, more positive-good defense of the institution, diverting his readers' attention from racial slavery. By appearing to be open to the possibility of white slavery, his defense of black slavery seems more liberal in nature. The scaffolding he constructs to justify white slavery, which politically he need not and cannot defend, is in the service of justifying black slavery, which politically he needs to defend and is more able to do.[111] Together, the two prongs of Fitzhugh's defense of southern slavery make his use of race as a critical determinant of status seem relatively benign, as one among many ways of deciding in which status any one individual may enjoy the most practical liberty. They also make the differences between a free North and a slave South appear relatively minor, as hardly the fodder for disunion and civil war.

Even if Fitzhugh's two-pronged defense of southern slavery is rather tortured, it allowed him to craft a more liberal defense of the institution than Dew had, as well as a more positive-good and contexualist one. The Fitzhugh-Dew comparison evidences the hypothesized development of the proslavery argument.

CONCLUSION

It would be easy to dismiss Fitzhugh, Dew, and the other defenders of southern slavery as racists and conclude that the institution could not possibly be defended on liberal grounds. Many scholars today would so dismiss them.[112] I am ready to admit that the defenders of southern slavery were racists and that their appeals to liberal principles were disingenuous. But to dismiss them is not to rebut them. To rebut them on liberal grounds is to argue, more convincingly than they, that liberal principles really oppose, rather than support, racial slavery and other forms of racial oppression. Arguably, the antislavery movement eventually adopted just such a strategy.

In offering his own theory of Civil War causation, President Lincoln said:

> The world has never had a good definition of the word liberty, and the American people, just now, are much in want of one. We all declare for liberty; but in using the same *word* we do not all mean the same *thing*. With some the word liberty may mean for each man to do as he pleases with himself, and the produce of his labor; while with others the same word may mean for some men to do what they please with other men, and the produce of other men's labor. Here are two, not only different, but incompatable *[sic]* things called by the same name—liberty.[113]

While his theory was not as nuanced as the ones offered by contemporary scholars, Lincoln did identify the essence of the struggle when he went on to debunk the proslavery definition of liberty as the definition of "the wolf at the sheep's throat."[114]

5

A "Guiding Principle" of Liberalism in the Thought of Frederick Douglass and W.E.B. DuBois

Gayle McKeen

Our question is: How do we understand American liberalism? Is it a more or less coherent "ism," one that intelligibly (if not comfortably) contains the views of such disparate thinkers as James Madison, Mercy Warren, George Fitzhugh, Martin Luther King Jr., and Milton Friedman, and the policies of such disparate figures as Ward Connelly, Donna Shalala, Al Sharpton, and Ross Perot? This eclectic list is a brief illustration of the difficulties of thinking of liberalism as anything like a coherent whole. And, as Harvey Mansfield has argued, "it is evident that liberalism, if it is a whole, is a whole that is afraid to be a whole—and therefore has difficulty in rousing partisans to its defense."[1] The difficulties of defending liberalism are preceded by the difficulties in understanding, characterizing, and defining it.

The essays in this collection point us to views of the liberal tradition in America particularly, and the tradition of American political culture more generally, as diverse and conflictual. J. David Greenstone argued that it was a mistake to think that "liberalism" simply provided the understandings and concepts of American political life. Within the liberal agreement on the importance, if not the substance, of consent, rights, and property, Greenstone argued, sufficient differences existed over "the nature of the human personality and a good society" as to constitute two different liberalisms.[2] These were, respectively, humanist liberalism, with its self-regarding character of materialist politics, and reform liberalism, which concerned itself with moral and substantive standards. Rogers Smith has taken issue with Greenstone's claim that liberalism has been dominant in American political culture, pointing out the prevalence of illiberal and undemocratic ideas—racism in particular, but also sexism and nativism. Going even further, Carol Horton encourages us to see the complexity of the ways in which liberalism has been combined with illiberal ideas and is thus more flexible and diverse than Greenstone thought, but more capable of containing conflicts than Smith realizes.

In this essay I would like to take up the perhaps unfashionable notion of liberalism as a kind of whole. By this I do not mean a consensus of the sort espoused by Louis Hartz, nor do I mean to argue that America and Americans have been shaped only (or even primarily) by ideas of freedom and equality. Rather, I assume that the central ideas of American liberalism continue to be of interest to us because they are useful, and that they are useful in part because they are dynamic. Thus I will focus not upon a "tradition" of thought or discourse in America but upon a process. That process is the one by which individuals who are members of a group that was formerly excluded from participation in the American political process—such as African Americans—come to see themselves and to construct their identity as individuals and citizens.

This approach has the advantage of showing liberal ideas not just in opposition to but in dialogue with illiberal and undemocratic ideas. (Indeed, one might go so far as to say that our substantive understanding of liberal principles evolves and takes shape through that very dialogue. One cannot help thinking of Lincoln in this connection.) African Americans and others were (and are) required to address and counter racist and other illiberal arguments against the recognition of their equal status as human beings and citizens. It is particularly useful for a consideration of American liberalism to trace the course of liberal arguments that were made not by the "dominant" members of society but by those who have done the tough work of persuading both themselves and others that the principles applied to them, too—even though the decks of custom and prejudice were stacked against them—and who have also done the tough work of making sense of and giving human meaning to pure principles in a complicated, contradictory, and impure world. In her essay, Carol Horton states, in connection with the issue of citizenship for the freedmen in the postbellum period, that the incorporation of a "previously excluded group into the polity was not a simple question of inclusion or exclusion; rather it was linked, in both concrete and abstract ways, to recalibrating the meaning of civic equality for all."[3] Yet what have been the terms of that recalibration in the cases of specific individuals? What language did they use? What aspects of American thought did they focus upon and make their own in an attempt to gain and preserve the freedoms and privileges that America in principle offered to them? What aspects of American thought did they reject? And, in their use of American ideas with a view to securing freedom and equality, might some understanding of American liberalism emerge that transcends Greenstone's bipolarity (and, for that matter, also takes the measure of the illiberal traditions discussed by Smith)?[4]

In this essay I will take up these questions by focusing on two well-known African-American thinkers: Frederick Douglass and W. E. B. DuBois. Having escaped slavery in 1838, Douglass joined the Garrisonian abolitionists in repudiating the government and the Constitution. However, by 1851 Douglass broke with the Garrisonians, having determined, as he argued in one of his most famous speeches ("What to the Slave Is the Fourth of July," 5 July 1852) that the Constitution was a "glorious liberty document."[5] Douglass's position did not change substantially thereafter, and his energies turned to what was in effect an attempt to educate both blacks and whites about the conditions of their freedom and prosperity. As Wilson Jeremiah Moses claims, Douglass attempted to create a "new America."[6] DuBois, however, was constantly evaluating and reevaluating his own understanding of the meaning of race in America. For DuBois (as for Douglass), democratic principles could be useful in helping him and other African Americans achieve a condition of freedom and opportunity in which they could develop their capacities and pursue their goals. DuBois claimed that as a young man he was attached to American principles because he was an American, but he came to assess those principles and their practice more objectively as he developed his understanding of the experience of the African American in America—of the black individual in a white world. Thus neither Douglass nor DuBois was attached to American principles simply as a "faith" or as a prejudice; each thought through the "truth" of those principles and the advantages they held for individuals like themselves. In my discussion of Douglass and DuBois, I do not intend to overlook or even to minimize their significant differences. Rather, I hope to bring out concerns, values, and understandings that are common to both in such a way as to contribute to the discussion of the liberal tradition in American politics, which is the theme of this collection of essays.

FREDERICK DOUGLASS

Douglass's hope to secure a place for his race in America led him to sustained reflection on individual identity, race, and human capacities. His understanding of the individual was clearly informed by the ideas of classical liberalism. He sought to draw attention to what he saw as the universal characteristics shared by all human beings: reason, speech, and the capacity for moral judgment. Indeed, for Douglass speech was a (perhaps the) defining characteristic of selfhood and humanity altogether. In an interesting—and little-noticed—piece titled "The Claims of the Negro Ethnologically Considered" (1854), Douglass explicitly takes up the question of what constitutes humanity. He states that "man is distinguished from all other animals" by his possession of faculties such as two-handedness, "his speech, his reason, his power to acquire and retain knowledge" as well as his hopes, fears, aspirations, and the ability to articulate them. Douglass goes on to attempt to demonstrate that the "Negro race...are part of the human family, and are descended from a common ancestry."[7] In a section headed "Ethnological Unfairness Towards the Negro," Douglass considers the attempts of ethnologists to distinguish blacks from Egyptians. The high civilization of the Egyptians led some ethnologists, such as Dr. Samuel George Morton, to try to prove that "the ancient Egyptians were totally distinct from the Negroes."[8] In a curious passage, Douglass suggests that there has been an evolution of American character, which will in the end make the question of the ancestry of both the white and the black American irrelevant:

> The lean, slender American, pale and swarthy, if exposed to the sun, wears a very different appearance to the full, round Englishman, of clear blonde complexion. One may trace the progress of this difference in the common portraits of the American Presidents. Just study those faces, beginning with WASHINGTON; and as you come thro' the JEFFERSONS, the ADAMSES, and the MADISONS, you will find an increasing bony and wiry appearance about those portraits, & a greater remove from that serene amplitude which characterizes the countenances of the earlier Presidents. I may be mistaken, but I think this is a correct index of the change going on in the nation at large — converting Englishmen, Germans, Irishmen, and Frenchmen, into Americans, and causing them to lose, in a common American character, all traces of their former distinctive national peculiarities.[9]

Indeed, Douglass goes on to appeal beyond physical description as a central feature of the definition of a people or nation, invoking language as that defining feature: "Language is held to be very important, by the best ethnologists, in tracing out the remotest affinities of nations, tribes, classes and families. The color of the skin has sometimes been less enduring than the speech of a people."[10]

The medium of Douglass's reshaping of American identity is language. Yet Douglass's use of the language of the status quo is more than the (mere) appropriation of the power of the status quo. For Douglass, identity is determined by language. A language that emphasizes rationality, universality, and equality places the power of self-determination in the hands of each individual.[11] Hence—and also through speech—Douglass urged both blacks and whites to take up their responsibilities to themselves, to help themselves.

One of Douglass's most oft-repeated exhortations to the members of his race was that they advance themselves through work, saving money, and accumulating property. Typical of Douglass's speeches is this passage from an address he delivered in Washington in 1886 urging his fellow (African-American) citizens not to despair:

> We have but to toil and trust, throw away whiskey and tobacco, improve the opportunities that we have, put away all extravagance, learn to live within our means, lay up our earnings, educate our children, live industrious and virtuous lives, establish a character for sobriety, punctuality, and general uprightness....[12]

These measures, though, are more than merely practical; they lead to the acquisition of character. In his *Narrative* (1845), for example, Douglass extols the virtues of work, condemns slavery for "darkening one's mental and moral vision," and strenuously warns against habits that dim one's judgments and capacities, such as drink. He continued to develop these themes in his later writings and speeches, such as the essay "What Are the Colored People Doing for Themselves?" (1848) and his lecture "Self-Made Men" (first delivered in 1859 and given more than fifty times thereafter). In "What Are the Colored People Doing for Themselves?" Douglass vigorously encourages the development of character. In "Self-Made Men," the path to character, and indeed to all good things, is paved with work:

> I am certain that there is nothing good, great or desirable which man can possess in this world, that does not come by some kind of labor, either physical or mental, moral or spiritual. A man may, at times, get something for nothing, but it will, in his hands, amount to nothing. What is true in the world of matter, is equally true in the world of mind. Without culture there can be no growth; without exertion, no acquisition; without friction, no polish; without labor, no knowledge; without action, no progress and without conflict, no victory. The man who lies down a fool at night, hoping that he will awaken wise in the morning, will rise up in the morning as he laid down in the evening.[13]

Alongside Douglass's exhortations to work and to attend to the development of character went his encouragement of the notion of merit and his corresponding discouragement of race pride. Douglass stated that he had always "attached more importance to manhood than to mere kinship or identity with any variety of the human family. Race, in the popular sense, is narrow. Humanity is broad. The one is special, the other is universal; the one is transient, the other permanent."[14] And individuals should strive as they might and expect to be evaluated on the basis of their achievements and their achievements alone: "For after all, our destiny is largely in our own hands.... If we succeed in the race of life, it must be by our own energies, and our own exertions. Others may clear the road, but we must go forward, or be left behind in the race of life."[15]

The "race of life" was for Douglass not a restless pursuit of power or wealth. Though he was realistic about the kind of work performed by most Americans (particularly black ones) and urged respect for all forms of needful labor,[16] he readily added that menial labor was a state one should seek a way out of as soon as possible, for man's "true dignity is not to be sought in his arms or in his legs, but in his head."[17] For work, and the economic progress that was its intended consequence, was but the foundation for the cultivation of moral and mental faculties; it is only with wealth that one can enjoy leisure and education and that one has the opportunity to pursue the most important thing: the cultivation of the human soul.

> As man is highest on the earth it follows that the vocation of the scholar is among the highest known to man. It is to teach and induce man's potential and latent greatness. It is to discover and develop the noblest, highest and best that is in him. In view of this fact no man whose business it is to teach should ever allow himself to feel that his mission is mean, inferior or circumscribed. In my estimation neither politics nor religion present to us a calling higher than this primary business of unfolding and strengthening the powers of the human soul. It is a permanent vocation.[18]

Thus we see that Douglass's exhortations to work and acquire material goods are made in conjunction with equally strenuous exhortations to cultivate character and the human soul.

Douglass understood that this proper ordering of the material and the spiritual was the enjoyment of meaningful human freedom. He also understood that this freedom was not simply a given, but required a context based on an understanding of the proper ordering of the relationship between the individual and the larger community of the nation or, indeed, of human beings altogether. Let me explain. First, Douglass saw that underlying Americans' various interpretations of human flourishing is a self-evident principle: We belong to ourselves. Douglass stated that one idea took possession of him even in childhood: "Every man is himself, is his self, if you please, and belongs to himself, and can only part from his self ownership, by the commission of crime."[19] This principle was evident to Douglass even in slavery. It was revealed to him in a highly Lockean way when, after arriving in New Bedford, Massachusetts, as a free man, he earned two silver half-dollars for bringing in and putting away a pile of coal: "To understand the emotion which swelled my heart as I clasped this money, realizing that I had no master who could take it from me—that it was mine—that my hands were my own, and could earn more of the precious coin—one must have been in some sense himself a slave."[20] All members of the larger society, then, must respect each individual's self-ownership in order for those individuals to make their way in the "race of life."

Second, in a sense Douglass valued the universal—all of humanity—over the particular, the race, or the nation. He sought to draw attention to the virtue involved in the honoring of that universal. Yet this is not a view with nationalist or totalitarian overtones, for the universal here is really the individual. This is suggested in Douglass's remark about the American founders in his Fourth of July oration. He calls them "statesmen, patriots and heroes" and goes on to say that they "loved their country better than their own private interests; and though this is not the highest form of human excellence, all will concede that it is a rare virtue."[21] Douglass does not say what the highest form of human excellence is, yet it is possible to infer that loving all humanity is a higher excellence than loving one's country. This point is made explicit in Douglass's praise of John Brown. In an address titled "Did John Brown Fail?" Douglass contrasted Brown with Patrick Henry in the following way: "Henry loved liberty for himself, but this man [Brown] loved liberty for all men, and for those most despised and scorned, as well as for those most esteemed and honored. Just here was the glory of John Brown's mission."[22] For Douglass, the best human effort seems to be to see that the liberty of one is inextricably linked with the liberty of all. On this level and on this understanding there is no real tension between individual and community, between individual aspirations and the aspirations of human communities, since liberty can be properly secured only in an environment in which this understanding is promulgated and cherished.

For Douglass our individual actions occur within a larger body, so to speak, and the success of the liberal principles of American society require a context that secures the condition of our making of ourselves what we can. That context requires an absence of prejudice as well as the presence of equality, fair play, and justice. Douglass exhorted whites again and again to "let the negro alone," by which he did not mean to encourage white complacency but to emphasize that blacks should be treated without prejudice, without pity, and with justice. In an 1894 address, Douglass listed a number of ways in which he thought the "race problem" could be solved:

> Let the white people of the North and South conquer their prejudices.... Let the American people cultivate kindness and humanity. Let the South abandon the system of "mortgage" labor, and cease to make the negro a pauper, by paying him scrip for his labor. Let them give up the idea that they can be free, while making the negro a slave. Let them give up the idea that to degrade the colored man, is to elevate the white man.... The whole thing can be done by simply no longer violating the amendments of the Consti-

tution of the United States, and no longer evading the claims of justice. If this were done, there would be no negro problem to vex the South, or to vex the nation.[23]

Whites and blacks alike must regard all individuals according to their accomplishments and not according to their race. The context necessary for the enjoyment of America's liberal principles is thus the sum of individual efforts: Only by each of us continually helping ourselves and assessing our goals and our treatment of others (our respect for their self-ownership) can any—and every—individual enjoy the liberties promised by the American republic. What those liberties make possible for Douglass is not unfettered freedom or self-indulgence, but each individual's tending to the cultivation of his or her own soul. To lose sight of this and to mistake justice as an advantage to be enjoyed by some or a few is to jeopardize not only the freedom of Americans to cultivate themselves, but the very future of America itself: "The true problem is…whether this nation has in itself sufficient moral stamina to maintain its honor and integrity by vindicating its own Constitution and fulfilling its own pledges, or whether it has already touched that dry rot of moral depravity by which nations decline and fall, and governments fade and vanish."[24]

Douglass's views of the individual and of a good society are layered and complex and are not easily reducible to a single formula. He takes account of the needs of human beings both as embodied creatures and as creatures not only capable of but defined by intellectual and spiritual capacities. He also takes account of the complex balance between individuals in a political community that encourages both the material and spiritual flourishing of its members. That balance is essential for the achievement and preservation of liberty.

This discussion shows that Douglass's thought contains many of the features of antebellum Whig political thought and culture, which have been discussed at length by scholars such as Daniel Walker Howe, Lawrence Kohl, and Greenstone himself, whose "reform liberalism" encompassed Whig values. Those Whiggish features include a concern with human potential, a strong emphasis on self-improvement and self-culture, the perception of a connection between individual and social betterment, the view that material things were a means for spiritual ends, and a tempered optimism about human progress. Moreover, both Douglass's goals and his style bear the stamp of Whiggish evangelism and nineteenth-century Romanticism.[25] It is time, then, for us to address explicitly Douglass's relation to his context and, more specifically, to Greenstone's "bipolarity" thesis. Was Douglass a reform liberal? Neither humanist liberal nor reform liberal? Both?

Readers of *The Lincoln Persuasion* will know that Greenstone intended to write a chapter on Douglass and Lydia Maria Child, and that this chapter was never written. Greenstone observed, however, that from the standpoint of his bipolarity thesis, "the extent to which Douglass avoided making a choice between these two perspectives [humanist and reform liberalism] is remarkable."[26] It is difficult to know exactly what Greenstone meant. Perhaps Douglass saw the choices as Greenstone saw them, but avoided choosing. Perhaps Douglass did not see himself faced with a choice between something like "reform" and "humanist" liberalism. For Daniel Walker Howe, "Douglass's political thought illustrates beautifully David Greenstone's conception of reform liberalism as a philosophy dedicated to national regeneration." Howe urges us to see that the context of Douglass's thought was Greenstone's "reform liberalism," "the self-conscious nurture of the human faculties, and the realization of human potential."[27] Furthermore, Howe attempts to "elaborate on and clarify Greenstone's model" by proposing that "humanist and reform liberals both believe that people have a right to self-realization, but only reform liberals believe that people have a duty to self-realization."[28]

Though a call to duty is implicit in Douglass's rhetoric—the duty to improve oneself, to practice temperance, value education, work hard, and be thrifty—Douglass spoke the language of rights more than he spoke the language of duty. A consideration of why this is so will help us to elucidate Douglass's own understanding of American liberalism and why, as I see it, it is not sufficiently explained by Greenstone's bipolarity model. Duty, as the Whigs understood it, drew upon commands of a sort that Douglass likely found difficult to trust. Those commands were biblical (duty to the Christian God), patriotic (duty to country), and filial (duty to family). Americans had relied upon such commands in the past in the service of the most unjust of ends—the maintenance of the institution of slavery—which gave them a dubious status. Rights, on the other hand, did not in Douglass's view ultimately draw upon specific religious, national, or partisan prejudices; thus they held the possibility of true universality. For example, an appeal to rights for blacks could not afford to be sectional (as the Whigs and Republicans had been) and remain silent on civil rights in the border states, the West, and the Midwest, let alone the South.[29] Rather, such an appeal *had* to be universal. The universality of rights and their accessibility to human reason made them as trustworthy a foundation as one could find for the social conditions that would make equality and individual development possible.

In seeing the matter in this manner, Douglass brought to light the inseparability of rights and duties. To speak the language of either rights or duties was, willy-nilly, to speak the language of the other. As we saw above, Douglass urged Americans to see that self-realization is attainable (and rights realizable) only when all members of society respect each other's self-ownership; whites and blacks alike must assess their goals and treatment of others. The enjoyment of the rights of each requires a duty to respect the rights of all; the two are impossible to separate without the loss of individuality and freedom. Indeed, for Douglass the separation of the two signals a corruption of the conditions that are necessary for the flourishing of the individual human being.

This interpretation of Douglass's thought helps us see why the humanist-liberal, "laissez-faire" strategy of self-help (recall his phrase "let the negro alone") that Douglass advocated was utterly compatible with his non-humanist-liberal call to moral standards and the cultivation of the human soul. Most important, it helps explain why Douglass's liberalism—unlike either humanist or reform liberalism—could not be combined with fundamentally illiberal ideologies such as racism. In the end, Douglass was clearly more like a reform liberal than a humanist one. Nevertheless, to describe him in that way is misleading. An attempt to explain Douglass's thought in terms of Greenstone's model could prevent us from seeing Douglass's own unique understanding of the meaning of American liberalism. Let us return, then, to our discussion of African-American understandings of American liberalism by turning to a discussion of W. E. B. DuBois.

W. E. B. DuBois

Readers of this essay who remember DuBois's elitism, his doctrinaire Marxism, and his expatriate life in Ghana may find it odd to find W. E. B. DuBois included in a discussion of the meaning of American liberalism. Yet DuBois's earlier work, particularly *The Souls of Black Folk* (1903), in addition to his later autobiographical work, such as *Dusk of Dawn* (1940), contain important reflections on the African-American self that help to illuminate the form of liberalism that I have suggested Douglass adumbrated. DuBois's vivid, poetic formulations contribute further substance and emotional meaning to Douglass's understanding of American liberalism. For DuBois, as for Douglass, work and wealth were for the sake of a higher goal: the cultivation of the individual soul. And like Douglass, DuBois stressed the importance of the social and political context for the enjoyment of meaningful liberty. I intend in this discussion to respect the differences between Douglass and DuBois, but to emphasize their shared concerns that bear on our question of understanding what American liberalism meant to these two men.

It was DuBois's reflections on the persistence of race prejudice in America that led him to articulate the "soul" of the African American. He uses various metaphors to characterize the psychological condition of the segregated African American. The most well-known of these metaphors is the "veil" of *Souls of Black Folk*, where DuBois relates an incident from his own childhood when he realized that he was different from the others (i.e., whites) and "shut out from their world by a vast veil." This condition, he goes on, allows no "true self-consciousness" but only allows one to see oneself "through the revelation of the other world."[30] *In Dusk of Dawn,* DuBois uses the metaphor of a "dark cave in a side of an impending mountain," from which prisoners (i.e., African Americans) look out and see the world. The passing throng of the outside world, however, scarcely notices them, and it "gradually penetrates the minds of the prisoners that the people passing do not hear; that some thick sheet of invisible but horribly tangible plate glass is between them and the world."[31] Those behind the glass do not think of themselves as individuals but as members of a group; they are "race men."[32] This feature of the inner life of African Americans suggests that to enjoy freedom one must be, and feel oneself to be, an individual, with a layered individual identity and not a narrow group identity. It is the sort of identity—and freedom—that was denied to Croatian writer Slavenka Drakulic´ by the recent war in the former Yugoslavia. She described its effects on her:

> Along with millions of other Croats, I was pinned to the wall of nationhood.... That is what the war is doing to us, reducing us to one dimension: the Nation. The trouble with this nationhood, however, is that whereas before, I was defined by my education, my job, my ideas, my character—and, yes, my nationality too—now I feel stripped of all that. I am nobody because I am not a person anymore. I am one of 4.5 million Croats.[33]

Ultimately, DuBois sought to transcend the veil, or to become free from the prison, to reach a place "beyond the color line." In order to do this, he urged a counsel of work and self-cultivation, not unlike that of Douglass; DuBois urged the members of his race to be responsible for their own uplift. In "The Conservation of Races" (1897), for example, DuBois wrote of the need for race organizations, of which the American Negro Academy was one. The academy, he argued, "should continually impress the fact upon the Negro people that they must not expect to have things done for them—they *must do for themselves;* that they have on their hands a vast work of self-reformation to do, and that a little less complaint and whining, and a little more dogged work and manly striving would do us more credit and benefit than a thousand Force or Civil Rights Bills."[34]

The meaning of "manly striving" was the nub of DuBois's well-known criticisms of the teach-them-practical-skills orientation of Booker T. Washington. For DuBois, work and the acquisition of skills and property were not enough; a liberal education was required to nourish men's souls, to give them ideals, to make them men. For DuBois, it was "foolish to ask what is the best education for one or seven of sixty million souls":

> Shall we teach them trades, or train them in liberal arts? Neither and both: teach the workers to work and the thinkers to think; make carpenters of carpenters, and philosophers of philosophers, and fops of fools.... And the

final product of our training must be neither a psychologist nor a brickma-
son, but a man. And to make men, we must have ideals, broad, pure, and
inspiring ends of living,—not sordid money-getting, not apples of gold.[35]

In *Souls,* DuBois looks to the persistence and evolution of a "higher individualism" which "the centres of culture protect." He urges that "there
must come a loftier respect for the sovereign human soul that seeks to know
itself and the world about it; that seeks a freedom for expansion and self-
development; that will love and hate and labor in its own way, untrammeled
alike by old and new."[36] Like Douglass, DuBois argued that the best human
efforts were devoted to the cultivation of those faculties which in some
degree all human beings share: the cultivation of the soul, self-understanding,
intellectual knowledge, and the development of speech and writing. This goal
requires one to set one's sights not upon the conditions that make the best
human efforts possible—such as wealth or politics—but upon those best
efforts themselves. As DuBois argued, it "would not do to concentrate all
effort on economic well-being and forget freedom and manhood and equality. Rather Negroes must live and eat and strive, and still hold unfaltering
commerce with the stars."[37]

Self-help and education, though, are necessary but not sufficient to transcend the veil or to free the prisoners from their cave. These metaphors make
clear that the relationship between those behind the veil or imprisoned in the
cave and those outside the veil or cave is a reciprocal one. The opacity (and
the ignorance) are mutual. Indeed, much of DuBois's career had as its aim the
understanding and articulation of "life within the veil" so that African
Americans may better understand themselves, and also that white Americans
may better understand both African Americans and themselves. A telling passage in *Souls* testifies to this. In "The Afterthought," DuBois pleads to "God
the Reader" to hear his cry: "Let the ears of a guilty people tingle with truth,
and seventy millions sigh for the righteousness which exalteth nations, in this
drear day when human brotherhood is a mockery and a snare."[38] What,
though, is the world like on the other side of the plate glass? What is the
responsibility of its inhabitants to the prisoners? The "outer world" (the
world of whites) is, DuBois states in *Dusk,* "also real and human and in its
essence honest." Some on the outside may have sympathy for the prisoners,
but because they are incapable of sharing the inner thought and experience
of the imprisoned, the "outside leadership will continually misinterpret and
compromise and complicate matters, even with the best of will"; it will
remain "impotent and unsuccessful until it actually succeeds in freeing and
making articulate the submerged caste."[39] Thus the "plate glass" (or the
"veil") cannot be removed by the prisoners themselves, and until the dominant class helps in removing it, individuality and freedom are denied. The

condition of the liberation of the imprisoned is true equal opportunity among groups:

> [I]t has been easy for me to realize that the majority of mankind has strug-gled through this inner spiritual slavery and that while a dream which we have easily and jauntily called democracy envisages a day when the envi-roning group looses the chains and compulsion, and is willing and even eager to grant families, nations, sub-races, and races equality of opportunity among larger groups, that even this grand equality has not come; and until it does, individual equality and the free soul is impossible.[40]

"Equality of opportunity" took on different meanings as DuBois later devised strategies for the improvement of the situation of the members of his race. Some of these strategies were economically oriented, such as his advo-cacy of a consumer movement[41] and democratic control of industry;[42] some were international in scope, as he sought to look beyond America to Africa and "the colored peoples of the world."[43] He states in *Dusk,* however, that his "newer emphasis" was "indeed a part of that original program [of agi-tation and self-assertion]; it is its natural and inevitable fulfillment."[44] In response to changing economic circumstances and the intransigence of racism, DuBois's new strategies sought the same goal—cultural expression and the flourishing of the individual soul—by different means.

To return to the cave metaphor, DuBois states that loosing the prisoners from their cave "would be a matter not simply of courtesy, sympathy, and help to them, but aid to all the world."[45] Later in *Dusk,* he claims (somewhat eliptically) that African Americans are the "spiritual hope of this land." Ego-tism aside, what could DuBois mean? Freeing the prisoners would help not only those imprisoned but those outside as well, for the prisoners' liberation requires the achievement of the "grand equality," the only equality that truly makes possible individual equality and the free soul, and not just for the liberated but for all. Like Douglass, then, DuBois makes clear that a proper *context* is necessary for the enjoyment of the rights and freedoms that are the promise of American liberalism. That context requires the efforts of each individual American to respect the "self-ownership" (to use Douglass's phrase) of every other individual American. Like that of Douglass, DuBois's "liberalism" cannot be contained within a bipolar understanding. The achievement of meaningful freedom requires on its face the development of each individual's capacities to a degree sufficient to enable him or her to cre-ate and sustain the political and social environment in which each individual can attempt to flourish. The understandings of DuBois and Douglass, then, share a transcendent quality. They both urge us to see that our own flour-ishing depends upon a context that guarantees to each and every individual the same opportunity to flourish. They also urge us to see that individuals are properly individual—and free—only when they understand in some degree the conditions of their individuality and freedom: a context that ensures justice, fair play, and an absence of prejudice, and that thus enables each individual to develop his or her "best" nature. Those conditions must be met universally within American society. If they are not, individuals are likely to be compelled to focus on their group identity, to the detriment of their freedom as individuals. Nevertheless, for DuBois especially but also for Douglass, the promotion of race identity (if not "race pride") was a strategy of considerable utility, but it was a strategy to be undertaken always with a view to the larger human aspirations of achieving individual equality and freedom.

At this point we must stop to consider whether *human* here means "male." Can its meaning be applied equally to women as well as to men? What did Douglass and DuBois intend? Douglass seemed to have thought that his understanding of the individual applied equally to women as well as to men. Though his alliance with the suffragists was fraught with tensions, he had attended the Seneca Falls Convention in 1848, was an effective champion of the suffragists' cause through the mid-1860s, and spoke often on behalf of women's rights in the 1880s and 1890s.[46] In an address titled "I Am a Radical Woman Suffrage Man" (1888), Douglass urged the same thing for the American woman as he urged for the African American: Let her alone.

> [W]oman does not ask man for the right of suffrage. That is something which man has no power to give. Rights do not have their source in the will or the grace of man. They are not such things as he can grant or withhold according to his sovereign will and pleasure. All that woman can properly ask man to do in this case, and all that man can do, is to get out of the way,...and let woman express her sentiments at the polls and in the government equally with himself. Give her fair play and let her alone.[47]

Douglass argued that the principle of self-ownership applies equally to women and to men: "[Woman] is herself, and can be nobody else than herself," he said.[48] Nevertheless, when speaking of "women" Douglass sometimes seemed to refer only to white women (and, probably more specifically, the white female activists for women's rights). For example, in an address in 1868 he argued that woman "has a thousand ways by which she can attach herself to the ruling powers of the land that we [African Americans] have not. If she wants to go to the Parker House she can go."[49]

DuBois was perhaps more mindful than Douglass of (or at least more outspoken about) the diversity and the reality of the experiences of African-American women. The situation of black women, for example, is a prominent theme in DuBois's *Darkwater: Voices from Within the Veil* (1920). DuBois was well aware of the painful choice between work and motherhood that many women face—"[o]nly at the sacrifice of intelligence and the chance to do their best work can the majority of modern women bear children"—and urged that women need both knowledge and economic independence.[50] The difficulties posed by work and family were particularly acute for black women, upon whom DuBois says "the crushing weight of slavery fell." Under slavery, there was no legal marriage, family, or control over children; black women were subjected to the degradation of being used sexually by white men.[51] The postemancipation economy, however, favored black women's labor over that of black men. By the first few decades of the twentieth century, DuBois noted, black women were more likely to be employed than black men and at a higher wage, especially in cities. DuBois anticipated the effect of women's work on the family:

> The family group…which is the ideal of culture with which these folk have been born, is not based on the idea of an economically independent working mother. Rather its ideal harks back to the sheltered harem with the mother emerging at first as nurse and homemaker, while the man remains the sole breadwinner. What is the inevitable result of the clash of such ideals and such facts in the colored group? Broken families.[52]

For DuBois, women's "uplift"—making women's economic freedom compatible with the requirements of the family and with women's own individual development—took its place alongside the color line as one of the great problems of the twentieth century. And there it remains.

CONCLUSION

Douglass and DuBois point us to what we might call a "guiding principle" of liberalism. This principle is located in the aspirations that both thinkers share to ensure what David Held has described as "the creation of the best circumstances for all humans to develop their nature and express their diverse qualities" and the enjoyment of equal rights and equal obligations in the creation of those circumstances.[53] One might point out quite fairly that on this understanding what makes liberalism an "ism," a whole, is its aspirations and not its actual practice. In the name of liberal freedoms, individuals every day of the week act in contradiction to the "transcendent" understanding of Douglass and DuBois. Nevertheless, Douglass and DuBois help us—without denying the importance of wealth or power—to set our sights on what is most important for all of us: the cultivation of our individual natures (our "souls," as Douglass and DuBois would have it) and the enjoyment of "autonomy." As DuBois argued in *Darkwater*, "[a] true and worthy ideal frees and uplifts a people; a false ideal imprisons and lowers."[54] Our collective life therefore requires that we pay attention to any and all factors that act as obstacles to the cultivation of our individual natures or that hinder our autonomy or that of any other member of our society. These obstacles might be legal, such as Jim Crow legislation. They might take the form of race prejudice or an inattentiveness to women's concerns. Or they might be economic. The increasing gap between the rich and poor in the late twentieth century—which itself has a racial dimension—threatens not only the ability of some individuals to cultivate themselves but social stability as well.

Before satisfying myself that I have arrived at a neat conclusion about the meaning of American liberalism through my reading of Douglass and DuBois, I must raise a very important question. Have I simply retold what Rogers Smith calls "the Tocquevillian story" from an African-American perspective? Smith argues that the Tocquevillian thesis "that America has been most shaped by the unusually free and egalitarian ideas and material conditions that prevailed at its founding" is too narrow, for inegalitarian ideologies and conditions "have shaped the participants and the substance of American politics just as deeply."[55] Smith goes on to examine the silence of mainstream approaches to American politics on the issues of race, ethnicity, and gender, arguing that a "multiple traditions" approach gives us a richer and more accurate understanding of American life and politics.

Rather than denying Smith's multiple traditions account, however, I believe that the account offered here of liberalism as a kind of whole presupposes those very traditions, particularly the tradition of ideologies that support racial inequality. Smith, David Ericson, and Horton all engage in the very important work of looking at ways in which liberalism has coexisted with, even "collaborated" with illiberal ideas. But it is equally important to look at the ways in which individuals who maintain liberal principles respond to that coexistence and that collaboration. In so doing, we see how these individuals give shape to our understanding of the meaning of liberal principles in (as I have said before) a complicated, contradictory, and impure world. Both Douglass and DuBois were especially mindful of the effects of racism upon the meaning, and fate, of American liberalism and its promises to actual and potential citizens. And like Smith, neither Douglass nor DuBois saw in that meaning and those promises the inevitable flowering of equality in America, as though guided by some teleological principle. What they did see was a possibility, the realization of which required conscious and constant labor. Douglass maintained hope in the possibility until the end of his life. That DuBois, however, despaired of its realization is well known, evidenced by his turn to Marxism and, ultimately, by his renunciation of his American citizenship. Whether we are able to maintain hope for equality in the face of a rich tradition of inequalities—products, as Smith shows, of both reason and prejudice—is the work of each of us, as individuals, to decide.

6

Liberal Equality and the Civic Subject: Identity and Citizenship in Reconstruction America

Carol Horton

J. David Greenstone's work on American liberalism captured the imagination of many who recognized something deeply compelling in his notion of a liberal tradition that was simultaneously consensual *and* conflictual, one that set the taken-for-granted terms of political discourse but established no common agreement on their meanings. Liberalism, he argued, represented a "boundary condition" of American political life. By this he meant that historically it has proven extremely difficult to frame politically successful ideas and practices in any idiom other than one that assumes the general principles of individual rights, private property, and government by popular consent as foundational to the political order.[1] At the same time, however, Greenstone believed that this broad liberal order contained a basic division between those he termed "humanist" liberals, who valorized the satisfaction of individual preferences, and "reform" liberals, who prioritized the development of human faculties. Consequently, he characterized the American liberal tradition as fundamentally bipolar, with major political conflicts, such as the antebellum division over slavery, being played out along these lines.[2]

The most influential alternative to this basic Greenstonian thesis has been developed by Rogers Smith, who holds that liberalism represents only one of several centrally important traditions in American political life. In particular, Smith argues, what he terms "republicanism" and "ascriptive forms of Americanism" have played equally important roles. Consequently, the best way to understand American political culture is in terms of a "multiple-traditions" approach. Particularly important here (due to its relative historical longevity) is what Smith views as the historical tendency of liberalism and ascriptive Americanism (i.e., racism, sexism, nativism) to combine with one another to produce a variety of politically effective, if logically inconsistent, ideological positions.[3]

This essay attempts to assimilate and supersede the conceptions of American liberalism developed by Greenstone and Smith by developing an alternative way of looking at both divisions within liberalism and its relationship with what Smith characterizes as "ascriptive Americanism." My key claim is that neither of these issues can be adequately understood without considering the capacity of liberal discourse to incorporate radically divergent conceptions of the individual subject, as well as his or her fundamental rights of citizenship, into its basic schema. This means that it is not sufficient simply to consider the ways in which different forms of liberalism alternatively value individual preferences and behaviors, as Greenstone did in his bipolarity thesis. Nor is it acceptable simply to posit that liberalism, racism, sexism, and nativism are clearly distinct traditions, as does Smith in his "multiple traditions" argument. Instead, it is necessary to dig analytically deeper, considering how the apparently neutral category of "the individual" is suffused with highly divergent cultural meanings in various forms of liberalism, even to the extent of constructing certain types of subjects (e.g., women, blacks) in explicitly inegalitarian terms.[4] The upshot of this analysis is that the true diversity of American liberalism is much greater than Greenstone inferred, as it has proven capable of containing many of the conflicts that Smith mistakenly places outside of its historical boundaries.

This essay attempts to demonstrate the validity of this alternative approach by means of a historical case study, rather than a purely theoretical exegesis.[5] Applying a different lens to the study of American liberalism allows us to focus sharply on various dimensions of it that have been previously blurred out of the picture. Although of course one case study cannot hope to be fully persuasive, it can provide a strong sense of what may be gained from this variety of analysis, and what is lost by refusing to consider its implications. Most ambitiously, I hope that it may lay the groundwork for further historical studies that could provide greater insight into the painful dilemmas of contemporary American liberalism, which is widely (and, I believe, correctly) perceived as being in a protracted state of crisis brought on largely by the racial and gender politics of the last several decades.[6] By demonstrating the true complexity of the American liberal experience, with its simultaneous ability both to defend and attack what many would today consider oppressive dogmas of racism and sexism, we may perhaps begin to craft a better sense of its contemporary liabilities and potential.

My specific focus in this essay is the contested nature of citizenship in Reconstruction America.[7] My key argument with regard to this case is that alternative constructions of the individual citizen—or, more formally, the civic subject—were systematically linked to different definitions of civic equality during this critical period in the nation's history. This argument is supported by an examination of three alternative positions prominent in the politics of the time, which I refer to as (1) anticaste liberalism, (2) phylogenetic liberalism, and (3) black republicanism. Each of these positions, I argue, represented a fundamentally different definition of citizenship that was directly related to alternative constructions of race, class, and gender. The key point of this case study is to provide an empirical grounding for the theoretical claims that (1) American liberalism has been substantially more diverse than Greenstone's bipolarity thesis allows, (2) this multiplicity has been critically structured by alternative constructions of the civic subject, and (3) contra Smith, the foundational nature of these constructions makes it impossible to consistently separate liberalism from ascriptive ideologies of race, class, and gender.

LIBERALISM AND RECONSTRUCTION

The period of Reconstruction (1863–1877) witnessed the development of an exceptionally rich and diverse array of contending American liberalisms. A key reason for this was that the formal emancipation of almost four million African slaves in 1863 necessarily threw the question of the fundamental nature of American citizenship into exceptionally sharp relief.[8] No longer legally defined as property, this huge and vitally important part of the American population was to be formally included as citizens of the American republic, which, after all, the victorious Union army had fought to defend. But what precisely did this mean, in solid, substantive terms? What concrete measures would have to be taken in order to secure the position of the freedpeople as civic equals? Articulating the freedpeople's status necessarily entailed explaining the general grounds of American citizenship as well. Whether pursued in the interests of racial justice or continued economic exploitation, the cultural and political exigencies of the period demanded that these questions be posed, debated, and defended with an exceptionally intense degree of urgency and vigor.

The stakes of this debate were tremendously high. Most immediately, of course, much of the quality and shape of the future lives of the freedpeople was directly on the line. Given, however, this group's central position in the national economic and political orders, what happened to them would have more or less direct repercussions for the entire country. Economically, black labor power was indispensable to the continuation of large-scale plantation agriculture in the postwar South. The key cash crops of cotton, sugar, tobacco, coffee, and rice produced in this region provided, in turn, vitally important goods and raw materials to the rapidly expanding manufacturing-based economy of the North. At the same time, the freedmen represented a potentially huge reservoir of reliable support for the Republican Party in the

South, particularly after the ratification of the Fifteenth Amendment in 1870. White party elites were, however, deeply divided over the issue of what this black support meant for the party, and over how much of a fight should be waged to protect it from southern Democrats eager to suppress or control it. As the developments of the succeeding decades would show, these issues would be pivotal to the basic shape of the two-party system as the nation moved into the twentieth century.[9] Consequently, while the civic status of the freedpeople was probably not a matter of great concern to most nonblacks living outside of the South, it was something that, whether they recognized it or not, would have an impact on them through its effect on the major political and economic structures that were a part of their lives. In this sense, the incorporation of one previously excluded group into the polity was not a simple question of inclusion or exclusion; rather, it was linked, in both concrete and abstract ways, to recalibrating the meaning of civic equality for all.

The significance of defining a national standard of citizenship was further compounded by the fact that the Civil War had produced a tremendous shift in both the cultural meaning and institutional structure of the United States. For the first time, there was a deep and widespread commitment to the "imagined community" of the nation; at the same time, there was a tremendous expansion of the institutional capacities of the federal government.[10] Consequently, a substantially new standard of civic equality could be not only set but potentially implemented both for the freedpeople and the nation at large. Although, of course, any program of political institution building operated under constraints that limited the scope of potentially realizable alternatives, this was nonetheless a period of relative openness and flux.[11] Old structures and ways of life had been decimated by the war, and no new pattern had as yet been consolidated.

ANTICASTE LIBERALISM

Certainly one prominent if ultimately unsuccessful construction of citizenship that emerged during this time operated on the assumption that this was indeed the case. This position, which I describe as anticaste liberalism, was premised on the idea that the Civil War had been fought over the issue of human equality, and that the triumph of the Union had set the grounds for a newly reconstructed constitutional order based on the principle of a national standard of citizenship. Rooted in the Enlightenment tradition of humanist universalism, heavily filtered through the Protestant moralism of the antebellum abolitionist movement, anticaste liberals held that a dramatic extension of federal power was necessary to ensure that African-American citizens would not be deprived of their civil rights due to continued racial discrimination. Without strong federal guarantees, they feared, new systems of racial caste would be established to perpetuate the legacy of slavery.[12]

Although this commitment to using federal power to combat racial discrimination was strongly supported by the African-American community, the primary base of anticaste liberalism was in the Radical wing of the Republican Party. Radical (as opposed to moderate and conservative) Republicans had strong ties to abolitionism, primarily representing the same "burned-over" districts of New England and New England migration where the movement had flourished. Reaching their peak of political influence around 1868, when reaction against the perceived excesses of presidential Reconstruction pushed many moderates at least temporarily into the Radical camp, Radicals were consistently on the cutting edge of the rapidly evolving course of federal civil rights law during the entire course of Reconstruction. Although always in a minority position in the party, the Radicals had enough strength and numbers to be highly influential, and they represented a prominent voice in national political debate.

Although passed after the period of their greatest power, the Civil Rights Act of 1875, as the last major piece of Reconstruction legislation, provides an excellent illustration of the logic of the anticaste position advocated by the Radicals and their allies. First proposed in the Senate by the prominent Radical leader Charles Sumner in May 1870, the Civil Rights Act of 1875 prohibited racial discrimination in places of public accommodation such as restaurants, inns, and theaters, as well as in public transportation and jury selection.[13] Highly controversial among Republicans, bitterly opposed by both Democrats and the overwhelming majority of the white South, and ultimately invalidated by the Supreme Court only eight years after its passage, the Civil Rights Act of 1875 was, nonetheless, historically significant in that it represented the culmination of the Radical commitment to using the power of the federal government to establish a newly egalitarian standard of national citizenship.[14]

This vision of citizenship was firmly rooted in the traditional liberal commitment to individual rights. Substantively, the Civil Rights Act of 1875 was held to represent the crowning achievement of a steadily expanding panoply of rights that had begun with emancipation.[15] The Thirteenth Amendment and the Civil Rights Act of 1866 had, Republicans agreed, established basic rights of liberty, property, and person, including contract, locomotion, state recognition of marital and parental status, and the opportunity to be parties and witnesses in judicial proceedings. Subsequently the Fourteenth Amendment had, in deliberately vague terms, protected the rights of national citizenship against state infringement, while the Fifteenth Amendment extended the franchise to all men regardless of race, color, or previous condition of servitude. Finally, the Civil Rights Act of 1875 was to guarantee equal access to basic public institutions. Repeatedly characterized by both Sumner and other supporters as the "capstone" needed to "crown and complete the great work of Reconstruction,"[16] this measure was presented as the final step necessary to ensure that the freedpeople would be uniformly protected against "unjust prejudices founded upon caste."[17]

This concept of caste was the pivotal point that brought together conceptions of civic equality and civic subject in this particular articulation of liberal discourse. The Radicals' objection to caste was fundamentally based upon the claim that, as Senator Daniel D. Pratt of Indiana asserted in the long debate over the bill, "God is no respecter of persons, and that he made of one blood all nations of men to dwell on the face of the earth." This reference to the singularity of blood was common, and, as will be seen below, stood in pronounced contrast to the phylogenetic liberal concept of a natural racial hierarchy. Humanist universalism was asserted both as an eternal truth and as the basic commitment of the United States as a nation: "I believe what our fathers who laid the foundations of our political edifice taught, [is] that all men are created equal."[18]

Any systemic pattern of racial discrimination violated this commitment to individual equality. Racial prejudice, asserted Senator Timothy Howe of Wisconsin, "is not a law of nature," but rather a belief taught and learned in particular environments. "We have but one creator and that is God, and he makes but one kind of men.... Those unequal conditions are an impeachment of society, not of creation."[19] To attribute racial inequality to nature rather than to social structure was both shameful and un-American. "This talk about superiority of race, about these distinctions in this Christian and democratic land, should pass away and pass away forever," stated Senator Henry Wilson of Massachusetts. "All that is high and noble and pure in the country is against recognizing these unchristian, inhumane, and undemocratic theories."[20]

The logical way to address such social problems was to prohibit the discriminatory practices that perpetuated them. Representative William J. Purman of Florida, for example, argued that "[c]olor is no crime, and the sacrilegious hands that would make it so...must be stayed by just and firm legislation."[21] In the same vein, Senator George Boutwell of Massachusetts, arguing in support of the section of the civil rights bill that prohibited racial segregation in the public schools, pointed out: "The theory of human equality cannot be taught in families, taking into account the different conditions of the different members of the families composing human society; but in the public school, where children of all classes and conditions are brought together, this doctrine of human equality can be taught, and it is the chief means of securing the perpetuity of republican institutions." Furthermore, Boutwell added, "inasmuch as we have in this country four million colored people, I assume that it is a public duty that they and the white people of the country…shall be assimilated and made one in the fundamental idea of human equality."[22]

Securing equal rights, however, was held to necessitate a fundamental restructuring of the federal system. As only the federal government could secure the rights of citizenship on a national basis, the entire federal system, Radicals argued, had been fundamentally recalibrated by the passage of the Reconstruction amendments. In particular, both the duties and the powers of the federal government had been radically expanded, while the autonomy of the states had been vastly curtailed. Senator Frederick Frelinghuysen of New Jersey, for example, claimed that the "Fourteenth Amendment goes much further than the old Constitution," as it "makes United States citizenship primary, and State citizenship derivative."[23] While nationalizing citizenship for all, the Reconstruction Amendments were particularly intended, the senator argued, "to do away with slavery—to wipe out every consequence of it." In keeping with this intent, Congress was "authorized to pass all laws appropriate to efface the existence of any consequences or residuum of slavery," as "freedom from discrimination is one of the rights of U.S. citizenship."[24]

While anticaste liberals favored a tremendous extension of federal power in this regard, they nonetheless cleaved to basic laissez-faire principles. Once the artificial barrier of caste was eliminated from the nation, they assumed, all individuals would have the equal opportunity to make their own way in life. "We know we have proven that equality is the true principle on which to run society; give it full play with no obstruction, and the machine will run noiselessly and without a jar."[25] Similarly, Representative (and future president) James Garfield of Ohio asserted, "I have never asked for [the black man] one thing beyond this: that he should be placed under the equal protection of the laws, with the equal right to all the blessings which our laws confer…and that the negro, guaranteed an equal chance in the struggle of life, may work out for himself whatever fortune his own merit will win."[26] Notably, three of the seven black congressmen who participated in the debates over the civil rights bill made similar statements, and none of the other four said anything in contradiction. "Place all citizens upon one broad platform; and if the negro is not qualified to hoe his row in this contest of life, then let him go down."[27]

Statements such as these point toward the implicit assumptions that were built into the anticaste liberal's explicit commitments to humanist universalism and racial equality. As many historians have documented, the universal subject of rights embraced by the Radical Republicans and their allies was fundamentally structured by a set of highly specific cultural assumptions. One of the most important of these assumptions, which flowed directly into the most vital political conflicts of Reconstruction, was that all individuals naturally shared a common economic rationality. Unless artificially blocked by some oppressive structure, all individuals, it was believed, would desire to engage consistently in productive and profitable work in order to accumulate goods and increase the comfort and respectability of themselves and their families.[28] Consequently, anticaste liberals believed that while slavery and any of its remaining traces would block such desires, the removal of these artificial barriers would immediately unleash them.[29]

By imputing this substantive content to the concept of the universal subject, anticaste liberals were able to maintain a tremendous faith in the fairness of the unfettered free market. Since everyone was assumed to share essentially similar commitments in this arena, ensuring true freedom of contract was thought to be the best means of maximizing both individual opportunity and social justice.[30] In this sense, the commitment to eliminating artificial barriers of caste was one and the same as the faith in the inherent, uncomplicated goodness of the untrammeled free market. In the same breath, in other words, was a truly radical desire to use federal power to prohibit racial segregation and discrimination in a wide range of public institutions and privately owned businesses and a deeply conservative belief in the inviolability of laissez-faire and the free-market order.

As Foner argues, this fundamental commitment to laissez-faire principles, along with its attendant assumption of universal economic rationality, had deeply undercut earlier radical proposals to foundationally restructure the southern economy that had been advanced by an influential minority of Republicans during the early years of Reconstruction.[31] The rapid evolution of the orientation and activities of the Freedmen's Bureau was particularly significant in this regard.[32] On the one hand, the creation of the bureau in 1865 represented the Republicans' commitment to using the power of the federal government to establish the concrete social conditions necessary to place the freedpeople on a meaningful standard of civic equality. On the other hand, such a radical intervention in the free-market order was conceived of as a highly temporary expedient, justified only by the exceptional circumstances of the initial transition from a system of slave to free labor. Consequently, the Freedmen's Bureau was built upon the assumption that fundamental change could be accomplished extremely quickly.

Naive as it appears in retrospect, such an assumption made sense given the widespread belief that both former masters and ex-slaves would naturally internalize the same economistic precepts once given the opportunity to do so and that the free-market system would naturally produce optimal results for all involved. Not surprisingly, such assumptions quickly ran into obstacles, which in turn forced a decisive showdown between radically different understandings of precisely what sort of concrete changes the Freedmen's Bureau had been commissioned to make. Although the most radical of the

Radical Republicans went substantially beyond the boundaries of anticaste liberalism by advocating land redistribution during the late 1860s, they were a tiny minority compared to the moderate faction that believed social mobility could be achieved without such extreme measures. Conservatives, alternatively, argued that the key issue was how to rapidly transform the freedpeople into a dependable class of agricultural laborers now that the old coercions of the slave system had been (at least theoretically) removed. Having grossly underestimated the scope of the task before them, both radicals and moderates were quickly overwhelmed by a combination of factors that had, in such circumstances, overdetermined the triumph of the conservative position.

Consequently, by 1866—only a year after its inception—the Freedmen's Bureau had become primarily devoted to the project of pressuring the freedmen to sign labor contracts with plantation owners on terms that generally allowed for neither meaningful choice nor social mobility. While ostensibly dedicated to furthering the classic liberal principle of freedom of contract, actual conditions in the South meant that even bureau officers dedicated to the cause of black empowerment were relatively powerless to prevent such principles from becoming complete travesties in terms of actual practice. In this sense, the substantive content of the anticaste construction of the universal subject was directly related to an attendant conception of civic equality. Universalist assumptions of economic rationality undergirded policy formation and institution building in a way that furthered the rapid legitimation of basic liberal principles, such as freedom of contract, within an entrenched system of economic hierarchy and inequality.

As should be evident, such an understanding of the meaning of civic equality and the universal subject was also bound up with particular understandings of different social groups. The concept of race, for example, was relevant only insofar as it was believed to provoke unjust prejudices that resulted in the creation of castelike barriers to individual rights and freedoms. Beyond this, race was a category that, it was assumed, should not have any political significance. While the importance of this anticaste proscription against racial segregation and discrimination should not be dismissed as inconsequential or otherwise undervalued—it was a politically important, socially radical, and highly controversial position to take—it was nonetheless very partial in scope. While supportive of government regulation of private enterprise to an extent that would not be widely accepted as legitimate until the mid-1960s, it rejected the claim, articulated by both the freedpeople and, in another context, the nascent national labor movement, that concentrations of economic power represented barriers to civic equality that could not be overcome simply by individual initiative. Beyond this, it also dismissed the meaning of race commonly shared by the freedpeople themselves, which, as will be discussed below, assumed the importance of recognizing both the historically conditioned connection of the individual to the group as well as the former slaves' connection to the land they had worked for generations.

In keeping with this conception of race, Radical Republicans did not, on the whole, accept class as a legitimate social category. In the logic of the anticaste view, there were individuals, and there were artificial barriers of racial caste that had to be eliminated, but there were no established groups that could be usefully located in critically different positions in the political economic order. One of the great appeals of laissez-faire, of course, both for anticaste liberals and for others who shared the same basic faith, was precisely that it was the one system that would prevent the establishment of the sort of fixed class structure that was commonly understood to have traditionally plagued Europe.[33] With every individual given the equal opportunity to rise or fall according to his own efforts, no system of either aristocratic privilege or proletarian subordination could (in theory) be maintained.

This widespread rejection of class as a useful category of analysis was directly connected to the anticaste commitment to the concept of a universal economic rationality that could easily be stimulated with the establishment of a free-market system, which would, in turn, create a harmony of interests between planters and field hands, capitalists and wage laborers, and so forth. As noted above, such a worldview was instrumental in undermining the effectiveness of critical Reconstruction policies, most notably the operation of the Freedmen's Bureau. Further, as Montgomery argues, this rejection of class analysis had the effect of making the guiding majority of Radical Republicans either uncomprehending of or hostile to the basic claims of what would soon be a rapidly expanding northern labor movement. Consequently, what would have been the best hope for a broad-based political alliance dedicated to the furtherance of egalitarian liberalism was critically undercut at a pivotal time in the nation's history.[34]

At the same time, anticaste conceptions of both civic equality and the civic subject were very much structured by gender. Just as the deeply classed nature of the meaning of race was generally overlooked, the profound linkage between gender and citizenship was largely disregarded. As Kerber and other feminist scholars have demonstrated, both the common understanding and legal structure of citizenship in the United States had been rooted in patriarchal principles and practices since the time of the founding of the republic.[35] The traditional construction of the universal subject had always been unproblematically male; women, it was widely assumed, were not, by their very nature, really individuals. Instead, they were organically tied to the patriarchal family, first as supportive daughters, then as nurturing wives and mothers. Consequently, the laissez-faire idealization of the economically rational, hardworking, and upwardly mobile individual was very much based upon a male image. True, women might labor outside of the home (particularly if they were black or poor), but even so, it was in the role of a helpmeet, not an individual actor who might aspire to achieve any meaningful measure of economic independence on her own.

Although many Radical Republicans, particularly those who had been involved in the more radical forms of abolitionism, had long supported the goal of female suffrage, their single-minded focus on the issue of racial caste caused them to explicitly relegate it to a much lower level of importance than the achievement of black manhood suffrage.[36] This insistence that it was much more important to secure the black man's right to vote than it was the woman's (and particularly the white woman's, as many white feminists indignantly pointed out) caused a major split in the feminist-abolitionist alliance when the issue came to a head over the status of the Fifteenth Amendment.[37] Although part of the feminist movement resisted, and continued to insist on the linkage of the two causes, the dominant wing of the feminist movement shifted to a single-issue focus on female suffrage, and, at the same time, increasingly adopted the openly racist and elitist appeal that respectable white women were clearly much more worthy of exercising the franchise than the ignorant and poverty-stricken men of an inferior race.[38]

In sum, while anticaste liberals articulated a dramatically new vision of national citizenship in tandem with a radical plan to restructure the basic constitutional order, they were also committed to a construction of the universal subject that erased class divisions, naturalized gender hierarchy, and denied the critical importance of economic subordination to the reproduction of racial inequality. The complexity of this radical vision underscores the importance of considering the cultural construction of the putatively universal "individual" when analyzing the structure of American liberalisms. The humanist universalism of the anticaste position was stunningly progressive for its time, presenting a strong moral rejection of anti-African racism at a time when "white supremacy" was a perfectly respectable, not to mention much more widely and ferociously shared, political principle. It is extremely unlikely that the racially egalitarian policies of Reconstruction, tapping directly into the culturally powerful narratives of Christianity and the founding, would ever have gone as far as they did without this sort of universalist commitment. At the same time, however, this universalism was neither truly universal nor entirely benign. Like any fixed commitment to a certain standard of political identity, it was, in many critical respects, partial and exclusionary.

PHYLOGENETIC LIBERALISM

The relative strengths of the anticaste construction of citizenship are particularly evident when compared to the most direct political competitor of its time, which I refer to as phylogenetic liberalism. In direct contrast to the humanist universalism asserted by the former, the phylogenetic position insisted that human beings were naturally divided up into different racial groups, which represented a prepolitical variety of species difference. Despite this particularist emphasis on racial difference, phylogenetic liberals nonetheless maintained a place for a universal subject of rights. Given their belief in natural inequality, however, both the recognition of human commonality and the substance of individual rights were extremely thin. Consequently, while phylogenetic liberals accepted that the basic purpose of the Reconstruction amendments was to enfranchise the freedpeople as civic equals, they defined both the nature of that equality and the import of the amendments in an extremely narrow way. Specifically, they held that national citizenship rights consisted of nothing more than the bare essentials of life, liberty, and property. They also held that the provision of these rights would do nothing to change the essentials of racial hierarchy, which was championed as an inevitable result of natural racial differences.

Again, the logic of this position is well illustrated by examining the key arguments advanced by the opponents of the Civil Rights Act of 1875 during the lengthy congressional debates over the legislation. While these arguments were primarily advanced by Democrats, who were solidly opposed to the measure, they did command some bipartisan support, with 16 percent of those voicing strong opposition to the bill being Republicans. Furthermore, this was almost certainly only the tip of the iceberg, as 11 percent of the votes against the bill in the House were cast by Republicans, as were 23 percent of those in the Senate.[39] At the same time, many Republicans avoided taking a position at all by absenting themselves from the debates and abstaining from the final vote.[40] This weak Republican support for measures disruptive of the racial status quo was indicative of a growing trend, as the power of the Radical faction increasingly faded and the dominant moderate-to-conservative wing became more and more disillusioned with Reconstruction. For the majority of these Republicans, phylogenetic liberalism represented a legitimate way of upholding the principles that their party had fought for during the Civil War, while finding common ground with moderate Southern Democrats willing to accept the basic principle of black citizenship (as long as it was placed firmly within the framework of white supremacy). The two groups could then enter into a productive alliance that would revive plantation agriculture and provide a healthy partner for Northern industry and investment.

"I understand by the term 'civil rights' rights appertaining to the individual as a free, independent citizen; and what are they?" asked Senator Lyman Trumbull, a moderate Republican from Illinois. "The right to go and come; the right to enforce contracts; the right to convey his property; the right to buy property—these general rights that belong to mankind everywhere."[41]

Strongly adhered to by most moderate and conservative Republicans, such a relatively minimal understanding of the rights of citizenship was one with which even moderate Democrats could agree, particularly given the actual conditions in which, as discussed above, such rights were being formally implemented. To be sure, such rights, minimal as they were, did represent a tremendous legal advance over the conditions of slavery, when neither simple physical mobility, contractual choice, nor property holding existed in either promise or actuality. Consequently, as will be discussed below, many southern whites and conservative Democrats vehemently rejected them as illegitimate extensions of the rights of white men to an inferior race. Thus it is important to emphasize that phylogenetic liberalism was not, despite its explicit embrace of racial hierarchy, a reactionary doctrine for its time. Indeed, one may safely say that it represented the moderate middle ground, especially in comparison to what was widely seen as the excessive radicalism of the anticaste position.

Again, the civil rights bill was a case in point. Many congressmen, such as Representative Aylett Hanes Buckner, a Democrat from Missouri, argued that it was "inconceivable that the provisions of the Fourteenth Amendment should have any application to the pretended rights" represented by the pending legislation. "The 'equal protection of the laws' could not have been designed for any such case. It could never have been contemplated that every citizen, male and female, black and white, foreign and native, should be accorded the enjoyment of every right in the same measure and in the same degree."[42] For the phylogenetic position, there was, in short, no contradiction between the maintenance of certain basic individual rights and the existence of systemic practices of racial discrimination.

"Social prejudice is a social liberty that the law has no right to disturb," asserted Representative Henry D. McHenry, a Democrat from Kentucky. While "the object of this bill is to abolish distinctions on account of 'race, color, or previous condition of servitude,'" he continued, "it in fact makes a discrimination against the white man on account of his color."[43]

Most objectionably, the civil rights bill, by proscribing racial discrimination in public accommodations and transportation, violated what should be the inviolable property rights of the white owners of these enterprises. As Representative J. Ambler Smith, a Democrat from Virginia, explained:

> [T]he right of property is so sacred that the Legislature of my State itself cannot dare to say to me, though one of her citizens, that I shall not decide for myself whom I shall admit and whom I shall exclude from *my* hotel. The assumption would be an impudent, unendurable usurpation and tyranny.... And so, sir, of my stage-coach, my steamboat, my theater—they are *my* property; and my State...cannot interfere with that property so long as I do not allow it to be a nuisance and to damage the public. If this be not so, then property, instead of being one of the great elements of society and a propul-

sion of honorable ambition and patriotic enterprise, would be a worthless bauble.[44]

Similarly, Representative Buckner characterized the bill as "such an interference with the rights of private property and the rules and regulations of society that no free people would tolerate such mischievous intermeddling."[45]

In addition to violating the property rights of whites, the civil rights bill was held to be an "odious form of race and class legislation," that, as Representative John M. Glover, a Democrat from Missouri, explained, signaled to the black man "that he is the especial ward and pet of the nation, to whom forty millions of white men should pay tribute and admiration."[46] As Representative Charles A. Eldredge, a Democrat from Wisconsin, further explained:

> To make the colored citizen feel that he is the pet, the especial favorite of the law will only feed and pander to that conceit and self-consequence which is now his weakest and perhaps most offensive characteristic. If he be made to feel that extraordinary provisions of law are enacted in his favor because of his weakness or feebleness as a man, the very fact weakens and enfeebles him. The consciousness that there is necessity for such legislation and protection for him must necessarily humiliate and degrade him. Such laws, too, are a constant reminder to him that he is inferior to the white race.

The bottom line, Eldredge concluded, was that there could "be no peace, no harmony, no confidence, no mutual respect, no feeling of equality between two races living together and protected from the infringement of each other's rights by different laws and different penalties."[47]

"So far as the law is concerned," asserted Eldredge, "the black man is in all respects the equal of the white. He stands and may make the race of life upon terms of perfect equality with the most favored citizen."[48] Like anticaste liberals, the phylogenetic position championed the laissez-faire vision of a nation of individuals forging their own destinies by virtue of their own effort and achievement. Once equal rights were established, there was nothing more for the law to do. Specifically, now that the Fourteenth and Fifteenth Amendments "have brought the colored race of this country upon the same plane with the white race," as Representative Glover stated, it was up to "the individuals of each [race] to work out their own destiny."[49]

While the anticaste position viewed racial discrimination and segregation as artificial and illegitimate barriers to civic equality that should be prohibited by federal law, the phylogenetic position viewed such practices as a natural and legitimate part of a social order that incorporated two extremely different, and inherently unequal, racial groups. From this perspective, the civil rights bill represented a draconian attempt to use the power of the federal government to impose "social equality" between the races in violation of both natural and constitutional law. While "the white people of the South" were "willing and desirous to give [black people] protection in every right and to concede to them equality before the law," explained Representative Eppa Hunton, a Democrat from Virginia, they would "resist by all legal means every attempt, whether in or out of Congress, to establish social equality between the races."[50]

This insistence that civil equality would logically result in racial hierarchy was rooted in the assumption that white supremacy was a divinely ordained bedrock of the natural order. As Representative Milton I. Southard, a Democrat from Ohio, argued:

> God himself has set His seal of distinctive difference between the two races, and no human legislation can overrule the Divine decree. Legislate as we may, the race passions and prejudices, the social tastes and inclinations, will remain, and forever keep the two classes upon terms of actual inequality.[51]

Similarly, Representative Glover held that "any legislation to counteract natural principles or to repeal natural laws or obliterate natural distinctions is impotent for good." Waxing sarcastic, he queried: "Why does not some learned gentleman introduce a bill to regulate the rainfall and to provide for the movements of the wind and tides? It would belong to the same class."[52]

To follow the dictates of the natural order, leaving the hierarchy of white supremacy and black subordination undisturbed, was held to be the only means of securing progress and harmony in race relations. As Representative James C. Harper, a conservative Democrat from North Carolina, argued, blacks and whites could live together for their mutual benefit—"side by side, in perfect peace, in perfect civil equality before the law, in the equal enjoyment of civil, moral, educational, and religious privileges"—as long as the prohibition against social equality was not violated.

> And so we should continue to live, each race helping the other, the whites teaching the blacks economy of time, improved methods of labor, and the cultivation of those qualities which give a man self-respect and the good will of his fellows. And the colored race, lending to the whites their strong arms and trained muscles, giving their labor for wages to support themselves and their families. Generations hence, should the negro exist that long, will see no change in the relations between the races, the whites acknowledging the civil equality of the blacks, and habituated to it; the blacks equally cognizant of and believing in their social and intellectual inferiority to the whites.[53]

To attempt to disturb this arrangement, however, was inevitably to generate violent white resistance and invite potentially disastrous social consequences. Representative Hiram P. Bell, a Democrat from Georgia, explained that the only reason that blacks and whites were able to coexist in their current state of "concord and peace" was that "the line of social distinction has been kept distinctly marked." Although the "colored people have never sought to cross or obliterate it," Bell claimed, the civil rights bill "seeks to blot it out." Such a move, Bell emphasized, would never stand:

> This attempt at its abolition invites the negro to take his position in the social scale with the whites. This will be resisted at the very threshold by all classes, and will never be submitted to or allowed, whatever consequences may result.[54]

At the same time, to attempt to legislate "social equality" was held to pose an equally dangerous threat to the integrity of the American constitutional order. Rejecting the anticaste argument that the Reconstruction amendments had fundamentally altered the shape of the federal system by significantly expanding the power of the national government, the phylogenetic position emphasized the inviolability of the original system as an indispensable bulwark against the growth of centralized power and despotic control. According to this perspective, the civil rights bill represented an illegitimate overextension of federal power that, once unleashed, would destroy the institutions of local self-government that formed the bedrock of the constitutional order. If "the construction which [Senator Sumner] and his associates have put upon the new amendments to the Constitution be received as the law of the country," stated Senator Orris S. Ferry, a Republican from Connecticut, "we may bid farewell to our hopes of American liberty for the generations to come."[55]

While the phylogenetic prohibition against "social equality" was, in this context, explicitly framed as a simple matter of natural racial difference, both the larger history of the concept and a deeper examination of its significance in this particular debate reveal that it was also profoundly connected to particular constructions of gender and class. There can be little question that one of the most powerful engines driving this virulent attack on "social equality" was the white supremacist prohibition against miscegenation—which was, of course, selectively focused on the sexual accessibility of white females to black males. (The sexual exploitation of black women by white men was, on the other hand, all too common; this, however, was discreetly accepted as one of the prerogatives of the ruling race.)[56] By this accounting, racial hierarchy was not only natural, but a key means of protecting the virtue of white women, who were, as is well known, held up as the primary, if weak and vulnerable, torchbearers of American civilization.

As has been repeatedly pointed out, the flip side of this superfeminization of white women was the defeminization of black women. Whites concerned with the health of plantation agriculture were scandalized when black women sought to remove themselves from the heavy physical labor of field work and devote themselves to home and family, in keeping with the idealized feminine prototype of the day. Race was such a central organizing principle of group difference that black women were not essentially viewed as "women" at all, in the sense that they were not seen as entitled to any of the same considerations and protections deemed appropriate for their white counterparts.[57]

The power of race to construct gender was repeated in the case of class. As in the case of anticaste liberalism, phylogenetic liberals had no operative category that explicitly referred to social structural divisions of wealth and poverty. If the former insisted upon describing such inequality as a result of individual differences, however, the latter essentially erased it by the intensity of the invocation of racial hierarchy. While, of course, far from unconcerned with the realities of material wealth and power, phylogenetic liberalism sent the implicit message that socioeconomic differences among whites were insignificant. What was important, in contrast, was their common bond as a part of the ruling race. In sum, phylogenetic liberalism racialized class out of existence as a general category, while shifting the double burden of race and class stigma to African Americans.

Given the intensity of anti-African racism in this construction of liberalism, its stated commitment to a minimal standard of universal rights may seem wholly inconsequential—a form of fraudulent window dressing that does not merit the dignity of recognition. To refuse to accept it as one historical variant of the basic liberal commitment to individual rights and civic equality is, however, mistaken. This is true for two key reasons. First, as overtly racist as this position was, it nonetheless represented what was, for the time, the politically moderate middle ground between the relative racial egalitarianism of the Radical Republicans and the unchecked racial virulence of what I refer to as white nationalism. Particularly prominent, of course, in the South, white nationalism distinguished itself from the more moderate position of phylogenetic liberalism in holding that black people were not simply inferior to whites but were so fundamentally different that they represented a "lower" order of being, unworthy of being accorded any rights whatsoever. Given this position, it logically followed that persons of African descent could not be considered citizens, even within a hierarchical system of white supremacy.[58]

Such views were prevalent throughout the course of Reconstruction. Louisiana's 1865 Democratic Party platform, for example, stated that "we hold this to be a Government of white people, made to be perpetuated for the exclusive benefit of the white race...people of African descent cannot be considered as citizens of the United States." Similarly, a New Orleans newspaper complained that "wicked demagogues" from the North were corrupting blacks and stirring up potentially dangerous trouble by instilling them with inappropriate notions of "rights":

> Negroes care nothing for "rights." They know intuitively that their place is in the field; their proper instruments of self-preservation, the shovel and the hoe.... Every real white man is sick of the negro, and the "rights" of the negro.[59]

Observers of everyday life in the Reconstruction South verified the prevalence of such views. A Freedmen's Bureau agent stationed in Greenville, South Carolina, for example, reported in 1866 that the "men that understand the Freedmen to have, or that they are entitled to any more rights than a horse are exceptions to the general rule."[60]

Beyond this issue of historical positioning, to define the phylogenetic position as outside the boundaries of American liberalism is to sanitize history in a way that is highly misleading. If the ways in which liberal universality can easily coexist with what now seem like wholly unacceptable constructions of group difference are not understood, simplistic calls for a "purified" standard of American liberalism, which assumes that it can easily purge itself of such "foreign" contaminants as racism and sexism, are strengthened. Bracketing such a position off from something like anticaste liberalism, which most contemporary liberals would be happy to claim as a part of the American liberal tradition, obscures the very important commonalities that they shared: an uncritical celebration of laissez-faire, an implicit endorsement of gender hierarchy, an atomized notion of individualism, and a refusal to consider the civic importance of entrenched patterns of socioeconomic inequality.

BLACK REPUBLICANISM

The common assumptions of anticaste and phylogenetic liberalism are set into sharper relief when compared to the alternative conception of citizenship that was dominant among the freedpeople themselves during Reconstruction. Following Foner, I refer to this position as black republicanism,[61] as it essentially represented a reworking of the key themes of eighteenth-century republican discourse in light of the particularities of the African-American experience.[62] In particular, this position emphasized both the embeddedness of the individual in the community and the connection between civil rights and economic independence. For the freedpeople, emancipation meant not simply the extension of individual rights, but the liberation of an entire people. At the same time, it was widely believed that neither could be achieved without the opportunity of economic self-sufficiency. Consequently, the issue of land redistribution and the provision of homesteads represented the first political priority of the overwhelming majority of the black public.

As contemporary historians have documented, southern blacks commonly considered the achievement of both individual and community autonomy to be a preeminently important component of their newly won freedom, and viewed land ownership as a vital precondition of that goal.[63] Similarly, with regard to the question of citizenship, land was widely understood to represent the economic foundation necessary for any meaningful extension of legal and political rights. As one Charleston resident succinctly explained to a northern journalist in 1865, "[W]ithout land, the old masters can hire or starve us, as they please."[64] During the same year, residents of Edisto Island, who, with the initial support of the Freedmen's Bureau, had settled upon abandoned plantation lands expecting to be given title to forty-acre plots, elaborated on this theme. Upon learning that the government now planned to restore the land to its former owners, the freedpeople formed a committee to write collective letters of protest to both President Andrew Johnson and General O. O. Howard, the commissioner of the Freedmen's Bureau. "General we want Homesteads; we were promised Homesteads by the government," they asserted. If the government reneged upon this promise, "we are left In a more unpleasant condition than our former...at the mercy of those who are combined to prevent us from getting land enough to lay our Fathers bones upon." Despite owning "property In Horses, cattle, carriages, & articles of furniture," being "landless and Homeless" rendered them once again subject to the will of their former owners. "We can not resist It In any way without being driven out Homeless upon the road," they explained. "You will see this Is not the condition of really freemen."[65]

Reinforcing this claim was the widely held belief that the freedpeople had a "right" to a portion of former slaveowners' lands. As one man protested when the U.S. Army came to evict him and others from land that they had settled on in Virginia:

> We have a right to the land where we are located. For why? I tell you. Our wives, our children, our husbands, have been sold over and over again to purchase the lands we now located upon; for that reason we have a divine right to the land.... And then didn't we clear the land, and raise the crops of corn, of cotton, of tobacco, of rice, of sugar, of everything. And then didn't those large cities in the North grow up on the cotton and the sugar and the rice that we made?... I say they have grown rich, while my people are poor.[66]

As such statements indicated, many southern blacks had a radically different understanding of the nature of the American political economy than was common among whites. Rather than seeing current economic arrangements as the outcome of a continually self-adjusting free-market system, they saw them as based in large part upon a long history of the exploitation of their labor. Consequently, the claim for a right to the land was not simply a contractual claim of individual former slaves against particular former owners, or even of the freedpeople as a collective against ex-slaveowners as a group. Rather, it was a claim on the nation itself, rooted in an assertion of the centrality of the African-American experience to the development of the country as a whole.

In this sense, black republicanism represented a way of combining universalist and particularist conceptions of citizenship that was quite different from even the obviously sympathetic position of anticaste liberalism. In recognizing the social and historical importance of group difference, black republicanism made a positive claim on American society, holding that, in the case of the freedpeople, civic inclusion necessitated particular measures that addressed the specific nature of the group experience. While anticaste liberalism similarly recognized the continued social significance of the experience of slavery, it viewed group difference as something that had to be made inconsequential in the public sphere in order to ensure the integrity of a universal standard of individual rights. While this goal was shared by the African-American community, black republicanism rejected any disaggregation of individual rights and group empowerment. Both had to be realized simultaneously if they were to be realized at all.

Framing the realization of the individual rights of the freedpeople so exclusively in terms of their status as a racially defined group, however, reinforced a broader tendency to ignore the significance of class, both within the black community and outside it. In fact, African-American political opinion was substantially divided along class lines, with the more affluent adhering to the laissez-faire assumptions embraced by anticaste liberalism and rejecting the economic claims represented by black republicanism. As Holt argues, the fact that the small—but, during Reconstruction, extremely important—group of prominent black political leaders came almost exclusively from the former group meant that there was a problematic disjuncture between the leadership and the broader public within the African-American community.[67] Further, as Emmer suggests, even if homesteads had been provided to the freedpeople, and they were consequently able to withdraw from plantation agriculture and the larger market economy within which it was embedded, it is likely that the sort of subsistence farming they would have engaged in would have kept most of them in a continual state of poverty.[68] Although this would probably have been greatly preferable to the actual outcome—continual poverty without land ownership under sharecropping—the point here is that what was really needed was a general democratization of the southern economy, rather than the placement of poor blacks on the margins of a highly inegalitarian system. This, of course, would have required an alliance with poor whites, which was almost certainly impossible at the time of Reconstruction. The more radical branches of the Populist movement would attempt such an alliance decades later, but only once economic discontent had built up to the boiling point among the economically disenfranchised of all races in the region.

Although the dynamics at work were extremely different in each case, it is nonetheless striking to note that neither anticaste liberalism, phylogenetic liberalism, or black republicanism connected citizenship to class structure. (Notably, it was not the case that such a class-centered conception of citizenship never existed in nineteenth-century America. On the contrary, such a position was already well embedded in the culture of the northern labor movement, and would soon rise to a position of national prominence following the collapse of Reconstruction.) If anticaste liberalism dissolved class into the logic of laissez-faire individualism, and phylogenetic liberalism racialized it out of existence, black republicanism both glossed over class differences within the African-American community and disconnected itself from a consideration of class differences more generally. While this disconnect made good sense given the generally rabid hostility of whites of all classes to any sort of program of black empowerment, it is nonetheless important to recognize that such deeply divergent political positions could still have such pronounced similarities.[69]

A similar point can be made with regard to gender. While there were certainly critical differences among each of the three positions, as well as different dynamics at work in the various social groups in which each was located, all, in one way or another, represented a deeply gendered conception of citizenship that relegated women to a dependent status of secondary importance. As Giddings documents, the prevailing vision of citizenship in the African-American community was deeply imbued with patriarchal conceptions of "manhood," and the fervent desire of black men to assert their rights was commonly expressed through a demand for increased dominance over black women. This was true both among individuals, within families, and in key community institutions such as, most notably, the church. "There is a great stir among colored men getting their rights, but not a word about the colored women," charged Sojourner Truth in 1867. "And if colored men get their rights, and not colored women theirs, you see the colored men will be masters over the women, and it will be just as bad as it was before." Although such public complaints were relatively rare, as many (probably most) black women believed that it was both right and necessary to secure the rights of black men before they could assert theirs, the pronounced linkage between masculinity and citizenship did not go unnoticed.[70]

In sum, while black republicanism differed dramatically from both phylogenetic and anticaste liberalism, it also shared certain commonalities with them, particularly along the lines of class and gender. The most critical difference among the three positions consisted of the different ways in which they constructed the meaning of race. While, of course, fundamentally opposed to phylogenetic liberalism's naturalization of racial hierarchy, black republicanism was also critical of anticaste liberalism's construal of race as a category that could be easily divorced from considerations of group history and economic inequality. This insistence upon the importance of race, however, did not entail a rejection of the liberal goal of achieving individual equality; on the contrary, the two goals were believed to be inextricably interrelated. The freedpeople did not make their claim to the land against the American nation, but as a fundamental part of it. Their special historical role as a group simply had to be recognized in order for their equality as individual citizens to be achieved.

CONCLUSION

Neither Greenstone's nor Smith's analytical framework is sufficiently robust to identify the critical dimensions of competing liberal constructions of the meaning of citizenship during Reconstruction. Greenstone's distinction between humanist and reform liberals is inadequate because it assumes an essentially singular conception of the individual subject, focusing on alternative valuations of what subjects *do* rather than who they *are*. Alternatively, Smith's "multiple-traditions" approach artificially separates discourses that were fundamentally intertwined, holding that "liberalism" and "ascriptive Americanisms" were clearly distinct and inherently incompatible species. As this case study demonstrates, alternative constructions of the civic subject provided the necessary basis for different conceptions of the fundamental rights of citizenship, with even the most explicit championship of the universal subject being imbued with a culturally distinct and practically consequential meaning. In short, the analysis of the *substance* and the *subject* of competing liberalisms must be joined in order to achieve a robust sense of their political significance.

7

Gendered Citizenship: Alternative Narratives of Political Incorporation in the United States, 1875–1925

Carol Nackenoff

[Dorothea Dix and Jane Addams] show…both an empathy for others and a desire to nurture, virtues that nineteenth-century American culture treated as out of place in the public world of competitive capitalism but central to the feminine province of family and home…. Addams explicitly stressed the need for a distinctively female perspective in reforming almost every facet of American society.[1]

For David Greenstone, Jane Addams was one of those figures whose political vision did not fit within Hartz's characterization of a Lockean, individualistic, state-fearing political culture. On this point, he was correct. He proceeded to identify Addams and many other figures who seemed to embrace a more positive, socially engaged state with Yankee Protestantism, a competing strain within the liberal tradition. Greenstone termed Addams's politics a "liberal politics of standards," which sought to supplant a politics of interest and provide all with the opportunity to develop their intellectual, moral, and cultural capacities. Rooting her values in those of New England Calvinism—a politics of conscience that even judged charity wanting if it led to egotism or self-congratulation—he argued that

> the goal was now the conversion of society into a community of brotherly love devoted to developing the rational and moral capacities, that is, the potential saintliness of every individual—precisely the goals of a liberal politics of standards.[2]

While the politics of individual rights and interests stood in tension with the politics of humanitarian reform, both were, Greenstone argued, inside the boundary conditions of a distinctive, patterned, liberal discourse in the United States. The Hartzian thesis remained vibrant if read metatheoretically: Our culturally conditioned words are Wittgensteinian "tools in a toolbox," available for widely different uses. Ambiguities over the meaning of concepts can—and do—lead to major conflicts; liberal creeds are not consensual. Nonetheless, we encounter "grammatical limits on what we can meaningfully say, think, and perceive." And if "words and deeds constitute each other," the words/practices nexus is a sticky one that leads us to expect slow, infrequent shifts in basic concepts and established practices. American political culture, bipolar though it has been, shapes and limits American liberal development.[3]

It is surely the case that political discourse and political practices are patterned, that political narratives are culturally and historically specific, and that these narratives are vital to the ways Americans struggle over politics. It is more problematic, however, to contend that all variants of American political thought fall within the confines of something defined as liberalism. Addams is one of those figures for whom I find this classification problematic. Republican concerns play on in Progressive-era struggles over the meaning of citizenship and its relationship to virtue. And the politics of citizenship is centrally bound up with the politics of gender, race, ethnicity, and class.

A liberal tradition that stretches to encompass all of this, I contend, ceases to have much explanatory power. I agree with Rogers Smith's contention that it is not clear what good is accomplished by using the term *liberalism* as expansively as many scholars now do.[4] If we are to understand the ways in which the politics of the limited American social welfare state were patterned, if we wish to think about political contingencies and possibilities, I do not think that variants on the American exceptionalism thesis will help us get there. I fear that Greenstone's bipolar categorizing approach diminishes our capacity to recognize potentially transformative worldviews. This posture places me at odds with quite a few contributors to this volume.

I offer support for my position in the form of a study of an important period in which the meaning of American citizenship was contested and reformulated. In examining the contested nature of citizenship and struggles over political identity during the Progressive era of American history, I share research interests with several other authors in this volume, especially Carol Horton and Rogers Smith, both of whom argue that the American political tradition is richer than Greenstone's bipolarism allows. I find, in support of Smith, that proponents of the cult of true womanhood blended, in different measures, liberal, republican, and ascriptive claims about civic identity, but I also argue that in the blend, new and potentially transformative visions were sometimes presented. These altered visions may even capture center stage in our political imagination. And while Smith especially stresses the ways in which political leaders and aspirants present "civic ideologies, or myths of civic identity that foster the requisite sense of peoplehood" in order to achieve political popularity, he thinks that the views of those who were ineligible to hold political office failed to shape American citizenship laws.[5] I treat as more central to the struggle over what it means to be a full member of the polity the views of those who contested their exclusion and who sometimes presented different visions of what citizenship might mean.

REVISIONING PUBLIC SPACES AND PUBLIC PURPOSES

The meaning of citizenship is historically contingent. The discussion is framed and the salience of citizenship is forged in a specific historical context in which identifiable portions of a population are either excluded from citizenship or are lesser citizens. One's own status and standing as a full member of the republic gains meaning by reference to the available alternatives; identity and self-definition as a citizen are forged in a conversation about otherness. Richard Slotkin calls this "definition by repudiation." Whatever their differences, a certain unity and identity of citizens is achieved by reference to what they have in common; for example, that they are not the children of Satan. In a different formulation, political life "aims at the construction of a 'we' in a context of diversity and conflict. But to construct a 'we' it must be distinguished from a 'them' and that means establishing a frontier."[6]

Entailed are unstated assumptions and arguments about what renders groups or individuals unfit for citizenship. Judith Shklar saw that slavery and servitude have been central to the way in which we think about citizenship. To be less than a full citizen is to approach the condition of slave; slavery always loomed in successive American political arguments for inclusion. Toni Morrison points out the central role Africans in America played in how white men defined their individualism, heroism, and virility. A "bound and unfree, rebellious but serviceable, black population" is the convenient group against which "all white men are enabled to measure these privileging and privileged differences."[7]

The public realm of modern citizenship had also been constructed upon the negation of female participation. Women were, Carole Pateman argues, subjects of the social contract. The ballot was a certificate of full membership in society, and paid labor separated the free man from the slave. Voting and earning, central attributes of the American citizen, were also marks of honor and civic dignity. Those who could not vote and who did not earn were mere subjects in a constitutional democracy. Voting was not simply about protecting one's rights and advancing one's interests; it was a mark of political agency and maturation. Citizenship and enfranchisement were *signs* of imputed virtue.[8]

Qualities associated with adult manhood were linked to qualities expected of a full participant in the life of the political community. As Pateman writes,

> [T]heoretically and historically, the central criterion for citizenship has been "independence," and the elements encompassed under the heading of independence have been based on masculine attributes and abilities.[9]

A man was an adult and an agent; he had the capacity for independence and self-sufficiency. Independence required autonomy, lest the agent be unduly influenced by and compromised by another. (Not all men were clearly "men.") Citizens were capable of boundary maintenance, self-discipline, and objectivity; they were responsible for their character.

In the United States, non-citizens have been understood to be non-white, non-male, non-adult, non-agents. They stand in a different relationship to the state than do citizens. It has been commonplace to presume that not-men required guidance, restraint, and sometimes protection. Not-men were more likely to become identifiable objects of policy making and policy discussion. Failing to measure up to the requisites of citizenship,

> one runs a high risk of entrapment in one of the categories of otherness derived from it…categories of abnormality license bureaucratic correction, discipline, regulation, exclusion, conquest, help, conversion, incentives, or punishment.[10]

By the late nineteenth century, amid large-scale immigration, labor struggles, the rise of Jim Crow legislation, and demands for female suffrage, an especially animated "conversation" about citizenship emerged. Visions of manliness, independence, and potency formulated by cultural elites not only were lampooned by Thorstein Veblen but were increasingly contested. New understandings of what constituted membership in the republic were in the making. Gender definition, independence, agency, and citizenship were drawn together in changing, contested narratives about American identity.

The strongest challenge to the moral authority of the man/independence/autonomy vision of citizenship was articulated in the Progressive era. During this period of rich, interlinked conflicts, the voices of those cast as less than full citizens revealed unstated rules and values in the polity. They sometimes revealed much more. As outsiders challenged their exclusion from full, mature, adult citizenship and the exclusion of their concerns from mainstream politics, they often challenged the frameworks linking autonomy, agency, independence, manliness, and citizenship. Talking back, they offered alternative narratives of citizenship.

As women challenged their exclusion from various aspects of public life during the Progressive era, the condition of the would-be new entrants became—in their eyes and potentially in the eyes of the broader society—an important or vital contribution to citizenship. Characteristics and experiences of the group were held to bring something essential or invaluable to the political life of the community. In emerging alternatives to male understandings of citizenship and agency, different qualities were valued, and the state itself was challenged to assume a new character.

Many feminists of this era sought something other—and sometimes more—than liberal theory, even in Greenstone's expanded liberal tent, tended to provide. Their vision extended beyond overturning restrictions on women as individuals and often beyond the individual as the unit of analysis. Maternal feminists such as Addams emphasized the corruption of the public realm as well as the dehumanizing features of a liberal capitalist state and the political culture underpinning it.

> Maternalists remind us of the inadequacy and limitations of a rights-based conception of the individual and a view of social justice as equal access. They…would have us recognize how, as interrelated "selves," we can strive for a more humane relational and shared community than our current political circumstances allow.[11]

It is hard to find in liberal theory the language and concepts to "understand the various kinds of human interdependence which are part of the life of both families and polities."[12]

In fact, the Progressive-era wave of women's activism could be seen as part of a veritable "democratic revolution," "a series of successive displacements of the line of demarcation between public and private." In this regard, turn-of-the-century feminists were part of the trajectory of workers' struggles of the late nineteenth century. The boundaries between public and private shifted by a "proliferation of new political spaces" rather than by the incursion of public authority into a pre-existing private realm.[13]

Women activists and women's organizations, so important in the expansion of notions of public responsibility, were not formally incorporated in deliberative bodies, yet they generated a narrative space for a new American public discourse of citizenship. Women were creating new languages about public space and new visions of the state. Women of different classes, races, and ethnicities were active in this struggle in different ways.

According to Mark Kann, classic accounts of an American liberal tradition are flawed because "individualism does not describe the historical norms or cultural practices of women…" from whom self-sacrifice is expected and for whom something more akin to civic virtue is the norm.[14] Adult white males are able to subscribe to individualism only because other members of the polity uphold other values. During the Progressive era, female activists insisted that these other values become public and universal values; individualism and prior notions of the individual subject came under heavy challenge.[15] These white activist claims, colored by race and class, nonetheless transgressed liberal boundaries.

This essay places Addams's world at center stage, for she was a central player in forging a gendered narrative of citizenship and an alternative vision of who we are. Addams's perspectives and criticisms in the name of social responsiveness touched every social and political institution—the family, the church, charitable institutions, business corporations, labor unions, political parties, and the institutions of racial coercion. To the female reformers and suffrage leaders of Addams's era, "it seemed perfectly clear that women were the only people in America capable of bringing about a new order in which democracy would find social as well as political expression."[16]

FROM AUTONOMY TO INTERDEPENDENCE

[M]uch of our ethical maladjustment in social affairs arises from the fact that we are acting upon a code of ethics adapted to individual relationships, but not to the larger social relationships to which it is bunglingly applied.[17]

Progressive-era women's highly articulated vision of citizenship stressed human interdependence. The good citizen was not the independent man. The city offered bountiful evidence of human dependence and interdependence; even infrastructure made the point. Addams's contemporary, Charlotte Perkins Gilman, noted that homes are now webbed together "by a network of pipes and wires."

Our houses are threaded like beads on a string, tied, knotted, woven together, and in the cities even built together; one solid house from block-end to block-end; their boasted individuality maintained by a thin partition wall. The tenement, flat, and apartment house still further group and connect us; and our claim of domestic isolation becomes merely another domestic myth.[18]

The modern city, bringing masses of people together, negated the self-sufficient household. More and more services were provided to the home by outside agents, public and private; water, light, and increasingly food supply were being socialized. There is now "a common dependency from which there is no escape." Building roads, providing drinking water, draining sewage, disposing of garbage, safeguarding food, and protecting children and homes could no longer be done by individuals themselves; they "can only be effectively done collectively." Addams emphasized "the futility of the individual conscience when woman insists upon isolating her family from the rest of the community and its interests."[19]

Woman in the metropolis "is utterly dependent upon the city administration for the conditions which render decent living possible." Anna Nicholes, the civil service commissioner of Cook County, Illinois, underscored the extent to which the functions of the home are connected with and controlled by the various departments of the central government. She noted how the politics of city hall permeate the home.[20] In Chicago machine politics, Addams further noted the pronounced dependence on the alderman, especially for poor and working people: "The long year round the fortunes of the entire family, down to the opportunity to earn food and shelter, depend upon the 'boss.'"[21]

A few miles south, at the University of Chicago, the theme of interdependence was also sounded. In *The Woman Movement from the Point of View of Social Consciousness* (1916), Jessie Taft, a student of George Herbert Mead, argued that "individuals are so interrelated and dependent that each one depends on the rest for obtaining his own ends." Health is a case in point, for "unless health is a common object of desire in a community and is sought for by each person with regard to all others, no one individual is safe from infection."[22]

Taft extended this argument to rights themselves, which were more properly viewed as dependent upon society for their existence than as absolute entities inhering in a self.[23] This alternative conception of rights generated a potent, if often underexplored, connection with African-American visions. It was shared by the aged ally of the woman's movement, Frederick Douglass, who saw only too well, with the rise of racial violence and Jim Crow, how inherently dependent upon others African Americans were for their rights. Douglass realized that citizenship was hollow unless government protected persons and rights. He considered independence synonymous with powerlessness and abandonment. "The first duty that the National Government owes to its citizens is protection," Douglass wrote.[24] Citizens depended on government for the enforcement of the claims of citizenship. Rights-bearers were dependent upon state and society. This was quite different from the perspective identifying citizenship with independence.

In Addams's view, men gravitate to ideals of individuality and independence, while women thirst for social action.[25] Social action served as a bridge from a self perceived as individual to a self perceived as interdependent. Working in urban slums, women in the settlement movement linked their sensitivity to social problems with their special qualities of feminine insight.

Female public campaigners such as Addams and Lillian Wald based their claims to the title of reformer in "specialized feminine perceptions of social justice," which included "women's ability to empathize with the weak and dependent." They believed "feminine intuition could both diagnose and direct social change."[26]

Women who based their claim to participation in the public realm upon the special characteristics of women asserted that women's nature would ennoble, uplift, and change the character of public life and discourse. "Those who sought to expand woman's role did so while defending the traditional conception of her nature," and women claimed to be especially equipped to recognize exploitation and see the true vision of a democratic society.[27]

Addams envisioned bringing women's brooms, caretaking skills, and the empathy and wisdom born of direct contact with immigrants and the urban poor into the definition of mature, ethical democratic citizenship. If female reformers would clean up urban machines and city administrations, care for the poor, and improve sanitation, suffragists would also pursue more caring policies and refrain from making war.[28] Feminine intuition and nature would tackle the problems of the industrial city, the nation, and the world. The house-cleaner government was a pervasive image, echoed in a late suffrage cartoon:

> Housekeeping is woman's work—no man denies that. Government is pub-
> lic housekeeping—practically everybody agrees to that. Isn't it foolish then
> to keep out of government the very people who have had most training for
> a large part of its function?[29]

The agents of economic and social injustice became gendered; females were not the designers and implementers of the rules of the business order. The diseases of the industrial order were deemed male diseases. Women, pro-claiming their noncomplicity, would counter the forces of materialism.[30]

Men were cast as notoriously bad housekeepers with a complete indif-ference to dirt, and "dirt means dead children." "Each little tombstone is a mute argument for giving the ballot to women, the natural enemies of dirt."

> Male-administration of government is mal-administration of government as
> proved by the perennial exposures of corruption in federal, state and munic-
> ipal government. Experience has proved that woman suffrage is a preven-
> tive of this malady.[31]

Addams often employed the metaphor of government as housekeeping, linking men with a predatory temperament and careless indifference to civic housekeeping. "Affairs, for the most part, are going badly in these great new centers"; males have been unable to solve the litany of urban ills:

Unsanitary housing, poisonous sewage, contaminated water, infant mortality, the spread of contagion, adulterated food, impure milk, smoke-laden air, ill-ventilated factories, dangerous occupations, juvenile crime, unwholesome crowding, prostitution and drunkenness, are the enemies which the modern cities must face and overcome, would they survive.[32]

Urban males, Addams thought, preferred to assess candidates on the basis of the national tariff or military policy, issues having to do "only with enemies and outsiders," thus ignoring the types of duties that had to be performed in the modern city.[33]

Despite the city's need for women's wisdom, Addams believed modern women were actually losing their capacity to participate in civic life. Traditional areas of women's concern were being increasingly absorbed into public business. The health department, bureau of street cleaning, and bureau of tenement house inspection had taken over functions that were once performed by the women of the community. Women were left "in a household of constantly narrowing interests."[34]

> Most of the departments in a modern city can be traced to woman's traditional activity; but, in spite of this, so soon as these old affairs were turned over to the city they slipped from woman's hands, apparently because they then became matters for collective action and implied the use of the franchise.[35]

As philanthropic activities passed from the private to the public sphere, women were often "forced to stand by and see the things they have started being done very badly because they can no longer help."[36]

Sounding a rearguard, defense-of-our-traditional-rights-and-prerogatives cry, Addams urged women to politics so as not to lose what they had claimed as their rightful sphere of expertise:

> [I]f women are to go on doing those things which they have always done they will have to have some share in the government which is now doing them. If not, these activities will be turned over altogether to the men.[37]

The image of the larger home—the social aspect of housekeeping—was part of a shared discourse:

> Woman's place is Home.... But Home is not contained within the four walls of an individual house. Home is the community. The city full of people is the Family. The public school is the real Nursery. And badly do the Home and Family need their mother.[38]

These public housekeeping concerns included regulation of industrial conditions, Americanization of urban immigrants, and addressing juvenile criminality, as through education and child-labor legislation. Women engaged in factory production often performed tasks similar to those they used to perform in the home (e.g., sewing, baking), but they no longer controlled working conditions; therefore, women's hours and working conditions should become objects of legislation. Young factory girls must not be left incapacitated for their future family life because of long hours and poor working conditions. Women and children of workers killed and disabled by industrial accidents were also matters for public concern, as were unemployed workers. Women who would fulfill their household duties must take part in the work of legislation.[39]

In Addams's world, the boundary between public and private could not be sharply delineated. Some activities and projects originating in philanthropic associations were entirely absorbed into the public sphere; in other cases, public institutions developed that still depended in part on the involvement of philanthropic associations (e.g., recommending family cases to the judge of the juvenile court for county aid). "There is perhaps no one thing in American life at present which is changing so rapidly as the dividing line between private beneficent effort and public governmental effort."[40]

In an image suggesting dynamism in the definition of public space, Addams speaks of a "wavering line between the public and private activities, so that you can scarcely tell what is philanthropy and what is public service." Would-be women citizens should see that the blurring of this line is going on all around them. Addams thought it outmoded and foolish to scowl upon as "unwomanly" women who continue to traffic in philanthropic activities when they have been taken over by the state.[41] Those whose social consciousness led them outside the narrow sphere of the home were truly womanly.

Addams considered the absorption of a woman in her own family circle selfish, a moral and civic failure. "We are under a moral obligation in choosing our experiences, since the result of those experiences must ultimately determine our understanding of life." She also believed that ideas and ethical values must evolve with changing conditions.[42]

> To attain individual morality in an age demanding social morality, to pride one's self on the results of personal effort when the time demands social adjustment, is utterly to fail to apprehend the situation.[43]

The language of social housekeeping was not confined to white middle-class feminists. African-American women activists also employed the imagery of social housekeeping. They too challenged the prevailing definition of public space and the boundaries between public and private. "African-

American women lived lives that knew no such artificial divisions.... They offered an interpretation of political life that emphasized the role of women as saviors of the race, justifying their activity because they were mothers."[44] Adella Hunt Logan, active in Alabama politics and lifelong member of the National American Women Suffrage Association (NAWSA), argued that African-American women could no longer refrain from meddling in politics, for they have learned "that politics meddle constantly with her and hers."

> Colored women feel keenly that they may help in civic betterment, and that their broadened interests in matters of good government may arouse the colored brother, who for various reasons has become too indifferent to his duties of citizenship....
>
> Good women try always to do good housekeeping. Building inspectors, sanitary inspectors and food inspectors owe their positions to politics. Who then is so well informed as to how these inspectors perform their duties as the women who live in inspected districts and in inspected houses, and who buy food from inspected markets?[45]

She enumerated many arenas in which good housekeeping gives women an interest in politics. Like her white middle-class counterparts, Logan frequently argued that women's greater involvement in politics furthered substantive policy goals. Even where women exercised only a partial franchise, she claimed, there have been policy benefits.[46]

But, Logan notes, "having no vote they [African-American women] need not be feared or heeded." African-American women and the families they sought to protect confronted an actively hostile state far more than did their white counterparts. Their power to shape public discourse and bend the state to their will was considerably weaker. "White women differed from African-American women in their ability to use the state to remedy social problems, but otherwise the dynamic was similar: women took the lead in remedying social problems."[47] Despite the overlapping discourse of social housekeeping, white feminists were not highly attentive to and did not tend to incorporate the insights of their African-American counterparts. As we will see, the nature of the claims they were building for citizenship confounded this issue.

There was not always agreement on the basis for woman's special claims upon public space. Quite often Addams and her contemporaries considered women's unique position to be primitive and instinctual. Women's interests were primordial and trustworthy; old maternal anxieties would, if shared by politicians, guide the city toward greater stability. Sometimes long home-based experience was held to yield a similar kind of expertise. And sometimes women's authority was traced to contact and involvement with urban immigrants and the poor. The question of "what home has to do with it" appeared to lead Addams and Gilman in one direction and politicians in another.

The science of the period offered a system of ideas readily adaptable to those seeking arguments for woman's innate uniqueness. Darwinism retained its hold on popular feminism during the early decades of the twentieth century, despite the fact it could be and was, in other hands, used to justify existing social institutions and roles. Feminists who based their authority in women's special nature derived considerable support from reigning beliefs about the relationship between biological differentiation and social evolution.[48]

Antoinette Brown Blackwell, the first ordained American female minister, paved the way in analyzing the implications of Darwinism for feminists in her 1875 work, *The Sexes Throughout Nature.* Blackwell accepted the argument of Darwin and Spencer that evolutionary divergence of males and females resulted from the different ways energy was used in the process of reproduction. Men developed powers of abstract reasoning; women developed the power of intuition. Her unique gloss lay in the argument that "intuition was not inferior to reason but rather an equivalent mental power and equally necessary to the proper functioning of society."[49]

According to the American followers of Spencer, sexual differentiation and sex role differentiation were markers of a particularly advanced state of civilization and characteristic of advanced races. Differentiation of civilized white male roles from civilized white female roles was an indication of an advanced status and a necessary stage in evolutionary progress. White women who espoused their advanced civilizing mission as highly specialized biological creatures embraced their differences from men as a signifier of the authority of white males and females to lead. Evolutionary theory of the late nineteenth century gave fuel to a sense of humiliation when white women were denied suffrage while black males and immigrant males (except Chinese and Japanese) could lay claim to it. Suffragists often voiced outrage at being classed below these men. Cartoons such as "The Political Companions of Women" depicted Frances Willard, president of the Women's Christian Temperance Union, alongside other disenfranchised denizens of the United States: Indians, the insane, criminals, and idiots.[50]

Addams read Spencer's 1873 *Study of Sociology* and accepted his position that "the female psyche and mind were of special significance in the evolutionary process because of the innate feminine capacity to empathize with the weak." She also appreciated Lester Ward's assertion that "the female was the prototype of the human being and the most highly evolved of the two sexes," a view at odds with some versions of evolutionary biology that accorded women a lesser role because of biological structure, cranial size, and the development of rational powers.[51] Although Ward cautioned that "like all instincts, [the maternal instinct's] acuteness and subtlety are proportioned to the narrowness of its purpose," he granted that woman's power instantaneously and accurately to judge what to do when her safety and that of her offspring were in jeopardy had become increasingly developed and complex with the progress of civilization.[52] Feminists also employed sociologist William I. Thomas's claim that life evolves from an anabolic (energy-storing) stage to a katabolic (energy-consuming) stage. He admitted that "[b]oth social feeling and social organization are thus primarily feminine in origin—functions of the anabolism of woman."[53]

Addams had met Scottish biologist and sociologist Patrick Geddes, coauthor with J. Arthur Thomson of *The Evolution of Sex* (1889), who argued that women's cell metabolism made them passive and nurturing, while males were warlike and aggressive. Geddes and Thomson posited an absolute difference between male and female cellular biology relating to the two laws of thermodynamics: that of conservation and that of irreversible degradation of energy in any system. "Male cells are 'katabolic,' that is, characterized by expenditure and breakdown, whereas female cells are 'anabolic,' conservative and constructive."[54] According to Geddes and Thomson, women were natural pacifists.

Suffrage cartoons frequently depicted woman's instinctual pacifism and what would be prevented if women were armed with the vote. "To bring peace, drive graft out of politics and close up forever Oriental harems and Occidental brothels requires woman suffrage, the most priceless possession of good civil government," one proclaimed. In another, a mother supports the weight of the world on her shoulders, Atlas-like, as three brigands battle on top and two children cling to the mother's skirts: "[T]he woman supports the world and protects her children, while the men waste property and kill each other. Woman suffrage will end such criminal foolishness. Only world suffrage means world peace."[55] Hoping to use their efforts to bring World War I to a speedy end, Addams and Carrie Chapman Catt issued a call for a convention in Washington in 1915, which led to the formation of the Woman's Peace Party.[56]

Addams, Catt, and many other feminists believed that "female and male natures had diverged in the course of evolutionary development and that society at large reflected this polarization." Catt held that "women have been given in greater perfection the gentler traits of tenderness and mercy, the mother heart, which goes out to the wronged and afflicted everywhere, with the longing to bring them comfort and sympathy and help."[57] For the natural evolution of society, they believed, women must not be confined to the home.

If males organized society and polity, then these organizations could be, and sometimes were, seen as reflecting physiological structures. Women would enter the public sphere bringing biologically based values, skills, and temperaments to bear on its institutions. This would produce a more egalitarian society, not just because women were now included, but because of what women cared about. Women, it was at least implied, could be better citizens than men.

One of the best statements of the Darwinist-influenced view of woman's biological contributions to the development of society and citizenship is found in Gilman's *Herland* (1915). Gilman organized an entire fictional society without men: a peaceful, noncompetitive society, reproducing by parthenogenesis and enjoying prosperity without distinctions of wealth. In this society, deep within the jungle, there is no concept of home, no private realm. Artificial characteristics commonly alleged to be innately feminine are stripped away from the women of Herland, but once artificial sex distinctions disappear, women remain biologically and psychologically distinct from men. They value peace, nurturance, industry, cooperation, motherhood, and a broader citizenship.[58] "Gilman criticized not innate female nature but its distortion in the course of evolution."[59] For the modern home to be more meaningful, Gilman argued, women must be able to enter the world of work, expanding their experiences and skills as men do. Consigned to the narrow circle of the home, women become selfish drones. Innately nurturant women need to be accorded larger roles in society if society is to benefit from female values.[60]

Addams and settlement house leaders did not base their entire argument about women's contribution to a larger citizenship on instinctual or home-based knowledge. Experience must also be born of contact with wider ills, and it is women who have invested their time and energy in cultivating such experience. According to Addams, "the fate of all the unfortunate, the suffering, and the criminal is daily forced upon woman's attention in painful and intimate ways."[61] We are unable "to see the duty 'next to hand' until we have become alert through our knowledge of conditions in connection with the larger duties."[62] Those who would develop a social morality "must be brought in contact with the moral experiences of the many in order to procure an adequate social motive." This contact with all kinds of life must be firsthand, not at arm's length or from books. A "wider acquaintance with and participation in the life about them" is essential for citizens, "for much of the insensibility and hardness of the world is due to the lack of imagination which prevents a realization of the experiences of other people."[63]

Differing types and degrees of experience with the larger life make it very difficult for people to understand each other. It is hard for people to free themselves from the individualistic point of view. "Most of the misunderstandings of life are due to partial intelligence, because our experiences have been so unlike that we cannot comprehend each other."[64]

Experience was a corrective to doctrine, for "experience gives the easy and trustworthy impulse toward right action in the broad as well as in the narrow relations." Contact with the moral experiences of the poor reveals that moral standards cannot be simply mechanical; the poor have much to teach the social worker. "We arrive at moral knowledge only by tentative and observant practice. We learn how to apply the new insight by having attempted to apply the old and having found it to fail."[65]

The charity worker learns from her encounter with others. Contact "not only increases her sense of social obligation but at the same time recasts her social ideals."

> She is chagrined to discover that in the actual task of reducing her social scruples to action, her humble beneficiaries are far in advance of her, not in charity or singleness of purpose, but in self-sacrificing action. She reaches the old-time virtue of humility by a social process.... She has socialized her virtues not only through a social aim but by a social process.[66]

The realization of democracy requires identification with the common lot; this identification "becomes the source and expression of social ethics." Participants in the settlement movement "aimed to blur class lines by helping their neighbors to achieve full participation in American democracy and social life."[67]

Addams's wider experience is a kind of social scientific inquiry. It is a mode of data collection; a broadening of the "sample" of life and thereby a testing and enlarging of views. The effort to build social consciousness through immediate experience throws out of the undertaking "all those who shrink before the need of striving forward shoulder to shoulder with the cruder men, whose sole virtue may be social effort."[68] Addams insisted that experience builds social perspective and combats insularity.

The search for social morality builds a democratic spirit, "for it implies that diversified human experience and resultant sympathy which are the foundation and guarantee of Democracy."

> To attempt to attain a social morality without a basis of democratic experience results in the loss of the only possible corrective and guide.... A man who takes the betterment of humanity for his aim and end must also take the daily experiences of humanity for the constant correction of his process.[69]

One must know of the lives of others, "not only in order to believe in their integrity, which is after all but the first beginnings of social morality, but in order to attain to any mental or moral integrity for ourselves or any such hope for society."[70]

The acquisition of social morality is a dialectical process. One's views and perspectives must be constantly tested by broader experience. Democracy requires a common belief in the *integrity*—the personhood and presumably morality—of the other. The privileged citizen acquires integrity only by developing the larger social morality.

Genuine experience cannot lead one astray, Addams believed, any more than scientific data can. And she had the utmost faith in "the illuminating and dynamic value of this wider and more thorough human experience." With faith in progress, Addams was confident that the social ethic was growing: "to see farther, to know all sorts of men, in an indefinite way, is a preparation for better social adjustment—for the remedying of social ills."[71]

If women interact with the poor on a far more sustained basis than men do, the implication is that women tend to develop the social ethic, while men are more likely to retain the individual, insular ethic. This leads to the feminist argument that women who have experience with the urban poor and their problems are better equipped for citizenship than are males who still retain industrial mentalities. In addition, the different experiences of men and women result in different views on public matters. The sensitivities of both men and women are essential if the city is to transcend its ills. If "government is undertaking, more and more those intimately human affairs which have to do with daily life and daily experience," women have a natural place in government.[72]

Addams considered the participation of women in public affairs necessary for the fulfillment of the polis. She argued that

> [i]f woman had adjusted herself to the changing demands of the State as she did to the historic mutations of her own household she might naturally and without challenge have held the place in the State which she now holds in the family.[73]

For Addams, "each advance in ethics must be made fast by a corresponding advance in politics and legal enactment." The state must have the right to regulate and control the industrial system, which "is in a state of profound disorder"; "there is no guarantee that the pursuit of individual ethics will ever right it."[74]

For many years Addams had focused on the municipal rather than the national franchise. By the time she embraced national suffrage, Addams would have concurred with Logan that "[w]omen who see that they need the vote see also that the vote needs them."[75]

TRANSCENDING INDIVIDUALISM: CITIZENSHIP AND THE SOCIAL ETHIC

> Even Mill claims that the social feelings of man, his desire to be at unity with his fellow-creatures, are the natural basis for morality, and he defines a man

of high moral culture as one who thinks of himself, not as an isolated individual, but as a part in a social organism.…

Upon this foundation it ought not to be difficult to build a structure of civic virtue.[76]

The alternative model of citizenship required transcendence of self-centeredness and the individualist ethic. The larger citizenship required social consciousness and concern for others. Women who would bring new values and standards to the American polity saw themselves allied with science and progress, with greater fellow-feeling and democracy.

Addams was influenced by the philosophy of Josiah Royce. She asserted "the virtues of social cooperation against the satisfaction of individual preferences, and the virtues of Royce's idealist philosophy against social Darwinist, laissez-faire doctrines that justified industrial capitalism."[77]

While Addams and her contemporaries were conversant with J. S. Mill's *The Subjection of Women,* it is Mill's *Utilitarianism* that was in the air, perhaps especially in Chicago. The firm foundation of utilitarian morality "is that of the social feelings of mankind; the desire to be in unity with our fellow creatures." As civilization advances, people "grow up unable to conceive as possible to them a state of total disregard of other people's interests." Strengthening social ties gives each person a stronger personal interest in consulting the welfare of others; "it also leads him to identify his *feelings* more and more with their good." And "he comes, as though instinctively, to be conscious of himself as a being who of course pays regard to others."[78] According to this philosophy, our own happiness is increasingly bound up with that of others.

Belief in a progressive science of politics based in increasing social consciousness was not, of course, confined to American women, though they influenced the language and perceptions of some of their male peers. Walter Lippmann was one of these. In 1914 he wrote of a political revolution in the making: "[T]he focus of politics is shifting from a mechanical to a human center." New statesmanship "proposes to fit creeds and institutions to the wants of men, to satisfy their impulses as fully and beneficially as possible." With this new tendency "to put men at the center of politics instead of machinery and things," he saw a turning toward "the creation of finer environments" and toward shaping our own destiny. "There is an ascendant feeling among the people that all achievement should be measured in human happiness. This feeling has not always existed…in America it belongs to the Twentieth Century."[79] Lippmann placed women in the forefront of this great movement.

Lippmann had considerable hope in the progress that might be attained through the social scientific understanding of psychology and the human personality.[80] Science could also help liberate women now. He seemed quite taken with Gilman's formulation that inefficient and outmoded home-based work is retarding human progress. Women "have got to adjust themselves to a new world," he wrote in 1914. Science must enter the home and help women specialize, saving the home from stupidity, inefficiency, and wasted labor. And women "must go into politics, of course, for no home exists that doesn't touch in a hundred ways upon the government of cities, states and the nation."[81]

Academic voices echoed some of these themes about progress, while questioning feminist claims to lead. University of Chicago psychologist Jessie Taft found humankind progressing from the objective consciousness of self (the Greeks) and the subsequent subjective consciousness of self (Kant and the French Revolution) to the reflective or social consciousness of self. Advanced civilization is just beginning to glimpse this third level of consciousness, which includes a belief in a science of society and an understanding of the social character of all human experience. With an avowed attraction to socialism, Taft echoed Marx and Engels when stipulating the greater chance for new forms of control and mastery, not only over nature but over social relations. With growing self-consciousness, Taft thought, we will no longer see merely economic relationships but will come to understand that we are engaged in a social relationship with those from whom we buy or to whom we sell, or with those who work for us or for whom we work. Becoming conscious of the social nature of our relationships teaches us that our goals are only realized in common. That "hard and unyielding individual with his boundless, empty freedom" disappears.

> That freedom that was supposed to reside in the individual is seen to be realized only through society. The individual is not economically or morally free except when he is able to express himself, to realize his ends through the common life.[82]

Again, the individual comes to take others naturally into account; it is a matter of the proper inclusion and analysis of data:

> [T]he value of his thought in handling social questions is tested just as it is in handling physical problems, by the adequacy with which it covers all the data involved. *Hypotheses which ignore the interests of entire classes of people, which fail to recognize existing social relations, will not work in the long run.*[83]

While Addams wrote of the activist woman's *experience* as the basis of a scientific knowledge of society and thereby social consciousness, Taft insists that the social scientist who systematically collects "data," who incorporates the interests of all classes, and who thinks as a social being will be in the vanguard of the movement for social consciousness and facilitate greater control over the human environment. Social scientists will lead in the progressive realization of "the reflectively conscious personality."

For the right attitude to prevail—for humans to understand the importance of unsatisfied and unexpressed impulses and to devote expert attention to such impulses—there must be "a sufficient number of people who are so socially sensitive and adaptable that they feel within themselves as their own the impulses and points of view of all classes and both sexes." The social scientific vanguard will make theory real. The woman's movement must serve the goal of producing these experts; indeed, this is its fundamental purpose.[84]

Taft rejected claims that woman's intuition and nurture were vital to the emergence of social consciousness. The movement of labor and the movement of women alike sought to address a tension between self and environment; these two movements often failed to understand how close their relation was and how they manifested a common problem in different aspects. However, while granting that these movements expressed real, unfulfilled impulses and an unhappiness over the untenable dualism of self and environment, Taft considered the highest goal of any social movement to be the production of social scientists whose hypotheses and data would increase social consciousness. Women as a class were not at the forefront of this effort. Subject to external authority and to the authority of fathers and husbands, women suffered double restrictions on their activities and social relations. As a class, women were more likely to remain childlike longer, and they were more lacking in self-consciousness than others in the history of the race.[85]

Academics interested in woman's nature had begun to abandon Darwin and biological assumptions in favor of environmental explanations of many kinds of human variation by 1900. Some of these academics were wary about concluding that reason and progress would bring about greater equality among the sexes. Columbia University–trained sociologist Elsie Clews Parsons believed that, rather than seeking progress, humans feared change and impeded progress. Sexual prejudice was part of a classification system by which women were deemed anomalous in comparison to men; rules and conventions regulating behavior followed.[86] Women were not likely to change unless social pressure and expectations about women's nature changed, and this was not likely to occur soon.

Academic feminists and social psychologists often disagreed with better-known feminists on political and social issues, including protective legislation for women and whether legislative remedies could end prostitution. In comparison with the preponderant feminist faith, these academic voices sounded faint and dissenting during the early years of the twentieth century.[87]

The most prevalent model of the female social engineer in the early twentieth century was the "sage or prophetess who claimed access to hidden wisdom by virtue of feminine insights," despite the rise to prominence of a few academically based female social scientists.[88] This model of feminine excellence created cultural heroines for one generation but did not transcend the era. Addams was the perfect model of the woman reformer.

EXPERIENCE, ENGAGEMENT, AND ETHICS

As female settlement house activists claimed status as social scientists, activist male social scientists in the university were in retreat. By the end of the nineteenth century, "objectivity" replaced advocacy in the work of most male social scientists. A wave of political repression had hit American universities between 1886 and 1894; many male social scientists who were politically active social planners were either fired or threatened with firing for advocating "radical" ideas. Experts who had previously been activists often became capable policy advisers, but "not as leaders of a crusade for social justice," and they were much less likely than before to work closely with popular social movements.[89] Thus, "the same forces that limited men's power to solve social problems actually promoted the power of women's political culture." Women such as Addams and Florence Kelley, sustained by institutions such as Hull House, were "undeterred by the repression experienced by their male colleagues in universities, [and] continued throughout their lives to affiliate closely with popular social movements, particularly those dominated by women." Projecting a secular and professional image, these women used social science as a reform tool. Settlement house women "could collect social data and use it to design remedies for social problems just as well as any university professor."[90]

Movement toward a more moral order required coordinated, concerted action by those willing to experiment and remain open. By the end of the nineteenth century, the old Yankee-Emersonian certainty about the existence of a single moral community was yielding to a sense of moral inquiry. New urban immigrant communities were built on norms and customs unfamiliar to American Protestants. "Right-minded Yankees could no longer make a moral appeal and then correctly anticipate either what others would do or even what their own consciences would tell them to do."[91]

Addams was drawn to John Dewey's pragmatism, where inquiry preceded collective action. Dewey served on the first board of Hull House and remained a friend of Addams. He insisted "on the decisive importance of an active, interpreting, human intelligence" and on the cultivation of every individual's cultural faculties. Ethical action toward all members of society was essential, for everyone had the capacity for moral and rational action.[92]

For Dewey, natural evolution was not yet finished; "claims about reality cannot be permanently and completely valid." Every assertion had to be open to further scrutiny; "every proposition concerning truths is really in the last analysis hypothetical and provisional." And "moral values…are determined in the course of deciding what actions we should take." If such a view leads to a belief in moral plurality rather than moral community, then inquiry is culturally conditioned and every truth is provisional. Different cultures make distinct contributions to this inquiry.[93]

Imbued with this perspective, Hull House residents would have to be taught by their neighbors. Addams refused to call them "clients" or "cases." Neighbors would "collaborate in the settlement's own work." Hull House "had to rely upon its neighbors, not just to implement its goals, but to determine just what those goals should be." Residents were to learn from mistakes. "Their method was experimental in Dewey's sense: perform an action, observe its effects, and modify one's behavior accordingly."[94]

"The ethics of none of us are clearly defined," Addams wrote, for we act only on "circles of habit" which are "based upon convictions we no longer hold." The settlement house was a method, not a solution. In the science of social reform, investigation and moral learning were inextricably linked.[95] Her criticisms of genteel reformers centered upon their unreflective moral certainty and rigidity when confronting urban immigrants.

Neither science nor reform movements should segregate politics from moral and social life. Addams saw this as a male mistake:

> The well-to-do men of the community think of politics as something off by itself; they may conscientiously recognize political duty as part of good citizenship; but political effort is not the expression of their moral or social life. As a result of this detachment, "reform movements," started by business men and the better element, are almost wholly occupied in the correction of political machinery and with a concern for the better method of administration, rather than with the ultimate purpose of securing the welfare of the people.[96]

While Hull House attempted two unsuccessful campaigns to oust a longtime corrupt alderman for the area, Addams found the choice between the aldermanic system and progressive reforms more difficult than many of her contemporaries did. Addams objected to the elitism of reformers, and their sense that the righteous do not need to be agreeable. She asked provocatively:

> Would it be dangerous to conclude that the corrupt politician himself, because he is democratic in method, is on a more ethical line of social development than the reformer, who believes that the people must be made over

by "good citizens" and governed by "experts"? The former at least are engaged in that great moral effort of getting the mass to express itself, and of adding this mass energy and wisdom to the community as a whole.[97]

There is a prescient criticism of the tendency of reform movements "to put more and more responsibility upon executive officers and appointed commissions at the expense of curtailing the power of the direct representatives of the voters." They then become negative influences and "lose their educational value for the mass of the people."[98]

Aldermen live near the masses of voters, know them intimately, and "minister directly to life and to social needs." They take care of the poor, pay funeral expenses, and distribute Christmas turkeys. The political success of these aldermen rests on an individualistic basis; it could hardly be otherwise in an ethnically heterogeneous ward where universal experiences "are perforce individual and not social." Constituents believe the alderman virtuous and heroic because his individual acts are kind and generous; "they are at the same time unable to perceive social outrages which the alderman may be committing."[99]

> Indeed, what headway can the notion of civic purity, of honesty of administration make against this big manifestation of human friendliness, this stalking survival of village kindness? The notions of the civic reformer are negative and impotent before it.[100]

The aldermanic code of behavior involves acting for the benefit of oneself or one's friends. Insiders belong "to a set of fellows who understand things, and whose interests are being cared for." Addams would find this "perfectly legitimate, and all in the line of the development of a strong civic loyalty, if it were merely socialized and enlarged." However, "it is a long step in moral progress to set the good of the many before the interest of the few, and to be concerned for the welfare of a community without hope of an individual return."[101] Ultimately, the alderman does the ethical development of the community no good.

A "fixer" impresses his constituents; many think "that the aldermanic power is superior to that of government." People see the alderman shielding them from the law and the police passing by illegal establishments owned or protected by their representative. "A certain contempt for the whole machinery of law and order is thus easily fostered." The undermining of civic loyalty and of respect for the power of law is a "cost" of the aldermanic system. The alderman "cares more for the feelings and pocket-books of his constituents than he does for the repute and cleanliness of his city." The entire community pays the price for corruption, but the "evils of corrupt government are bound to fall heaviest upon the poorest and least capable," who experience the disease-carrying public water and garbage in the streets.[102]

But even the most corrupt aldermen are better champions of democracy than reformers and proceed upon a sounder theory. "The real leaders of the people are part of the entire life of the community which they control, and so far as they are representative at all, are giving a social expression to democracy." Machine politicians are not frightened by democracy, as are a certain type of businessmen, who have lost their faith in the people.[103] Reformers, businessmen, and social scientists who shun public engagement are all guilty of failing to learn from experience.

Compared to elite reformers, "the poor turned out to have the more genuinely sympathetic, neighborly, and self-sacrificing moral code."[104] Addams here gives Mill a Rousseauean twist, arguing that the simplest people have fellow-feelings upon which a politics of social consciousness can and should build. "Primitive" humans, such as the urban ethnic poor, have a ready willingness to help friends and neighbors in need, whatever the inconvenience to themselves.

Addams tends to identify immigrants as childlike and having a primitive, simple moral code. They have a sense of goodness, but for people at an early stage of moral evolution (Addams mentions southern Italian peasants), "abstract virtues are too difficult for their untrained minds to apprehend." Good personal example is essential. "It is obvious that ideas only operate upon the popular mind through will and character, and must be dramatized before they reach the mass of men."[105] This primitive sense of goodness is a better instinct upon which to build a social morality than the businessman's ethic and individualistic morality of the adult male. Women, with their housekeeping skills, are more in touch with the childlike and simple. But children need guidance.

This preference for primitive goodness and a sense of social interdependence carried over from the urban arena to labor struggles. Addams placed hope in the common turn-of-the-century assertion that America was passing from an age of individualism to an age of association. Action carried out along the line of associated effort is "more highly developed"; even if inefficient, it "may represent a finer social quality and have a greater social value than the more effective individual action."[106] The struggles of cooperating, associated workingmen against even the most benevolent individual employer exemplify the higher value of association.

The ethics of the mass of men surpass that of the employer. Their desire for self-expression, self-government, and the amelioration of their condition is nobler than the employer's desire to provide for their good as he sees fit. Workingmen have a more general vision and a greater sense of morality than the industrialist. They talk of justice and brotherhood, attempt to inspire and encourage each other, and appeal to the "identity of the interests of workingmen the world over." Addams admires the proletarian sentiment that "the injury of one is the concern of all." The social virtues "express themselves in associated effort." Working people know that an individual employer is lodged in an industrial system with competitors and that their wages and conditions in a trade do not depend merely on their employer's goodwill. They know that the relationship is not merely one between individuals.[107]

For Addams, "the real sin of capitalism was not the economic fact that capitalists made profits, but the social consequence that the poor had no genuine (rather than merely formal) opportunity for cultural expression and self-development."[108] Because of business demands, employers are often cut off from the emerging social ethic and "from the great moral life springing from our common experiences. This is sure to happen when he is good 'to' people rather than 'with' them, when he allows himself to decide what is best for them instead of consulting them."[109]

Addams helped workers form organizations, sided regularly with workers in Chicago strikes, and bitterly attacked George Pullman's paternalism toward his striking workers. In the Pullman strike, she noted how much the men resented the extension of industrial control into domestic and social arrangements. "They felt the lack of democracy in the assumption that they should be taken care of in these matters, in which even the humblest workman has won his independence." Pullman did not consult worker feelings or needs; his attitude was rather that of the artist toward his creation. The benefactor too frequently fails to cultivate a frank equality with his or her beneficiaries, "and there is left no mutual interest in a common cause." The performer of too many good deeds may lose his or her capacity to recognize good in others.[110]

In an attempt to aid and educate working people, the middle-class moralist or industrialist "has constantly and traditionally urged upon the workingman the specialized virtues of thrift, industry, and sobriety—all virtues pertaining to the individual." But in a highly organized, complex, and interdependent environment,

> if a workingman is to have a conception of his value at all, he must see industry in its unity and entirety; he must have a conception of it that will include not only himself and his immediate family and community, but the industrial organization as a whole.[111]

Working men and women need the kind of education that develops an understanding of interdependence; "if the workingman is to save his life at all,...he should get a sense of his individual relation to the system." It is intellectually and morally deadening to be engaged in "feeding a machine with a material of which he has no knowledge, producing a product, totally unrelated to the rest of his life, without in the least knowing what becomes of it, or its connection with the community." What workers need is a social consciousness of the value of their work, a sense of participation and pleasure in the end use of the product, and "some historic conception of the development of industry and the relation of [their] individual work to it."[112] Addams's goal was to help workers move beyond the relatively passive experience of exhausting factory labor "to the active interpretation that makes one's life and actions form an intelligible whole." Every human had the capacity to develop this perspective. Armed with such sentiments, Addams enthusiastically attended the Progressive Party convention of 1912 and voted for Eugene Debs in 1920. She thought that individuals could learn to appreciate the interests uniting labor and capital. She also favored industrial cooperation over more militant class-conscious worker movements.[113]

For Addams, we are interdependent in the project of democracy. "All parts of the community are bound together in ethical development." Addams concludes that "this is the penalty of democracy…that we are bound to move forward or retrograde together."[114]

GENDERED VISIONS, PUBLIC VISIONS

Progressive-era debates about membership in the polity and the terms of citizenship gave rise to new visions of progress and political incorporation in the United States. The ramifications of these debates were broad. Wider understandings of citizenship paved the way for and shaped the American version of the welfare state.

Gendered rhetoric of citizenship pervaded the public sphere. Neither gender spoke in unison, yet it is fair to conclude that masculinist political rhetoric, with its emphasis upon manliness, autonomy, vigor, and independence, was gradually and at least temporarily displaced by feminist rhetoric. Gendered visions of the state and of the meaning of citizenship became public visions.

Mark Kann's assertion that historically "ours was a Lockean liberalism that required, incorporated, and perpetuated republican civic virtue according to an engendered division of labor" helps us understand the need to qualify claims for the pervasiveness of the liberal tradition.[115] As the cult of true womanhood permeated the suffrage movement, women insisted that their civic labor could no longer be private or merely family-directed, but rather that notions of citizenship and state had to be transformed.

The Progressive vision was, in considerable measure, a female vision, inspired by the rhetoric of social responsibility. As Skocpol has forcefully argued, "women's politics played a much more central role in progressivism than most historians have heretofore acknowledged." Turn-of-the-century women made "collective and hegemonic demands—that is, demands not only for themselves but also on behalf of the entire society—to a degree highly unusual for any broad category of people in American politics."[116] Sklar concurs that "to an extent unequaled elsewhere, middle-class American women were crucial and central to the responses state and federal governments made to social pressures created by massive immigration and rapid industrialization and urbanization." In the United States, "so much of the path to the welfare state [was] blazed by middle-class women" because their activism "served as a surrogate for working-class social-welfare activism." Political mobilization by these women "formed the largest coalitions that broke through the malaise and restructured American social and political priorities at the municipal, state, and federal levels."[117]

While most still lacked the ballot, "women became civically involved in a polity where plenty of 'space' was available for new forces who favored collective as opposed to distributive, patronage-oriented policies."[118] In preparation for a new leadership role, women's clubs and branches of NAWSA provided a training ground for public life. They staged parliamentary debates, read and discussed scholarly works of the day, entertained distinguished visitors, including Beatrice Webb and Eleanor Marx, and discussed political questions such as "Free Trade," "Socialism in the Home," "Bismarck and His Policy," and "The Eight Hour Day."[119]

Women activists were more supportive of an expanded public sector than were their male counterparts. Their associations generally supported the expansion of governmental responsibility for the welfare of the able-bodied. Shorter hours and higher wages plus safer work sites would create sounder citizens and improve society.[120] Women's groups lobbied for legislation that they "boldly claimed was in the moral best interest of society as a whole."[121] Maternal values were presented as progressive democratic values.

Women's vision of citizenship included much of what T. H. Marshall termed "social rights." This vision refused to accede to the separation of ethics from politics or to accept an individualistic ethos. Women's political culture had faith in democratic processes and in the "capacity of large social organizations—like state and federal governments—to respond positively to social needs." The state was not an enemy of human liberty; rather, it was "a potential guarantor of social rights."[122]

It would appear that Progressive-era maternalists did have "an advantage in defining what the public interest meant." The rhetoric used by these women proved effective with legislators and civic leaders; it claimed to rise above narrow partisanship in the name of selfless morality. Organized American women, in a structurally and culturally privileged position, were able to attract support from male elites and shape the agenda of progressive politics.[123] Their critique of individualism was heard in a way that class-based critiques were not.

Influenced by the rhetoric of the social ethic, political leaders began to envision American identity and strength differently by the time of Wilson's first inauguration. Presidents increasingly mentioned women's positive influence in public life or noted approvingly the growth of those virtues that women liked to claim as their special domain.

In his first inaugural address, Wilson invoked the great moral force of American life.

> Nowhere else in the world have noble men and women exhibited in more striking forms the beauty and the energy of sympathy and helpfulness and counsel in their efforts to rectify wrong, alleviate suffering, and set the weak in the way of strength and hope.[124]

He aspired to find and perfect "the means by which government may be put at the service of humanity"; men, women and children must be shielded "in their lives, their very vitality, from the consequences of great industrial and social processes which they can not alter, control, or singly cope with." "Sanitary laws, pure food laws, and laws determining conditions of labor which individuals are powerless to determine for themselves are intimate parts of the very business of justice and legal efficiency." Four years later, Wilson celebrated the "significant changes in the spirit and purpose of our political action." Americans were attempting to "lift our politics to a broader view of the people's essential interests."[125]

Elected after ratification of the Nineteenth Amendment, Warren G. Harding extolled woman's contribution to politics in terms of her special talents and virtues:

> [W]e may count upon her intuitions, her refinements, her intelligence, and her influence to exalt the social order. We count upon her exercise of the full privileges and the performance of the duties of citizenship to speed the attainment of the highest state.[126]

He proclaimed that "service is the supreme commitment of life" and pledged "an administration wherein all the agencies of Government are called to serve." Harding found American strength, greatness, and citizenship to be home-centered. In an inventory of what the nation stands for, his successor, Calvin Coolidge, declared that American government stands "attentive to the intuitive counsel of womanhood."[127]

CONCLUSION: POLITICAL TRADITIONS AND POLITICAL POSSIBILITIES

This alternative vision of citizenship had some real, if limited, success in attacking the truncation of public space and the impoverished vision of citizenship of the era. But these broader visions failed to completely transform or dislodge resilient autonomy-based understandings of citizenship. By the mid-1920s, "powerful backlashes developed against policy gains that had already been achieved."[128] As we stand at the end of the twentieth century, the vision offered by Addams and her contemporaries seems no longer to purchase much legitimacy in public space. One might well conclude that "[a]ll normative concerns have increasingly been relegated to the field of private morality, to the domain of 'values,' and politics has been stripped of its ethical components."[129]

Do the limits of the power of this vision vindicate claims for the brute strength of Hartzian liberalism, or even of the boundary conditions of a more bipolar liberal discursive community? Was this as far as rules of the language game somehow allowed Americans to think and move? Is this a mapping with which a reified political culture confronts political actors, holding out certain roles, cues, and prospects for would-be participants in social transformation? I don't think so. Let me instead modestly examine some reasons for the limited extent to which this particular vision of citizenship was successful, while allowing some possibility of a broader historical contingency.

Maternalism helped some women attain more masculinized, paternalistic public roles. After the Civil War, white middle-class women increasingly sought out and began to assume "the masculinized, powerful role of 'protector'" through their work as missionaries, with the settlement house movement, Indian reform, and temperance. This protector or rescuer role provided a vehicle through which some women could transcend domesticity and "could demonstrate independence and autonomy."[130] This was an important role for women looking to influence politics and society. Increasing numbers of these women altered their status "from 'dependents' in need of protection to 'protectors' of 'working girls,' 'primitives,' immigrants, Indians and others, and in so doing they created a recognized political role for themselves."[131]

White middle-class women exerted control and demonstrated their own public competence by taking care of those who were not capable of doing so themselves; in so doing, they helped negotiate their way through the state. Addams is one woman who derived some title to citizenship on behalf of women for representing and caring for urban dependents. Settlement houses around the nation

> dispensed educational and social services to surrounding working-class residents, and got involved in politics on their behalf. They organized social and instructional clubs, ran day nurseries, agitated for better city services, and—over time—pursued new social legislation on behalf of the less privileged.[132]

In another sense, too, the maternalist legacy was not simply liberal. Maternalist policy underlined responsibilities to dependents. "Policies toward the 'dependent' classes of wage-earning women and children set precedents for state intervention that later could be extended to wage-earning men and to non-wage-earning women and children."[133] This continuum underscores the extent to which the narrative structure of the welfare state remained rooted in the notion of dependency. Recipients of many kinds of benefits were dependents—wards or brides of the state—and not fully citizens. With the rise of the welfare state, many recipients of state benefits lost out in terms of citizenship. "To be on welfare is to lose one's independence and to be treated as less than a full member of society."[134] Thus the victory of the limited welfare state was hollow in terms of redefining the social ethic—the social web of interdependence—that Addams and some of her contemporaries envisioned.

Despite Addams's best efforts to avoid it, the maternalist framework itself appeared to generate a trap. Motherhood of necessity conjured up dependents who required nurturing. A mothering, nurturing relationship was one among those who might someday be equals but were not at that point in time. Addams disliked the "doing for" model of women's leadership, stressing instead interdependence, but it seems to have followed almost necessarily from the imagery of the cult of true womanhood.

When using maternalist rhetoric and drawing upon analogies to the home, women very easily conflated the asymmetrical mother-child bond with that between the middle-class woman and the immigrant, or that between white women and Native Americans or African Americans. Because mothering and housekeeping, associated with women's traditional roles, remained so central to Addams's claim to authority in public spaces, the imagery of caring and interconnection that influenced policy visions was modeled on parent-child relations rather than the special bonds forged among equal citizens. While maternalism opened up some opportunities to radically revision the state, relations of dependence and asymmetry that were so prevalent in much of its rhetoric were not liberal relations of equality.

Maternalist imagery created dependents and reinforced tiered citizenship. It did not ultimately dislodge the independence/autonomy model of citizenship, but rather paved the way for some privileged women to approximate male standards of independence and autonomy. A class fragment of white women not only gained the vote and an additional avenue to speak for themselves, but had given themselves leave to speak in public for all women.

Maternalism may have created a sense of responsibility for public caring, but the model of caring also tended to affirm the infantilization of recipients. Dependents who were objects of policy, such as female recipients of welfare, could be told what to do and how to do it. These attempts to regulate behavior were much like the mother's attempt to control unruly or wayward children lacking in mature judgment. The social welfare state formulated, with women's help, in the United States was in many ways a maternal social welfare state.

The dynamic interaction of race and gender also constitutes a key piece of this story, and it is linked to the discourse of republican virtue. While speaking of "woman" without racial specification, NAWSA leaders and other prominent feminists increasingly meant white women. This was quite clear among white suffrage leaders by the 1890s; suffrage leaders turned increasingly to arguments based in inegalitarianism. Egalitarianism was supplanted by the politics of virtue.[135] Suffrage and virtue could no longer be dissociated, and virtue was measured relationally. Smith's ascriptivism and republicanism were intermingled, not separated, in this discourse, as Horton has noted.

Women argued their claim to citizenship by contrasting their virtue with the corruption and greed of a male-dominated economy and polity. They argued their virtue by contrast with that of the foreign-born immigrant, and with the level of civilization enfranchised African-American males had attained. If Addams insisted that the argument for women's incorporation was compatible with the claim that other, "simpler" peoples had much to teach Americans about compassion and the social ethic, hers was a relatively lonely voice. Such a discourse of virtue limited the appeal of this vision of citizenship across racial, ethnic, and class lines.

While contributing to the creation of new political spaces, feminists did not speak with one voice about who could be readily incorporated as citizens. Claims to entry that were framed in terms of white female cultural and moral superiority relative to non-Caucasians sometimes fueled the immigration restriction movement. Gilman's maternalist vision sent women outside the home to seek independence; she regarded self-sufficiency as critical to citizenship. She also became a highly vocal supporter of immigration restriction. Those "below a certain grade of citizenship," who are not self-supporting, who are not fully capable of entire personal responsibility, and who might degenerate into becoming social burdens or criminals, exist in a different relationship to the state than do (real) citizens. They might require compulsory state supervision and tutelage.[136] Supporters of the cult of true womanhood frequently rejoined white males over the citizenship status of African Americans and immigrants.

Skocpol argues that within the vast array of women's organizations, grassroots community organizations and intellectual leaders worked together well, establishing cross-class gender goals and even being able to speak at times with one voice.[137] I contend, however, that the terms of political incorporation of women are incomprehensible without understanding the centrality of race in American politics. Twentieth-century politics was shaped in no small measure by the limits within which activists were able to rethink the meaning of citizenship during the suffrage struggle. While the cult-of-true-womanhood arguments of white and African-American feminists looked much alike, African-American women were not fully accorded the status of "true women" by their white counterparts.[138] White women belonged to the civilizing race and generally insisted on their authority to speak for and make claims on behalf of the interests of others. African-American, immigrant, and poor and working-class women may have become objects of state and national policy making, but they were often deemed suspiciously lacking in the virtue that "real" citizens possess. They lacked real personhood. Though they spoke, they would continue to be spoken for. The suffrage struggle had missed the opportunity to extend the meaning of citizenship by learning from multiple experiences with exclusion.

Maternalism had another confounding legacy. It "tie[d] one's identity as a social critic to acquiescence in the traditional stereotype of women."[139] Even if women left the home, they maintained they were merely extending it. However, if women chose or were compelled to leave home—or curtailed those community works that helped legitimate their claim to know—the special, intuitive and/or experiential source of their authority was severely jeopardized. So, too, was the claim to a unity of interest.

If public officials recognized a broader vision of the state and accepted some version of the social ethic as part of official conceptions of citizenship, they did not always remember (or wish to remember) the extended definition of home. Linking virtue to the home, rather than escaping from narrow definitions of it, President Harding sought a nation of homes "where mothers, freed from the necessity for long hours of toil beyond their own doors, may preside as befits the hearthstone of American citizenship." If "the cradle of American childhood [is] rocked under conditions so wholesome and so hopeful that no blight may touch it in its development," *this* is the "education so essential to best citizenship."[140] Harding's desire for a home-centered citizenship echoed arguments for protective legislation for women in the workplace. Reflecting how strongly traditional homes figured in women's allotted roles in the absence of the expanded definition women tried to give those roles, by the outset of the New Deal, federal legislation—followed by state and local legislation—began to bar married women from civil service work.[141] While feminist leaders active in reworking the definition of the public did not contend the private realm was superior to the public, male public officials linked women's title to virtue closely to their home-based activities. The state would play an important role in preserving the home in the name of citizenship.

Race, class, ethnicity, republicanism, patriarchy, and liberalism all figure importantly in the story of what white reform women won, and what they failed to win. In part because they could not adequately clarify or convince others "what home has to do with it" (to borrow from a popular feminist tract), these women failed to move their transformative vision further in the postsuffrage era. The failure to transcend a specifically gendered conception of a larger citizenship limited the public life expectancy of these women's social vision. And because their discourse of virtue was so closely specified by race and class, it was hard to extend the meaning of the social ethic beyond caring for dependents.

The constitution of a "we" is part of the process of defining citizenship. Who we are is also a statement about what we do. Gilded Age elite male reformers, critical of patronage parties, were frequently ridiculed as unmanly and politically impotent.[142] In the Progressive era, many of the new reformers were adamantly feminine. Could men regard transformative visions of state and citizenship, and the reforms undertaken in the name of these visions, as collective action done in their name, indeed, in the name of all citizens? In part, the limited duration of what Progressive-era women helped achieve reflected discomfort with a feminized state.

The late-twentieth-century politics of citizenship also suggests that the broader vision of citizenship remains a specifically gendered vision. The politics of exclusion prevails, as does deep doubt that we constitute a nation of shared values. The legacy of Addams's vision of interdependence and of growing social consciousness appears relatively weak amid growing social insularity and political polarization. Without the continual mobilization and deployment of an authoritative alternative rhetoric of citizenship, the narrative underpinnings of both the welfare state and of more inclusive visions of American political identity are gradually being deprived of lifeblood.

It can hardly be accidental that masculinist politics and rhetoric in the 1980s accompanied the assault on both the limited welfare state and on feminism. The demise of the welfare state is most closely associated with a president with a distinctively "masculine" public image and rhetoric: Ronald Reagan. George Bush became a "wimp" in part because of his supposed lack of stomach for the visionary politics of his predecessor. To be for government, especially for social welfare programs, is seen as feminine. Gender gap research suggests that women are more likely than men to support governmental social programs. Male imagery helped reseize the political agenda from an era seen as bankrupt, soft, feminized.

Creating a "we" in political discourse is a matter of negotiation and struggle. Women activists in the Progressive era were attempting to reformulate a collective identity, yet "part of the knowledge revealed in political discourse is the scope and validity of the claim entered in saying 'we': i.e., who turns out to be willing and able to endorse that claim."[143]

Public space is contested space. The alternative narrative of citizenship, which became in part and for a time a public vision, needed to cross not only class lines but also race and gender lines if it was to become the basis of an enduring collective vision.

The liberal tradition is not the only discourse in America. It keeps company with more exclusionary as well as more communal visions of citizenship, state, and society. The debates between competing narratives of autonomy and interdependence, individual and community, competition and cooperation, and exclusion and inclusion are fertile and dynamic. Alternative visions remain potentially transformative.

Liberalism, Political Culture, and the Rights of Subordinated Groups: Constitutional Theory and Practice at a Crossroads

Ronald Kahn

Redefining the rights of subordinated groups and protecting these groups from arbitrary action by government, private groups, and individuals are tasks that traditionally belong to the Supreme Court, lower federal courts, and state courts. Supreme Court decisions with regard to race since the 1950s and gender since the 1970s have played a major, even dramatic, role in improving the life chances of African Americans and women in our nation. However, in the 1990s constitutional theory and practice face new questions regarding the rights of previously identified subordinated groups before the law and which groups, if any, should be added to the list.

Defining what constitutes a subordinated group deserving of protection by the courts is far more difficult today than in previous decades. There are several reasons for this. First, there are fewer situations today in which groups are formally denied access to government. Second, as our nation becomes more diverse, issues arise each day as to what constitutes a majority or minority. Finally, questions as to what constitutes a subordinated group have become more ambiguous and conflictual than in the past due to the rise of identity politics as well as to the view that inequalities for individuals and groups are cumulative in terms of race, class, gender, national origin, and ethnicity. Constitutional theory, therefore, is at a crossroads as to how to define what constitutes equal protection before the law, when to define a fundamental right or interest, and when to find substantive violations of the due process clauses of the Fifth and Fourteenth Amendments. One need only look at the public debates over affirmative action and the rights of homosexuals to see evidence that constitutional thought is at an impasse as to how to define the rights of subordinated groups.

I draw upon J. David Greenstone's "Against Simplicity: The Cultural Dimensions of the Constitution" in considering whether constitutional theory, and the American liberal tradition upon which it draws, are equal to the important task of redefining the rights of subordinated groups.[1] In his article, Greenstone sought to explore the range of real restraints on political actors that are imposed by the United States Constitution through its authoritative interpretation(s).[2] He was seeking to make sense of the transformative possibilities of constitutional theories in light of the conflictual and consensual elements of American political culture. In this essay, I consider how constitutional scholars, political scientists, and legal practitioners must recast their thinking about constitutional theory, Supreme Court decision making, and the process of constitutional change if a redefinition of the rights of subordinated groups is to occur. In order to help us redirect our focus, I will introduce the concepts of social, economic, or political "pictures in precedents" and social, economic, and political "pictures in cases" as tools that will enable us to link theory, practice, and precedents in deciding new cases involving the rights of subordinated groups.

In the following section of the essay, I suggest why the unitary, consensual vision of American political culture cannot help us understand constitutional change in general or change in the area of the rights of subordinated groups in particular. I argue for the use of Greenstone's alternative vision of the constitutional regime. This vision contains three liberal but very different approaches to basic constitutional issues: a *republican* account, in which political events are interpreted in terms of the opposition between citizens who can be trained in civic virtue and concerns about the possible usurpations of power by public officials; a *humanist liberal* account, which emphasizes the tension between the value of the autonomous individual pursuing privately determined goals and the need for effective cooperation in pursuit of broadly shared collective interests; and a *reform liberal* account, which emphasizes the interpretation of constitutional norms in terms of a tension between holding individuals to appropriate moral standards and a social obligation to ensure that every person has an opportunity to develop his or her faculties.[3] Then, in the third section, I draw upon Greenstone's rejection of a unitary, consensual liberal regime to argue that it would be better to view the world of constitutional theory and practice as consisting of a tension between instrumental liberalism and constitutive liberalism. Here I argue for the constitutive liberal approach. In the fourth section I offer a brief analysis of constitutive liberalism at work in the decision-making process of the Supreme Court. In the fifth section I suggest how the rights of subordinated groups might be redefined under constitutive liberalism, drawing upon

Greenstone's three accounts of American political culture. I argue that what is needed in such a redefinition is a way to meld social, economic, and political change with the normative premises found in the republican, humanist liberal, and reform liberal accounts of our culture. Finally, in the sixth section, I argue that through the use of the concepts of pictures in precedents and pictures in cases we can begin the process of imaging social change through law and secure the needed redefinition of the rights of subordinated groups.

THE LIMITS OF A UNITARY, CONSENSUAL VISION OF AMERICAN POLITICAL CULTURE TO OUR UNDERSTANDING OF CONSTITUTIONAL CHANGE

The Prevailing Doctrinal View and Its Radical Critique

Greenstone argues that many scholars view the existing constitutional order according to one of two dominant patterns, each cohesive in its own interests and commitments. These patterns are the "prevailing *doctrinal* view," which treats the Constitution as "the ultimately authoritative text for adjudicating legal disputes," and its *"radical critique,"* which sees the Constitution as "a weapon wielded by one economic interest or another."[4] Here, as in much of Greenstone's scholarship, unitary models of political reality and thought—meaning models that view cultural values as consensual in nature—are viewed as being too simplistic to provide an adequate understanding of the relationship between political thought and action; that is, they do not respect the frequently dialectical fabric of American thought and politics.

According to Greenstone, the doctrinal account is flawed because it assumes that the regime's fundamental premises require a basically impartial polity and judicial system, while strict impartiality is simply not possible. It thus incorrectly assumes that the Constitution consists of neutral principles and that the courts and other agencies that interpret the Constitution are devoted to the dispassionate adjudication of these essentially neutral principles.

Greenstone criticizes those that hold a formal doctrinal view of the Constitution, such as Herbert Wechsler and Robert Bork, for assuming that "the Constitution expresses and implements a consensual political logic that precludes conflict over fundamental issues within the American legal system."[5] Judges, for Greenstone, do not find law merely on the basis of neutral principles, nor is the Constitution composed of neutral principles. The doctrinal account also ignores the Constitution's social bases and biases. Procedures that are neutral on their face may promote inequalities in practice. In the United States, the effects of liberal politics reinforce the effects of liberal economics.

The radical critique of the doctrinal approach also is flawed for Greenstone because it incorrectly assumes that courts regularly sanction outcomes that have a pronounced class bias or other type of social bias and that law is simply an instrument for achieving partisan objectives, typically those of the socially and economically privileged.[6] The problem with the radical critics is that they "ignore the fact that the United States does have a constitutional regime...[and that] the American Constitution imposes a range of real restraints on political actors that the free market does not impose on buyers and sellers."[7] In the United States, the Constitution and constitutional rules are regarded as final and determinative. "As a text," Greenstone argues, "the Constitution is not indefinitely deconstructable.... American constitutional practice exacts obedience from all comers."[8]

Greenstone also finds that the two approaches share several areas of agreement that oversimplify the place of law and the courts as forums for social change. First, each approach emphasizes the role of political interests. For holders of the doctrinal approach, it is the view that there is an impartial adjudication among political interests; for their radical critics, it is the dominance of a single faction. Second, the two sides agree that "the Constitution specifies the rules of the game, fair or unfair, within which the clash among economic groups or particular litigants takes place." Third, each approach agrees that "the constitutional order has legitimated some modes of conflicts while proscribing others, such as the open resort to violence by private parties." The fourth area of agreement is that "certain substantive constitutional issues are no longer matters of active dispute."[9]

Thus, according to Greenstone, the problem with both accounts of the role of law and the courts in our society is that they "treat political issues as conflicts of interest. Neither account...views the Constitution primarily as a cultural system that helps Americans understand and cope with intrinsically puzzling or ambiguous events." Greenstone sees both approaches as buying into a consensus perspective on American political culture, one based on the premise that "clashes over cultural matters can be ignored because American political culture as a whole is so powerfully, uniformly liberal."[10]

The agreement on the consensual nature of American political culture obscures for both groups the relevance of culture to politics. Each view agrees on the existence of a fundamental consensus in the American political order, acknowledging our polity's "thoroughly liberal character," but neither view takes into account the complexity of that liberal character.[11]

The problem for Greenstone is that the doctrinal and radical views agree on the consensual nature of American political culture, a narrow definition of interests, the manner in which the struggle is conducted, and even who wins and loses. From the doctrinal perspective, Greenstone argues, "[t]he Constitution is the liberal framework that all politically active groups accept. For the radical critics, a dominant liberal culture has systematically, via the Constitution, excluded all significant alternatives to a liberal, capitalist society." In either case, Greenstone argues, "political conflict is restricted in the economic sphere to the clash of specific interests.... Both the doctrinal and radical views implicitly adopt a consensual view of American political culture as the point of departure, however much they differ on the normative merit of the consensus."[12] Having accepted the consensual nature of our culture, each group "obscures the possibility that a culture can be pervasively liberal without being *consensually* so."[13]

They also are forced to focus on specific conflicts of interest, thereby failing to sufficiently emphasize that the citizens of a liberal polity must reconcile the value of liberal autonomy with the need for political authority as well as the overall needs of society. From the latter perspective, the problem is that purely self-regarding individuals or groups will often fail to secure desirable, or even indispensable, collective goods, such as law and order, economic prosperity, or a protected environment.

The Constitutional Regime under a Dialectical Vision of Political Culture

Greenstone views the Constitution, and the other rules and legal norms of our constitutional regime, in far different ways than do scholars who hold a static vision of political culture. For Greenstone, constitutions are not as self-enforcing as those who emphasize a consensual view say they are. He writes, "To talk about operative constitutions is to talk about certain socially accepted and culturally significant rules—whether or not they are formally part of the written document. In the American context, such rules limit political life, and also help pattern both its conflictual and consensual features." So political life, as a starting point, has both conflictual and consensual features that are meaningful.[14]

Greenstone notes that constitutions have three types of rules: constitutive provisions, precepts, and norms.[15] *Constitutive provisions* specify the members of the body politic, identify key political institutions and assign them particular powers and responsibilities, and establish the rights and obligations of citizens and public officials. Examples are rules regarding the presidential veto and congressional override. Constitutive rules most fully resist deconstruction. "Without settled meanings, these provisions could not establish the framework essential for a complex political life."[16] *Precepts* advise actors about their most effective courses of action. In democratic politics, precepts informally shape the constitutional order by giving cues as to when to act and when not to act. Precepts must be open to revision as new ideas and developments offer better prospects for success. For example, Greenstone notes that precepts surround members of the American legislature and executive on using the mass media in appealing to the public and on using technical experts in the budgetary process. Also, one might see Greenstone's formulation of precepts in action by examining appeals to and uses of independent prosecutors.[17] Norms or *ethical ideals* express enduring cultural and philosophical commitments. They are "authoritatively asserted by public officials, enshrined in a polity's basic charter, and rooted in practices of long standing." First Amendment liberties and egalitarian values from the Civil War and women's suffrage amendments are obvious examples of norms or ethical ideals for Greenstone.[18] Because ideals and commitments are often not fully realized, they identify projects that a regime continues to pursue. They invite reformulation and revision and thus include elements of permanence and change. Indeed, when they are wholly accepted and come to define existing practices, they become constitutive provisions. For example, minorities now have a right to vote. But the larger goal of racial equality is a norm because it has yet to be realized. Disputes over interpretations of the meaning of "equality" may also readily emerge with regard to this norm. To understand the process through which constitutional law redefines the rights of subordinated groups we need to explore how these three types of rules interact with the republican, humanist liberal, and reform liberal accounts of American political culture.

Republican, Humanist Liberal, and Reform Liberal Constitutionalism

The question still remains as to how change is negotiated in our nation through appeals to the republican, humanist liberal, and reform liberal accounts of American political culture. Greenstone argues that republicanism emphasizes constitutive provisions in the Constitution. Political events are interpreted in terms of opposition between the good of citizen virtue and the evil of usurpation of power by government officials, such as with regard to questions of impeachment. Moreover, in many instances, the language of constitutive provisions is that citizens are good and public officials are bad. This language determines how the government is molded. Note that there is a normative statement in republicanism: Structures of citizen power and of weak officials will produce adherence to the Constitution.

In the humanist liberal case, the emphasis is on precepts that facilitate effective action to secure individual liberty. Events are interpreted in terms of the tension between the value of the autonomous individual pursuing privately determined goals and the need for effective cooperation in pursuit of broadly shared objectives. As explored below, precepts are developed to preserve a viable political market; they specify key actors, procedures, and institutions to deal with market failure.

Reform liberalism emphasizes the importance of constitutional norms. They are interpreted in terms of a tension between holding individuals to appropriate moral standards and an obligation to see that every person has the opportunity to develop his or her faculties. Do we trust moral rules to keep citizens in line, or do we trust that individuals can do well if we support opportunities for them to develop their faculties?

Greenstone argues that simplicity is not basic to our constitutional order. A charter or constitution that includes both norms and precepts, which by definition are in a continual or permanent state of becoming, will not function smoothly on behalf of any single project or goal. Those who hold the doctrinal view, as well as its radical critics, cannot accept the view that norms and precepts are in a state of constant revision, or that constitutive rules, precepts, and norms vary in prominence depending on the problems facing the nation. That Greenstone has outlined the full complexity of our nation's constitutional regime in terms of republican, humanist liberal, and reform liberal constitutionalism is less important than his having disclosed many of the value conflicts that inform the regime.[19]

INSTRUMENTAL AND CONSTITUTIVE LIBERALISM: RECONCEPTUALIZING GREENSTONE'S CATEGORIES

I want to restructure Greenstone's argument, building on the problematic nature of static or consensual visions of American political culture. It might be useful for purposes of understanding constitutional theory and practice to think of two primary strands of thinking about political culture in general and, more specifically, how American political culture informs our understanding of law and legal change.

The primary differences between the doctrinal approach and its radical critique are the assumptions each has about the role of principles and ideas in Supreme Court decision making. At the core of the doctrinal approach is the view that justices take legal precedents, constitutional principles and interpretation, and the separation of law and politics seriously, while its radical critics contend that these elements are taken for granted in order to perpetuate the economic and social inequalities of our capitalist nation.

The doctrinal and radical approaches to constitutionalism have a far too simplistic vision of our political culture and constitutional regime. The underlying reason for the differences between the doctrinal and radical approaches is a difference in viewpoint over the question of whether or not constitutional knowledge, theory, and practice should be based on scientific naturalism. Scientific naturalists argue that the only real knowledge is that which is gained through the study of empirical data, using scientific methods. For something to be knowledge, it must be related to particular factual referents, and scientific replication of the findings must be possible. What Greenstone calls the radical critique of doctrinalism is a modern-day version of legal realism, with its faith in scientific data and a debunking of the independent effects on judging of legal norms, such as *stare decisis* and the institutional need of courts to support respect for the rule of law. Doctrinalists, in contrast, argue that at the core of constitutional law is a respect for foundational values and deductions from such values. Doctrinalists totally reject the scientific naturalist basis of law. They view judging as simply mechanical and refuse to consider how social, economic, and political facts might enter the process of judicial decision making.[20]

I have written elsewhere that our analysis of Supreme Court decision making has been harmed in important ways by political scientists in the legal realist/behavioral tradition who argue that Supreme Court justices decide cases based on the policy outcomes they desire and then use precedent, constitutional principles, and the decision-making process simply to justify those policy preferences. I have argued how such assumptions have caused behavioral political scientists to fail to explain the process of Supreme Court decision making generally, and Warren, Burger, and Rehnquist Court jurisprudence in particular.[21] These assumptions also have led behavioralists to grossly underestimate the place of constitutional and political theory as well as the interpretive community in the process of constitutional change. Those who adhere strictly to a doctrinal approach or its radical critique commit the same error. Building on Greenstone's insights, I argue that it might be useful to conceive of two discrete approaches to constitutional choice and theory. I will call these two approaches instrumental liberalism and constitutive liberalism .[22]

Instrumental Liberalism

Instrumental liberals "see the *existing* constitutional order as exhibiting a single dominant pattern, which in each case is defined by one relatively cohesive set of interests and commitments." Thus for Greenstone, the "prevailing *doctrinal* view," which treats the Constitution "as the ultimately authoritative text for adjudicating legal disputes," and its "radical critique," which sees the Constitution "as a weapon wielded by one economic interest or another," are instrumentally liberal because they assume a consensus on the cultural values underlying the Constitution.[23] To the list of instrumental liberals, I would add political scientists who use the attitudinal model of Supreme Court decision making. These scholars argue that Supreme Court justices simply follow their own personal attitudes and policy desires rather than precedent, the institutional needs of the court, the rule of law, or long-standing polity and rights principles.[24] Scholars who view Supreme Court justices as making decisions in order to secure strategic advantage over other justices also should be considered instrumental liberals.[25]

Instrumental liberalism is called "instrumental" because it assumes that ideas, such as the rule of law and *stare decisis*, do not have an independent effect on judicial action. Instrumental liberalism assumes that ideas are used by judges to fulfill instrumental objectives. The instrumental liberal approach is based upon the assumption that human action can be explained by unitary causes.

We see instrumental liberalism not only in the scholarship of modern-day legal realists, such as critical legal, attitudinal, and rational-choice scholars. We also see it among originalists, and even in the more complex pluralist formulations of Supreme Court decision making by Robert Dahl,[26] Gerald Rosenberg,[27] and Mark Graber.[28]

Thus instrumental liberal analysis of Supreme Court decision making can be of the right or left. This model fits any legal scholar or practitioner who does not have a complex view of history and ideas and who does not see such ideas as the rule of law and stare decisis as part of a set of basic institutional and rights values that have an independent effect on Supreme Court decision making and the development of constitutional law. While the Constitution does not speak for itself, it is important to include in one's approach to decision making some notion of the Supreme Court's formulation of decisions through the application of polity and rights principles, especially if one is to have a nonstatic vision of constitutional law.

Constitutive Liberalism

Constitutive liberalism rejects the consensual values of instrumental liberalism and simple doctrinalism. Constitutive liberals view precedent, constitutional principles, and basic polity and rights principles as fundamental to Supreme Court decision making. It is constitutive because it assumes that there are no preconceived policy or outcome desires that drive a particular Court decision. Constitutive liberalism is not simply analogous to the static doctrinal approach that Greenstone explores and rejects. Rather than viewing decision making as static, constitutive liberalism sees Supreme Court decision making as dynamic (though bounded). The Court has to apply polity and rights principles in light of a changing social, economic, and political environment as it decides cases.

One can better understand the limitations of conceiving the world of constitutional law in instrumental liberal terms if we ask how the outside world influences Supreme Court decision making. If Supreme Court decision making is not the simple application of doctrine and precedent, the direct result of the policy desires of individual justices, or the indirect result of the needs of social, economic, and political elites, as Greenstone argues, we must better articulate theoretically, as well as through empirical studies of Supreme Court decision making, the link between social, economic, and political changes in the outside world and constitutional law and theory.

SUPREME COURT DECISION MAKING, CONSTITUTIVE LIBERALISM, AND LEGAL CHANGE

Social Facts and the Bounded Evolution of Constitutional Law

To examine how justices bring the outside world into Supreme Court decision making while sustaining a rule of law is to explore the relationship between the interpretive community of legal scholars, political theorists, journalists, and the informed public and constitutional theory and practice. Although law, politics, and society are viewed by many as autonomous of one another, the role of the scholar is precisely to suggest how Supreme Court decision making resonates with social, economic, and political facts, and, most important, how this process of resonance occurs. This can be done in a two-stage process. The first stage is to identify the use of polity and rights principles in a Supreme Court decision-making process that is viewed heuristically as constitutive in nature. In such an analysis, we study the cases internally. We compare the use of polity and rights principles in cases within and among different doctrinal areas, and see how changes in polity and rights principles and in their juxtaposition inform Supreme Court decision making.

In the second stage, we ask how the recognition and definition of political, economic, and social facts change over time and how changes in the definition of social facts inform changes in constitutional law.[29] An example of this is the effects of changing views of the health menace to bakers and of employer and employee bargaining relationships in *Lochner v. New York* (1905) compared to post-*Lochner* jurisprudence. In *Lochner,* the Supreme Court found a New York state working-hours law unconstitutional, asserting that "there is no danger to the employee in a first-class bakery and so far as unsanitary conditions are concerned the employee is protected by other sections of the law."[30] The Court then determined that "[t]he statute in question was never intended as a health provision but was purely a labor law."[31] As primarily a labor law, the statute was found to violate a right of contract which the *Lochner* Court declared an implied right under the due process clause of the Fourteenth Amendment. The employer and employee were to be viewed as equally free to buy or sell labor. Beliefs about social, economic, and political facts entered this case at two different levels: first, as a question relevant to the regulation of health and safety by the state, and second, as part of what constitutes a "right of contract" and whether the Court should be concerned about the relative bargaining power of employers and employees.

The central holdings of *Lochner* were challenged in a number of rulings, culminating in *West Coast Hotel Co. v. Parrish* (1937), a case in which the Supreme Court upheld a minimum-wage law for women. What is significant about *West Coast* is that it rejected many of the central premises of *Lochner,* including the notion that the state could not limit the contract rights of employer and employee and the definition of the social facts regarding employer and employee bargaining power. In *West Coast* the Court wrote, "The exploitation of a class of workers who are in an unequal position with respect to bargaining power and are thus relatively defenseless against the denial of a living wage is not only detrimental to their health and well being but casts a direct burden for their support upon the community."[32]

Having identified the use of polity and rights principles in the American constitutional regime and undertaken internal case analyses within different Supreme Court eras, the constitutive liberal's next step is to embark upon the difficult task of explaining doctrinal change. The Supreme Court's definition of polity and rights principles, while adhering to long-held liberal principles, such as the separation of public and private space, is informed by changes in constitutional and political theory. There is a dialogue between the Supreme Court and prevailing visions of political institutions and individual agency that inform the constitutional and political theory of the day. Within these theories, there will be new definitions of what social, economic, and political facts explain the plight of subordinated groups and how these facts affect the ability of political institutions to protect (or infringe upon) such constitutional values as personal liberty, due process, and equal protection.

Transformative or evolving constitutional theory asks us (and Supreme Court justices) to rethink polity and rights principles, the nature of social facts, and legal precedents. Unlike instrumental liberals, the primary objective of constitutional theory and practice for constitutive liberals is not to simply apply the logic of law or to assume that law, precedent, and foundational values are epiphenomenal to people's lives. Constitutive liberals ask us to reconsider the nature of public and private space in order to rethink the responsibilities of government and expectations of individual agency. This allows the constitutive process of Supreme Court decision making to be the basis for political and social change through a reformulation of what constitutes personal liberty, due process, and equal protection today as compared to prior eras.

There is a concept of "bounded evolution" in the constitutive liberal vision of doctrinal change. Perhaps the new doctrine is an improvement over the past, perhaps it is not. In using the term "bounded evolution," I do not assume a teleological (or progressive) view of doctrinal change. Apart from such normative glosses, constitutive liberalism seeks to rethink the nature of political responsibility and legitimacy as social facts change. The constitutive liberal examines how evolving definitions or interpretations of social conditions gain general acceptance from the interpretive community and the wider public as debates about rights and the powers of government reach the print and broadcast media. Without considering these public forums, we are left with the imposition of the intellectual elites' values upon the general public.

New formulations of the relationships among the foundational values of liberalism inform new definitions of rights and the role of the courts and other governmental institutions in the process of constitutional change. An important role for the interpretive community is to develop new theories informed by the nonstatic tenets of liberalism. The interpretive community must make sense of social, economic, and political change, and it must relate those changes to how definitions of personal liberty, due process, and equal protection should be altered in light of those changes.

Supreme Court Decision Making, "Social Facts," and Legal Change

The constitutive liberal must incorporate social, economic, and political facts into her analysis and not simply apply principles or precedents as if they were merely a matter of logic. At the same time, the constitutive liberal must not assume that the presence of facts demonstrating social, economic, and political inequalities automatically constitutes a constitutional violation. Except for the most trivial cases, there is no way to define in pure factual terms that a constitutional violation has occurred. Therefore, the constitutive liberal must somehow make choices as to how to incorporate social, economic, and political facts into constitutional theory and practice while protecting long-held constitutional values.

If there is a normative decision-making component to law, it involves the application of the complex cultural ideas of our liberal society to constitutional theory. Such a theory provides the normative benchmarks with which courts can define polity and rights principles in specific contexts and cases. Constitutive liberalism is not inherently based on polity principles; there is a need to consider the importance of social facts when defining constitutional theory and practice. The problem for constitutional scholars lies in introducing social facts into constitutional theory while ensuring that the categories of that theory are not static or bias-laden but instead are sufficiently dynamic and complex in the sense of their application and fairness. If the courts have an autonomous effect on the life chances of citizens through their power of rights definition and doctrinal change, law in the liberal state should be viewed as in a condition of constantly becoming.

To have a normative force that can inform legal change, constitutional theory must do more than get the interpretive community and wider public to accept a particular vision of social reality and the plight of subordinated groups. It must link the facts and plight(s) of subordinated groups to fundamental constitutional principles. Although such principles are constantly being interpreted, they have a foundational constancy that perpetuates their normative strength.

Reconceiving the Rights of Subordinated Groups in Constitutional Theory and Practice

If we are to aid subordinated groups, we must develop a system of interpretation that moves us beyond the interest group model of liberalism.[33] It is not possible to secure the moral force of law or the normative principles of liberalism if the formation of rights principles is viewed simply as a battle of the weak versus the strong. Traditionally, it is argued that when there is a polity malfunction, the courts must step in to ensure equal access to government for all citizens. Alternatively, nonoriginalist scholars have argued that courts must step in when there is a violation of fundamental individual rights specified in the Constitution. However, a statement of fundamental rights or substantive wrongs in policy terms is not enough to justify court intervention into the political arena. There has to be a linkage of court action to a morally acceptable vision of why a subordinated group needs the help of the courts.

Ronald Kahn

Constitutional Theory and the Rights
of Subordinated Groups

I turn now to the role of constitutional theory in constitutional change. The role of constitutional theory traditionally has been to provide an intellectual basis, through the establishment of normative guidelines, for court intervention. It also seeks changes in the bases on which courts decide cases, by proposing linkages between foundational constitutional values and constitutional law. While there are different levels of constitutional theory, those theories that are most wide-ranging, such as those of John Hart Ely and Cass Sunstein, seek to develop a theory of court intervention into the political arena that builds upon visions of polity and rights principles in the Constitution and their place in Supreme Court decision making.

Constitutional theory builds upon expectations of judicial decision making, the rule of law, and methods of constitutional interpretation that have developed since the eighteenth century. Therefore, constitutional theory builds upon ideas about ethical relativism, legal realism, the rise of scientific naturalism and non-Euclideanism in law and social science, and, presently, post- and multiculturalism. The manner in which linkages are made to foundational values helps retain the moral force of law while also allowing for change. It is these linkages that are indispensable to developing a constitutional theory that will help redefine the rights of subordinated groups. We need to develop a theory of the rights of subordinated groups that enables us to connect constitutional theory to the moral force of ideas. The only viable method for doing this is to make linkages to our political culture, in light of the changing social, economic, and political conditions that place people at risk of rights violations. Only the linkage of social facts to the long-standing tensions in American political culture will compel justices, judges, political leaders, and citizens to redefine the rights of subordinated groups.

Political culture offers the normative basis for thinking about constitutional questions, the possible bases for court intervention into the political arena, and definitions of fundamental rights. Social facts are necessary in the redefinition of the rights of subordinated groups because reformulations of rights must be built on the actual treatment members of subordinated groups face from the government and other citizens, considered in light of prevailing conceptions of liberty, justice, and political system failures. However, sociological data do not, in themselves, constitute rights or the basis for rights, especially today, when formal denials of access to government are no longer major constitutional questions. Therefore, in order to consider issues of the rights of subordinated groups, we must somehow relate social, economic, and political facts and basic normative elements in our political culture to ways in which polity and rights principles are defined, and then apply new constitutional theories as benchmarks for judicial consideration of specific constitutional issues as informed by the justices' dialogue with the interpretive community. In doing this, we must reexamine contemporary theories in light of a more complex vision of our political system and liberal culture.

For example, Ely views the Constitution, even with the Civil War amendments, not as a document with fundamental rights, but rather as a set of procedures to keep the political system open to minorities.[34] Scholars such as Ely argue for a constitutional theory of polity malfunction, and against viewing the Constitution as a document that rests on fundamental moral values. We need to ask whether this view of polity malfunction and of the role of fundamental rights can sustain a redefinition of the rights of subordinated groups into the future.

Another set of constitutional scholars, the civic republicans, argues that if we are to protect the rights of subordinated groups and make more sustainable, equitable public policy, we must include more groups in our nation's deliberations. We also need to consider whether a civic republican focus on political participation can form the basis for a redefinition of the rights of subordinated groups.[35]

A theory of the rights of subordinated groups must be convincing in terms of the aspects of our political culture that are generally emphasized, definitions of polity malfunction, and the linkages that are made to polity and rights principles that justices and judges actually use when they make constitutional choices. There must be rules (on-off switches, really) in constitutional theory that tell us when we should leave a decision to "raw politics" and when we should not. A linkage is needed between social facts, definitions of polity malfunction, and the basic elements of our political culture that are highlighted in a particular theory, so that a theory of the rights of subordinated groups can secure acceptance in the interpretive community and among the broader public. And finally, there must be a theory, rather than just practice. Only theories and theoretical arguments can educate other scholars, jurists, and the wider interpretive community.[36]

GREENSTONE'S THEORY OF THE AMERICAN CONSTITUTIONAL REGIME: REPUBLICANISM, HUMANIST LIBERALISM, AND REFORM LIBERALISM

Let us return to Greenstone's vision of the American constitutional regime. We do this not to argue that his particular interpretation of American political culture is necessarily the one to draw upon in redefining the rights of subordinated groups. Rather, it offers a picture of some elements of our constitutional regime that could be incorporated into a constitutional theory that adequately redefines the rights of subordinated groups.

Republicanism, which has gained a renewed influence among constitutional scholars, argues for an independent, virtuous, and participatory citizenry uplifted by labor, virtue, and a devotion to the general good of the community. In the founding period, holders of landed property and those working the soil were viewed as more virtuous than holders of financial wealth created by economic manipulation. Republicans feared standing armies, and favored citizen leaders elected for short terms in office and institutional checks and balances. The framers, as republicans, remained supportive of a liberal creed, but had no comprehensive vision of human well-being. Questions of individual and social good were left to the citizens themselves. Republican public-spiritedness solved the liberal problem of coordinating autonomous, even warring, individuals. Republicanism trusted political institutions to create a situation where individual virtue could flourish. However, in the American context, republicanism was one member of a family of liberal beliefs, all devoted to the ideal of individual liberation.[37] For Greenstone, republicanism became a liberal vaccine against a liberal disease.

Republican views of citizen vigilance against government remain today. Republican norms reject the political analogue to market relationships in which individuals simply seek personal advantage. Republicanism tells citizens to sacrifice their own interests to preserve a liberal regime. This results in the collective quality of representation being present, without any notion of collective will. Greenstone argues that "ideas of limited government, virtue, corruption, separation of powers, and, of course, individual rights" are aspects of "a real American liberal consensus."[38] What remains in dispute are broader social and philosophical questions, as well as the nature of human personality and the good society, which are addressed in more comprehensive liberal theories.

Humanist liberals accord the highest value to the welfare of the individual and the liberty of an individual to define his or her own welfare. A good society satisfies individual desires and preferences in an equitable way, as citizens define their own goals with a minimum of external constraint from government. Liberty is not an affirmative right to resources from government; it is a right not to be infringed upon by government. Because politics is not economics, the role of politics is not to satisfy a complex set of preferences that require government action. Government, instead, must keep citizens from infringing on the freedom of one another and must deal with the effects of collective-action problems. It must deal with market failure when private exchanges among rational, self-regarding individuals are not sufficient. Greenstone argues that for humanist liberals "it is this tension between the preferences of autonomous individuals and the need for government intervention that creates a concern for constitutional rules."[39]

Humanist liberals, with an eye to preserving a viable political market, are concerned with precepts that specify key actors, procedures, and institutions to deal with market failure. Directions on maneuvering in such well-defined situations provide a very thin cultural dimension to humanist liberalism.

For Greenstone, the difference between the reform and humanist sides of liberalism has less to do with concepts of class or group interests than with vastly different cultural and philosophical commitments. Humanist and reform liberals share a cultural commitment to implementing private preferences and to the maintenance of a good society, defined as supporting liberty and fair procedure. The difference between humanist and reform liberalism reflects a deep ambiguity in liberal thought over the scope of individual autonomy.[40] Should individuals judge their own well-being and the basic goals they ought to pursue, or should individuals simply determine the means with which to pursue such goals?

Humanist liberalism says that individuals should choose goals as well as means, provided the freedom of others to do likewise is respected. Reform liberals draw on Kant and the Puritans to argue that human beings have an obligation to develop their physical, intellectual, and aesthetic faculties.[41] Reform liberals argue for the development of language, mathematics, and the practical and moral knowledge vital to daily living, with the criteria for individual competence established by the community or culture. There is a collective sense of responsibility for creating a society in which individuals can develop their faculties, with those faculties that encourage human development being more valid than those that do not. Constitutional principles that transcend equal access draw on reform liberal values. We see this in the area of the Supreme Court's definition of fundamental rights and interests. For example, in *Plyler v. Doe* (1982), the Supreme Court refused to allow Texas to charge tuition for public schools to children of illegal aliens.[42] Doing so would have impeded these children from developing the knowledge, education, and personal faculties necessary to fulfill their roles as citizens. The court would not permit the state to aid in the process of creating such a class of citizens.

Reform liberals are liberals, like humanist liberals, because the individual is still the primary unit of action. However, standards of evaluation for what these individuals' faculties should be and how government is to help secure them dominate only reform liberal thinking. Therefore, humanist and reform liberals hold very different pictures of our constitutional regime.

The values of reform liberals gained strength from the Civil War and women's suffrage amendments, which were products of antislavery and feminist movements that espoused reform liberal values. Because distinctions of race and gender were merely physical, they were not constitutionally acceptable. Blacks and women were human beings with distinctively human capacities of self-development.[43] Therefore, the Civil War and women's suffrage amendments identify polity principles, such as the power and responsibility of Congress to enforce equal protection of the law under the Fourteenth Amendment and to prevent racial and sexual discrimination in the exercise of voting rights under the Fifteenth and Nineteenth Amendments.

Reconceptualizing Liberal Dialectics in Supreme Court Decision Making

Reform liberalism has a critique of bourgeois society, a critique that is internal to the liberal enterprise. It flows from the debates between humanist and reform liberals and others who emphasize different strands of our political culture. The radical critique of liberalism may emphasize, as does the reform liberal, the impact of poverty or hopelessness on the opportunity for self-development. At other times, the conflict may essentially be a conflict over what the Constitution means, in doctrinal terms, as those who hold the prevailing doctrinal view emphasize. As we discussed above, the doctrinal and radical accounts overlook the basic division within the American constitutional regime between humanist and reform liberals; that is, the division between those who have faith in the constitutional regime as a set of fair procedures for citizens with different personal faculties (the humanist liberals) and those who argue that society-fostered self-development is a necessary ingredient for social change (the reform liberals). Thus, the conflict between humanist and reform liberals is fundamentally a conflict over which cultural norms should prevail.[44]

Historically, reform liberals have sought to use the courts to support the development of human faculties when political institutions have failed to do so, frequently arguing that such faculties are linked to changing definitions of the requirements of engaged citizenship. But Greenstone did not discuss our nation's specific attempts to incorporate social change into legal theory and practice, or the specific terms of the relationship among political culture, judicial power, and doctrinal change. However, constitutional decisions that seek to further reform liberal values raise unavoidable questions about the respective role of political institutions and the courts as venues for social change. Does the objective of developing human faculties call for limits on government power, or is the government required by the Constitution to support the development of human faculties, with individual citizens choosing whether to take advantage of such opportunities?

At a certain level, the conflict over polity- and rights-based constitutional theory and practice is a conflict over which aspect of our political culture to emphasize. Scholars who emphasize simply keeping the political process open seem to be quite similar to Greenstone's humanist liberals, with their faith in doctrine, legal process, and process norms. As many scholars have so cogently argued, it is impossible to simply be process-oriented, because a process theory requires a notion of justice.[45]

For reform liberalism, the question of when courts should intervene is a question not simply of equal access and lack of prejudice, but of whether courts should require the state to intervene so that self-development, as a right, is facilitated. When the *Plyler* Court guaranteed illegal Mexican immigrant children the opportunity, through education, to ensure their self-development as future United States citizens, it followed reform liberal principles by taking an active role in limiting disabilities imposed on immigrant children. It implicitly stated that proactive legal measures were indeed necessary in order to ensure equal rights under the Constitution.

Humanist and reform liberals both accept values of representation, individual rights, and such polity principles as the separation of powers, but they are divided on the fundamental philosophical and cultural question of whether the state should be in the business of actively promoting individual self-development. Therefore, in the American context, the conflict over what the Constitution means is not simply a question of applying precedent and formulating a decision that fits existing precedents to the facts in a case. Conflicts over what the Constitution means involve complex matters of political culture and social practice, including whether one sees American political culture through the eyes of a humanist liberal or those of a reform liberal.

In some respects, Greenstone accepts the Hartzian analysis while reinterpreting Hartz from a static model to a dynamic one. Political debate over constitutional principles based on the acceptance or rejection of reform and humanist liberal values is at the core of constitutional change. The lack of organized class antagonisms in the United States commends us to view or conceptualize issues of rights in self-development terms, not in terms of social justice in regard to the fruits of capitalism. Therefore, constitutional issues are critical because we must frame rights in terms not simply of outcomes but of the delivery of goods so that self-development can occur. Framing issues in this way requires us to ask what the individual is doing to "qualify" for government support in terms of his or her own acts of self-development.

The humanist liberal's faith in political and economic structure means that he or she is antagonistic to a powerful government that could potentially stifle the market system. However, even reform liberals might oppose some government programs that undermine individual initiative or the right of a citizen to be left alone. Opposition to state power weakens support of the welfare state; many fear that a state so empowered might go beyond fostering self-development and move toward making citizens wards of the state.

If republicanism, with its call for more deliberation, is not a genuine alternative to the static consensus view of the doctrinal approach and its radical critique, then how can we expect it to be the basis for a new constitutional theory to transform the rights of subordinated groups?[46] Moreover, if Hartzian liberalism has within it the need for independent citizens and the fear of government corruption, but civic republicanism does not, will civic republicanism truly protect the independence of minority groups and viewpoints?

Greenstone views the relationship of history to political culture as a core force for change. In the United States, liberalism functions as what is known as a boundary condition: a set of relatively permanent features of a particular context that affect causal relationships within it. A boundary condition must be behavioral and ideological, and it must be explanatory in the sense that it describes those operative rules (standards of correct performance) that define the regime. The concepts of humanist and reform liberalism fit this bill.[47]

Complex Liberalism, Supreme Court Decision Making, and Social Change

Supreme Court decision making, constitutional theory, and their intersection with our political culture offer a way for our society to confront new problems by redefining the nature of individual rights and the powers of government. However, since the Constitution and its underlying rights and polity principles are not self-defining, we need to better understand the process of constitutional change and the role of social, economic, and political facts and differing elements of the American constitutional regime, including republican, humanist liberal, and reform liberal values, in that process of change. Only through such an understanding can we construct a constitutional theory that will guide the redefinition of the rights of subordinated groups.

Whether change is required by our constitutional regime depends on how we define the principles that we, as a nation, and the Supreme Court, in its decision-making process, view as important. Political leaders regularly seek to redefine the powers of government as well as the nature of citizen roles and rights. One merely has to look at the overtly political issues pertaining to racial minorities, gays, and immigrants in states such as California and Colorado. The Supreme Court responds to these attacks in different ways: The *Casey* decision supported the right of abortion choice for women; the *Bowers* decision supported the criminalization of sodomy and the rejection of a right of sexual intimacy among homosexuals; and the *Romer* decision outlawed a state's imposition of a more difficult political process for homosexuals who seek to secure antidiscrimination legislation.[48] The numerous affirmative action decisions of the 1990s promise to change our concept of affirmative action, since definitions of *majority* and *minority* mean little in many political venues. Similarly, the upcoming cases on the rights of legal immigrants will ensure that the rights of subordinated groups will be at the center of our political and legal agenda for years to come.

American liberalism is a stable boundary condition that affects how we see the impact of social change on our political system, with the courts acting as interpreters of the American liberal tradition. However, given the formal separation of the political and the economic, we may have to meet the effects of having or not having control of economic power through the medium of humanist and reform liberal principles.

Can reliance on such a paradigm result in a transformative constitutional theory for subordinated groups in our nation? Whether we rely on a constitutional theory of subordinated groups based on humanist or reform liberal principles or view the Supreme Court as instrumental or constitutive in nature is central to how we view the possibilities for transformative constitutional theory and a transformative role for the court.

Any constitutional theory that is developed must adhere to central liberal values if it is to attain the level of legitimacy that is necessary to support social change. The sometimes unarticulated premises about society and culture that become manifest through political and constitutional choices are key elements in change. Changes in practices and the meaning of such practices are also central to social change. In real-world political action there may not be a direct causal relationship between words and deeds. However, there is a closer relationship between liberal boundary conditions and the constitutional choices courts make, because constitutional theory and practice build upon and consciously reconsider the nature of what constitutes public and private space and action.

Debates over boundary conditions and whether and what polity and rights principles apply in a given case or doctrinal area are central to the process of change in constitutional principles, citizen rights, the role of the courts, and the power of political institutions. Debates among constitutional scholars who emphasize humanist or reform liberal values, or an amalgam of such values, are debates about whether the American liberal tradition should envision new rights and on what basis new rights should be viewed as legitimate.

Humanist and Reform Liberalism and Social Change through Law

Since each justice has within him- or herself aspects of the values found within the republican, humanist liberal, and reform liberal strands of American political culture (or some other definition(s) of our culture and how cultural values relate to each other), we need a way to identify these values and explain how they make their way into Supreme Court decision making. One way to do this is to explore the choice of polity and rights principles that a justice brings to a case and analyze how they are employed. Though one can easily study the use of polity and rights principles by particular justices to see whether they accept republican norms about the political process, it is a much different task to study the role of humanist and reform liberal values in their decisions.

It is the reform liberal aspect of our political culture that is least understood and least admired in constitutional theory and law. One reason for this is that instrumental liberals automatically assume that reform liberal values are policy desires that "dictate" decisions. Critics of doctrinalism will view reform liberal values as simply means used by courts to appease the weak and to support dominant social and economic groups. Many legal scholars formally reject the sliding-scale approach to equal protection doctrine articulated by Justice Thurgood Marshall, while using sliding scales in their own jurisprudence. We see this in the determination of what constitutes fundamental rights and interests that require court protection. Legal scholars unfairly reject Marshall's call for looking at the nexus between the relative importance of government benefits a citizen is deprived of, such as welfare or education, and the specific constitutional guarantee in question, such as a right to travel, to vote, or to procreate, or the right to privacy.[49]

Thus, it is reform liberal values, not republican or humanist liberal values, that raise the most interesting questions for understanding Supreme Court decision making and the process of doctrinal change, especially regarding the plight of subordinated groups. Reform liberal values also raise the most interesting questions about how the legal process inserts social, economic, and political facts into constitutional theory and practice.

Moreover, the acceptance of the Supreme Court's nonmajoritarian difficulty—that we should not trust its nine justices to make decisions that affect public policy—is viewed by many scholars as the prime reason to trust majoritarian politics to decide the extent to which society should help various individuals and groups. Scholars and jurists who reject the significance of the Court's nonmajoritarian difficulty are more at ease in accepting the reform liberal strand of American constitutionalism. They also view judicial review as an unproblematic use of Supreme Court power, especially when it is used to interpret and protect rights that are clearly implied by the words of the Constitution. Ironically, the values of reform liberalism are central to scholars who study modern nonoriginalist constitutional theory and practice. At the same time, these values are among those that are most contested as bases for court action yet most necessary for the protection of the rights of subordinated groups.[50]

PICTURES IN PRECEDENTS:
IMAGING SOCIAL CHANGE
THROUGH LAW

I would like to use the concepts of "pictures in precedents" and "pictures in cases" as a way to help us understand how reform liberal values, and really all strands of liberal constitutionalism, make their way into nonoriginalist constitutional decision making. Instead of conceiving of justices as only applying polity and rights principles, it may be useful to argue that justices create mental pictures in precedents, really social constructs, which they relate to pictures in cases. In so doing, they ask what the pictures in precedents are that apply to the given case before them. They ask whether the picture in precedents that they envision as controlling in a case (or doctrinal area) is qualitatively different from the new picture before them. Considering pictures in precedents and pictures in cases allows us to better answer the question in each case of whether and what rights or polity principles are at issue.

We have already discussed *Lochner v. New York* (1905), a case that had perhaps the most notable picture in precedent in constitutional history. It defined a relationship between employer and employee that was built on social facts and polity and rights principles but which was renounced in later cases, culminating in *West Coast Hotel v. Parrish* (1937).

One can see the place of pictures in precedents in numerous areas of modern constitutional law. If one analyzes cases involving government aid to religion and questions of the separation of church and state, one can envision a child sitting in a parochial school (and a parochial educator in that school). Viewing that picture gives us a more precise and holistic view of the act of judging than simply segmenting the case into its many separate issues, which also must be done as part of the act of constitutional interpretation and analysis. When we create such a picture in precedents, we see that precedents require us to leave the child alone. That picture is at the core of school prayer decisions and cases involving direct aid to parochial education.

When we move to the question of state aid to parents of all school-children, one does not have that picture, even though children are aided in going to parochial schools. Also involved in this picture is the notion that the parochial-school child should not be kept from being helped in acquiring the necessary tools to be a functioning citizen of secular society. Cases show that some aid to parochial-school children is allowed for the economic good of the nation and for the children's self-development as people and citizens, as long as it is distributed in a way that does not violate that picture in precedent. Both scholars who support traditional *Lemon v. Kurtzman* test standards for establishment-clause cases and those who want to move to a simple noncoercion test would agree on the picture in precedent, even though the different tests they advocate result in different levels of support for state aid to parochial education and for school prayer.[51] Pictures in precedents replace traditional case analysis. They help us to better understand which aspects of liberal constitutional values are viewed by nonoriginalists as not at issue and which are viewed as at issue in a particular case in a way that analysis of the application of polity and rights principles does not. *Lee v. Weisman* (1992) is an easy case, to a degree, because the picture is set by the religion clauses of the First Amendment: no school prayer at graduation ceremonies.

We see pictures in precedents at work in the area of fundamental rights and interests under the equal-protection clause. In *Plyler* the Supreme Court said that the undocumented children of illegal Mexican immigrants cannot be forced to pay for public school while other students pay no fees. The court in *Plyler* talked of a future discrete and insular class of citizens who would not be allowed the same chance as other children to gain an education. Reform liberal values of the importance to each child of the right to fulfill her own abilities and destinies abound in *Plyler*. However, prior cases suggested that illegal aliens had few, if any, equal-protection rights, with the possible exception of some basic procedural rights. We ask whether there are pictures in precedents that can help explain this case. We find them in the pictures in precedents of *Brown v. Board of Education* (1954), the case that banned racial segregation in schools, compared with *Plessy v. Ferguson* (1896), which allowed racial segregation on railroad cars. We find them in *Brown* in the notion that education is so central to a child's chance for self-development as a citizen that to allow racial segregation is to deny that development. We find it in cases that highlight the belief that children are not responsible for their conditions and, at times, actions. We find it in *San Antonio Independent School District v. Rodriguez* (1973), which suggested that a total denial of access to public education—as opposed to the different levels of spending across school districts, which was at issue in the case—might raise constitutional questions.[52] These pictures in precedents *Brown* and *Rodriguez* help explain *Plyler*. I am asking that we not view constitutional law cases simply as consisting of arguments, although the analysis of arguments must occur along with pictures in precedents. Pictures in precedents are important because they offer a more refined view of how justices choose among the elements of our political culture, such as the elements of republicanism, humanist liberalism, and reform liberalism.

When pictures in precedents are dominant in a doctrinal area, they make it more difficult for both "conservative" and "liberal" justices to reject precedents rather than follow them because they must reject clear pictures in precedents that numerous prior courts have used as starting points for analysis. Unfortunately, for originalists, pictures in precedents cannot play a major role in the development of doctrine because their picture of social facts and of polity and rights principles is fixed in the founding period of the part of the Constitution that is in question. Pictures in precedents and cases allow us to ask how changing social, economic, and political facts inform the Supreme Court's analysis of whether basic constitutional principles, such as the prohibition of a state-established religion or state-endorsed religious practice, are being maintained. For example, in *Lee v. Weisman* (1992), moderate Justice Kennedy talks of peer pressure among middle-school students to attend graduation in the 1990s as a reason why there should not be school prayers at graduation ceremonies. Justice Powell in *Plyler* talks of the desires of the United States government and industry for cheap Mexican labor as reasons for illegal-alien children to seek an education. It is the effect of changing social, economic, and political facts on whether pictures in precedents can be sustained in the future that triggers new definitions of rights.

I am not arguing that facts alone explain the outcome in cases, as we saw in the facts presented on gender and arrests for drinking and driving in the landmark gender rights case *Craig v. Boren* (1976). In that case, while the Supreme Court noted there was a statistical correlation between gender and arrests for drunk driving, it viewed the data as resulting from archaic gender stereotypes held by police and the young people they stop.[53] The pictures in precedents in gender cases change after *Boren*. The court will no longer accept preference for men or women under the law as a simple matter of legislative preference. A new picture in precedent is developed. The court will add the filigree around these pictures in precedents, with some fitting and some not. This is not simply judges choosing the policy outcomes they desire, as attitudinalists emphasize, because the picture has staying power over time. It is usually only refined; it is rarely changed in a significant way.

Perhaps the most dramatic recent example of the role of pictures in precedents in constitutional change is found in *Casey*, a case that upheld the central tenets of the right of abortion choice that were first enunciated in *Roe v. Wade* (1973).[54] In *Casey*, the Rehnquist Court argued that settled expectations in a right to abortion choice that were created in *Roe* in 1973 must be continued in 1992. Important to this view was the Court's reading of the social facts in 1973 as compared to 1992. The role of women in the workforce and changing sexual mores provided clear evidence to the Court that the liberty interests of women that were at risk in 1973 if childbirth was forced upon them were even more at risk in 1992. These social facts seemed so important that the Court talked about a woman's right of personhood, an equal-protection concept, rather than simply a right of privacy. Also, to overturn *Roe*, given that the right of abortion choice had proven to be workable to new generations of citizens and had become a settled expectation among those citizens, would place the Supreme Court as an institution and the rule of law itself at risk. This situation was quite different from the situation when the court had to overturn the pictures in precedents that were central to *Lochner.*

Thus, pictures in precedents build on constitutive liberal theories of constitutional decision making and interpretation. They speak to the inability to segregate constitutional issues into simple polity and rights principles. They help us see that a new definition of rights is not merely a choice among policy outcomes, but may be "required" because the picture in the new case is so similar to the picture in precedents that to deny the right is to deny fundamental constitutional values. For example, in order to uphold Colorado's Amendment 2 in *Romer v. Evans* (1996), the Supreme Court would have had to disavow important pictures in precedents under the equal-protection clause.[55] In *Romer,* the Court said that lesbians, gays, and bisexuals cannot be required to amend the Colorado Constitution rather than secure through normal political processes state and city laws to protect themselves from discrimination. To require gays to amend the state constitution in such instances would force the court to reject long-held pictures in precedents that citizens are equal before the law—that all citizens and classes of citizens should be expected to face the same political process in securing favorable legislation, especially when the group seeking to change the law is likely to be subjected to discrimination by the majority. Pictures in precedents will help us study the process through which the Court makes choices in the future as to whether reform liberal, humanist liberal, or republican values will inform these choices.

America's complex liberal culture cannot be analyzed merely in terms of doctrinalism or its radical critique. Nor should one view American liberalism as simply instrumental in nature, for such an outlook fails to take into account the dialectical nature of American law, politics, and culture. In deciding cases, the Supreme Court does not simply thrust its policy desires to the fore or follow election returns and decide cases based upon them. Rather, the Court employs precedent, polity and rights principles, and ideas from America's complex liberal culture. Although one strand of our culture may be emphasized over another in a given case, all have contributed to Supreme Court decision making.

Among republicanism, humanist liberalism, and reform liberalism, though, it is reform liberalism that most significantly contributes to a discussion of the redefinition of the rights of subordinated groups. In redefining the rights of subordinated groups, one must look at the everyday situations and interactions of the members of those groups in light of more complex definitions of social, economic, and political inequalities. Our objective should be to ascertain the degree of subordination involved and possible remedies. In order to do this, we must incorporate social, economic, and political facts into the analysis, but in such a way so as to be consistent with constitutional principles and structural processes as they have been reconceptualized by constitutional scholars and the wider interpretive community. Pictures in precedents allow us to measure the degree and nature of change in our political culture while adhering to the rule of law and other constitutional values and mores. Pictures in precedents also allow us to understand the various points of emphasis in our political culture that allow the Supreme Court, lower federal courts, and state courts to be transformative in nature. Finally, pictures in precedents will allow us to take into account the constitutive nature of Supreme Court decision making and its influence on legal and social change. Further study regarding the extent and limits of pictures in precedents in explaining Supreme Court decision making and doctrinal change will allow us to better explain the relationship of law and culture. In so doing, we build on Greenstone's admonition "against simplicity" in the study of American law and politics.

Situated Rationality: A Preface to J. David Greenstone's Reading of V. O. Key's THE RESPONSIBLE ELECTORATE

Ira Katznelson

More than twenty years have passed since David Greenstone delivered a paper entitled "V. O. Key's Pragmatism" to the Foundations of Political Theory Group at the annual meeting of the American Political Science Association.[1] Never published, the paper marks something of a missed opportunity both for the intellectual venue of historically oriented studies of American political development within which Greenstone worked and for the elaboration of "rationality" as a core concept in political science. By way of a close, appreciative analysis of Key's much-criticized posthumous volume, *The Responsible Electorate,* Greenstone's essay was motivated by skepticism about both the approach to rationality by the then-ascendant behaviorist strand of the discipline and understandings of human agency that are too thin, as in the vision of the individual as a simple utility-maximizer. Greenstone's subtitle—"'Rationality' Is a Predicate of Voting and Not a Cause"—and its aphoristic opening citation from Wittgenstein—"We are trying to get hold of the mental process of understanding which seems to be hidden behind those coarser and therefore more readily visible accompaniments"—signaled that his ambition far transcended the paper's genre, an extended book review.[2]

And so it was. From the start of his career, Greenstone had been wrestling with questions his teachers Louis Hartz and Grant McConnell, building on Tocqueville, had posed about the status of liberalism and the braiding of associational participation and exclusion in American political development. The body of work Greenstone had produced before his consideration of Key and his discovery of Wittgenstein had married Hartz's ambition and scope (and his Marxisant agenda) to McConnell's penchant for crisp conceptualization and empirical scholarship (and his postpluralist ambition).[3] Between Greenstone's lines was a continuing and manifestly restless search for a theory of interest and action appropriate to agency inside what he later called (in an elaboration of Hartz's metatheory, following Wittgenstein's discussion of norms of correct performance in the *Investigations*) the "boundary conditions" of the country's liberal regime.[4] In *Labor in American Politics*, Greenstone had wrestled with the inadequacies of Marxist notions of objective interest and of mirror-image pluralist scholarship, which highlighted subjective interests at the expense of structure, by preferring Ralf Dahrendorf's Weberian, authority- and conflict-oriented reconstruction of Marxist theory.[5] This achievement, Greenstone claimed, provided nondeterministic tools for understanding the contingent but not unguided process by which members of the working class had become effective collective political actors in the United States. In *Race and Authority in Urban Politics*, the linkage between structure and agency was provided by the sociological concepts of role and role interests. Individuals in specific social roles do possess interests, he and Peterson argued, and it is the task of the analyst to understand when, how, and why these become recognized interests.[6] In "Group Theories" he showed that the absence of just such an approach to interest and action in pluralist theory (even in the work of critics such as McConnell) had made pluralism incapable of accounting for large-scale social movements.

Greenstone, in short, had been seeking a concept of rationality capable of coupling a macroscopic understanding of the relatively durable, if multidimensional, qualities of American liberalism with the microanalysis of individual and group behavior. From the start to the conclusion of his truncated career, he believed that only with a concept of rationality superior to those offered by overly structural and determinist theories (whether based on Marx, Durkheim, or Parsons) or by increasingly popular but undersocialized and disembedded formal models based on instrumental rationality could empirical and normative democratic theory thrive.

Greenstone understood that if his preferred ways of working were to be able to hold their own against other powerful currents of political science, an alternative approach to issues of agency, rationality, and interest would have to be elaborated. It was this proactive imagination and quest for novel solutions that drew him to Key via Wittgenstein. Key, in Greenstone's view, had done more than question a mechanical behaviorist epistemology or rattle the cage of mainstream studies of political participation. More important, he had made a conceptual breakthrough with respect to our understanding of rationality. Properly attended to, his understanding of rationality could come to undergird political science with a particular kind of pragmatist philosophical orientation, which could allow the discipline to keep its behavioral and empirical gains without making the undue sacrifices required by a credulous positivism or understandings of rationality that are too lean. Wittgenstein, in turn, provided Greenstone with tools for a reading of Key that aimed to tease out these meanings and implications, especially those aspects that Key himself did not articulate with sufficient boldness or directness.

We now know that Greenstone's paper on Key was written in midcareer, at just the moment he was shifting emphasis, as it were, from McConnell's questions and behavioral studies about the terms and character of interest group life in America to Hartz's on the traits and limits of the country's liberalism based mainly on a treatment of ideas and debates about the nature of the regime. More than any other text Greenstone wrote in his career, "V. O. Key's Pragmatism" illuminates the junction of these issues and emphases. As such, for all its sketchiness and convolution, it represents one of his most incisive contributions. My treatment of this paper proceeds in two steps. First, I underscore the elements of Key's book Greenstone found so compelling, then, elaborating on his perspective, I consider some more general implications of his reading of Key for political science. I close with an appreciative assessment of the advantages of the course Greenstone charted but also with an inventory of difficult issues he charged his readers to resolve.

THE SIGNIFICANCE OF KEY FOR GREENSTONE

Greenstone opened his consideration of *The Responsible Electorate* by observing how Key's "last, incomplete, and posthumously published book...has been most unevenly received by our profession"(p. 1).[7] After a burst of initial enthusiasm, it had been treated as an unworthy curiosity, methodologically flawed, substantively deficient, and something of a dead end. Greenstone thought this dismissal to be wrongheaded. The tough-minded critiques of Philip Converse and Michael Margolis,[8] among others, which had taken Key to task for failing to conform to "the criteria for issue voting described in the *American Voter*,"[9] Greenstone argued, had misunderstood the fundamental difference between the behaviorism within whose fold they were writing and Key's pragmatism.[9]

Greenstone argued that Key's much-maligned approach to voter rationality based on findings of parallelism between voting and policy preferences and a focus on switchers (whom the literature often had represented as the least informed voters) in fact constituted something of a breakthrough. Key's critics had been disturbed by his reliance on the relationship between issues and voting. As Margolis put it, "All the book really demonstrated was a simple bivariate relationship between issue positions and vote. Key never asked if voters perceived the party they voted for to be in agreement with them on any given issue. Nor did he examine whether those who voted for a party with a particular issue position in fact identified with that party to begin with—let alone examine the effects of any more subtle control variables. Moreover," he continued, "Key failed even to check whether or not voters cared about the issues for which he claimed they voted."[10] In complementary fashion, Converse castigated Key for his silence about political psychology, that is, for his failure to specify the reasoning process voters used in casting their votes. If voters are rational, the behavioral critics reproached, their reasoning process must be a good one and we must look for it empirically; otherwise, citizens' votes can be said to be otherwise caused.

Nonetheless, Margolis did concede the book's "resurrection of the rational voter" had value because it implicitly promoted the line of inquiry "as originally described in the *American Voter*. Voters must know about the issues, the party positions, and the current government policies. Voters must care about how the issues are resolved."[11] By underscoring rationality at a time when much behavioral research had emphasized its absence, Key also had contributed to orienting the discipline to a then-emerging rational-choice focus, which imputed rationality to voters and other agents in the sense of pursuing their preferences efficiently (and thus elided the steps both Key and especially his behaviorist critics thought necessary to establish the existence of such rational behavior).[12]

Greenstone did not so much reject inductive behaviorism or deductive model building as insist that Key's pragmatist reorientation of rationality should anchor inquiry of both kinds. Greenstone's paper focused primarily on the still-regnant behaviorism and on the behavioral challenge to Key. It served as a rejoinder to Converse, Margolis, and other like-minded critics by arguing that their call for a demonstration of political psychology in action is not the same as a presentation of rationality; it merely constitutes one of a number of plausible hypotheses about the origins of instrumentally rational voting. Perhaps good reasoning is necessary to rational voting, but perhaps not, Greenstone argued; this is (merely though not trivially) an empirical question. Key, he claimed, had considered the concept of voter rationality not as a cause that explains why individual voters choose as they do but as a predicate "which describes the vote (and thus the voter)." For Key, voter rationality is thus entwined with the issue "of the broader meaning of our mental predicates, an issue that occupied both Ryle and Wittgenstein"(p. 2).[13] From this angle, "the most fundamental issue is whether we should derive our concept of rationality from a neo-positivist or pragmatist version of scientific inquiry." Since he had opted for the latter, Key had been warranted in his interpretation of "electoral decisions as *intentional judgments* on governmental performance and policy"(p. 3).

Inside this mode of inquiry the reasoning process provides only one amongst other possible causal accounts. Drawing primarily on Wittgenstein's *Investigations* but also on the pragmatism of Dewey and Peirce, Greenstone argued Key's position was this: "*Whatever the source* of the voter's decision—be it a good intuition, a vague but accurate impression, or careful reasoning—what counts is that the voters do align their issue position and partisan choices."[14] But he added a proviso, a critical one that is both temporal and historical: "Before we can confidently consider the voters rational they must exhibit a course of conduct...in which such partisan choice alignments are repeated"(p. 10). Again following Wittgenstein, Greenstone did not conceive of understanding, rationality, and purposiveness as mental processes. Rather, as Greenstone wrote in one of the paper's pivotal passages, we use such terms "to indicate that we have mastered and are using techniques necessary or appropriate for participating in the social contexts that constitute our life—the games, forms of life, customs and the like which Wittgenstein himself so often discusses.... Rationality, on this account, therefore characterizes the behavior of someone in an existing context" (p. 11). Rationality is a marker of how we code our relational experiences using the ordinary language and concepts of our social settings; it is right to call this rational when we use these tools successfully, as in voting (p. 12). It thus was essential for Key that he could operationalize this idea, as he did by counting as rational votes both cases where people with issue positions choose the "appropriate" party and where they change issue positions based on party loyalty (which has been labeled the rationalization problem). Key was criticized for not making preferences fixed and causal, but this, Greenstone rightly notes, is one of his text's great strengths, for a voter's preference is not prior to the "voter's empirical inquiry about the political situation"(p. 26). Rationalization, from this perspective, is no less rational than issue voting and perhaps, given its systemic consequences for liberal democracy, even more so (p. 27). Key, Greenstone observes, was indifferent to the problem of the causal direction of the shift in voting and issue preferences precisely "because his concern with the pragmatics of 'voter rationality' led him away from the question of causality as such, and to the question of systemic consequences." For Key, Greenstone wrote, "this concept entailed considerations of democratic theory (when are rulers controlled or influenced?) rather than political psychology (when do voters reason well?)"(p. 20).

Key thus married the idea of a course of conduct to the Deweyite notion of appraisal and in so doing bridged structure and action, as well as fact and value, in a powerful mix of context, intention, and behavior. Further, he refused to treat rationality as independent of the pragmatic/normative dimension of the control of government, for without such a prospect no voting can be rational. Steeped in these considerations, Key had embedded his approach to rationality inside democratic theory by focusing on how the existence of switchers who move across party lines from one presidential election to the next create a climate in which governing elites are disciplined by their fear of losing popular support;[15] hence "this shifting sector of the electorate must play a basic role in the workings of a democratic system."[16] Greenstone comments that "Key's 'must' here suggests that one of the most important, and necessary, features of voter rationality...is its contribution toward disciplining the government." Rationality, from this perspective, not only is contextual but is systemic, with important normative consequences. "And even though his *operational* definition for rational voting—aligning one's policy position and electoral choices—does not refer to such systemic consequences, he suggests here," Greenstone's appraisal continues, "that we are entitled to label such voters rational only if they in fact function as an electorate to exert popular control over their rulers. And that switchers do exercise just such influence is one of the major themes of *The Responsible Electorate*"(p. 18).

This orientation to switchers and this benign neglect of the rationalization problem so vexing for the behavioral critics were central to Key's consideration of rationality as akin to what Wittgenstein called a language game, as making sense only inside a distinctive mode of practice and discourse. In such settings there are no noncircular criteria available for independent appraisals. For Key, neither party nor issue preference can be treated as a priori. Rather, "compatible with voter rationality," he "licenses the voter to choose the part of his set of political beliefs he will change when confronted with the 'recalcitrant' fact that a favored party (or candidate) has endorsed a policy the voter initially opposed." Key was criticized for his refusal to fix the policy preferences of the voter before his analysis begins. By contrast, Greenstone avers, his great contextual strength lay in just this refusal to situate "the voter's empirical inquiry" prior to an evaluation "about the political situation"(p. 26). This approach, of course, constitutes an alternative not only to the behavioral insistence that voters' preferences be treated as analytic—that is, as prior to empirical situations—but to comparable moves made, implicitly or explicitly, by most rational-choice theorists.

In Key's hands, voter rationality thus provides the bridges between individual-level and system-level rationality and between intentionality and structure that we cannot do without, Greenstone noted, if we want to have "an acceptable theory of American politics"(p. 30). His approach to such a task was neither antibehavioral nor opposed to rational-choice analysis, but, he believed, the precondition of both. How Greenstone thought so, and what the implications of this thought might be not just for behaviorism and rational choice but for the new historical institutionalism within which he felt most comfortable, are the subjects to which I now turn.

The Significance
of Greenstone's Key

Greenstone's pragmatist rejection of neopositivist views of causation and rationality in accord with some of the late Wittgenstein's deepest insights hardly constituted a rejection of the possibility of systematic, scientific inquiry, but it did counsel a basic reorientation, which he left understated by staying largely within the confines of a review essay. His brief "final note," however, touches on this larger purpose and its considerable ramifications for the practice of political science. The behaviorists, Greenstone claimed, are missing a coherent approach to rationality, preferring induction to imputations of rationality; in turn, deductive approaches to the study of politics build models which predict behavior based on an analytic a priori assumption about the existence of individual-level rationality understood as instrumental goal seeking, leaving to the side questions about the content of rationality.

Greenstone thought Converse's ambivalent approach to rationality in his survey of scholarship on public opinion and voting behavior to be representative of the ambivalence of behavioral political scientists. "I have never found the concept of rationality sufficiently clear," Converse had written, "to be depended on in inductive work." For this reason, he explicitly preferred to focus on issue voting than on "questions of the prevalence of rationality."[17] Yet in "The Nature of Belief Systems in Mass Publics," Converse had noted how "such basic dimensions of judgment as the liberal-conservative continuum" may be associated with "political behavior" that "increasingly approximates that of sophisticated 'rational' models, which assume relatively full information."[18] Greenstone thought Converse and his fellow behaviorists had grappled with their unease by unduly restricting rationality "to designate only those processes of reasoning which successfully draw valid inferences from factually correct premises" (p. 29). Greenstone sought, instead, to find a secure place for rationality as integral to the view of human subjects political science requires, without embracing the shortcut of rational-actor models based on highly stylized and often implausible sets of assumptions about rational behavior.

Greenstone's alternative invokes Wittgenstein's treatment of mental processes. How, he had asked, do we know that a student has "understood" how to proceed accurately with a series of numbers when continuing a series after a degree of instruction by his teacher? This is "a question which parallels Key's concern with the criteria for saying a vote has been cast rationally." Wittgenstein had argued it is a mistake to assume that the student can continue the series up to a certain point because of the possession and understanding of the relevant algebraic formula as a tool of good reasoning, just as Key had rejected as a test of rationality the possession by a voter of "an appropriate calculus which, given correct information, specifies which party or candidate to support. Wittgenstein replies," Greenstone continues, "that—while the formula *may* occur to the student enabling him or her to continue the series—having the formula is in fact *neither* a necessary nor sufficient condition for understanding how to do so" (p. 9). Of course, it is possible that the student possesses and deploys such an exact method of thought to get the right answer, but the student also may not. As Wittgenstein wrote, "He watches A with a series of tension, and all sorts of vague thoughts go through his head. Finally, he asks himself: 'What is the series of differences?' He finds the series 4, 6, 8, 10 and says: 'Now I can go on.'... B says nothing at all and simply continues the series. Perhaps he had what may be called the sensation 'that's easy!' (...for example...a light quick intake of the breath)."[19] It was in this context that Greenstone noted an analogy with Key's position that regardless of the source of the voter's decision, ranging from intuition to the possession of an algorithm, what matters is the alignment the voter chooses between issues and party voting and how this is done as part of a pattern of conduct over time. Voting, but not voting alone, is a site of intelligent and directed action when "we have mastered and are using techniques necessary or appropriate for participating in the social contexts that constitute our life—the games, forms of life, customs and the like which Wittgenstein himself so often discusses"(p. 11). Rational action thus cannot be understood only as the instrumental pursuit of goals, but of that pursuit in specific circumstances:

> Rationality, on this account, therefore characterizes the behavior of someone in an existing context—for example having to vote in an election—with respect to some possible state of affairs such as that created by a particular public policy or other government action. We are entitled to say that a voter is rational not if he reasons well, but if he in fact casts his vote in a way that seems most likely to increase the probability that the desired state of affairs will come to pass. (p. 11)

Rationality does not require a process of reasoning capable of drawing "valid inferences from factually correct premises" (p. 29), nor does it exist as an individual-level assumption. Rather, rationality is a contextual, configurative, and interactional predicate. "Rationality" marks out a school of "phenomena which, as Wittgenstein puts it, presents us with 'a complicated network of similarities' that can best be described as 'family resemblances.'" We can distinguish rational action, including voting, from nonrational and irrational action, but only "in so far as the intention exhibited by the voting behavior (the vote for a party with a given policy position) parallels *other behavioral indications* of intention—which include but surely need not be restricted to the voter's verbal expression of policy positions on which Key relied" (p. 29). Such activity may be interpreted as intentional only when embedded in the context of a given situation. Rationality, in short, requires the specification of *macro*conditions.

In effect, Greenstone was trying to transcend the two theories of human rationality, drawn from cognitive psychology and economics, that had found the greatest acceptance in political science. Though he shared their covering designation of "rational" as denoting "behavior that is appropriate to specified goals in the context of a given situation," he was uneasy not only with procedural or bounded rationality, which treats thinking as information processing by actors lacking in capacity and information (this discomfort was the basis of his criticism of Converse's and Margolis's stress on thinking and information processing) but also with substantive rationality drawn from decision theory and neoclassical economics, which takes for granted the possession of a utility function that consistently orders preferences and choices among alternatives and the ability of actors to choose a course of conduct with the greatest utility.[20]

The boundedly rational *Homo psychologicus* of cognitive science and the objectively rational *Homo economicus* of economic theory have provided philosophical anthropologies for behavioral studies with an affinity, respectively, for political psychology and for rational-choice approaches based on the presumption that actors possess accurate models of the political order and the choices available to them. Greenstone's reading of Key was motivated by discomfort with these options and by a search for an alternative approach to microfoundations appropriate to the context-thick historical and institutional approach exemplified by his own scholarship on labor, race, and American liberalism. Of course, Greenstone focused in his appreciation of Key on the shortcomings found on the cognitive-behavioral side, but the larger body of his scholarship demonstrates a recurrent concern with the shortcomings of economic rationality. These included problems of metapreferences, preference formation, and preference change; the uncertain status of selfishness and self-regarding behavior; a devaluation of the discursive and the deliberative, let alone the altruistic; the status of the irrational and nonrational; stillness when it comes to questions about the external social, structural, and contextual determination of the person; an excessive voluntarism; credulousness about the actual existence of choices, especially in circumstances of unequal power; the universalism of the idea that all social groupings ultimately are based on common foundations; the commitment to an individualism that is at odds with the ontological independence of large-scale associations; and the still-unresolved collective-action problem.

But Greenstone also understood that whatever the flaws of procedural and substantive rationality, the absence of appropriate microfoundations for historical institutionalism exacted a very considerable cost, for without such underpinnings this kind of inquiry is susceptible to the sins of methodological collectivism, teleology, and at least an implicit functionalism. Concerned by this deficiency, Greenstone read Key via Wittgenstein and the American pragmatists as groping for a third way. Greenstone's consideration of Key inquires, in effect, whether historical institutionalism does or can possess microfoundational affinities of its own or whether it must borrow and deploy the resources of cognitive psychology and microeconomics despite the considerable tensions attendant on the introduction of either approach inside a thoroughgoing historical and configurative analysis. Is the only alternative doing without a coherent philosophical anthropology?

Greenstone struggled with Key's pragmatism to suggest that indeed there is the third option of what might be called *situated rationality.* This approach does not so much compete with as incorporate the best features of bounded rationality (especially its realist sense of constraints on individuals not only because of their cognitive limits as decision makers but as a consequence of restrictions imposed by structural situations) and rational choice (especially its focus on strategic settings and mutually dependent interaction). However, the rationality proffered by Greenstone can only be inferred over time. It makes sense only in particular normative and institutional settings that are culturally and structurally thick, not just strategically lean. It depends on conventions and relationships. It links the internal and external environments of persons. It transcends methodological individualism and collectivism to focus on relationships as the key units of analysis. It is agnostic about whether there really are choices in all "choice" situations. It locates behavior within the rules and practices that constitute regimes. It makes room for culture, and it incorporates identities and what ordinarily is seen as the nonrational. It treats the actor as an information processor. It does not oppose rationality and norm-guided action or norms to outcome-oriented motivations or norms and self-interest. It makes institutions, understood both as rules and contexts, central to inquiry. It shows how developing experiences and traditions change frameworks for strategic decisions. It helps link individual and collective decision. It marries holism and individualism dynamically. It is open to a science of preference formation.

In these ways, Greenstone's paper succeeds in demarcating a set of tough problems and in pointing to a way we might work through them. These virtues are not easy to access, however. The essay makes its points indirectly, by way of a review, and even as an example of this genre, it presents a particularly difficult and elliptical sketch. This abstruseness also proves a strength, however. For precisely because the text's character and content hardly are self-evident, it challenges readers to reflect on how a situated and embedded approach to rationality might be developed further.

Indeed, "V. O. Key's Pragmatism" might have been entitled "Refuse to Choose." Its search for an appropriate microfoundation for macroanalysis is replete with potentially productive tensions and analytical contradictions, which are turned in the direction of balanced commitments. It is consistent with methodological individualism, but not when it is too strong, and with methodological holism when it is not too determinative. It refuses too emphatic an antinomy beween decision-based rational theory tilting toward radically autonomous individuals and normatively based sociopsychological models that run the risk of a rigid social determinism. It considers the benefits of action and participation without assuming that the nature of the goods sought or the benefits of participation are consistent across historical situations. It implicitly sympathizes with the rational-choice critique of the fallacy of composition, which reasons from the collectivity to the individual, at the same time as it insists on a socially constructed notion of the person. It treats strategies as embedded in the past and conditional on the future. It revivifies culture without according it too deterministic a place in its analysis. It leaves open the balance among cultural, intentional, and structural determinations of beliefs, norms, values, and desires, and it leaves open whether these mental attributes are rational, irrational, or nonrational. It embeds politics in forms of life and language without eliminating its autonomous aspects. It refuses simple or linear rankings of preferences, understanding that preferences exist at multiple levels arrayed in situational hierarchies. It implicitly contains a theory of periodization, flagging particular formative moments, as well as a concern with sequencing. In short, Greenstone's paper does not so much present a full-blown alternative to dominant ways of conceptualizing rationality as offer an insistent invitation to those of us unhappy with the standard orientation to develop such an alternative, while exhorting that criticism is not enough. After all, as he put it, rationality is a concept "too important to live without" (p. 28).

Conclusion

David F. Ericson

In this concluding essay of the volume, I would like to consider the liberal consensus thesis as a series of research questions. The thesis variously presents itself as an empirical question, a political (or, equally, hermeneutic) question, a comparative question, and a methodological question. It also raises the hoary question of the relation between theory and practice, the question that most interested J. David Greenstone.

In the most obvious sense, the liberal consensus thesis is an empirical question, and many of the essays in this volume (Ericson, Horton, McKeen, Nackenoff, Smith) treat it as such. Did various historical actors appeal to political principles that we would consider liberal principles? Or, better, did various historical actors appeal to the same set of political principles, whether or not we would consider them liberal principles? On one level, it is immaterial to the thesis what those principles were, much less what we, or the historical actors themselves, call(ed) them.[1]

As an empirical question, the liberal consensus thesis has a quantitative dimension. Taken most literally, the thesis is that all political actors throughout American history have appealed to the same set of liberal principles. In its softer, more credible versions, the thesis is that most political actors throughout American history have appealed to a similar set of liberal principles.[2] We might also want to make qualitative distinctions within the universe of American historical actors and sample only the members of that universe whom we consider sufficiently important or profound.[3] Still, we would have to sample a large set of actors to either prove or disprove the liberal consensus thesis in any of its significant variants. Some of the essays in this volume (Ericson, Horton) start to build the case for the thesis, while others (Nackenoff, Smith) start to build the opposite case. However, in order to build either case, we clearly face a formidable research agenda.[4]

Yet, obviously, the liberal consensus thesis is not merely an empirical question, and none of the essays in this volume treats it merely as such. The thesis also has significant political and hermeneutic dimensions. It is an important political (and historical) fact whether historical actors thought a liberal consensus existed or not, just as it is an important point of interpretation whether we think a liberal consensus exists or not. For historical actors, their belief in a liberal consensus (or lack thereof) told them what arguments to present and not to present. For researchers, our belief in a liberal consensus (or lack thereof) tells us what questions to research and not to research. We are also more likely to frame research questions that transcend the initial issue of whether a liberal consensus exists through the lens of whether we think such a consensus exists. So, for example, we will ask the question whether what is public in the United States has been characterized by progressive enactments of liberal principles (Green); whether liberal principles have been sufficiently resonant to allow the Supreme Court to adequately protect the rights of subordinated groups (Kahn); whether the standards of correct performance provided by liberal principles for rational voting are too narrow (Katznelson); and whether liberal principles (or any other comparable set of principles) have substantially guided American political development (Orren and Skowronek). As a research question, the liberal consensus thesis requires us not only to count cases but to be conscious of how we count them, and of how the historical actors themselves did.[5]

On this level, the nature of the consensual principles does matter. While consensus presents a peculiar set of political and research problems, liberalism does, too. The continued existence of American slavery into the nineteenth century offers an excellent example of this phenomenon, which is why it was then part of so many political agendas and is currently part of so many research agendas. For historical actors, the fundamental problem was how to either defend or attack the institution on the basis of liberal principles or, alternatively, how the continued existence of the institution revealed the shortcomings of those principles. For researchers, the problem is similar, except now the problem appears as one of consistency and, possibly, hypocrisy, or as the disproof of a certain historical thesis. The brilliance of the work of David Brion Davis, among others, on the history of slavery consists in showing how the institution became a major intellectual and political problem only with the widespread acceptance of Enlightenment principles, a Gestalt shift that henceforth presented contemporary actors and subsequent researchers with a peculiar set of problems.[6] The point of this work is not that slavery, or any other institution, is problematic only from a liberal perspective. Rather, the point is that existing institutions become problems, and problems with a distinctive shape, depending on the perspective of the contemporary actors and subsequent researchers who contemplate them.[7]

The liberal consensus thesis is also a comparative question. Falling under the umbrella of American exceptionalism, the thesis is a challenge for comparative research. How exceptional was (is) the United States as a consensual society? How exceptional was (is) it as a liberal society? Of course, the null hypothesis may well be valid. Scholarly attacks on American exceptionalism are profuse and suggestive, but they tend to be energized by research agendas other than testing the liberal consensus thesis.[8] The same generalization applies to the growing number of comparative studies of slavery.[9] Following his own admonition in *The Liberal Tradition in America*, Hartz and several colleagues initially tested the liberal consensus thesis from a comparative perspective in *The Founding of New Societies*.[10] Yet it still is the case that we have barely begun to explore the comparative dimensions of the thesis.

The primary reason for this lack of comparative research is obvious. Such research requires a considerable amount of time, effort, and, often, money. It surely presents a case for collaborative efforts not only between Americanists and comparativists but among members of each group. Such efforts have generally not been rewarded by the discipline or the academy, certainly not in proportion to the resources that they require. Cross-national studies are risky investments of research capital.[11] I confess to being as guilty of not "being comparative" as anyone else. My best excuse is that while comparative research is the only way of ultimately proving the liberal consensus thesis, the thesis must at some point be proven, or disproven, on its American "side," an imposing enough task in itself.

Finally, the liberal consensus thesis is a methodological question. At this point in the controversy over the thesis, I think we would all agree that it simplifies our "dependent variable": the reality of American political thought and practice. That reality clearly is a complicated mix of principles of many different sorts, including liberal, republican, ascriptive, feudal, and Protestant ones. The key question, then, is whether the liberal consensus thesis *over*-simplifies that reality. Or, alternatively, how much do we gain or lose by adding other "independent variables" to our explanatory theories? On this level, the liberal consensus thesis is that liberal principles provide the main currents of American political thought and practice, and the rest is background noise. The contrary view is that at least some of the background noise is not really that but rather part of the main currents. Again, this disagreement can be settled only empirically. It does, however, raise some troublesome methodological questions concerning the relative merits of single-factor and multiple-factor explanations of phenomena. The laws of parsimony and diminishing returns are certainly relevant to assessing those relative merits.[12]

We introduce another wrinkle when we break the whole into its constituent parts and consider the political ideas and actions of individual actors as our dependent variables. Now, the question appears as one of whether different traditions of political ideas influenced individual actors and, if so, how the actors combined ideas from those different traditions. Did they do so coherently or incoherently? Did they rank-order the traditions or ideas? Which did they consider primary and which secondary? In considering these questions, we should avoid the temptation to treat the actors as sieves for the

traditions that influenced them, an approach that would clearly reify the traditions.[13] There is inevitably a qualitative dimension to these questions as
well. Some actors—the ones we tend to study—combined "their" traditions
and ideas more coherently than others did. If we sample only the actors we
consider more profound or more significant, we might well prejudice the
result in favor of the liberal consensus thesis. But then we come back to the
question of the universe we are sampling when we either assert or deny the
thesis. In any case, we should not preclude the possibility that multiple traditions existed only as they were synthesized by individual actors, that any
given sample of actors might have synthesized those traditions in similar
(though presumably not identical) ways, and that in this respect multiple traditions could really have been one tradition. The McKeen essay, in particular, reminds us of the possibility of a "whole" to American political thought
and practice.[14]

I have already identified several areas of further research. First, we need
to keep building the case either for or against the liberal consensus thesis by
analyzing individual cases. Second, we need to assess how a metabelief in a
liberal consensus or lack thereof might have affected individual actors as well
as our own research. Third, we need to engage in more comparative research
on whether the United States was (is) uniquely a consensual (liberal) society
or not. Fourth, we need to consider more deeply the question of what counts
as evidence either for or against the thesis.

However, above all, we need to look more closely at the relation between
political principles and practices. While the Green, Kahn, Katznelson, and
Orren and Skowronek essays take this research question most seriously, all
the essays in the volume at least implicitly address the relation between
political principles and practices. Ultimately, any argument about the presence (or absence) of a liberal consensus must show how the presence (or
absence) of both consensus and liberal principles affected actual political
practices and events. If we more explicitly attach intellectual and political
debates to actual political practices and events—no matter what perspective
we adopt—we would truly be carrying on the Greenstonian tradition. We
would then be exploring the "forms of life" he was so adept at elucidating.[15]
In this sense, the essays in this volume represent the beginning of an extended
discussion of, and contestation over, the particular forms of life that have
defined American politics.

Notes

Introduction

1. Louis B. Hartz, *The Liberal Tradition in America: An Interpretation of American Political Thought Since the Revolution* (New York: Harcourt Brace Jovanovich, 1955).
2. See Charles A. Beard, *The Rise of American Civilization* (New York: Macmillan, 1933). Hartz, of course, did not establish the paradigm alone, but he does now appear preeminent. See Daniel T. Rodgers, "Republicanism: The Career of a Concept," *Journal of American History* 79 (1992): 13–14; Rogers M. Smith, "Beyond Tocqueville, Myrdal, and Hartz: The Multiple Traditions in America," *American Political Science Review* 87 (1993): 555.
3. Bernard Bailyn, *Ideological Origins of the American Revolution* (Cambridge, Mass.: Belknap Press, 1967); Gordon S. Wood, *The Creation of the American Republic, 1776–1787* (Chapel Hill: University of North Carolina Press, 1969); J. G. A. Pocock, *The Machiavellian Moment: Florentine Political Thought and the Atlantic Republican Tradition* (Princeton, N.J.: Princeton University Press, 1975). For republican revisionism as a paradigm shift, see Rodgers, "Republicanism," pp. 11–12.
4. J. David Greenstone, "The Transient and Permanent in American Politics: Standards, Interests, and the Concept of the 'Public,'" in J. David Greenstone, ed., *Public Values and Private Power in American Politics* (Chicago: University of Chicago Press, 1982), pp. 3–33; "Political Culture and American Political Development: Liberty, Union, and the Liberal Bipolarity," *Studies in American Political Development* 1 (1986): 1–49; *The Lincoln Persuasion: Remaking American Liberalism* (Princeton, N.J.: Princeton University Press, 1993).
5. James T. Kloppenberg, "The Virtues of Liberalism: Christianity, Republicanism, and Ethics in Early American Political Discourse," *Journal of American History* 74 (1987): 9–33. See also Isaac Kramnick, "The 'Great National Discussion': The Discourse of Politics in 1787," *William and Mary Quarterly,* 3d series, 45 (1989): 3–32; and Peter S. Onuf, "Reflections on the Founding: Constitutional Historiography in Bicentennial Perspective," *William and Mary Quarterly,* 3d series, 46 (1989): 350–51, 353–54.
6. Rogers M. Smith, *Civic Ideals: Conflicting Visions of Citizenship in U. S. History* (New Haven, Conn.: Yale University Press, 1997).
7. For a similar case about religious outsiders in American political history, see R. Laurence Moore, *Religious Outsiders and the Making of Americans* (Cambridge, Mass.: Harvard University Press, 1984).

C h a p t e r   1

1. Louis Hartz, *The Liberal Tradition in America: An Interpretation of American Political Thought Since the Revolution* (New York: Harcourt, Brace, 1955).
2. Malcolm X, "The Ballot or the Bullet," in Sue Davis, ed., *American Political Thought: Four Hundred Years of Ideas and Ideologies* (Englewood Cliffs, N.J.: Prentice-Hall, 1996), pp. 416–28; see also p. 384 (quoting Malcolm X on the "rampant racism" of white Americans).
3. To my chagrin, the book's index, which I prepared myself, has no entries for "race," "gender," "African Americans," or "women," for example, though there are some pertinent discussions in the text. Rogers M. Smith, *Liberalism and American Constitutional Law* (Cambridge, Mass.: Harvard University Press, 1985; rev. ed., 1990).
4. Alasdair MacIntyre, *Whose Justice? Which Rationality?* (Notre Dame, Ind.: University of Notre Dame Press, 1988), pp. 8–9, 11.
5. Herbert Croly, *The Promise of American Life* (New York: E. P. Dutton, 1963 [1909]); Michael Lind, *The Next American Nation: The New Nationalism and the Fourth American Revolution* (New York: Free Press, 1995); Michael J. Sandel, *Democracy's Discontent: America in Search of a Public Philosophy* (Cambridge, Mass.: Harvard University Press, 1996).
6. MacIntyre, *Whose Justice*, pp. 164–82, 401–3.
7. Hartz, *Liberal Tradition*, pp. 3–32.
8. These statements are based on a rather extensive reading of American political writing and speeches in the eighteenth and twentieth centuries, along with much less extensive knowledge of English sources. Note, however, that writers such as Locke, Cato, Adam Smith, Jeremy Bentham, David Ricardo, and the Millses, all of whom are often identified with liberalism, each used different titles for their systems of thought, when they used any such labels at all.
9. L. T. Hobhouse, *Liberalism* (New York: Oxford University Press, 1964 [1911]), pp. 9–43. Hobhouse's work was one of the key works in English broadening the use of the term *liberalism* to go beyond the program of the Liberal Party (with which Hobhouse was nonetheless greatly concerned) to refer to a body of theory that he dated back to Locke (p. 32). More generally, he described "the historic beginning of liberalism" as a "protest" against a preexisting "authoritarian order" of royal absolutism, "a protest religious, political, economic, social and ethical" in nature (pp. 14–15).
10. See Hobhouse, *Liberalism*, pp. 63–127; John Dewey, *Liberalism and Social Action* (New York: Capricorn Books, 1963 [1935]). Dewey dated the use of the term *liberalism* to "the first decade of the nineteenth century" but traces its ideas further back, to Locke. He then goes on to define, as Hobhouse did, a post-laissez-faire "new" liberalism (p. 3). Though both these authors discussed liberalism as a nineteenth-century term, the nineteenth-century examples of the actual use of the word that they invoked were essentially confined either to discussions of the English Liberal Party, the Manchester school of laissez-faire economics, or cognate continental parties and movements. In 1928 Hoover identified a "liberalism" that stressed economic freedoms, but that was not, he insisted, purely a "system of laissez-faire" as much as it was the "true spirit in the American sys-

tem" for the preceding "hundred and fifty years." He offered this definition in opposition to the more interventionist forms of "new liberalism." See Herbert Hoover, "Rugged Individualism," in Richard F. Hofstadter and Beatrice K. Hofstadter, eds., *Great Issues in American History*, vol. III: *From Reconstruction to the Present Day, 1864–1981*, rev. ed. (New York: Vintage Books, 1982), pp. 333–34.

11. *Strecker v. Kessler*, 95 F. 2d 976 (1935).

12. *West Virginia Board of Education v. Barnette*, 319 U.S. 624 (1943).

13. Though I cannot report systematic data at this point, over the last fifteen years I have read not only a very large number of primary documents, political speeches, presidential proclamations, and judicial decisions from the nation's founding through the Progressive era, but also most of the leading political science texts of those years. One finds analyses featuring terms such as *civil liberty, freedom, Americanism, equal rights, the nation, the state, progressivism*, and especially *democracy*, but rarely if ever *liberalism*.

14. See, for example, Thomas F. Gossett, *Race: The History of an Idea in America* (New York: Schocken Books, 1963); George M. Fredrickson, *The Black Image in the White Mind: The Debate on Afro-American Character and Destiny, 1817–1914* (New York: Harper & Row, 1971). Cf. Kenneth Dolbeare, *American Political Thought*, rev. ed. (Chatham, N.J.: Chatham House, 1984). Dolbeare's text does not include any extended defenses of racial hierarchy in the United States, much less any identification of racism as a tradition of thought in the country. Virtually all modern textbooks on American political thought resemble Dolbeare's in these regards.

15. *Korematsu v. United States*, 323 U.S. 214 (1944), at 233; *Webster's Collegiate Dictionary*, 5th ed. (Springfield, Mass.: G. & C. Merriam, 1942), p. 818.

16. *Webster's Encyclopedic Unabridged Dictionary of the English Language* (New York: Gramercy Books, 1989), p. 1184.

17. The eighteenth- and nineteenth-century works are cited and discussed in Rogers M. Smith, *Civic Ideals: Conflicting Visions of Citizenship in U.S. History* (New Haven, Conn.: Yale University Press, 1997), pp. 105, 174, 203–4, 292–93, 359–60, 364–65. See also Madison Grant, *The Passing of the Great Race* (New York: Charles Scribner, 1926 [1916]); Carl Campbell Brigham, *A Study of American Intelligence* (Princeton, N.J.: Princeton University Press, 1923); Richard J. Herrnstein and Charles Murray, *The Bell Curve: Intelligence and Class Structure in American Life* (New York: Free Press, 1994), pp. 1–16, 269–315, 642–43; J. Philippe Rushton, *Race, Evolution and Behavior: A Life History Perspective* (New Brunswick, N.J.: Transaction Publishers, 1995), pp. 1–16.

18. Lind, *Next American Nation*, pp. 369–71.

19. Hartz, in fact, offered no concise definition of liberalism, but these elements were recurringly stressed in *The Liberal Tradition*. See, for example, pp. 4–6, 12, 50–66, 302–9.

20. For Hartz's 1964 reformulations, see Louis Hartz, *The Founding of New Societies* (New York: Harcourt, Brace, 1964), pp. 16–17, 49–50, 60–62, 102. For discussion, see Smith, *Civic Ideals*, pp. 20, 25, 507 n. 5.

21. J. David Greenstone, *The Lincoln Persuasion: Remaking American Liberalism*

(Princeton, N.J.: Princeton University Press, 1993), pp. 41–44. Cf. Smith, *Civic Ideals,* pp. 20, 512 n. 14.

22. Greenstone, *Lincoln Persuasion,* pp. 35–65. To prove my sincerity in this praise, let me note that the framework nicely captures the differences I had with Shklar, which I referred to above. I wanted to defend a kind of "reform liberalism," while her "liberalism of fear" was, then at least, more a form of "humanist liberalism." Both of us were, however, wary of moving too far toward socialism. My criticism of Greenstone's framework is that while it helps explain such conflicts among liberals, it fails to reflect adequately the important currents in American thought that are not primarily liberal.

23. Greenstone, *Lincoln Persuasion,* pp. 105–17, 124–27, 133–39, 148–53. Cf. Smith, *Civic Ideals,* p. 548 n. 1. In her essay in this volume, Louisa Bertch Green suggests that for Greenstone, American liberalism did not include any substantial commitment to equality, only to individual rights, private property, and government by consent. Hence, perhaps, squaring liberalism with racial hierarchies might not be impossible. See Louisa Bertch Green, "The Liberal Tradition in American Politics: A Slow Boat to Democracy," p. 45 in this volume. Cf. Greenstone, *Lincoln Persuasion,* p. 36 n. 1. Yet if all individuals are said to have rights, and government is to be by the consent of all the governed, certain significant forms of egalitarianism are implied. Both slavery and Jim Crow laws denied African Americans very basic economic as well as political rights.

24. See David F. Ericson, *The Shaping of American Liberalism: The Debates over Ratification, Nullification, and Slavery* (Chicago: University of Chicago Press, 1993), pp. 1, 10–26, 132–35, 158–63, 179; Ericson, "Dew, Fitzhugh, and Proslavery Liberalism," p. 68 in this volume. Cf. Smith, *Civic Ideals,* pp. 204–5, 550–51 nn. 23–25, 566 n. 10.

25. Gayle McKeen, "A 'Guiding Principle' of Liberalism in the Thought of Frederick Douglass and W. E. B. DuBois," pp. 100, 114 in this volume.

26. Carol Horton, "Liberal Equality and the Civic Subject: Identity and Citizenship in Reconstruction America," p. 116 in this volume.

27. Carol Pateman, *The Sexual Contract* (Stanford, Calif.: Stanford University Press, 1988), pp. 38, 41, 54, 92–94.

28. Horton, "Liberal Equality and the Civic Subject," p. 243 n. 5 below. Horton goes on to map out different versions of liberalism—the most attractive of which is termed "black republicanism"—that include a "phylogenetic liberalism." This form of liberalism posits the division of mankind into "inherently unequal" races who nonetheless all possess some bare minimum of rights (pp. 126–32, 246 n. 58). But it is bare indeed. This minimum includes sharply attenuated economic as well as political rights. Black rights to buy and sell goods were sharply constrained under the Black Codes and later Jim Crow laws. Hence it seems to me too minimal to qualify as a form of liberalism as Hartz defined it, even though, as Horton rightly insists, its adherents did hold other liberal positions and were less extreme than the genocidal racists she terms "white nationalists."

29. Smith, *Civic Ideals,* pp. 5–9, 29–30, 36–39, 82, 517 nn. 44 and 48, 526 n. 36.

30. Horton, "Liberal Equality and the Civic Subject," p. 116 in this volume. Ira Katznelson has repeatedly made these points to me in conversation and has suggested them in several essays, most recently in "Liberal Maps for Technology's

Powers: Six Questions," *Social Research* 64 (1997): 1333–37. In this essay, Katznelson indicates that "Locke's focus on rationality and Mill's on unenlightened peoples and places" now and in the past "combine" to "produce new masses and underclasses of excluded people" deemed insufficiently rational and enlightened for full rights (p. 1334).

31. See, for example, Sydney A. Ahlstrom, *A Religious History of the American People* (New Haven, Conn.: Yale University Press, 1973), esp. pp. 295–359.

32. Barry Alan Shain, *The Myth of American Individualism: The Protestant Origins of American Political Thought* (Princeton, N.J.: Princeton University Press, 1994), esp. pp. 32–83, 320–28; Ahlstrom, *A Religious History*, pp. 360–84; Smith, *Civic Ideals*, pp. 74–77, 83–85.

33. Ahlstrom, *A Religious History*, pp. 648–729, 1070–78; Martin Luther King Jr., "Letter from Birmingham Jail," in Sue Davis, ed., *American Political Thought: Four Hundred Years of Ideas and Ideologies* (Englewood Cliffs, N.J.: Prentice-Hall, 1996), pp. 406–28; Smith, *Civic Ideals*, pp. 103–4, 142–43, 205, 210–11, 246–47, 273–77, 353–55, 430–31.

34. John Hope Franklin and Alfred A. Moss Jr., *From Slavery to Freedom: A History of Negro Americans*, 6th ed. (New York: Alfred A. Knopf, 1988), pp. 89–90; Smith, *Civic Ideals*, pp. 70–86, 103–6, 112, 208.

35. Smith, *Civic Ideals*, pp. 30–39, 70–86, 197–212, 410–19. I believe the analysis there also shows how and why, under changing economic, intellectual, and political conditions, American political actors have transformed prevailing civic ideologies and altered institutions in light of these changes. Hence I think the approach of that work is not so devoid of meaningful "development" as is suggested in the Karen Orren and Stephen Skowronek essay in this volume, "In Search of Political Development," pp. 33–34. I think the argument of that essay can, however, frutifully be used to enrich the understanding of development in *Civic Ideals*, though I cannot undertake that task here.

36. For such an analysis, see Smith, *Civic Ideals*, pp. 138–40, 165–66, 353–56.

C h a p t e r   2

1. Louis Hartz, *The Liberal Tradition in America: An Interpretation of American Political Thought Since the Revolution* (New York: Harcourt, Brace, 1955).

2. Alan Brinkley, *The End of Reform: New Deal Liberalism in Recession and War* (New York: Knopf, 1995).

3. Eldon Eisenach, *The Lost Promise of Progressivism* (Lawrence: University Press of Kansas, 1994).

4. Lawrence Goodwyn, *Democratic Promise: The Populist Moment in America* (New York: Oxford University Press, 1976).

5. Victoria Hattam, *Labor Visions and State Power: The Origins of Business Unionism in the United States* (Princeton, N.J.: Princeton University Press, 1993).

6. Eric Foner, *Reconstruction: America's Unfinished Revolution, 1863–1877* (New York: Harper & Row, 1988).

7. David F. Ericson, *The Shaping of American Liberalism: The Debates over Rat-*

ification, Nullification, and Slavery (Chicago: University of Chicago Press, 1993); Gordon Wood, *The Creation of the American Republic, 1776–1787* (Chapel Hill: University of North Carolina Press, 1969).

8. Anne Norton, *Alternative Americas: A Reading of Antebellum Political Culture* (Chicago: University of Chicago Press, 1986).

9. Samuel P. Huntington, *American Politics: The Promise of Disharmony* (Cambridge, Mass.: Harvard University Press, 1980).

10. J. David Greenstone, *The Lincoln Persuasion: Remaking American Liberalism* (Princeton, N.J.: Princeton University Press, 1993).

11. Rogers M. Smith, "Beyond Tocqueville, Myrdal, and Hartz: The Multiple Traditions in America," *American Political Science Review* 87 (1993): 549–66; *Civic Ideals: Conflicting Visions of Citizenship in U.S. History* (New Haven, Conn.: Yale University Press, 1997).

12. J. David Greenstone, "Political Culture and American Political Development: Liberty, Union, and the Liberal Bipolarity," *Studies in American Political Development* 1 (1986): 1.

13. Theda Skocpol, *Protecting Soldiers and Mothers: The Political Origins of Social Policy in the United States* (Cambridge, Mass.: Harvard University Press, 1992), p. 56.

14. Karen Orren and Steve Skowronek, "Institutions and Intercurrence: Theory Building in the Fullness of Time," *Nomos: Political Order* 38 (1994): 111–46.

15. Paul Pierson, "When Effect Becomes Cause: Policy Feedback and Political Change," *World Politics* 45 (1993): 600.

16. Pierson, "When Effect Becomes Cause," p. 595; Elmer E. Schattschneider, *The Semi-Sovereign People* (New York: Holt, Rinehart, and Winston, 1960).

17. Paul Pierson, "Path Dependence, Increasing Returns, and the Study of Politics," unpublished manuscript.

18. Walter Dean Burnham, "Periodization Schemes and Party Systems: 'The System of 1896' as a Case in Point," *Social Science History* 10 (1986): 285.

19. Kenneth A. Schepsle, "Studying Institutions: Some Lessons from the Rational Choice Approach," *Journal of Theoretical Politics* 1 (1989): 131–47.

20. Jack Knight, *Institutions and Social Conflict* (New York: Cambridge University Press, 1995).

21. J. David Greenstone, "The Transient and Permanent in American Politics: Standards, Interests, and the Concept of the 'Public,'" in J. David Greenstone, ed., *Public Values and Private Power in American Politics* (Chicago: University of Chicago Press, 1982), pp. 3–33.

22. Again, see Smith, "Beyond Tocqueville" and *Civic Ideals*.

23. Charles Bonaparte quoted in Robert Wiebe, *The Search for Order, 1877–1920* (New York: Hill and Wang, 1967), p. 60.

C h a p t e r   3

1. For comments on this and earlier versions of the essay, I would like to thank David F. Ericson, J. Ronald Green, Russell Hardin, Stephen Holmes, James D.

Johnson, Rogers M. Smith, Kimberly Stanton, Cass Sunstein, Gayle McKeen Waller, and two anonymous reviewers.

2. See J. David Greenstone, *The Lincoln Persuasion: Remaking American Liberalism* (Princeton, N.J.: Princeton University Press, 1993), and Louis Hartz, *The Liberal Tradition in America: An Interpretation of American Political Thought Since the Revolution* (New York: Harcourt Brace Jovanovich, 1955).

3. Greenstone, *Lincoln Persuasion*, p. 36 n. 1; pp. 36–46, 50–65.

4. See Rogers M. Smith, "Beyond Tocqueville, Myrdal, and Hartz: The Multiple Traditions in America," *American Political Science Review* 87 (September 1993): 549–66; p. 549, emphasis added. See also his *Civic Ideals: Conflicting Visions of Citizenship in U.S. History* (New Haven, Conn.: Yale University Press, 1997).

5. See Smith, "Beyond Tocqueville," pp. 549–50; J. David Greenstone, "The Transient and the Permanent in American Politics: Standards, Interests, and the Concept of 'Public,'" in J. David Greenstone, ed., *Public Values and Private Power in American Politics* (Chicago: University of Chicago Press, 1982), pp. 3–33. Cf. Eric Hobsbawm, "Introduction: Inventing Traditions," in Eric Hobsbawm and Terence Ranger, eds., *The Invention of Tradition* (Cambridge: Cambridge University Press, 1983), pp. 1–15, esp. pp. 2 and 5.

6. Smith, "Beyond Tocqueville," p. 549.

7. Even as late as 1911, "equality" scarcely figures in L. B. Hobhouse's account of liberalism; "social liberty" (pp. 192–94) is closest in substance. Hobhouse was asking if democracy is "in substance as well as in form a *possible* mode of government"; there is no reference to the United States, but the fact that he asks the question would indicate that the United States did not present to the world an overwhelmingly persuasive case of accomplished democracy—Smith is right in saying that we haven't a case to present. Hobhouse does, however, refer to democracy as "the necessary basis of the *[coming]* Liberal idea" (Hobhouse, *Liberalism* (New York: Henry Holt and Company, 1911), pp. 192–94, 226–27; emphasis added).

8. Milton Rosenberg, *Extension 720*: "Remembering David Greenstone," WGN Radio, Chicago, 14 October 1993; Greenstone was a frequent guest on Rosenberg's weekly program *Extension 720* to discuss local and national political issues.

9. Smith, "Beyond Tocqueville," p. 549.

10. Smith, "Beyond Tocqueville," p. 549.

11. See, for example, Enrique Krauze, *Mexico: Biography of Power; A History of Modern Mexico, 1810–1996,* translated by Hank Heifetz (New York: Harper Collins, 1997), ch. 1; and Carole Pateman, *Participation and Democractic Theory* (Cambridge: Cambridge University Press, 1970). See also Hobsbawm and Ranger, eds., *Invention of Tradition*.

12. For an account of conflicting socializations, see Pateman, *Participation and Democratic Theory*.

13. These attitudes are human if not humane, irrespective of time or regime form. See, for example, discussion of the sixteenth-century observations of Bartolomeo de las Casas and others, in Krauze, *Mexico*, p. 32.

14. Smith, "Beyond Tocqueville," pp. 549–66.
15. See, for example, R. Laurence Moore, *Religious Outsiders and the Making of Americans* (Cambridge, Mass.: Harvard University Press, 1984). One could say that some humans have habits if not traditions of protecting hard-won privileges and of extending them to others only with reluctance.
16. Smith, "Beyond Tocqueville," p. 550.
17. See Laurence Tribe, *Constitutional Choices* (Cambridge, Mass.: Harvard University Press, 1985), pp. 175–76, 205–7. For a good general account of the development of liberalism and of democratic theory and practices, see David Thomson, *Europe Since Napoleon*, 2d ed. (New York: Alfred A. Knopf, 1965). See also R. R. Palmer, *The Age of Democratic Revolutions: A Political History of Europe and America, 1760–1800* (Princeton, N.J.: Princeton University Press, 1959).
18. Affirmative action measures, adopted in large part because of the demonstrable discrepancies between procedural and substantive representation, have been continuously under attack for favoring women, African-Americans, and so forth, over white males. Formal representation, such as numerical or proportional representation, based on single factors (color or gender, for example) is not necessarily substantive, since such formulations assume that one African-American or a few, or one woman or a few, can represent all African-Americans or women—that race or gender is the single salient criterion. The partial fallacy of this assumption has long been recognized. See, for example, J. S. Mill, *Considerations on Representative Government*, chs. 4, 6, 7; see also Charles R. Beitz, *Political Equality: An Essay in Democratic Theory* (Princeton, N.J.: Princeton University Press, 1989); Brian Timmons, "Fraudulent 'Diversity,'" *Newsweek*, 12 November 1990, p. 8; Jake Lamar, "Whose Legacy Is It, Anyway?" *New York Times*, 9 October 1991, p. A15; Nicholas Lemann, "Taking Affirmative Action Apart," *New York Times Magazine*, 11 June 1995, pp. 36–43, 52, 54, 62, 66; and Lisa Anderson, "Law Review Masks Diversity in a New Admission System," *New York Times*, 7 July 1995, p. C16.
19. Cf. Gordon S. Wood, *Representation in the American Revolution* (Charlottesville: University Press of Virginia, 1969), esp. pp. 2–11; and John Phillip Reid, *The Concept of Representation in the Age of the American Revolution* (Chicago: University of Chicago Press, 1989).
20. Recall that in the early 1980s political cartoonist Gary Trudeau created a strip in which the president responds to an aide who has just proposed a woman for the most recent vacancy on the Supreme Court, "Ha, ha, ha! Did you forget? We already have a woman on the Supreme Court!"
21. See, for example, Kathleen L. Barber, *Proportional Representation and Election Reforms in Ohio* (Columbus: Ohio State University Press, 1995). Cf. Beitz, *Political Equality; Wesberry v. Sanders*, 376 U.S. 1 (1964); and *Reynolds v. Sims*, 377 U.S. 533 (1964).
22. See Barber, *Proportional Representation*. Cf. Stanley Cavell, *Pursuits of Happiness: The Hollywood Comedy of Remarriage* (Cambridge, Mass.: Harvard University Press, 1981), pp. 36–37; and Charles E. Lindblom, "Review of *The Public Interest* by Richard E. Flathman," *American Political Science Review*, December 1967: 1008–9.

23. Cf. Jürgen Habermas, *The Structural Transformation of the Public Sphere: An Inquiry into a Category of Bourgeois Society*, translated by Thomas Burger from the 1962 German edition (Cambridge, Mass.: MIT Press, 1989); David D. Laitin, "Marginality: A Microperspective," *Rationality and Society* 7 (January 1995): 31–57; James M. Buchanan, "Individual Rights, Emergent Social States, and Behavioral Feasibility," *Rationality and Society* 7 (April 1995): 141–50; and Benjamin I. Page and Robert Y. Shapiro, *The Rational Public* (Chicago: University of Chicago Press, 1992).

24. For a discussion of these differences, see, for example, Wood, *Representation*, ch. 1.

25. Cf. Krauze, *Mexico*, pp. 8, 13, 14, 15.

26. See, for example, Gerald E. Frug, "The City as a Legal Concept," *Harvard Law Review* 93 (April 1980): 1057–154; Grant McConnell, *Private Power and American Democracy* (New York: Vintage, 1970); and Robert A. Lively, "The American System: A Review Article," *Business History Review* 29 (March 1955): 81–96.

27. Socialism is a good example. The equation of socialism with a strong public sphere and the American ambivalence about the latter makes up part of the contradiction we are examining here. "The American people, in an inconsistency incomprehensible to doctrinaires, oppose socialism yet manifest a tendency to support specific measures that may be in principle socialistic" (V. O. Key Jr., *Public Opinion and American Democracy* [New York: Alfred A. Knopf, 1961], 1961, p. 125; see also p. 59 n. 3; p. 516 n. 7; cf. p. 269, table 11.1; p. 444, table 17.5; p. 465, table 18.3. See also Herbert McClosky and John Zaller, *The American Ethos: Public Attitudes Toward Capitalism and Democracy* [Cambridge, Mass.: Harvard University Press, 1984], esp. pp. 135, table 5–2; 220; 233; and 301–2).

28. Cf., for example, Richard Goldstein, "Visitation Rites: The Elusive Tradition of Plague Lit," *The Village Voice Literary Supplement*, October 1987, pp. 6–7; Richard Epstein, *Takings: Private Property and the Right of Eminent Domain* (Cambridge, Mass.: Harvard University Press, 1985), ch. 1; and Peter Ordeshook, *Game Theory and Political Theory: An Introduction* (Cambridge: Cambridge University Press, 1986), p. xii and chs. 1 and 2.

29. See Stephen Holmes, *Benjamin Constant and the Making of Modern Liberalism* (New Haven, Conn.: Yale University Press, 1984), pp. 241–61.

30. Cf., for example, Plato's *The Republic*; Richard Sennett, *The Fall of Public Man* (New York: Alfred A. Knopf, 1977); Robert B. Reich, ed., *The Power of Public Ideas* (Cambridge, Mass.: Ballinger, 1988); Alan Stone, *Public Service Liberalism: Telecommunications and Transitions in Public Policy* (Princton, N.J.: Princeton University Press, 1991); and John Kenneth Galbraith, *Economics and the Public Interest* (Boston: Houghton Mifflin, 1973).

31. See, for example, Jon Elster, ed., *Rational Choice* (New York: New York University Press, 1986); and Brian Barry and Russell Hardin, eds., *Rational Man and Irrational Society?* (Beverly Hills, Calif.: Sage Publications, 1982).

32. See Holmes, *Benjamin Constant*, esp. the epilogue, "The Public and the Private."

33. For example, in the introductory essay to *Public and Private in Social Life*, of their edited volume (New York: St. Martin's Press, 1983), Stanley I. Benn and

Gerald F. Gaus divided "public" into three dimensions—access, agency, and interest (pp. 7–11). This articulation of what is public into relationship, parties, and reasons provides no common ground for analysis of and comparison among the three measures. See also Benn and Gaus's other essay in that volume,"The Liberal Conception of the Public and the Private," pp. 31–65. Cf. Frug, "The City as a Legal Concept."

34. See, for example, Anne Wells Branscomb, *Who Owns Information? From Privacy to Public Access* (New York: Basic Books, 1994); John Mark Hansen, *Gaining Access: Congress and the Farm Lobby, 1919–1981* (Chicago: University of Chicago Press, 1991), esp. pp. 11–25; David R. Mayhew, *Congress: The Electoral Connection* (New Haven, Conn.: Yale University Press, 1979); Barry D. Karl, "Public Administration and American History: A Century of Professionalism," *Public Administration Review* 36 (Sept./Oct. 1976): 489–503; and David B. Truman, *The Governmental Process: Political Interests and Public Opinion* (New York: Alfred A. Knopf, 1951), pp. 333–35.

35. *The Concise Oxford English Dictionary* defines *access* as "a right or means of approaching." The implication is that there is someone or something that approaches and someone or something that is approached, but access refers neither to the approacher nor to the one approached but to the approaching, to what connects them.

36. See Russell Hardin's discussion of asymmetries in public and collective goods in *Collective Action* (Baltimore, Md.: Johns Hopkins University Press, 1982), pp. 67–89; see also A. John Simmons, *Moral Principles and Political Obligations* (Princeton, N.J.: Princeton University Press, 1979).

37. See John Dewey, "Search for the Public," in *The Public and Its Problems* (Chicago: Swallow Press, 1954), pp. 12ff.

38. See Branscomb, *Who Owns Information?*

39. See Frug, "The City as a Legal Concept." This essay is a thorough analysis of a complex social entity in which the question "Is it public?" is treated as a substantive one. The essay sustains the emphasis on measuring both the direct and the representative access encompassed by the situation to demonstrate that a city—a "public" entity—is not public in all its features.

40. On consent theory, see Simmons, *Moral Principles and Political Obligations,* chs. 3 and 4; see also Frederick C. Mosher, *Democracy and Public Service* (New York: Oxford University Press, 1968), esp. ch. 1.

41. On nonreciprocity, see Robert Goodin, *Reasons for Welfare: The Political Theory of the Welfare State* (Princeton, N.J.: Princeton University Press, 1988), pp. 134–37; see also Hardin, *Collective Action,* pp. 67–89, and Mosher, *Democracy and Public Service,* ch. 1.

42. See, for example, Greenstone, "The Transient and the Permanent," pp. 15–18.

43. See, for example, "Support Is Found for Broad Change in Health Policy," *New York Times,* 6 April 1993, p. 1A.

44. Cf. Mosher, *Democracy and Public Service,* chs. 1 and 7; Cass R. Sunstein, *The Partial Constitution* (Cambridge, Mass.: Harvard University Press, 1993); Page and Shapiro, *Rational Public;* Brian Barry, *Justice as Impartiality* (New York: Oxford University Press, 1995); Greenstone, "Against Simplicity: The Cul-

tural Dimensions of the Constitution," *University of Chicago Law Review,* 55 (1988): 428–49; and Karl, "Public Administration and American History."

45. Cf. H. L. A. Hart, *The Concept of Law* (Oxford: Clarendon Press, 1982), p. 56; and Michael Walzer, *Spheres of Justice* (New York: Basic Books, 1983).

46. See Dewey, *Public and Its Problems,* pp. 12ff.

47. For a recent version of the argument that follows from Madison's and Tocqueville's warnings against the tyranny of the majority, see Lani Guinier, *The Tyranny of the Majority: Fundamental Fairness in Representative Democracy,* foreword by Stephen L. Carter (New York: Free Press, 1994), esp. ch. 1; see also Beitz, *Political Equality.*

48. However, see Lemann, "Taking Affirmative Action Apart."

49. See John Hart Ely, *Democracy and Distrust: A Theory of Judicial Review* (Cambridge, Mass.: Harvard University Press, 1980), pp. 55–70.

50. See Peter Applebome, "In Alabama, Blacks Battle for the Authority to Govern," *New York Times,* 31 January 1992, p. A8, and Chris Stern Hyman, "New York Protects Bad Doctors," *New York Times,* 29 July 1995, p. 15, which reports on a ruling of the New York State Court of Appeals that "the [New York] Legislature should weigh which interests should prevail, the doctor's or the public's."

51. Cf. Minxin Pei, "Is China Democratizing?" *Foreign Affairs* 77 (Jan./Feb. 1998): 68–82.

52. Thanks to Russell Hardin for pressing the case of closed committees. See Hyman, "New York Protects Bad Doctors." See also "Senate Rejects Attempts to Force Hearings on Packwood Charges," *New York Times,* 3 August 1995, p. A1, a report on a partisan vote in the Senate to keep the hearings closed.

53. See Greenstone, "The Transient and Permanent," pp. 15–18.

54. See Mosher, *Democracy and Public Service,* chs. 1 and 7, and Karl, "Public Administration and American History," pp. 489–503.

55. For a discussion of differing emphases on liberty, equality, and rules within liberalism, see Steven Kautz, *Community and Liberalism* (Ithaca, N.Y.: Cornell University Press, 1995).

56. The condition of scarce resources may be absolute (i.e., only a specified quantity of something exists), or it may result from a monopoly of a sought-after resource by an individual or group; cf. Goodin, *Reasons for Welfare,* pp. 264–67.

57. See Sunstein, *Partial Constitution,* esp. pp. 3–39. Cf. Robert J. Sternberg and John Kolligian Jr., eds., *Competence Considered* (New Haven, Conn.: Yale University Press, 1990), especially the essays by David Elkind, "Introduction: Changing Conceptions of Competence," pp. 1, 2, 3, 7–8, and by Ellen J. Langer and Kwangyang Park, "Incompetence: A Conceptual Reconsideration," pp. 149–50, 161.

58. The interests of the excluded are commonly overlooked or are assumed to be negligible, because "it is easier that way"; see, for example, Sol Worth and John Adair, *Through Navajo Eyes: An Exploration in Film Communication and Anthropology* (Bloomington: Indiana University Press, 1975), esp. pp. 42–62.

59. See Jerome K. Bruner, *Toward a Theory of Instruction* (Cambridge, Mass.: Harvard University Press, 1971), especially chs. 2, 3, and 6.

60. See, for example, Julius Jacobson, *The Negro and the American Labor Movement* (New York: Anchor, 1968).
61. See Mosher, *Democracy and Public Service,* chs. 1 and 7.
62. Cf. Clifford Geertz, *Local Knowledge* (New York: Basic Books, 1983); Paul Starr, *The Social Transformation of American Medicine: The Rise of a Sovereign Profession and the Making of a Vast Industry* (New York: Basic Books, 1982); Daniel Kevles, *The Physicists: The History of a Scientific Community in Modern America* (New York: Vintage Books, 1979); Frederick Suppe, ed., *The Structure of Scientific Theories,* 2d ed. (Urbana: University of Illinois Press, 1977); Diana Crane, *Invisible Colleges: Diffusion of Knowledge in Scientific Communities* (Chicago: University of Chicago Press, 1972); Thomas Kuhn, *The Structure of Scientific Revolutions,* 2d ed. (Chicago: University of Chicago Press, 1970); and Claude Lévi-Strauss, *The Savage Mind* (Chicago: University of Chicago Press, 1966).
63. No one, presumably, would claim that there is not a valid case to be made for certain exclusions—as when, for example, for differing reasons, illegal aliens, convicted felons, the insane, and children are not allowed to vote. In Hobbes's time, for example, those excluded by common consent were "Children, Fooles, and Mad-men that have no use of Reason" (*Leviathan,* pt. 1, ch. 16 [London: Dent, 1979]).
64. See Brian Barry, *Political Argument* (London: Routledge & Kegan Paul, 1963), p. 193.
65. Goodin, *Reasons for Welfare,* pp. 264–67.
66. See J. A. W. Gunn, *Politics and the Public Interest in the Seventeenth Century* (London: Routledge & Kegan Paul, 1969). It is possible to recognize in this point the argument made by the Chrysler Corporation, in the 1970s, to win government aid to rescue Chrysler from bankruptcy; the demise of Chrysler, it was argued, would be sufficiently detrimental to the national economy to be also destructive of the public interest. This is a good example of a compelling and selective (if possibly erroneous) single-vector argument.
67. See Duncan Snidal, "Public Goods, Property Rights, and Political Organizations," *International Studies Quarterly* 23 (December 1979): 532–66; see also Michael Taylor, *Community, Anarchy, and Liberty* (Cambridge: Cambridge University Press, 1982), pp. 39–48; Dennis C. Mueller, *Public Choice* (Cambridge: Cambridge University Press, 1979); and Hardin, *Collective Action.*
68. Cf. Hanna Pitkin's discussion of her pre-Wittgensteinian view of representation in the introduction to *The Concept of Representation* (Berkeley: University of California Press, 1967).
69. Introductory address to the annual meeting of the National Alliance of Media Arts Centers, Walker Art Center, Minneapolis, Minnesota, spring 1983.
70. Hobhouse, *Liberalism,* pp. 232–33, emphasis added; Krauze, *Mexico,* pp. 8, 13–15.
71. L. B. Green, "Horace Mann and the Bipolarity of the American Liberal Tradition," unpublished paper delivered at the Spring Institute of the Department of Sociology, University of Chicago, 21 April 1980.

72. Russell Hardin, "Democracy on the Margin," in *Understanding Democracy: Economic and Political Perspectives* (Cambridge: Cambridge University Press, 1997), edited by Albert Breton, Gianluigi Galeotti, Pierre Salmon, and Ronald Wintrobe, pp. 249–66.

Chapter 4

1. If we loosely define liberal principles as appealing to ideas of personal liberty, equal worth, private property, and government by consent, the alternatives appeal to some notion of hierarchy, whether based on race, gender, ethnicity, religion, or birthright. Liberal proslavery arguments would then not deny the personal worth of the slaves but rather claim that, all appearances to the contrary, they do enjoy personal liberty and private property and are ruled by their own consent, and that to the extent they do not enjoy these social goods, it is so other members of society can enjoy greater shares of them. Illiberal proslavery arguments would, in contrast, deny the equal worth of the slaves, as members of an inferior race, gender, ethnicity, religion, or birthright, and claim that they are, therefore, properly enslaved to their superiors.
2. Louis Hartz, *The Liberal Tradition in America: An Interpretation of American Political Thought Since the Revolution* (New York: Harcourt, Brace, 1955), pt. 4. For Hartz's "paradigmatic" influence, see Daniel T. Rodgers, "Republicanism: The Career of a Concept," *Journal of American History* 79 (1992): 13–14.
3. Hartz, *Liberal Tradition*, pp. 18–19.
4. Hartz, *Liberal Tradition*, pp. 148, 172–73, 182–83.
5. Eugene D. Genovese, *The Political Economy of Slavery: Studies in the Economy and Society of the Slave South* (New York: Vintage, 1967), pp. 3–4, 13–14, 34–35; *The World the Slaveholders Made: Two Essays in Interpretation* (New York: Pantheon, 1969), pp. 123–24, 129–31, 165–66, 184–85, 237–38. Genovese's more recent work better fits the "multiple traditions" approach discussed below: Eugene D. Genovese, *The Slaveholders' Dilemma: Freedom and Progress in Southern Conservative Thought, 1820–1860* (Columbia: University of South Carolina Press, 1992); *The Southern Tradition: The Achievement and Limitations of an American Conservatism* (Cambridge, Mass.: Harvard University Press, 1994).
6. Rogers M. Smith, "Beyond Tocqueville, Myrdal, and Hartz: The Multiple Traditions in America," *American Political Science Review* 87 (1993): 549–66; *Civic Ideals: Conflicting Visions of Citizenship in U.S. History* (New Haven, Conn.: Yale University Press, 1997).
7. James Oakes, *Slavery and Freedom: An Interpretation of the Old South* (New York: Knopf, 1990), pp. xiii–xiv, 62–64, 75–77, 179–80. For earlier versions of this argument, see James Oakes, *The Ruling Race: A History of American Slaveholders* (New York: Knopf, 1982); "From Republicanism to Liberalism: Ideological Change and the Crisis of the Old South," *American Quarterly* 37 (1985): 551–71.

8. Kenneth S. Greenberg, "Revolutionary Ideology and the Proslavery Argument: The Abolition of Slavery in Antebellum South Carolina," *Journal of Southern History* 42 (1976): 365–84; *Masters and Statesmen: The Political Culture of American Slavery* (Baltimore: Johns Hopkins University Press, 1985), ch. 5.

9. In *The Shaping of American Liberalism*, I argue for understanding liberalism and republicanism not as opposites but as genus and species. David F. Ericson, *The Shaping of American Liberalism: The Debates over Ratification, Nullification, and Slavery* (Chicago: University of Chicago Press, 1993), chs. 1–2.

10. In using individual proslavery figures to understand the movement as a whole, the question of the proper sample arises. Obviously, if we analyze more religious figures, the movement appears more religious; if we analyze more racist figures, it appears more racist; if we analyze more liberal figures, it appears more liberal; and so forth. Smith fastens on the southern ethnologists to illustrate the racist tendencies of the movement (Smith, *Civic Ideals*, pp. 24–25, 203–5). This choice, however, is not a felicitous one. As William Stanton argues in his definitive study of scientific racism, the southern ethnologists were marginalized in the antebellum South because of clerical resistance to their "findings." Perhaps more significantly, Stanton notes that they did not themselves use their findings to defend slavery since they considered themselves objective scientists. William Stanton, *The Leopard's Spots: Scientific Attitudes Toward Race in America, 1815–1859* (Chicago: University of Chicago Press, 1960), pp. 149, 160, 192–94. Both Greenberg and George Fredrickson, moreover, argue that scientific racism was at least strongly contested by more liberal racial views in the antebellum South. See Greenberg, *Masters and Statesmen*, pp. 89–90; George M. Fredrickson, *The Black Image in the White Mind: The Debate on Afro-American Character and Destiny, 1817–1914* (Middletown, Conn.: Wesleyan University Press, 1987 [1971]), pp. 76–90. Of course, Smith claims one of my choices, George Fitzhugh, is not a felicitous one, either (Smith, *Civic Ideals*, pp. 24, 204). This claim, though, is based on the erroneous assumption that Fitzhugh, atypically, advocated "white slavery," when he did not. Based on my own reading of the proslavery literature, it seems to me that Fitzhugh was a fairly typical defender of slavery, more so than Josiah Nott.

11. To be perfectly clear, I am *not* denying the illiberal tendencies of the proslavery movement emphasized by other scholars; I am only repudiating their emphasis on those tendencies.

12. Hartz, though, is clear about his preference for single-factor explanations. Hartz, *Liberal Tradition*, p. 21. Cf. Smith, *Civic Ideals*, p. 39.

13. J. David Greenstone, *The Lincoln Persuasion: Remaking American Liberalism* (Princeton, N.J.: Princeton University Press, 1993), pp. 50–63. For earlier versions of this argument, see J. David Greenstone, "The Transient and Permanent in American Politics: Standards, Interests, and the Concept of the 'Public,'" in J. David Greenstone, ed., *Public Values and Private Power in American Politics* (Chicago: University of Chicago Press, 1982), pp. 3–33; "Political Culture and American Political Development: Liberty, Union, and the Liberal Bipolarity," *Studies in American Political Development* 1 (1986): 1–49. Greenstone identifies two forms of American liberalism: humanist liberalism and reform liberalism. While the claim is that proslavery thought fits under humanist liberalism

and antislavery thought under reform liberalism, Greenstone died before he could fully elaborate this claim or a correlative theory of civil war causation. Almost all the essays in this volume discuss Greenstone's "bipolarity" thesis; the Kahn essay does so most extensively.

14. This topic is beyond the scope of the present study. Yet it is clear that many of the arguments that were used to defend racial slavery before the Civil War were used after the war to defend continued racial oppression. See Fredrickson, *Black Image,* pp. 187–89; Genovese, *Southern Tradition,* pp. 7–8, 23. It is also clear that many of these arguments were, as Smith shows, ascriptive ones, but I, again, would place greater stress than he does on the degree to which these later movements also offered liberal arguments. Cf. Smith, *Civic Ideals,* ch. 11.

15. Proslavery and antislavery figures did respond to each other's arguments, even if, as seems likely, their target audiences were not each other but more moderate opinion in their respective sections of the country.

16. Greenstone, *Lincoln Persuasion,* pp. 42–50.

17. Hartz, *Liberal Tradition,* pp. 147–48, 153–54, 170, 180, 189–90. Cf. Gaines M. Foster, "Guilt over Slavery: A Historiographical Analysis," *Journal of Southern History* 56 (1990): 665–94; Charles Grier Sellers Jr., "The Travail of Slavery," in Charles Grier Sellers Jr., ed., *The Southerner as American* (New York: Dutton, 1966), pp. 40–71.

18. It is difficult to believe that many of the proslavery arguments I will be examining were not offered disingenuously, though I would not want to underestimate the all-too-human power of self-justification. The state of our private consciences is, in any case, unfathomable; the nature of our public arguments is not.

19. After all, as David Brion Davis has shown, the prima facie case was *for* slavery until the Enlightenment. David Brion Davis, *The Problem of Slavery in Western Culture* (Ithaca, N.Y.: Cornell University Press, 1966), esp. chs. 13–14; *The Problem of Slavery in the Age of Revolution* (Ithaca, N.Y.: Cornell University Press, 1975), pp. 39–49.

20. *Selections from the Letters and Speeches of the Hon. James H. Hammond of South Carolina* (New York: John F. Trow, 1866), p. 124 ("Two Letters on the Subject of Slavery in the United States, Addressed to Thomas Clarkson, Esq.," 1845). [Hereafter cited as Hammond, with page numbers from this source.]

21. Here I am excluding clerical defenses of slavery whose primary purpose was to win the battle of the scriptures with their antislavery counterparts. For example, cf. George D. Armstrong, *The Christian Doctrine of Slavery* (New York: Negro Universities Press, 1969 [1857]); Albert Barnes, *The Church and Slavery* (Detroit: Negro History Press, 1969 [1857]).

22. Albert Bushnell Hart and Edward Channing, eds., *American History Leaflets: Colonial and Constitutional* (New York: A. Lovell, 1893), no. 10 ("Governor McDuffie's Message on the Slavery Question," November 1835), pp. 4–5. [Hereafter cited as McDuffie, with page numbers from this source.]

23. For the Declaration's emerging exemplary status, see Philip F. Detweiler, "The Changing Reputation of the Declaration of Independence: The First Fifty Years," *William and Mary Quarterly,* 3d series, 19 (1962): 557–74.

24. E. N. Elliott, ed., *Cotton Is King, and Pro-slavery Arguments: Comprising the Writings of Hammond, Harper, Christy, Stringfellow, Hodge, Bledsoe, and*

Cartwright, on this Important subject (New York: Johnson, 1968 [1860]), p. 44 (hereafter cited by author of essay and page number). Ironically, proslavery figures argued that no one at the time thought blacks were included in the Declaration of Independence any more than they thought women were. See Chancellor Harper, *Cotton Is King*, p. 556.

25. See Christy, *Cotton Is King*, pp. 168, 198, 226.

26. However, as we shall see, proslavery figures did contend blacks were benefiting, morally and intellectually, from their enslavement to southern whites. Proslavery figures were also quick to point out that it was not an either/or choice between enslaving and educating blacks, though they claimed the abolitionists were forcing slaveholders into that position by "agitating" their slaves. See Hammond, pp. 142–43 ("Letters to Clarkson").

27. John C. Calhoun, *Works* (New York: D. Appleton, 1851–56), IV:508, 511 ("On the Oregon Bill," 27 June 1848).

28. Calhoun, *Works*, IV:511–12 ("On the Oregon Bill"). Cf. William W. Freehling, "Beyond Racial Limits: Paternalism over Whites in the Thought of Calhoun and Fitzhugh," in *The Reintegration of American History: Slavery and the Civil War* (New York: Oxford University Press, 1994), pp. 84, 93.

29. Proslavery figures commonly claimed the British government was responsible for instituting slavery in the United States. Similarly, they accused the British government of blocking colonial efforts to abolish the slave trade. See Albert Bledsoe, *Cotton Is King*, p. 381; Christy, *Cotton Is King*, p. 41.

30. Hammond, p. 119 ("Letters to Clarkson"). Cf. Oakes, *Slavery and Freedom*, pp. 71–72.

31. Bledsoe, *Cotton Is King*, pp. 314–16. Note that Bledsoe is not content to redefine slavery solely in terms of an exchange of liberty for subsistence. See below.

32. See Wilfred Carsel, "The Slaveholders' Indictment of Northern Wage Slavery," *Journal of Southern History* 6 (1940): 504–20; Greenberg, *Masters and Statesmen*, p. 94.

33. Bledsoe, *Cotton Is King*, p. 313.

34. See Greenberg, *Masters and Statesmen*, pp. 98–99.

35. Hammond, p. 319 ("Speech on the Admission of Kansas, Under the Lecompton Constitution, Delivered in the Senate of the United States," 4 March 1858).

36. Thomas Jefferson, *The Portable Jefferson*, edited by Merril D. Peterson (New York: Viking, 1975), p. 568 ("Letter to John Holmes," 22 April 1820).

37. See Larry E. Tise, *Proslavery: A History of the Defense of Slavery in America, 1701–1840* (Athens: University of Georgia Press, 1987), ch. 5.

38. *Portable Jefferson*, p. 568. The literature on Jefferson's views on race and slavery is profuse. Especially valuable are: William Cohen, "Thomas Jefferson and the Problem of Slavery," *Journal of American History* 56 (1969): 503–26; Paul Finkelman, *Slavery and the Founders: Race and Liberty in the Age of Jefferson* (Armonk, N.Y.: M. E. Sharpe, 1996), chs. 5–6; John C. Miller, *The Wolf by the Ears: Thomas Jefferson and Slavery* (New York: Free Press, 1977); Robert E. Shalhope, "Thomas Jefferson's Republicanism and Antebellum Southern Thought," *Journal of Southern History* 42 (1979): 3–26.

39. The African colonization movement was in full-scale retreat by the mid-1830s because of its meager results and also because of the vigorous attacks it had sus-

tained from both proslavery and antislavery figures. The movement, however, enjoyed a miniresurgence in the 1850s since it did seem like such a convenient (even if totally impractical) response to the dilemma of how to end slavery without committing oneself to creating a racially egalitarian society. See Fredrickson, *Black Image,* pp. 25–28, 43–46, 115–17, 147–49; P. J. Staudenraus, *The African Colonization Movement, 1816–1865* (New York: Octagon, 1980), chs. 14–18. But cf. William W. Freehling, "'Absurd' Issues and the Causes of the Civil War: Colonization as a Test Case," in *Reintegration of American History,* pp. 138–57.

40. See Harper, *Cotton Is King,* pp. 616–20; McDuffie, pp. 7–10.
41. The defenders of slavery were certain that even if emancipation went relatively smoothly, the freed slaves would still suffer from intense racial discrimination, as in the American North. See Hammond, p. 40 ("On the Justice of Receiving Petitions for the Abolition of Slavery in the District of Columbia," 1 February 1836).
42. Daniel Mallory, ed., *The Life and Speeches of the Hon. Henry Clay* (New York: Van Ambringe and Bixby, 1844), II:375 ("Petition for the Abolition of Slavery," 7 February 1839).
43. See Christy, *Cotton Is King,* pp. 216–21.
44. McDuffie, pp. 9–10. This version of the argument has been labeled the "*Herrenvolk* democracy" argument: "inferior-race" slavery facilitates "superior-race" democracy. See Richard J. Ellis, "Legitimating Slavery in the Old South: The Effect of Political Institutions on Ideology," *Studies in American Political Development* 5 (1991): 342–45; Fredrickson, *Black Image,* pp. 61–64.
45. McDuffie, p. 10.
46. Harper, *Cotton Is King,* p. 625.
47. See Fredrickson, *Black Image,* chs. 2–5; Leon F. Litwack, *North of Slavery: The Negro in the Free States, 1790–1860* (Chicago: University of Chicago Press, 1961), chs. 3–6.
48. See Hans Kohn, *American Nationalism: An Interpretative Essay* (New York: Macmillan, 1957), esp. ch. 3; Frederick Merk, *Manifest Destiny and Mission in American History: A Reinterpretation* (New York: Random House, 1963), chs. 1–2; Paul C. Nagel, *One Nation Indivisible: The Union in American Thought* (New York: Oxford University Press, 1964), esp. chs. 4–5; Ernest Lee Tuveson, *Redeemer Nation: The Idea of America's Millennial Role* (Chicago: University of Chicago Press, 1968), ch. 3.
49. See Amos A. Phelps, *Lectures on Slavery and Its Remedies* (Boston: New England Anti-Slavery Society, 1834), p. 23; Louis Ruchames, ed., *The Abolitionists: A Collection of Their Writings* (New York: Capricorn, 1964), p. 83 ("Declaration of Sentiments of the American Anti-Slavery Society," December 1833); John Greenleaf Whittier, *The Prose Works* (Boston: Houghton Mifflin, 1892), III:33 ("Justice and Expediency: or, Slavery Considered with a View to Its Rightful and Effectual Remedy, Abolition," 1833).
50. McDuffie, p. 8. Edmund Morgan has explored this historical "paradox." See Edmund S. Morgan, "Slavery and Freedom: The American Paradox," *Journal of American History* 59 (1972): 5–29; *American Slavery, American Freedom: The Ordeal of Colonial Virginia* (New York: Norton, 1975).

51. McDuffie, p. 10.
52. See Genovese, *Slaveholders' Dilemma,* pp. 10–13; Bertram Wyatt-Brown, "From Piety to Fantasy: Proslavery's Troubled Evolution," in *Yankee Saints and Southern Sinners* (Baton Rouge: Louisiana State University Press, 1985), pp. 156, 167.
53. Harper, *Cotton Is King,* p. 618; Hammond, p. 172 ("Letters to Clarkson").
54. Calhoun, *Works,* III:179 ("Remarks Made During the Debate on His Resolutions, in Respect to the Rights of the States and the Abolition of Slavery," 10 January 1838).
55. Calhoun, *Works,* II:629 ("On the Reception of Abolition Petitions," 6 February 1837).
56. See Greenberg, *Masters and Statesmen,* pp. 119, 121, 123; Tise, *Proslavery,* pp. 360–62.
57. See Christy, *Cotton Is King,* pp. 129, 218.
58. *The Papers of James Henry Hammond* (Washington, D.C.: Library of Congress, 1823–1875), reel 14 (untitled speech, 8 November 1860), p. 27.
59. I will refer to the version of Dew's essay reprinted in *The Pro-Slavery Argument; as Maintained by the Most Distinguished Writers of the Southern States, Containing the Several Essays, on the Subject, of Chancellor Harper, Governor Hammond, Dr. Simms, and Professor Dew* (New York: Negro Universities Press, 1968 [1852]), pp. 287–490. (Dew's essay was originally published as a separate pamphlet in late 1832.) For more contemporary reviews of the Virginia debate, see Alison Goodyear Freehling, *Drift Toward Dissolution: The Slavery Debate of 1831–1832* (Baton Rouge: Louisiana State University Press, 1982), ch. 5; Joseph Clarke Robert, *The Road to Monticello: A Study of the Virginia Slavery Debate of 1832* (New York: AMS Press, 1971 [1941]), ch. 3. The debate was instigated by Thomas Jefferson Randolph's proposal that the state adopt a postnati emancipation scheme patterned after the one his grandfather, Thomas Jefferson, had sketched in the 1780s but never proposed. The ensuing debate largely, though not solely, split the legislature along geographic lines between eastern, slaveholding Virginia and western, nonslaveholding Virginia, a split that eventually led to separate statehood for West Virginia. The debate ended with a token victory for the antislavery legislators—a resolution declaring slavery an evil institution—but with the defeat of all their specific proposals. A similar debate never again took place in Virginia or any other slave state. Dew, a professor of political economy and law at the College of William and Mary, wrote a critical review of the debate at the suggestion of Governor John Floyd. His review was clearly intended for a Virginia audience, to try to reunify the state behind slavery. See Dickson D. Bruce Jr., *The Rhetoric of Conservatism: The Virginia Convention of 1829–1830 and the Conservative Tradition in the South* (San Marino, Calif.: Huntington Library, 1982), p. 187; Fredrickson, *Black Image,* p. 44; Kenneth M. Stampp, "An Analysis of T. R. Dew's *Review of the Debate in the Virginia Legislature," Journal of Negro History* 27 (1942): 381–82; Tise, *Proslavery,* p. 71.
60. Not surprisingly, then, scholars seem divided on the question of whether Dew was "necessary-evil" or "positive-good." Cf. Bruce, *Rhetoric of Conservatism,*

pp. 179–80; Fredrickson, *Black Image,* pp. 44–46; A. G. Freehling, *Drift Toward Dissolution,* pp. xii–xiii, 203; Ralph E. Morrow, "The Proslavery Argument Revisited," *Mississippi Valley Historical Review* 48 (1961): 82; Robert, *Road to Monticello,* pp. v, 46; Stampp, *"Analysis of Dew's Review,"* pp. 382–83; Tise, *Proslavery,* pp. 71–72, 288–89.

61. The traditional explanation of this shift is that it was a response to the rise of Garrison abolitionism in the North. The problem with this explanation is that the "effect" seems to have preceded the "cause." (As we will see, Dew himself appears unaware of the Garrison abolitionists.) A more likely explanation is that the shift was part of an elite attempt to stifle internal dissent against slavery as southern political and intellectual leaders increasingly identified the institution with an embattled southern way of life. Cf. Fredrickson, *Black Image,* pp. 43, 48; William B. Hesseltine "Some New Aspects of the Proslavery Argument," in Richard N. Current, ed., *Sections and Politics: Selected Essays by William B. Hesseltine,* (Madison: State Historical Society of Wisconsin, 1968), p. 71; Morrow, "Proslavery Argument Revisited," p. 94; Kenneth M. Stampp, "The Fate of the Southern Antislavery Movement," *Journal of Negro History* 28 (1943): pp. 13–14; Tise, *Proslavery,* pp. 286, 308.

62. Dew even thinks the northern abolitionists agree that emancipation requires removals (p. 421), seemingly unaware of the Garrison abolitionists, who advocated not only emancipation without removals but immediate emancipation. (It would not have been surprising if he had been unaware of the Garrisonians when he wrote his essay, given that they were only beginning to organize and publish antislavery tracts in 1832.) Though his reference for "abolitionists" in the essay is the Virginia legislators who had proposed various emancipation schemes during the recent legislative debate, today we would say, as the Garrisonians did, that they were not really abolitionists but colonizationists. See Lydia Maria Child, *An Appeal in Favor of [That Class of] Americans Called Africans* (New York: Arno, 1968 [1833]), p. 101. Indeed, these legislators sought, with temporary success the following year, state funding for colonizing free blacks in Africa. Both William Jenkins and Tise argue that Dew's primary target was the colonization movement. They also argue that his essay paralleled Garrison's *Thoughts on African Colonization* (Boston: Garrison and Knapp, 1832) in undercutting the movement in the United States. William Sumner Jenkins, *Pro-Slavery Thought in the Old South* (Gloucester, Mass.: Peter Smith, 1960 [1935]), pp. 87–88; Tise, *Proslavery,* pp. 70, 72–73.

63. Dew actually considers two other cost-shifting measures—reopening the slave trade with Latin America (p. 379) and securing federal subsidies for African colonization (pp. 413–14, 418–20)—but he rejects both as morally and/or politically indefensible.

64. Dew believes the Southampton (Nat Turner) rebellion precipitated the legislative debate (pp. 289–90). He also believes emancipation without removals in Virginia would encourage white flight from the state because of the increased threat of racial violence (p. 443). This eventuality would, of course, separate the two races in Virginia, or rather outside it, but hardly in a way Dew could have found acceptable.

65. Dew alleges such a compulsory labor system has already been instituted in Haiti (pp. 441–42).

66. Dew claims that many of the slaves themselves know they are better off than free blacks (p. 428); that slaves in border areas attempt to escape less often than slaves further south because they are better acquainted with the wretched conditions of free blacks in the North (p. 428); and that West Indian slaves often reject offers of freedom from their masters and, when emancipated, welcome a return to slavery (pp. 424, 426–28, 437).

67. Dew does not even discuss the ability of the slaves to participate in their own *collective* self-government, as if that possibility were totally inconceivable to him.

68. Dew, indeed, offers internal improvements as a general panacea for all Virginia's problems, including the deep geographic divisions exposed by the recent legislative debate (pp. 479–80). His proposal also suggests how he was not a traditional southern sectionalist, because, at least on the state level, he favors more, not less, government (p. 478), and because he envisions Virginia becoming a more urban and commercial state, more like the states to its north than to its south (pp. 478–79). The second count follows from his climatological theory: Virginia may well be too far north to sustain a prosperous slave economy (p. 484). Tise stresses how proslavery figures, in general, were not traditional southern sectionalists. Tise, *Proslavery,* pp. 71–72, 291, 323, 327–28, 333–35.

69. Cf. A. G. Freehling, *Drift Toward Dissolution,* pp. 206–7.

70. In these passages, Dew often conflates the two ideas that the African slaves are not ready for freedom (as if someday they might be) and that they are naturally unsuited for freedom (because they belong to an inferior race). As already suggested, this equivocation was typical of the defenders of slavery.

71. See pp. 351, 354, 421. Dew had also earlier argued that the British government was responsible for blocking Virginia's efforts to abolish the slave trade prior to independence (pp. 352–53).

72. See *Portable Jefferson,* pp. 214–15.

73. On this point, Dew offers an implicit critique of northerners for their narrowly utilitarian values (pp. 455–56). Dew appears ambivalent toward the North. While he is a defender of southern slavery, he also admires northern progress (pp. 429, 446–47, 478–79). Cf. Genovese, *Slaveholders' Dilemma,* pp. 14–18.

74. At one point, Dew refers to the northern states as "what are called free States" (p. 466).

75. This passage is the same one McDuffie would quote in his famous gubernatorial message.

76. Here Dew presents his version of the "*Herrenvolk* democracy" argument.

77. Dew calculates that only three slave revolts have been attempted in the two hundred years of the existence of southern slavery: one in Virginia (Nat Turner, 1831); one in South Carolina (Denmark Vesey, 1822); and (perhaps) one in Louisiana (a reference to the 1811 slave uprising near New Orleans?) (p. 471). Cf. Herbert Aptheker, *American Negro Slave Revolts* (New York: International Publishers, 1963 [1943]), pp. 249–51, 268–72, 293–306.

78. Dew primarily has the protective tariff in mind as a federal policy that he thinks unjustly (and unconstitutionally) benefits the North at the expense of the South (pp. 486–89).

79. As already noted, Dew admits Virginia may be too far north to enjoy the optimal conditions for slave labor.

80. Native-born slaves were freed every seventh year, but Dew observes that they could always choose to remain slaves (p. 318). He also observes that in densely populated areas where food is scarce, such as in China and India, people still sell themselves into slavery (pp. 318–19).

81. These natural-law theorists—Hugo Grotius, Thomas Rutherforth, Cornelis van Bynkershoek, and Emmerich de Vattel, as well as Locke—specify such circumstances as that the war is a just one and that the captives have committed acts for which they may be justly executed.

82. Dew, in fact, believes the opposite, that southern slavery began in the injustices of the African slave trade (pp. 345–48). However, his claim that southerners were not themselves responsible for those original injustices becomes important here.

83. Dew notes that the status of slave has historically been an extremely common one (pp. 294–95) and that statuses analogous to it remain so (pp. 295–96). He later pursues the most prominent of these analogues, that of serfdom (pp. 437–40).

84. Part of Dew's point is that the end of serfdom in Poland did not end the dependent relations between the parties involved. See pp. 437–39.

85. Dew considers these legislators irresponsible for even broaching the slavery issue (p. 293).

86. All my references to *Cannibals All* will be from George Fitzhugh, *Cannibals All! or, Slaves Without Masters* (Cambridge, Mass.: Belknap, 1960 [1857]). Fitzhugh was a self-educated Virginian who became a small slaveholder through marriage and assumed the role of proslavery polemicist rather late in life. He was an avid reader of abolitionist tracts and British social criticism and liberally quoted from those sources in his own writings. Beginning in the late 1840s, he published a torrent of proslavery essays in several major Virginia newspapers and Southern literary journals. His two books, *Cannibals All* and *Sociology for the South, or the Failure of Free Society* (New York: Burt Franklin, 1965 [1854]), heavily borrowed from what he and others had written elsewhere, though *Cannibals All* is the more original and maturer work. Fitzhugh sought a broader audience than Dew had. He wanted the northern abolitionists to personally respond to his arguments, even wrote them letters to that effect, and was disappointed when they did not. In 1855 he took the unusual step of traveling north to visit one leading abolitionist, Gerrit Smith (a distant cousin), and to speak jointly with another, Wendell Phillips. See pp. 9–10, 97–106, 257–59.

87. Fitzhugh's two-pronged defense of southern slavery has led to three confusions in the secondary literature. First, Fitzhugh does favor stronger government, even a stronger federal government (pp. 247–48). Though he never specifies exactly what he has in mind, it seems safe to assume that he, like Dew, was thinking of internal improvements and other policies that would "thicken" American society. His dedication of *Cannibals All* to Governor Henry Wise lauds Wise's pursuit of internal improvements on the state level (p. 3), something Dew had advocated more than twenty years before. While both Fitzhugh and Dew are good examples of defenders of slavery who were not traditional southern sec-

tionalists, Freehling and Genovese clearly overstate the case in referring to Fitzhugh as a "statist." W. W. Freehling, "Beyond Racial Limits," p. 102; Genovese, *Slaveholders' Dilemma*, p. 26. Second, Fitzhugh does suggest the possibility of white or working-class slavery in *Cannibals All.* He quotes, at length, two articles from British journals on this possibility. However, the first article, from *Jerrod's Magazine,* proposes working-class slavery with tongue firmly in cheek (pp. 153–57), and the second, from the *Edinburgh Review,* only broaches the idea that British workers might be better off as slaves without actually proposing their enslavement (pp. 159–64). Similarly, Fitzhugh's 1858 essay "Origin of Civilization," which is often cited in this context, asserts that whites would make (and have, in the past, made) better slaves than blacks without offering any concrete proposal to that effect. George Fitzhugh, "Origin of Civilization—What Is Property?—Which Is the Best Slave Race?" *DeBow's Review* 25 (1858): 662–63. Cf. George Fitzhugh, "Southern Thought," *DeBow's Review* 23 (1857): 338–39, 347–48; "The White and Black Races of Men," *DeBow's Review* 30 (1861): 448–49, 454. It seems safe to conclude that for Fitzhugh, as in the articles he quotes, the idea of white slavery was rhetorical, not, as several scholars have suggested, something he seriously intended. See Ellis, "Legitimating Slavery," p. 349; Fredrickson, *Black Image,* pp. 59–60; Jenkins, *Pro-Slavery Thought,* p. 304; Smith, *Civic Ideals,* pp. 24, 205. Third, Fitzhugh does make some strikingly illiberal pronouncements in *Cannibals All.* Not surprisingly, then, Hartz singles out Fitzhugh as the exemplary proslavery polemicist who abandoned liberalism for the "feudal dream"; Harvey Wish, in his biography of Fitzhugh, and C. Vann Woodward, in his critical introduction to the reprint of *Cannibals All,* also interpret Fitzhugh as choosing "Filmer over Locke"; and even scholars who are critical of Hartz and view the antebellum South as torn between slavery and liberalism place Fitzhugh on the illiberal side of that divide. See Genovese, *World the Slaveholders Made,* pp. 123–24, 127, 129–31, 157–58; Hartz, *Liberal Tradition,* pp. 145–46, 157, 164–65, 171, 182–83; Oakes, *Slavery and Freedom,* pp. 179–80; Harvey Wish, *George Fitzhugh: Propagandist of the Old South* (Gloucester, Mass.: Peter Smith, 1962 [1943]), pp. vii–viii, 32, 224, 301–3; C. Vann Woodward, editor's introduction to *Cannibals All,* pp. viii–xi, xix–xx, xxxi, xxxiv–v, xxxviii. Dispelling this third confusion is the main purpose of this section of the essay—not to deny Fitzhugh's illiberal pronouncements but to demonstrate the primacy of his liberal arguments.

88. Though Fitzhugh's timing of the South's shift from "necessary evil" to "positive good" seems in error, the shift was not necessarily a clean one. As we shall see, even his own defense of slavery is not purely positive-good.

89. Fitzhugh does assume Hobbes would agree with his "cannibals all" premise (pp. 215, 218–19). He does not, however, discuss the specifics of Hobbes's solution to the political problems that premise raises, where some points of disagreement would undoubtedly emerge.

90. Like Dew, Fitzhugh refers to free society as "what is falsely called Free Society" (p. 72). He also refers to the "so-called liberty and equality" in which free societies place men (p. 36) and contends that in free societies "miscalled freemen" perform the same offices slaves perform in slave societies (p. 221).

91. Dew made this same argument.

92. In chapter 10 of *Cannibals All* ("Our Best Witnesses and Masters in the Art of War"), Fitzhugh quotes the abolitionists, ad nauseam, on the failures of free society. However, even as the abolitionists criticized northern free society, they strongly defended it against southern slave society. See Jonathan A. Glickstein, "'Poverty Is Not Slavery': American Abolitionists and the Competitive Labor Market," in Lewis Perry and Michael Fellman, eds., *Antislavery Reconsidered: New Perspectives on the Abolitionists* (Baton Rouge: Louisiana State University Press, 1979), pp. 195–218; Daniel J. McInerney, "'A State of Commerce': Market Power and Slave Power in Abolitionist Political Economy," *Civil War History* 37 (1991): 101–19; Ronald G. Walters, *The Antislavery Appeal: American Abolitionism after 1830* (New York: Norton, 1978), ch. 7.

93. Here Fitzhugh also seeks to debunk the abolitionists as racists. Cf. Lawrence J. Friedman, *Gregarious Saints: Self and Community in American Abolitionism, 1830–1870* (Cambridge: Cambridge University Press, 1982), ch. 6; William Pease and Jane H. Pease, "Antislavery Ambivalence: Immediatism, Expediency, Race," *American Quarterly* 17 (1965): 682–95.

94. However, as we have seen, Fitzhugh identifies many analogues to slavery. He certainly never suggests that nations that have abolished serfdom should reinstitute it. (Nor did Dew.) Fitzhugh's defense of serfdom is evidence that he believed protective institutions can increase the sphere of personal liberty, not that he believed in the "feudal dream."

95. In addition, Fitzhugh claims British workers are worse off than the serfs of eastern Europe and central Asia (pp. 79–80); cites the *Edinburgh Review* to the effect that Russian serfs would be worse off if freed (p. 161); contends West Indian slaves, prior to emancipation, were better off than British workers (pp. 24–25); quotes the *London Globe* to the effect that emancipation has significantly worsened the condition of West Indian workers (pp. 184–85); and asserts West Indian workers were formerly freer as slaves than they are currently as free persons (p. 185).

96. Fitzhugh also argues that in this sense slaves are freer than their masters (pp. 16, 18, 80–81, 204, 235).

97. See Greenberg, *Masters and Statesmen*, pp. 90, 101–2.

98. In Fitzhugh's view, Locke and the other modern philosophers he criticizes in chapter 7 of *Cannibals All* ("Liberty and Slavery") would also be guilty of this "oversight." This chapter should be read as an attack on abstract philosophy, not as a rejection of liberal principles. The central theme of the chapter reflects the central theme of the book: The attempts Blackstone, Montesquieu, and Paley made to define "liberty" and "slavery" really show, *sub voce*, how those two statuses merge into one another.

99. Again, Fitzhugh does not make clear what "more of protection" entails, though he does make clear that it means more than more government (pp. 247–48). He attributes the North's ability to sustain itself so far to the way the frontier acts as a safety valve for its discontents but that, of course, is not a long-term solution (pp. 11, 40, 199, 255, 259).

100. Fitzhugh contends racial prejudice also contributes to the present-day animus against racial slavery: Whites hate black slavery because they hate blacks. He

thus ascribes northern antislavery sentiments to the fact that racial prejudice is stronger in the North than in the South (p. 201). (This claim is certainly more credible than the similar claim he leveled against the abolitionists in trying to debunk their antislavery sentiments.) He ascribes the cruelty of West Indian slavery to the fact that in the West Indies, unlike in the American South, most of the slaves were "unseasoned" (pp. 79, 200). While Fitzhugh, like Dew, refuses to defend the African slave trade in *Cannibals All*, he was to endorse southern efforts to revive the trade within a year of completing the book. Cf. George Fitzhugh, "The Conservative Principle, or, Social Evils and Their Remedies; Part II—The Slave Trade," *DeBow's Review* 22 (1857): 449–62; "The White Slave Trade," *DeBow's Review* 24 (1858): 273.

101. Fitzhugh's reference for white "slaves" is the serfs of eastern Europe and central Asia (p. 200).

102. Note how Fitzhugh blurs the source of racial inequality in this passage. See below.

103. Fitzhugh clearly recognizes this conclusion as a generalization: Not all blacks are, or should be, slaves, and not all whites are, or should be, free persons. He does nonetheless make a fairly sweeping racial generalization about who is best suited to which status.

104. Fitzhugh's only reference to the possibility of abolishing southern slavery is to say that it would be "a curse" to the slaves and those around them (p. 199). He does, however, twice refer to the (according to him) disastrous consequences of emancipation in the British West Indies (pp. 24–25, 184-85).

105. In a private letter of 11 April 1855 to his friend and fellow proslavery polemicist, George Frederick Holmes, Fitzhugh had confessed: "I assure you Sir, I see great evils in slavery, but in a controversial work, I ought not to admit them" (quoted in W. W. Freehling, "Beyond Racial Limits," p. 102). Such confessions are precisely what we would expect if a dynamic toward positive-good defenses of slavery had existed in the antebellum South.

106. Fitzhugh, though, does not focus his proslavery consequentialism totally on nonslaveholding whites. He also claims broader benefits for whites, blacks, the North, the South, and the world as a whole (pp. 201–2, 221, 232).

107. See Child, *Appeal*, p. 81; John W. Blassingame, ed., *The Frederick Douglass Papers, Series One: Speeches, Debates, and Interviews* (New Haven, Conn.: Yale University Press, 1979–82), II:289 ("Slavery's Northern Bulwarks," 12 June 1851); Wendell Phillips, *Speeches, Lectures, and Letters* (Boston: Lee and Shepard, 1891 [1863]), I:82 ("Simms Anniversary," 12 April 1852).

108. I take this untenability to be the reference for Fitzhugh's statement that "no sane man in America proposes to makes slaves of white men" (quoted in W. W. Freehling, "Beyond Racial Limits," p. 100, from *Richmond Enquirer, 12* September 1856).

109. Fitzhugh even suggests that this philosophical struggle has been a long-standing partisan struggle more than a sectional one (pp. 255–56); that it will ultimately be settled in the North rather than between the North and the South (p. 254); and that the loss of the frontier will mandate the victory of the "more government" party, now the Democratic Party (pp. 30, 255).

110. Fitzhugh's own commitment to the union seems evident. In praising Governor Wise in the dedication as someone who loves both his state and the union (p. 3), Fitzhugh was undoubtedly also speaking of himself. Later, he accuses the abolitionists of seeking to "involv[e] us in civil and fraticidal war" (p. 232). He also claims Virginia intends to cling to the union "as long as honor permits" because it "cannot bear the thought of" disunion (p. 234). Fitzhugh did not support secession until *after* Lincoln's election; committed southern secessionists had been working assiduously to precipitate the event throughout the year. Cf. Fitzhugh, "Disunion Within the Union," *DeBow's Review* 28 (1860): 1–7; "The Message, the Constitution, and the Times," *DeBow's Review* 30 (1861): 162–63.

111. See W. W. Freehling, "Beyond Racial Limits," pp. 97–100.

112. Rogers Smith exemplifies this tendency. The Horton essay in this volume offers a related critique.

113. Abraham Lincoln, *The Collected Works of Abraham Lincoln,* edited by Roy P. Basler (New Brunswick, N.J.: Rutgers University Press, 1953), VII:301–2 ("Address at a Sanitary Fair, Baltimore, Maryland," 18 April 1864).

114. Lincoln, *Works,* VII:302. Lincoln, though, makes clear that the proslavery definition has some currency in the North. He also makes clear that the blackness of the sheep in this case is significant.

Chapter 5

1. Harvey C. Mansfield Jr., *The Spirit of Liberalism* (Cambridge, Mass.: Harvard University Press, 1978), p. 16.

2. J. David Greenstone, *The Lincoln Persuasion: Remaking American Liberalism* (Princeton, N.J.: Princeton University Press, 1993), p. 53.

3. Carol Horton, "Liberal Equality and the Civic Subject: Identity and Citizenship in Reconstruction America," p. 118 in this volume.

4. Consideration of the question of bipolarity in particular addresses issues that are current in American political thought, for other "bipolarity" models of American liberalism—such as that which turns on the perceived defects of the self-regarding individualism of classical liberalism and a liberalism grounded either in moral principles or a notion of community—are not only the subject of much debate in the academy but find expression in public discourse in the multiple calls for a re-creation of community in American life.

5. Frederick Douglass, *The Frederick Douglass Papers, Series One: Speeches, Debates and Interviews,* edited by John W. Blassingame (New Haven, Conn.: Yale University Press, 1982), II:502.

6. Wilson Jeremiah Moses, *The Golden Age of Black Nationalism, 1850–1925* (New York: Oxford University Press, 1978), p. 97.

7. *Frederick Douglass Papers,* II:502.

8. *Frederick Douglass Papers,* II:504.

9. *Frederick Douglass Papers,* II:514–15.

10. *Frederick Douglass Papers,* II:517.

11. The link between Douglass's increasing awareness of speech (and hence literacy) and his sense of selfhood has a true career. Recent and impressive work on Douglass's multiple autobiographies has shown the extent to which Douglass rewrote episodes of his life in order to present them with new meaning. See Eric J. Sundquist, "Frederick Douglass: Literacy and Paternalism," in William L. Andrews, ed., *Critical Essays on Frederick Douglass* (Boston: G. K. Hall, 1991), p. 124; see also David Leverenz, "Frederick Douglass' Self-Refashioning," *Criticism* 29 (1987): 341–70; Houston A. Baker Jr., "Autobiographical Acts and the Voice of the Southern Slave," in Charles T. Davis and Henry Louis Gates Jr., eds., *The Slave's Narrative* (New York: Oxford University Press, 1985); John W. Blassingame, "Introduction to Series One," *Frederick Douglass Papers*, I:xxi–lxix.

12. *Frederick Douglass Papers*, V:237–38. Douglass went on to characterize the consequence of such efforts in the following manner: "[A]nd we shall raise up powerful friends who shall stand by us in our struggle for an equal chance in the race of life. The white people of this country are asleep, but not dead" (p. 238).

13. *Frederick Douglass Papers*, V:555. Douglass goes on in the following paragraph to scorn an unthinking reliance upon religion in place of work: "Faith, in the absence of work, seems to be worth little, if anything.... In the old slave times colored ministers were somewhat remarkable for the fervor with which they prayed for knowledge, but it did not appear that they were remarkable for any wonderful success. In fact, they who prayed loudest seemed to get least. They thought if they opened their mouths they would be filled. The result was an abundance of sound with a great destitution of sense."

14. *Frederick Douglass Papers*, IV:625.

15. *Frederick Douglass Papers*, V:74. Nonetheless, Douglass was nothing if not realistic about the situation of the black individual in America and the strategy of race-based associations. In an address delivered at the opening of the Douglass Institute in Baltimore in 1865, Douglass said: "I once flattered myself that the day had happily gone by when it could be necessary for colored people in this country to combine and act together as a separate class, and in any representative character whatsoever. I would have had them infuse themselves and their works into all the political, intellectual, artistical and mechanical activities and combinations of their white fellow countrymen.... I may say that I still hold this opinion in a modified degree. The latent contempt and prejudice towards our race, which recent political doctrines with reference to our future in this country have developed, the persistent determination of the present Executive of the nation, and also the apparent determination of a portion of the people to hold and treat us in a degraded relation, not only justify for the present such associate effort on our part, but make it eminently necessary." See *Frederick Douglass Papers*, IV:90–91. See also Douglass's defense of a national convention of blacks in 1883: "No reasonable man will ever object to white men holding conventions in their own interests, when they are once in our condition and we in theirs, when they are the oppressed and we the oppresors. In point of fact, however, white men are already in convention against us in various ways and at many points. The practical construction of American life is a convention against us." See *Frederick Douglass Papers*, V:91.

16. *Frederick Douglass Papers,* V:620.
17. *Frederick Douglass Papers,* V:622.
18. *Frederick Douglass Papers,* V:622.
19. *Frederick Douglass Papers,* IV:42.
20. Frederick Douglass, *Life and Times of Frederick Douglass* (New York: Macmillan, 1962 [1892]), p. 210. Emphasis in the original.
21. *Frederick Douglass Papers,* II:364.
22. *Frederick Douglass Papers,* V:22.
23. *Frederick Douglass Papers,* V:604.
24. *Frederick Douglass Papers,* V:444.
25. Daniel Walker Howe, *The Political Culture of the American Whigs* (Chicago: University of Chicago Press, 1979), and his *Making the American Self: Jonathan Edwards to Abraham Lincoln* (Cambridge, Mass.: Harvard University Press, 1997); Lawrence Frederick Kohl, *The Politics of Individualism: Parties and American Character in the Jacksonian Era* (New York: Oxford University Press, 1989).
26. Greenstone, *Lincoln Persuasion,* p. 190.
27. Howe, *Making the American Self,* pp. 155–56.
28. Howe, *Making the American Self,* p. 140.
29. See the discussion of the National Republicans and party ideology in John Gerring, "Party Ideology in America: The National Republican Chapter, 1828–1924," *Studies in American Political Development* 11 (1997): 44–108, esp. pp. 94–96.
30. W. E. B. DuBois, *The Souls of Black Folk* (New York: New American Library, 1969), pp. 44–45.
31. W. E. B. DuBois, *Dusk of Dawn: An Essay Toward an Autobiography of a Race Concept* (New York: Schocken Books, 1968 [1940]), p. 131.
32. DuBois, *Dusk of Dawn,* p. 132.
33. Slavenka Drakulic´, "Overcome by Nationhood," in *The Balkan Express: Fragments from the Other Side of War* (New York: Norton, 1993), p. 51.
34. "The Conservation of Races," in *W. E. B. DuBois: Writings,* edited by Nathan Huggins (New York: Library of America, 1986), pp. 823–24. Emphasis in the original.
35. DuBois, *Souls,* p. 119.
36. DuBois, *Souls,* p. 138.
37. DuBois, *Dusk of Dawn,* p. 7.
38. DuBois, *Souls,* p. 278.
39. DuBois, *Dusk of Dawn,* p. 132.
40. DuBois, *Dusk of Dawn,* p. 137.
41. DuBois, *Dusk of Dawn,* pp. 208f.
42. DuBois, *Dusk of Dawn,* pp. 288f.
43. For example, DuBois, *Dusk of Dawn,* pp. 275–81.
44. DuBois, *Dusk of Dawn,* p. 311.
45. DuBois, *Dusk of Dawn,* pp. 130–31.
46. The source of that tension was the question whether black men would get the vote before, or at the same time as, white women. Susan B. Anthony, for example, said at a meeting of the American Equal Rights Association, founded in

1866, that she "would sooner cut off my right hand than ask the ballot for the black man and not for woman." Quoted in William S. McFeely, *Frederick Douglass* (New York: Norton, 1991), p. 266. For a brief summary of the height of the tension between Douglass and the suffragists, see McFeely, *Frederick Douglass,* pp. 265–69.

47. *Frederick Douglass Papers,* V:383. See also *Frederick Douglass Papers,* V:350 ("Give Women Fair Play," March 1888).

48. *Frederick Douglass Papers,* V:255.

49. *Frederick Douglass Papers,* V:255 ("Who and What Is Woman?," 24 May 1886).

50. W. E. B. DuBois, *Darkwater: Voices from Within the Veil,* in *The Oxford W. E. B. DuBois Reader,* edited by Eric Sundquist (New York: Oxford University Press, 1996), p. 565.

51. DuBois, *Darkwater,* pp. 568–69.

52. DuBois, *Darkwater,* p. 573.

53. The "guiding principle" that emerges from Douglass's and DuBois's thought bears important similarities to the "principle of autonomy" that David Held sets out in his *Models of Democracy.* See David Held, *Models of Democracy,* 2d ed. (Oxford: Polity Press, 1996), esp. ch. 9.

54. DuBois, *Darkwater,* p. 500.

55. Rogers M. Smith, "Beyond Tocqueville, Myrdal, and Hartz: The Multiple Traditions in America," *American Political Science Review* 87 (1993): 549. See also Rogers M. Smith, *Civic Ideals: Conflicting Visions of Citizenship in U.S. History* (New Haven, Conn.: Yale University Press, 1997).

C h a p t e r   6

Earlier versions of this paper were presented at the 1996 annual meeting of the American Political Science Association, San Francisco, California, and at the conference "The Liberal Tradition in American Politics: Consensus, Polarity, or Multiple Traditions," University of Chicago, November 1996. Thanks to David Ericson and Rick Valelly for helpful comments and suggestions.

1. This is the working definition of liberalism provided in J. David Greenstone, *The Lincoln Persuasion: Remaking American Liberalism* (Princeton, N.J.: Princeton University Press, 1993). The definition employed in this paper is essentially similar, although it additionally assumes that liberals must be committed to a market economy, the rule of law, and the ethical primacy of liberty and individualism in the public realm.

2. Greenstone, *Lincoln Persuasion,* introduction, ch. 2.

3. This argument was first set forth in Rogers M. Smith, "Beyond Tocqueville, Myrdal, and Hartz: The Multiple Traditions in America," *American Political Science Review* 87 (1993): 549–66, and is fully developed in Smith, *Civic Ideals: Conflicting Visions of Citizenship in U.S. History* (New Haven, Conn.: Yale University Press, 1997).

4. To be clear, I am not arguing that racism (or sexism, or nativism) is foundational or in any sense indispensable to liberalism. Rather, I am arguing that because lib-

eralism is a highly plastic discourse, it is fully capable of assimilating highly disparate constructions of the individual into its basic schema—including those that attach a clear importance to his or her social location in a particular racial, gender, or national group.

5. Although I do not develop the case here, I believe that a theoretically informed historical or contextual approach is by far the best means of studying liberal politics, which is all too commonly presented in a highly idealized and abstract manner. See Smith, *Civic Ideals,* pp. 11–12, for a fuller elaboration of an essentially similar position.

6. Left-leaning academics, for example, routinely dismiss liberalism as necessarily committed to racial, gender, and class oppression. Meanwhile, conservative academics and pundits attack much of contemporary feminism, multiculturalism, and so forth as inherently illiberal and socially destructive.

7. In formulating this case study, I am deeply indebted to the excellent secondary literature on postemancipation societies, particularly Eric Foner's work on the United States. See, in particular, Foner, *Reconstruction: America's Unfinished Revolution, 1863–1877* (New York: Harper & Row, 1988), as well as his *Free Soil, Free Labor, Free Men: The Ideology of the Republican Party Before the Civil War* (New York: Oxford University Press, 1970) and *Politics and Ideology in the Age of the Civil War* (New York: Oxford University Press, 1980). Other works that particularly influenced my thinking include Ira Berlin et al., *Slaves No More: Three Essays on Emancipation and the Civil War* (New York: Cambridge University Press, 1992); W. E. B. DuBois, *Black Reconstruction in America, 1860–1880* (New York: Atheneum, 1992 [1935]); Gerald David Jaynes, *Branches Without Roots: Genesis of the Black Working Class in the American South, 1862–1882* (New York: Oxford University Press, 1986); Thomas C. Holt, *The Problem of Freedom: Race, Labor, and Politics in Jamaica and Britain, 1832–1938* (Baltimore: Johns Hopkins University Press, 1992); Leon F. Litwack, *Been in the Storm So Long: The Aftermath of Slavery* (New York: Vintage Books, 1979); David Montgomery, *Beyond Equality: Labor and the Radical Republicans, 1862–1872* (New York: Alfred A. Knopf, 1967); Montgomery, *The American Civil War and the Meanings of Freedom* (New York: Oxford University Press, 1987); and Julie Saville, *The Work of Reconstruction: From Slave to Wage Laborer in South Carolina, 1860–1870* (New York: Cambridge University Press, 1996).

8. The four million figure is taken from Montgomery, *The American Civil War and the Meanings of Freedom,* p. 2.

9. See Stanley P. Hirshson, *Farewell to the Bloody Shirt: Northern Republicans and the Southern Negro, 1877–1893* (Bloomington: Indiana University Press, 1962); J. Morgan Kousser, *The Shaping of Southern Politics: Suffrage Restriction and the Establishment of the One-Party South, 1880–1910* (New Haven, Conn.: Yale University Press, 1974); and C. Vann Woodward, *Origins of the New South, 1877–1913* (Baton Rouge: Louisiana State University Press, 1971 [1951]).

10. Foner, *Reconstruction,* pp. 23–24. See also Stephen Skowronek, *Building a New American State: The Expansion of National Administrative Capacities, 1877–1920* (New York: Cambridge University Press, 1982).

11. As Valelly, for example, argues, while the goal of maintaining the viability of the black vote in the South was shared by many Republicans, it was severely hindered by both the divergent economic interests of their base constituencies in the region and the difficulty of controlling the tidal wave of violent white resistance that swept through the South in reaction to Reconstruction. Richard M. Valelly, "Party, Coercion, and Inclusion: The Two Reconstructions of the South's Electoral Politics," *Politics and Society* 21 (1993): 37–67.

12. This analysis of anticaste liberalism is based upon "Race, Liberalism, and American Political Culture," my Ph.D. dissertation, Department of Political Science, University of Chicago, 1995. Although this interpretation is original to that work, the literature that addresses similar issues is enormous. In particular, legal scholars have, for obvious reasons, devoted extensive attention to the question of the original meaning of the Fourteenth Amendment. For a succinct review of this literature, see William E. Nelson, *The Fourteenth Amendment: From Political Principle to Judicial Doctrine* (Cambridge: Harvard University Press, 1988), pp. 1–7. Of the existing literature, the work of Robert J. Kaczorowski ("Revolutionary Constitutionalism in the Era of the Civil War and Reconstruction," *New York University Law Review* 61 [1986]: 863–940) and Harold M. Hyman and William M. Wieck (*Equal Justice Under Law: Constitutional Development, 1835–1875* [New York: Harper & Row, 1982]) comes closest to the view presented here, as both stress that at least a sizable bloc of Radical Republicans held that the Reconstruction amendments had nationalized the rights of citizenship and given the federal government the power to enforce those rights in both the public and private sectors. In contrast to my analysis, however, both portray this as representing a general commitment to a more robust conception of nationalism and citizenship, rather than tying it to the racially specific concept of caste. Notably, the view represented by these scholars is less influential than that represented by works such as Raoul Berger's *Government by Judiciary: The Transformation of the Fourteenth Amendment* (Cambridge Mass.: Harvard University Press, 1977) and Earl Maltz's "Reconstruction Without Revolution: Republican Civil Rights Theory in the Era of the Fourteenth Amendment," *Houston Law Review* 24 (1987): 221–79, which emphasize that the Republican Party was overwhelmingly committed to the traditional federal structure and a relatively minimalist conception of citizenship rights.

13. The original version of the bill had also prohibited racial segregation in the public schools, as well as in churches and cemeteries. The school clause, in particular, was extremely controversial, however, and was eventually dropped in a crucial compromise measure.

14. The *Civil Rights Cases* of 1883 (109 U.S. 3) declared the key portions of the Civil Rights Act of 1875, which prohibited racial discrimination in public accommodations and transportation, unconstitutional.

15. Hyman and Wieck, *Equal Justice Under Law,* p. 396.

16. Charles Sumner, *The Works of Charles Sumner* (Boston: Lee & Shepard, 1883), XIV:412; Sumner, *Works,* XV:288.

17. Quote of Representative Robert B. Elliott, a black congressman from South Carolina. See U.S. Congress, House and Senate (1873–1874), 43d Cong., 1st sess., *Congressional Record*, vol. 2, pts. 1 and 6: 407.

18. Irving J. Sloan, ed., *American Landmark Legislation* (Dobbs Ferry, N.Y.: Oceana Publications, 1976), I:284.

19. Sloan, *American Landmark Legislation*, I:306–7.

20. Sloan, *American Landmark Legislation*, I:609.

21. *Congressional Record* (1873–74), p. 425.

22. Sloan, *American Landmark Legislation*, I:295.

23. *Congressional Record* (1873–74), p. 3454.

24. *Congressional Record* (1873–74), p. 1874.

25. Stated, once again, by Senator Frelinghuysen; *Congressional Record* (1873–74), p. 3451.

26. See U.S. Congress, House and Senate (1875), 43d Cong., 2nd sess., *Congressional Record*, vol. 3, pts. 2 and 3: 1004.

27. Stated by Representative Richard H. Cain of South Carolina. See *Congressional Record* (1875), p. 957. African-American representatives were first seated in Congress following the enactment of the Fifteenth Amendment in 1870. (Although the first black man to be elected was John Willis Menard in 1868, who represented a district encompassing New Orleans, Louisiana, he was not allowed to take his seat following a governmental decision that it was "too early" to admit a black to Congress. See Annjennette Sophie McFarlin, *Black Congressional Reconstruction Orators and Their Orations, 1869–1879* [Metuchen, N.J.: Scarecrow Press, 1976], p. 177. Between 1870 and 1877, during the 41st to the 44th Congresses, a total of sixteen black men served in Congress, including fourteen in the House and two in the Senate. The height of black representation during this period was reached during the 43d and 44th Congresses, following the elections of 1872 and 1874, which had placed first seven and then eight black men in Congress (for a total of twelve individual congressmen). These Congresses set a record that would not be surpassed until the commencement of the 91st Congress in 1969. See Maurine Christopher, *Black Americans in Congress* (New York: Thomas Y. Crowell, 1976), pp. 309–11.

28. This perspective must be distinguished from the simpler and narrower belief that individual behavior is primarily motivated by economic concerns. Particularly given the context of the times, the argument that the freedpeople would be motivated to work hard in order to make economic gains for themselves and their families inherently had a strong moral as well as egalitarian dimension, in that it countered the widely made claim that they were too lazy to work without coercion and too dissolute to care about respectability. See Foner, *Reconstruction*, pp. 132–33.

29. See Foner, *Reconstruction*, pp. 28–29.

30. Foner, *Reconstruction*, pp. 164–70.

31. The following discussion of the Freedmen's Bureau is based primarily upon Foner, *Reconstruction*, pp. 68–69, 142–70.

32. Thanks to Rogers Smith for pointing out the importance of addressing the significance of the Freedmen's Bureau in the context of anticaste liberalism.

33. Foner, *Reconstruction,* p. 484.

34. Montgomery, *Beyond Equality;* see also DuBois, *Black Reconstruction.*

35. Linda K. Kerber, *Women of the Republic: Intellect and Ideology in Revolutionary America* (Chapel Hill: University of North Carolina Press, 1980).

36. The prioritization of black male suffrage was also greatly aided by the traditional connection between military service and citizenship. See Mary Frances Berry, *Military Necessity and Civil Rights Policy: Black Citizenship and the Constitution, 1861–1868* (Port Washington, N.Y.: Kennikat Press, 1977). (Thanks to Rick Valelly for pointing this out to me, as well as providing the citation.)

37. Foner, *Reconstruction,* pp. 255–56, 447–48, 472–73.

38. Following this split, the mainstream suffragist movement also shifted from arguments based on principles of gender neutrality and equal rights to ones based on more traditional notions of gender difference, claiming that women naturally possessed a superior moral sensibility, which would, if tapped, elevate the quality of political life. See Ellen Carol DuBois, "Outgrowing the Compact of the Fathers," *Journal of American History* 74 (1987): 836–62; see also Nackenoff's essay in this volume.

39. For the descriptions of the voting patterns from which these figures were drawn, see Alfred Avins, "The Civil Rights Act of 1875: Some Reflected Light on the Fourteenth Amendment and Public Accommodations," *Columbia Law Review* 66 (1966): 912, and his "Racial Segregation in Public Accommodations: Some Reflected Light on the Fourteenth Amendment from the Civil Rights Act of 1875," *Western Reserve Law Review* 18 (1967): 1279; see also Sloan, *American Landmark Legislation,* p. 232.

40. William Gillette, *Retreat from Reconstruction, 1869–1879* (Baton Rouge: Louisiana State University Press, 1979), p. 205.

41. Alfred Avins, ed., *The Reconstruction Amendments' Debates* (Richmond: Virginia Commission on Constitutional Government, 1976), p. 642.

42. *Congressional Record* (1873–74), p. 428.

43. U.S. Congress, House and Senate (1872), 42d Cong., 2d sess., *Congressional Globe,* vol. 45, pts. 2 & 6: 218.

44. *Congressional Record* (1875), p. 157.

45. *Congressional Record* (1873–74), p. 428.

46. *Congressional Record* (1873–74), p. 4.

47. *Congressional Record* (1875), p. 984.

48. *Congressional Record* (1875), p. 984.

49. *Congressional Record* (1873–74), p. 4.

50. *Congressional Record* (1873–74), p. 119.

51. *Congressional Record* (1873–74), p. 3.

52. *Congressional Record* (1873–74), p. 4.

53. *Congressional Globe* (1872), p. 370.

54. *Congressional Globe* (1873–74), p. 3.

55. Avins, *The Reconstruction Amendments' Debates,* pp. 624–25.

56. See, for example, Litwack, *Been in the Storm So Long,* pp. 265–66.

57. Paula Giddings, *When and Where I Enter: The Impact of Black Women on Race and Sex in America* (New York: Bantam Books, 1984), p. 63.

58. Such a position placed white nationalists outside of the boundaries of American liberalism as it existed in the postemancipation context, since they flatly refused to accept the constitutional change which had incorporated blacks as citizens. The fact that this ideology was highly prevalent among southern whites during this period demonstrates that liberalism has by no means been a consistently hegemonic presence in American political culture. By the same token, however, phylogenetic liberalism was clearly considered to be a temperate and legitimate position precisely because it did (at least ostensibly) accept the new constitutional framework, in accordance with the fundamental liberal principle of the primacy of the rule of law.

59. Litwack, *Been in the Storm So Long,* p. 260.

60. John A. Carpenter, "Atrocities in the Reconstruction Period," *Journal of Negro History* 47 (1962): 240.

61. Following Ericson and Greenstone, I consider nineteenth-century republicanism to be a variant of American liberalism. While this terminology may be confusing, it is consistent with the literature and helps to differentiate this position from the others examined. See, in general, David Ericson, *The Shaping of American Liberalism: The Debates over Ratification, Nullification, and Slavery* (Chicago: University of Chicago Press, 1993), as well as Greenstone, *The Lincoln Persuasion,* pp. 51–53.

62. Eric Foner, "Rights and the Constitution in Black Life During the Civil War and Reconstruction," *Journal of American History* 74 (1974): 863–83; Foner, "Reconstruction and the Black Political Tradition," in Richard McCormick, ed., *Political Parties and the Modern State* (New Brunswick, N.J.: Rutgers University Press, 1984), pp. 53–69. See also Berlin et al., *Slaves No More,* ch. 2; Litwack, *Been in the Storm So Long;* Montgomery, *The American Civil War and the Meanings of Freedom;* and Saville, *The Work of Reconstruction.*

63. See, for example, Foner, "Rights and the Constitution in Black Life"; Litwack, *Been in the Storm So Long,* pp. 399–408; Montgomery, *The American Civil War and the Meanings of Freedom.*

64. Quote altered to conform to standard English. Cited in Foner, "Rights and the Constitution in Black Life," p. 871.

65. Quoted without alteration from letter reprinted in Berlin et al., "The Terrain of Freedom: The Struggle over the Meaning of Free Labor in the U.S. South," *History Workshop* 22 (1986): 127–28.

66. Quoted in Foner, "Rights and the Constitution in Black Life," p. 871 (modified from this source to conform more closely to standard English).

67. Thomas Holt, *Black over White: Negro Political Leadership in South Carolina During Reconstruction* (Urbana: University of Illinois Press, 1977).

68. Pieter C. Emmer, "The Price of Freedom: The Constraints of Change in Postemancipation America," in Frank McGlynn and Seymour Drescher, eds., *The Meaning of Freedom: Economics, Politics, and Culture After Slavery* (Pittsburgh: University of Pittsburgh Press, 1992), p. 36.

69. This was not uniformly true, as many blacks were involved in the labor movement (despite the fact that white unions continued to exclude them), forming,
for example, the National Colored Labor Union in 1869. While this involvement may have had more of an impact on black republicanism with regard to
class issues than I indicate here, if this was the case, it is not noted in the generally excellent secondary literature on the subject. Consequently, my working
assumption is that it did not.

70. Giddings, *When and Where I Enter,* p. 65. Again, see also Nackenoff's essay in
this volume.

Chapter 7

1. J. David Greenstone, "Dorothea Dix and Jane Addams: From Transcendental-
ism to Pragmatism in American Social Reform," *Social Service Review* 53
(December 1979): 531.

2. Greenstone, "Dorothea Dix and Jane Addams," pp. 529, 532, 534, 536–37;
quote, p. 536.

3. J. David Greenstone, "Political Culture and American Political Development:
Liberty, Union, and the Liberal Bipolarity," *Studies in American Political Development* 1 (1986): 1–49, esp. 9–17.

4. See Rogers M. Smith, "Liberalism and Racism: The Problem of Analyzing
Traditions," pp. 9–27 in this volume.

5. Rogers M. Smith, *Civic Ideals: Conflicting Visions of Citizenship in U.S. History* (New Haven, Conn.: Yale, 1997), pp. 6–7.

6. Richard Slotkin, *Regeneration Through Violence* (Middletown, Conn.: Wesleyan University Press, 1973), p. 22. See also Michael Rogin's discussion in
Ronald Reagan: The Movie (Berkeley: University of California Press, 1987), esp.
chs. 2, 5; Chantal Mouffe, "Democratic Citizenship and the Political Community," in Chantal Mouffe, ed., *Dimensions of Radical Democracy* (New York:
Verso, 1992), p. 234.

7. Judith Shklar, *American Citizenship: The Quest for Inclusion.* (Cambridge,
Mass.: Harvard University Press, 1991), pp. 1, 16–17; Toni Morrison, *Playing
in the Dark* (Cambridge, Mass.: Harvard University Press, 1992), pp. 44–45,
63–65.

8. Carole Pateman, *The Sexual Contract* (Stanford, Calif.: Stanford University
Press, 1988); Shklar, *American Citizenship,* pp. 2–3, 14, 51–52.

9. Carole Pateman, *The Disorder of Women: Democracy, Feminism and Political
Theory* (Stanford, Calif.: Stanford University Press, 1989), p. 185.

10. William E. Connolly, *Identity/Difference: Democratic Negotiations of Political
Paradox* (Ithaca, N.Y.: Cornell University Press, 1991), p. 21.

11. Mary Dietz, "Context Is All: Feminism and Theories of Citizenship," in Chantal Mouffe, ed., *Dimensions of Radical Democracy* (New York: Verso, 1992),
p. 73. Dietz's reference is to a much more recent group of difference feminists.

12. Mary Shanley, quoted in Dietz, "Context Is All," p. 67.

13. Ernesto Laclau and Chantal Mouffe, *Hegemony and Socialist Strategy,* cited in
Kirstie McClure, "On the Subject of Rights: Pluralism, Plurality and Political

Identity," in Chantal Mouffe, ed., *Dimensions of Radical Democracy* (New York: Verso, 1992), p. 122.

14. Mark E. Kann, "Individualism, Civic Virtue, and Gender in America," *Studies in American Political Development* 4 (1990): 46. Kann includes, along with women, young men, of whom military service and self-sacrifice are also expected.

15. See Horton's essay in this volume for a critique of David Greenstone's corrective to Hartz for its failure to adequately conceptualize the individual subject.

16. Jill Conway, "Women Reformers and American Culture, 1870–1930," *Journal of Social History* 5 (Winter 1971/72): 172–73.

17. Jane Addams, *Democracy and Social Ethics,* edited and with an introduction by Anne Firor Scott (Cambridge, Mass.: Belknap Press, 1964 [1902]), p. 221.

18. Charlotte Perkins Gilman, *The Home, Its Work and Influence* (New York: Source Book Press, 1970 [1903]), p. 330.

19. Gilman, *The Home,* p. 330. Anna E. Nicholes, cited in Shailer Mathews, ed., *The Woman Citizen's Library,* vol. 9, *The Larger Citizenship* (Chicago: The Civics Society, 1913), pp. 2148–9; Jane Addams, "Why Women Should Vote" (New York: National American Women's Suffrage Association, 1912), pp. 4–5.

20. Addams, "Why Women Should Vote," p. 2; Nicholes, cited in Mathews, *Woman Citizen's Library,* pp. 2143–4.

21. Addams, *Democracy and Social Ethics,* p. 262.

22. Jessie Taft, *The Woman Movement from the Point of View of Social Consciousness* (Chicago: University of Chicago Press, 1916), p. 49.

23. Taft, *The Woman Movement,* p. 49.

24. Frederick Douglass, "Southern Barbarism," in Philip Foner, ed., *The Life and Writings of Frederick Douglass* (New York: International Publishers, 1955), IV:437.

25. Jane Addams, *Twenty Years at Hull House* (New York: Macmillan, 1925 [1910]), ch. 18; Addams, *Democracy and Social Ethics,* p. 86.

26. Conway, "Women Reformers," pp. 171, 166–67.

27. Rosalind Rosenberg, "In Search of Woman's Nature," *Feminist Studies* 3 (Fall 1975): 142; Conway, "Women Reformers," pp. 169, 171.

28. See Addams, *Democracy and Social Ethics;* U.S. suffrage cartoons, Sophia Smith Collection, Smith College, Northampton, Mass.

29. "To the Male Citizen: If This Is Womanly—Why Not This?" suffrage cartoon, Sophia Smith Collection.

30. Addams, "Why Women Should Vote," p. 19. Conway claims that men were "discarded as irrelevant in the planning of Hull House and other women's settlements because they were thought of as 'less Christian' in spirit than women and motivated to action almost entirely by commercial rewards." See Conway, "Women Reformers," p. 171.

31. "For a good job of a clean sweep *SHE can't be beat,*" suffrage cartoon, Sophia Smith Collection.

32. Jane Addams, "The Modern City and the Municipal Franchise for Women," (1906), pp. 2, 4 (quote p. 2); Jane Addams, "Women and Public Housekeeping" (1910?), p. 1. Both these essays are in the Schlesinger Library History of Women microfilm collection.

33. Addams, "The Modern City," pp. 1, 4–5; Addams, "Women and Public Housekeeping," p. 2.
34. Addams, "Why Women Should Vote," p. 14.
35. Addams, "Women and Public Housekeeping," p. 2; Addams, "The Modern City," p. 5; Addams, "Philanthropy and Politics," p. 2130.
36. Addams, "Philanthropy and Politics," pp. 2124–5; Addams, "Why Women Should Vote," p. 18.
37. Addams, "Philanthropy and Politics," pp. 2137.
38. Addams, "Why Women Should Vote," p. 1; Retha Childe Door, *What Eighty Million Woman Want,* quoted in Paula Baker, "The Domestication of Politics: Women and American Political Society, 1780–1920," *American Historical Review* 85 (June 1984): 632.
39. Addams, "The Modern City," p. 8; Addams, "Why Women Should Vote," pp. 3, 8, 14; Addams, "Philanthropy and Politics," pp. 2129, 2131–5, 2139, and passim.
40. Addams, "Philanthropy and Politics," p. 2140.
41. Addams, "Philanthropy and Politics," pp. 2129, 2141.
42. Addams, "Why Women Should Vote," p. 15; Addams, *Democracy and Social Ethics,* pp. 4, 9–10. See also Anne Firor Scott, introduction to *Democracy and Social Ethics,* p. xxvi.
43. Addams, *Democracy and Social Ethics,* pp. 2–3.
44. Eileen Boris, "The Power of Motherhood: Black and White Activist Women Redefine the 'Political,'" in Seth Koven and Sonya Michel, eds., *Mothers of a New World: Maternalist Politics and the Origins of Welfare States* (New York: Routledge, 1993), pp. 213–14.
45. Adella Hunt Logan, "Colored Women as Voters," *The Crisis* 4 (September 1912): 243, 242.
46. Adella Hunt Logan, "Woman Suffrage," *The Colored American Magazine* 9 (September, 1905): 488.
47. Adella Hunt Logan, "Colored Women as Voters," p. 242; Kathryn Kish Sklar, "The Historical Foundations of Women's Power in the Creation of the American Welfare State, 1830–1930," in Seth Koven and Sonya Michel, eds., *Mothers of a New World* (New York: Routledge, 1993), p. 72.
48. Rosenberg, "In Search of Woman's Nature," p. 142.
49. Rosenberg, "In Search of Woman's Nature," pp. 142–43.
50. "The Political Companions of Women," suffrage cartoon, Sophia Smith Collection.
51. Conway, "Women Reformers," pp. 171–72.
52. Lester Ward, "Genius and Woman's Intuition," *Forum* (June 1890), pp. 401–2. Ward dismissed extended claims for woman's instinctual powers. He contended that intuition is subjective and egoistic and that its loudest demand is for individual existence. He also contended that intuition is associated with the coarser bodily wants and is far removed from a concentration of mental faculties upon ideals and the abstract (p. 405).
53. Thomas, "On a Difference in the Metabolism of the Sexes," quoted in Rosenberg, "In Search of Woman's Nature," p. 144.

54. Conway, "Women Reformers," p. 172; Mark Seltzer, "The Naturalist Machine," in *Sex, Politics, and Science in the Nineteenth Century Novel* (Baltimore: Johns Hopkins University Press, 1986), p. 135 (quoting Geddes and Thomson, *Evolution of Sex).*

55. "The European Situation," suffrage cartoon, Sophia Smith Collection.

56. Scott, introduction to *Democracy and Social Ethics,* p. lxiv. Addams was instrumental in forming the Women's International League for Peace and Freedom and served as president until her death. African-American leader Mary Church Terrell was another member of the Woman's Peace Party.

57. Rosenberg, "In Search of Woman's Nature," p. 144 (citing Jane Addams, *Newer Ideals of Peace,* and quoting Carrie Chapman Catt, "Evolution and Woman's Suffrage," a speech delivered 18 May 1893).

58. Charlotte Perkins Gilman, *Herland* (New York: Pantheon, 1979 [1915]).

59. Rosenberg, "In Search of Woman's Nature," p. 145 (citing Charlotte Perkins Gilman, *The Man-Made World, or Our Androcentric Culture and Women and Economics.)*

60. See Gilman, *The Home;* Rosenberg, "In Search of Woman's Nature," p. 146.

61. Jane Addams, "The Larger Aspects of the Woman's Movement," *Annals of the American Academy of Political and Social Science* 14 (November 1914): 2.

62. Addams, "Why Women Should Vote," p. 12.

63. Addams, *Democracy and Social Ethics,* pp. 5, 9.

64. Addams, *Democracy and Social Ethics,* pp. 93, 175, and passim.

65. Scott, introduction to *Democracy and Social Ethics, p.* xlvii. Addams, *Democracy and Social Ethics,* esp. ch. 2 ("Charitable Effort"); quotes pp. 5, 274 (referencing an unnamed recent lecturer).

66. Addams, *Democracy and Social Ethics,* pp. 8, 9, 68–69.

67. Addams, *Democracy and Social Ethics,* p. 11; Theda Skocpol, *Protecting Soldiers and Mothers: The Political Origins of Social Policy in the United States* (Cambridge, Mass.: Harvard University Press, 1992), p. 345.

68. Addams, *Democracy and Social Ethics,* p. 274.

69. Addams, *Democracy and Social Ethics,* pp. 7, 176.

70. Addams, *Democracy and Social Ethics,* pp. 176–77.

71. Addams, *Democracy and Social Ethics,* pp. 7, 8, 9, 68–69.

72. Addams, "Philanthropy and Politics," p. 2138.

73. Addams, "If Men Were Seeking the Franchise," *Ladies' Home Journal* 30 (June 1913): 21.

74. Addams, *Democracy and Social Ethics,* pp. 166, 167.

75. Logan, "Colored Women as Voters," p. 243.

76. Addams, *Democracy and Social Ethics,* pp. 268–69.

77. Greenstone, "Dorothea Dix and Jane Addams," pp. 553, 535. Addams encouraged the study of Royce at Hull House.

78. J. S. Mill, *Utilitarianism,* in *Essential Works of John Stuart Mill,* edited with an introduction by Max Lerner (New York: Bantam, 1961), pp. 217–18.

79. Walter Lippmann, *A Preface to Politics* (Ann Arbor: University of Michigan Press, 1962 [1914]), pp. 67–68, 70–71.

80. Walter Lippmann, *A Preface to Politics,* pp. 68–69.

81. Walter Lippmann, *Drift and Mastery* (New York: M. Kennerley, 1914), pp. 217, 215–16, 224.

82. Taft, *The Woman Movement*, pp. 42, 48, 50–52; quotes pp. 51, 52.

83. Taft, *The Woman Movement*, p. 51. Emphasis added.

84. Taft, *The Woman Movement*, pp. 56–57.

85. Taft, *The Woman Movement*, pp. 56, 53, 57, 45–46.

86. Among these academics were University of Chicago–trained psychologist Helen Thompson (Woolley), author of *Psychological Norms in Men and Women* (1903), and University of Chicago sociologist William I. Thomas, whose social-biological views had moderated over time. See Rosenberg, "In Search of Woman's Nature," pp. 146, 147; p. 150 (citing Elsie Clews Parsons, *Fear and Conventionality* and *Social Rule.*)

87. See Rosenberg, "In Search of Woman's Nature," p. 152 (on Parsons and Thomas).

88. Conway, "Women Reformers," pp. 167–69, 174.

89. Sklar, "Historical Foundations of Women's Power," pp. 58 (citing Mary O. Furner, *Advocacy and Objectivity*), 59.

90. Sklar, "Historical Foundations of Women's Power," pp. 59–60, 65–67.

91. Greenstone, "Dorothea Dix and Jane Addams," pp. 546–47, 553; quote p. 548.

92. Greenstone, "Dorothea Dix and Jane Addams," pp. 544–45.

93. Greenstone, "Dorothea Dix and Jane Addams," pp. 550–51.

94. Greenstone, "Dorothea Dix and Jane Addams," pp. 552–53.

95. Greenstone, "Dorothea Dix and Jane Addams," p. 552 (citing Addams's *Twenty Years at Hull House*, ch. 8).

96. Addams, *Democracy and Social Ethics*, pp. 222–23.

97. Addams, *Democracy and Social Ethics*, pp. 3, 247 (on the campaign to unseat the local alderman).

98. Addams, *Democracy and Social Ethics*, p. 223.

99. Addams, *Democracy and Social Ethics*, pp. 224, 225–26, 240.

100. Addams, *Democracy and Social Ethics*, p. 240.

101. Addams, *Democracy and Social Ethics*, pp. 268, 226–27.

102. Addams, *Democracy and Social Ethics*, pp. 233, 244, 250, 260.

103. Addams, *Democracy and Social Ethics*, pp. 224–25; quote p. 224.

104. Greenstone, "Dorothea Dix and Jane Addams," p. 552.

105. Addams, *Democracy and Social Ethics*, quotes pp. 229, 227.

106. Addams, *Democracy and Social Ethics*, pp. 137–38.

107. Addams, *Democracy and Social Ethics*, pp. 147, 149, 143, 144, 214, 158–59.

108. Greenstone, "Dorothea Dix and Jane Addams," pp. 540–41.

109. Addams, *Democracy and Social Ethics*, pp. 154–55.

110. Greenstone, "Dorothea Dix and Jane Addams," p. 540; Addams, *Democracy and Social Ethics*, pp. 144–46.

111. Addams, *Democracy and Social Ethics*, pp. 212–13.

112. Addams, *Democracy and Social Ethics*, pp. 213–14.

113. Greenstone, "Dorothea Dix and Jane Addams," p. 543, 540; Jane Addams, *The Second Twenty Years at Hull House* (New York: Macmillian, 1930), ch. 2. The Debs vote cited in Greenstone, "Dorothea Dix and Jane Addams," p. 540.

114. Addams, *Democracy and Social Ethics*, pp. 263–64, 256.

115. Mark E. Kann, "Individualism, Civic Virtue, and Gender in America," p. 80.

116. Skocpol, *Protecting Soldiers and Mothers,* pp. 354, 318.

117. Sklar, "Historical Foundations of Women's Power," pp. 44–45.

118. Skocpol, *Protecting Soldiers and Mothers,* p. 318.

119. Letters and columns in the *Women's Tribune,* the weekly vehicle of NAWSA. On discussion topics at the Chicago Women's Club in the early 1880s, see Sklar, "Historical Foundation of Women's Power," pp. 63–64.

120. Sklar, "Historical Foundations of Women's Power," pp. 68–69.

121. Skocpol, *Protecting Soldiers and Mothers,* pp. 355, 318.

122. Sklar, "Historical Foundations of Women's Power," p. 68.

123. Skocpol, *Protecting Soldiers and Mothers,* pp. 372, 368, 319, 354, 363.

124. Woodrow Wilson, "Inaugural Address" (4 March 1913), in *Inaugural Addresses of the Presidents of the United States: From George Washington 1789 to Lyndon Baines Johnson 1965* (Washington, D.C.: United States Government Printing Office, 1965, pp. 200–2.

125. Wilson, "Inaugural Address" (4 March 1913), pp. 200–2; Wilson, "Inaugural Address" (4 March 1917), p. 203.

126. Warren G. Harding, "Inaugural Address," (4 March 1921), p. 212.

127. Harding, "Inaugural Address" (4 March 1921), p. 213; Calvin Coolidge, "Inaugural Address" (4 March 1925), p. 223.

128. Skocpol, *Protecting Soldiers and Mothers,* p. 319.

129. Mouffe, "Democratic Citizenship and the Political Community," p. 230.

130. Louise Michele Newman, *Laying Claim to Difference: Ideologies of Race and Gender in the U.S. Woman's Movement, 1870–1920,* Ph.D. dissertation, Department of History, Brown University (Ann Arbor, Mich: University Microfilms International, 1992), p. 78.

131. Peggy Pascoe, *Relations of Rescue: The Search for Female Authority in the American West, 1874–1939* (New York: Oxford University Press, 1990); Newman, *Laying Claim to Difference,* p. 110. Alice Fletcher and Frances Willard saw their movements as embodying attempts to rescue and liberate nonwhite women.

132. Skocpol, *Protecting Soldiers and Mothers,* p. 344.

133. Sklar, "Historical Foundations of Women's Power," p. 58.

134. Shklar, *American Citizenship,* p. 22.

135. Aileen S. Kraditor, *Ideas of the Woman Suffrage Movement, 1890–1920* (New York: Columbia University Press, 1965), pp. 126–27.

136. Charlotte Perkins Gilman, "A Suggestion on the Negro Problem," *American Journal of Sociology* l (July 1908): 78–85. The quoted phrase is hers.

137. Skocpol, *Protecting Soldiers and Mothers,* pp. 372, 368, 319, 354, 363.

138. Confronted with the need to confront racial stereotypes and assert their own worthiness in society and polity, African-American women activists were generally less concerned than was Addams with learning from their poorer brothers and sisters. These women sought to lift the poor while setting the values and standards to be met. See Boris, "Power of Motherhood," p. 222.

139. Conway, "Women Reformers," pp. 166–67.

140. Harding, "Inaugural Address" (4 March 1921), p. 213.

141. Barbara Hobson, "Feminist Strategies and Gendered Discourses in Welfare States: Married Women's Right to Work in the United States and Sweden," in

Seth Koven and Sonya Michel, eds., *Mothers of a New World* (New York: Routledge, 1993), pp. 396–429.

142. "Men whose loyalty to a party was questionable were referred to…as the 'third
sex' of American politics, 'man-milliners,' and 'Miss-Nancys.'" See Paula Baker,
"Domestication of Politics," p. 623, n. 27.

143. Hannah Pitkin, *Wittgenstein and Justice: On the Significance of Ludwig
Wittgenstein for Social and Political Thought* (Berkeley: University of California Press, 1972), p. 208.

Chapter 8

I would like to express my appreciation to the James Monroe Professorship
Research Fund and the Ronald E. McNair Post-Baccalaureate Program, Oberlin College, for financial support. I am indebted to McNair Fellow Susan Den-
nehy and research assistants Sara Marcus and Steve Manthe, who ably assisted
at various stages of this project, and to the editors of this volume for their very
helpful suggestions.

1. J. David Greenstone, "Against Simplicity: The Cultural Dimensions of the Constitution," *University of Chicago Law Review* 55 (1988): 428–29. Whether one
considers Greenstone's work on labor, in *Labor in American Politics* (Chicago:
University of Chicago Press, 1969), or on the political power of the poor in
cities, in *Race and Authority in Urban Politics* (New York: Russell Sage Foundation, 1973; coauthored with Paul E. Peterson), or on the historical foundations of liberalism, in *The Lincoln Persuasion: Remaking American Liberalism*
(Princeton, N.J.: Princeton University Press, 1993), or on the underclass, in
"Culture, Rationality, and the Underclass," in Christopher Jencks and Paul E.
Peterson, eds., *The Urban Underclass* (Washington: Brookings Institution,
1991), his scholarship has always considered whether the American political tradition could sustain the important task of incorporating the weak and less
advantaged into our nation's political, social, and economic system. Also,
Greenstone's scholarship is about understanding (and at times furthering) the
transformative potential of our nation in a way that is true to important constitutional values, even when such values were denied in the short run by those
who call themselves progressive. This project—my search to understand the
constitutive nature of Supreme Court decision making, my rejection of instrumental assumptions about Supreme Court decision making, and my search to
explore constitutional theories that can help in the (re)definition of the rights of
subordinated groups—is testimony to Greenstone's vision as a scholar and as
a person. I see in the many wonderful scholarly projects that are reported in this
volume additional testimonies to Greenstone.

2. Greenstone, "Against Simplicity," p. 431.
3. Greenstone, "Against Simplicity," p. 435.
4. Greenstone, "Against Simplicity," p. 428.
5. Greenstone, "Against Simplicity," p. 430.
6. Greenstone, "Against Simplicity," p. 431.

7. Greenstone, "Against Simplicity," p. 431.

8. Greenstone, "Against Simplicity," pp. 431–32.

9. Greenstone, "Against Simplicity," p. 432.

10. Greenstone, "Against Simplicity," p. 432.

11. Greenstone, "Against Simplicity," p. 434.

12. Greenstone, "Against Simplicity," p. 435.

13. Greenstone, "Against Simplicity," p. 435. At this point, I note that the problems that Greenstone has identified for scholars and practitioners who subscribe to either the doctrinal approach or its radical critique can also be found to an even greater degree among scholars who use the attitudinal or rational-choice approach. Attitudinalists assume that the law is simply the result of the policy wants of judges, while rational-choice scholars assume that law and constitutional choices are simply the result of the strategic desires of legal actors. Both approaches to Supreme Court decision making assume a static, consensual model of liberal and legal values that Greenstone so persuasively argues against.

14. Greenstone, "Against Simplicity," p. 436.

15. Greenstone, "Against Simplicity," p. 436.

16. Greenstone, "Against Simplicity," p. 437.

17. See Stephen Skowronek, *The Politics Presidents Make: Leadership from John Adams to Bill Clinton* (Cambridge, Mass.: Harvard University Press, 1997), p. 29, for a superb study of how presidents differ in the degree to which they engage in "order-shattering, order-affirming, and order-creating impulses of presidential action." In part, this book is about how presidents seek to be successful but are limited in their success by the ways of acting developed during prior regimes and the willingness of the public to rethink these precepts.

18. Greenstone, "Against Simplicity," p. 437.

19. We shall leave that task to colleagues such as Rogers Smith and others in collateral essays in this volume.

20. See Ronald Kahn, *The Supreme Court and Constitutional Theory, 1953–1993* (Lawrence: University Press of Kansas, 1994), p. 70.

21. See Kahn, *Supreme Court and Constitutional Theory,* chs. 3, 6.

22. See Ira Katznelson, "Situated Rationality: A Preface to J. David Greenstone's Reading of V. O. Key's *Responsible Electorate*," in this volume, for an argument against instrumental notions of rationality in "mainstream" political science.

23. Greenstone, "Against Simplicity," p. 428.

24. See Jeffrey A. Segal and Harold J. Spaeth, *The Supreme Court and the Attitudinal Model* (New York: Cambridge University Press, 1993), for the most sophisticated presentation of the attitudinal approach.

25. See Lee Epstein and Jack Knight, *The Choices Justices Make* (Washington, D.C.: Congressional Quarterly Press, 1997), for an important new statement of this approach.

26. See Robert Dahl, "Decision-making in a Democracy: The Supreme Court as a National Policy-maker," *Journal of Public Law* 6 (1957): 279–95, and the many scholars who accept Dahl's instrumental vision of justices as policy makers.

27. See Gerald Rosenberg, *The Hollow Hope: Can Courts Bring About Social Change?* (Chicago: University of Chicago Press, 1991).

28. See Mark Graber, "The Non-Majoritarian Difficulty: Legislative Deference to the Judiciary," *Studies in American Political Development* 7 (1993): 35–73.
29. By the term "social facts," I mean social, economic, and political facts about the real world; the social, economic, and political structural facts of life that inform the life chances of citizens and groups. Social facts can be seen at two levels—*social facts, writ small,* and *social facts, writ large.* Social facts writ small are simply social, economic, and political facts. They center on facts simply as facts, as parts of arguments. Social facts writ small have very little transformative potential. Social, economic, and political facts embedded in theories or landmark cases, or social facts writ large, interact with social, economic, and political facts writ small in cases before the Supreme Court and become embedded as part of precedents. One way to overcome the problems in the use of social facts writ small that have been identified by Howard Gillman, Michael McCann, William Haltom, and other political scientists in Ronald Kahn, ed., [Symposium On] "Social Facts, Constitutional Theory, and Doctrinal Change," *Law and Courts* 5 (Summer 1995): 3–15, is to take seriously the constitutive nature of Supreme Court decision making and the dialectical nature of doctrinal change. Social facts, defined instrumentally as social facts writ small, are incompatible with how the process of constitutive decision making occurs, for their use violates key elements of the rule of law, in which the legitimacy of court choices is a central objective. We must look at the role of social facts in constitutional decision making with a conscious regard for the process through which law gains its moral force by means of the juxtaposition of the conflicting values of our nonstatic liberal political culture. See Ronald Kahn, "Precedential Social Facts and the Rights of Subordinated Groups in Post-Pluralist America" (paper delivered at the 1998 annual meeting of the American Political Science Association, Boston, Massachusetts, 4 September 1998), for a comparison of the place of social facts writ large, or what I there call "precedential social facts," in the development of constitutional law in the areas of affirmative action and capital punishment. Social facts writ large are at the core of "pictures in precedents," which are explored more fully in the sixth section of this essay. See also Ronald Kahn, "Bringing the Outside World into Supreme Court Decision-making: Changing 'Social Facts' and Doctrinal Change," in Howard Gillman and Cornell W. Clayton, eds., *The Supreme Court and American Politics: New Institutionalist Approaches* (Lawrence: University Press of Kansas, 1999), for a discussion of how Supreme Court justices' beliefs about social reality inform the development of constitutional doctrine.
30. *Lochner v. New York,* 198 U.S. 45, at 49 (1905).
31. *Lochner v. New York,* 198 U.S. 50.
32. *West Coast Hotel v. Parrish,* 300 U.S. 379, at 399 (1937).
33. Ironically, Robert Dahl, and Cass Sunstein in *The Partial Constitution* (Cambridge, Mass.: Harvard University Press, 1993) both rely on an interest group model of liberalism, though viewing it from quite different perspectives. Rogers Smith talks about the limits of a consensual and interest group model of liberalism in "Liberalism and Racism: The Problem of Analyzing Traditions," in this volume, and in the recently published *Civic Ideals: Conflicting Visions of Citizenship in U.S. History* (New Haven, Conn.: Yale University Press, 1997).

34. See John Hart Ely, *Democracy and Distrust: A Theory of Judicial Review* (Cambridge, Mass.: Harvard University Press, 1980). Ely's vision of pluralist democracy was accepted as a given by many scholars, even though his vision of the political system and Constitution is problematic. It harbors the problems of a static view of political culture that are not too different from those Greenstone found in the doctrinal approach and its radical critique.

35. See Frank Michelman, "The Supreme Court 1985 Term, Forward: Traces of Self Government," *Harvard Law Review* 100 (1986): 4–77. See also Bruce Ackerman, *We the People 1: Foundations* (Cambridge, Mass.: Harvard University Press, 1991) and *We the People 2: Transformations* (Cambridge, Mass.: Harvard University Press, 1998).

36. Even theoretically informed statements of practicing constitutional law, no matter how insightful, as seen in Laurence Tribe, *Constitutional Choices* (Cambridge, Mass.: Harvard University Press, 1985), cannot provide the moral force for a transformative constitutional theory.

37. Greenstone, "Against Simplicity," p. 439.

38. Greenstone, "Against Simplicity," p. 442.

39. Greenstone, "Against Simplicity," p. 443.

40. Greenstone, "Against Simplicity," p. 444.

41. Greenstone, "Against Simplicity," pp. 444–45.

42. *Plyler v. Doe,* 457 U.S. 202 (1982).

43. Greenstone, "Against Simplicity," p. 447.

44. Greenstone, "Against Simplicity," p. 447.

45. For example, see Laurence Tribe, "The Puzzling Persistence of Process-Based Constitutional Theory," *Yale Law Journal* 80 (1980): 1063.

46. See Ronald Kahn, *The Supreme Court and Constitutional Theory,* pp. 211–49, for the argument that constitutional theories built upon civic republican values are a poor guide to understanding Supreme Court decision making. There, I argue for a more complex ideational basis for making constitutional choices.

47. Cf. Karen Orren and Stephen Skowronek, "In Search of Political Development," in this volume, for an argument against the transformative potential and analytic usefulness of the concepts of political culture and liberalism for understanding American political development. The Green, Horton, and Smith essays, at least in part, take divergent views of the matter.

48. See *Planned Parenthood of Southeastern Pennsylvania v. Casey,* 505 U.S. 833 (1992), *Bowers v. Hardwick,* 478 U.S. 186 (1986), and *Romer v. Evans,* 116 S. Ct. 1620 (1996).

49. See Kahn, *The Supreme Court and Constitutional Theory,* pp. 145–47, 156–58, for a fuller discussion of this point.

50. I note that the recent budget agreement suggests that even Republican conservatives have or will listen to reform liberal values and accept them as part of our political culture.

51. *Lee v. Weisman,* 505 U.S. 577 (1992). See Ronald Kahn, "God Save Us from the Coercion Test: Constitutive Decision-making, Polity Principles, and Religious Freedom," *Case Western Reserve Law Review* 43 (Spring 1993): 983–1020.

52. *San Antonio Independent School District v. Rodriguez,* 411 U.S. 1, at 55 (1973).

53. *Craig v. Boren*, 429 U.S. 190, at 208, note 22 (1976).
54. *Planned Parenthood of Southeastern Pennsylvania v. Casey*, 505 U.S. 833 (1992).
55. *Romer v. Evans*, 116 S. Ct. 1620 (1996).

C h a p t e r   9

1, V. O. Key, *The Responsible Electorate: Rationality in Presidential Voting, 1936–1960* (Cambridge, Mass.: Harvard University Press, 1966). I presented a first verbal cut at this paper at the Workshop in American Politics at the University of Chicago in May 1996 and the first written draft at the Conference on the Liberal Tradition in American Politics, also at the University of Chicago, in November 1996. For their questions and comments, I particularly want to thank Joseph Cropsey, Michael Dawson, Uday Mehta, Norman Nie, John Padgett, Lloyd Rudolph, Rogers Smith, Sue Stokes, Steven Walt, and the editors of this volume.

2. Greenstone's citation reads: "We are trying to get hold of the mental process of understanding which seems to be hidden behind those coarser and therefore more readily visible accompaniments. But...even supposing I had found something that happened in all those cases...why should *it* be the understanding? And how can the process of understanding be hidden, when I said 'now I understand' *because* I understood! And if I say it is hidden—then how do I know what I have to look for? I am in a muddle" (Ludwig Wittgenstein, *Philosophical Investigations* [New York: Macmillan, 1958], I, par. 153). Over the years, Greenstone gave me much of what he was writing to read in draft. He presented me with this paper when it was finished with the unusual flourish of an announcement that he had really figured something out that had been worrying him for some time. The unwillingness of the *American Political Science Review* to publish this article was one of his keenest professional disappointments.

3. J. David Greenstone, *Labor in American Politics* (New York: Knopf, 1969); J. David Greenstone and Paul E. Peterson, *Race and Authority in Urban Politics: Community Participation in the War on Poverty* (New York: Russell Sage Foundation, 1973); J. David Greenstone, "Group Theories," in Fred I. Greenstein and Nelson Polsby, eds., *Handbook of Political Science* (Reading, Mass.: Addison-Wesley, 1975).

4. J. David Greenstone, *The Lincoln Persuasion: Remaking American Liberalism* (Princeton, N.J.: Princeton University Press, 1993), pp. 36–48.

5. Ralf Dahrendorf, *Class and Class Conflict in Industrial Society* (Stanford, Calif.: Stanford University Press, 1959).

6. Greenstone and Peterson, *Race*, p. 52.

7. The page numbers inserted in the text refer to the 1977 APSA annual meeting draft. I do not know if there was another, subsequent version.

8. Philip F. Converse, "Public Opinion and Voting Behavior," in Fred I. Greenstein and Nelson Polsby, eds., *Handbook of Political Science* (Reading, Mass.: Addison-Wesley, 1975); Michael Margolis, "From Confusion to Confusion: Issues

and the American Voter (1956–1972)," *American Political Science Review* 71 (1977): 31–43. It was the publication of Margolis's paper that impelled Greenstone to write his convention paper during the course of the late spring and summer of 1977.

9. Margolis, "Confusion," p. 32. His reference, of course, was to Angus Campbell, Philip Converse, Warren Miller, and Donald Stokes, *The American Voter* (New York: John Wiley, 1960).

10. Margolis, "Confusion," p. 32.

11. Margolis, "Confusion," p. 42.

12. The pioneer work, of course, was Anthony Downs, *An Economic Theory of Democracy* (New York: Harper & Row, 1957).

13. Gilbert Ryle, *The Concept of Mind* (New York: Barnes and Noble, 1949).

14. John Dewey, "The Logic of Judgments and Practice" (1915) and "Ethical Subject Matter and Language" (1945) in Amelie Rorty, ed., *Pragmatic Philosophy: An Anthology* (New York: Doubleday Anchor, 1966); Charles Sanders Peirce, *The Collected Papers of Charles Sanders Peirce* (Cambridge, Mass.: Harvard University Press, 1934).

15. When the number of switchers grows dramatically, "critical elections" ensue. See V. O. Key Jr., "A Theory of Critical Elections," *Journal of Politics* 17 (1955): 3–18.

16. Key, *Responsible,* p. 10.

17. Converse, "Public Opinion," pp. 119, 125; cited in Greenstone, "Situated Rationality," p. 28.

18. Philip Converse, "The Nature of Belief Systems in Mass Publics," in David Apter, ed., *Ideology and Discontent* (Glencoe, N.Y.: Free Press, 1964), p. 227; cited in Greenstone, "Situated Rationality," p. 28.

19. Wittgenstein, *Philosophical Investigations,* I, par. 151; cited in Greenstone, "Situated Rationality," p. 10.

20. Herbert A. Simon, "Human Nature in Politics: The Dialogue with Psychology in Political Science," *American Political Science Review* 79 (1985): 294. The discussion that follows draws on this essay, which first was presented as the James Madison Lecture at the annual meeting of the American Political Science Association in 1984. See also his "Rational Decision Making in Business Organizations," *American Economic Review* 69 (1979): 493–513; *Models of Thought* (New Haven, Conn.: Yale University Press, 1979); and *Models of Bounded Rationality* (Cambridge, Mass.: MIT Press, 1982).

C o n c l u s i o n

1. It certainly appeared to be immaterial to Hartz, which was probably the reason he spent so little time defining liberalism. As we proceed, we can, at any point, usefully separate his thesis into two separate questions: (1) Did consensus exist? (2) If so, was it a liberal consensus? I would also insist that the "failure" of historical actors themselves to use the term *liberal* or *liberalism* to refer to their own political principles is a red herring. Compare Smith's essay on this point.

2. Obviously, this formulation leaves open a number of judgment calls, such as how many is most and how similar is similar.

3. This formulation also begs several questions, such as how to assess historical significance or intellectual profundity.

4. Many other scholars have, of course, contributed to building these cases; it would be pointless (and potentially embarrassing) to try to list them all here.

5. Unfortunately, we are all more likely to look at what fits our point of view rather than at what does not fit, and we tend most often to interpret objects of study as fitting rather than as not fitting.

6. See David Brion Davis, *The Problem of Slavery in Western Culture* (Ithaca, N.Y.: Cornell University Press, 1966), chs. 13–14; *The Problem of Slavery in the Age of Revolution* (Ithaca, N.Y.: Cornell University Press, 1975), ch. 1. See also Winthrop D. Jordan, *White over Black: American Attitudes Toward the Negro* (Chapel Hill: University of North Carolina Press, 1968), ch. 7; Duncan J. Macleod, *Slavery, Race and the American Revolution* (Cambridge: Cambridge University Press, 1974), ch. 1; Duncan Rice, *The Rise and Fall of Black Slavery* (New York: Harper & Row, 1975), ch. 5.

7. This point also raises important questions about the relation between political principles and practices, which I will discuss shortly.

8. See esp. Michael Kammen, "The Problem of American Exceptionalism: A Reconsideration," *American Quarterly* 45 (1993): 1–43.

9. See esp. Orlando Patterson, *Slavery as Social Death: A Comparative Study* (Cambridge, Mass.: Harvard University Press, 1982). See also Seymour Drescher, "The Long Goodbye: Dutch Capitalism and Antislavery in Comparative Perspective," *American Historical Review* 99 (1994): 44–69; Stanley M. Elkins, *Slavery: A Problem in American Institutional and Intellectual Life* (New York: Grosset & Dunlap, 1963 [1959]), pp. 52–80; Laura Foner and Eugene D. Genovese, eds., *Slavery in the New World: A Reader in Comparative History* (Englewood Cliffs, N.J.: Prentice-Hall, 1969); George M. Fredrickson, *Black Liberation: A Comparative History of Black Ideologies in the United States and South Africa* (New York: Oxford University Press, 1995); Eugene D. Genovese, *The World the Slaveholders Made: Two Essays in Interpretation* (New York: Pantheon, 1969), ch. 2; Herbert S. Klein, *Slavery in the Americas: A Comparative Study of Virginia and Cuba* (Chicago: University of Chicago Press, 1967); Martin Klein, *Breaking the Chains: Slavery, Bondage, and Emancipation in Modern Africa and Asia* (Madison: University of Wisconsin Press, 1993); Peter Kolchin, "Some Recent Works on Slavery Outside the United States: An American Perspective," *Comparative Studies in Society and History* 28 (1986): 767–77; Frank Tannenbaum, *Slave and Citizen: The Negro in the Americas* (New York: Vintage, 1963 [1947]); Robin W. Winks, ed., *Slavery: A Comparative Perspective* (New York: New York University Press, 1972); C. Vann Woodward, "Protestant Slavery in a Catholic World," in *Slavery and Racism in the North/South Dialogue* (New York: Oxford University Press, 1971), pp. 47–77.

10. See Louis B. Hartz, *The Liberal Tradition in America: An Interpretation of American Political Thought Since the Revolution* (New York: Harcourt, Brace, 1955), pp. 4, 28; *The Founding of New Societies: Studies in the History of the*

United States, Latin America, South Africa, Canada, and Australia (New York: Harcourt, Brace, 1964).

11. Reiterating what we all know: Comparativists dismiss Americanists who "dabble" in comparative research, and vice versa; coauthored books do not count proportionately to single-author books; securing funding for cross-national studies itself requires a lot of time, effort, and, in many cases, money.

12. On one hand, the more independent variables we use, the more variance in the phenomenon we explain. On the other hand, the more independent variables we use, the "messier" our explanation of the phenomenon becomes and the less we may actually contribute to understanding it. Cf. Hartz, *Liberal Tradition*, p. 21; Rogers M. Smith, "Beyond Tocqueville, Myrdal, and Hartz: The Multiple Traditions in America," *American Political Science Review* 87 (1993): 550; Rogers M. Smith, *Civic Ideals: Conflicting Visions of Citizenship in U.S. History* (New Haven, Conn.: Yale University Press, 1997), p. 39.

13. Political traditions could then also function as dependent variables as long as we keep in mind that they are, at least partially, constructs and as long as we are open to the possibility that historical actors also affected the traditions that affected them. See esp. J. G. A. Pocock, *Virtue, Commerce, and History: Essays on Political Thought and History* (Cambridge: Cambridge University Press, 1985), ch. 1.

14. Again, compare Smith's essay on these points.

15. In this, Greenstone was, of course, adapting Wittgenstein's "ordinary language" philosophy to the study of American politics. See J. David Greenstone, *The Lincoln Persuasion: Remaking American Liberalism* (Princeton, N.J.: Princeton University Press, 1993), pp. 47, 49, 62–63; Ludwig Wittgenstein, *Philosophical Investigations* (New York: Macmillan, 1953), pp. 11, 88, 226.

Contributors

David F. Ericson is an associate professor of political science at Wichita State University.

Louisa Bertch Green works in the development department at the Columbus Museum of Art and is a doctoral candidate in political science at the University of Chicago.

Carol Horton is an economic development consultant based in Chicago and has taught at Macalester College.

Ronald Kahn is the James Monroe Professor of Politics and Law at Oberlin College.

Ira Katznelson is the Ruggles Professor of Political Science at Columbia University.

Gayle McKeen is an assistant professor of political science at the University of the South.

Carol Nackenoff is an associate professor and chair of the political science department at Swarthmore College.

Karen Orren is a professor of political science at the University of California at Los Angeles.

Stephen Skowronek is a professor of political science at Yale University.

Rogers M. Smith is an associate professor of political science at Yale University.

Index

Access; *see also* Representation
  best use, 56, 60–64
  as criteria to measure what is
    public, 54–55
  generality, 56, 57–59
Accountability, as criteria to measure
  what is public, 56
Addams, Jane, 5, 137, 141
  experience as social scientific
    inquiry, 151, 156–61
  "liberal politics of standards," 137
  vs. alderman system, 143, 157–58
Affirmative action policies, 61, 62, 171

Bailyn, B., 1
Beard, Charles, 1
Blackstone, William, 85
Blackwell, Antoinette Brown, 148
Bledsoe, Albert, 72
Bork, Robert, 173
Boutwell, Senator George, 120–21
Brigham, Carl Campbell, 17
Buckley, William F., 12
Buckner, Aylett Hanes, 127, 128
Burke, Edmund, 12, 84
Bush, George, 168

Calhoun, John C., 19, 71, 77–78
Catt, Carrie Chapman, 149
Citizenship, 4–5, 21; *see also*
    Reconstructionist era citizenship
  different visions, 139–42, 161–63
  interdependence vs. autonomy,
    142–52
  and the social ethic, 152–56, 162
Civil Rights Act of 1875, 119, 126
Class
  and African-American political
    opinion, 134

not a social category for Radical
    Republicans, 123–24
  and phylogenetic liberalism, 131
  and the Populist movement, 135
Clay, Henry, 74
Consent
  and racial slavery, 72–73
  virtual or direct, 50–51
Consequentialist proslavery
    arguments, 69, 73–76
  "maximum-liberty" argument,
    75–76
  "positive-good" argument, 73–74,
    82–88
Constitutional theory
  defining equal protection, 171
  doctrinal view and radical critique,
    173–75, 177–78
  instrumental liberalism, 178–79
Constitutive liberalism, 5, 172,
    179–80, 182–83
Contextualist proslavery arguments,
    69, 76–78
Courts
  and redefining rights of
    subordinated groups, 171–72,
    183–85, 188–90, 191, 196–97
  and resonance of decision making,
    180–82, 193–97
Croly, Herbert, 12
Cyclical historical view, 1

Darwin, Charles, 17
  Darwinism and feminism, 148,
    150, 155
Declaration of Independence, and the
    proslavery movement, 70–71
Democratization
  and inclusiveness, 60–64

process vs. thing, 46–48
slow pace, 3, 43, 66
Deontological proslavery arguments,
    69, 70–73
  biblical argument, 70
Development
  as a core concept, 3, 32
  displacement phase, 38–39
  rearrangement phase, 39–40
  vs. liberalism as study focus, 29
Dew, Thomas R., 19, 69, 95
  antiabolitionist, 78–79
  "necessary evil" argument, 79–82
  "positive good" argument, 82–88
Dewey, John, 15, 16, 55, 57, 156–57,
    203
Discursive pluralism, 2
Douglass, Frederick, 4, 20, 101–8
  alliance with suffragists, 112, 143
  praise of John Brown, 105
  "race problem" solutions, 105–6
  self-belonging, 104–5
  speech defining humanity, 101–2
DuBois, W. E. B., 4, 20, 45, 101,
    108–13
  context and liberty, 108, 111
  and experiences of African-
      American women, 112–13
  and Marxism, 114
  race prejudice and the "veil"
      metaphor, 108–9, 110

Edwards, Jonathan, 23
Eldredge, Charles A., 128
Ely, John Hart, 184, 185
Enlightenment rationalism, 22, 24, 25
Equality
  not as a principal belief in American
      political foundations, 45–46, 65
  "social" vs. "legal," 129–30
Ericson, David, 19–20, 21, 44
Federal government, to combat racial
    discrimination, 119, 122
Feminists
  and the American welfare state, 5
  and the house-cleaner government
      image, 144–46

and labor, 155, 159–60
  maternalist trap, 165
  maternalist vision, 141
  and the Progressive vision, 161
  and settlement house social
      scientists, 156
  and the vision of African-American
      women, 146–47, 167
"Fit" within time periods concept,
    33–34
  and incongruity, 35–36
Fitzhugh, George, 69, 96
  proslavery as protective institution
      argument, 88–93
  proslavery as a southern institution,
      93–97
Freedmen's Bureau, 122–23, 133
Frelinghuysen, Senator Frederick, 121

Garfield, James, 121
Garrison abolitionists, 67, 101
Geddes, Patrick, 149
Gender
  and anticaste conceptions during
      Reconstruction, 124–125
  and citizenship concepts, 135, 138,
      168
  and citizenship visions, 139–42
  superfeminization of white and
      defeminization of black women,
      130–31
Genovese, Eugene, 67
Gilman, Charlotte Perkins, 142, 150
Glover, John M., 128
Goodin, Robert, 63
Grant, Madison, 17
Greenberg, Kenneth, 68
Greenstone, J. David, 6, 19, 27, 44,
    199
  concept of rationality, 200–1, 205,
      207
  founding period principles, 44
  liberal bipolarity, 1, 52, 65, 99,
      106, 107, 136
  liberalism as a "boundary
      condition," 115, 138, 182
  political language analysis, 1

and problem of culture and
development, 32
vision of the Constitution, 173,
175–76, 185–88

Hammond, James Henry, 72, 73, 77
Hardin, Russell, 66
Harding, Warren G., 163, 167
Harper, Chancellor, 75, 77
Hartz, Louis, 1, 9, 12, 199
liberal consensus, 19, 24, 30–31,
44, 68, 100, 211–13
"liberal tradition," 14–15
theory problems with racism and
sexism issues, 19
Held, David, 113
Herrnstein, Richard J., 17
Historical-institutionalists, 36
Hobhouse, L.T., 15
Hoover, Herbert, 16
Howard, General O.O., 133
Howe, Daniel Walker, 106
Hull House, 156–58
Humanist liberalism, 1, 19, 172, 177,
186–87, 189, 191–92
Humboldt, Wilhelm von, 15
Huntington, Samuel, 32

Institutional learning, 36–37

Jefferson, Thomas, 15, 22, 26, 44
election as a "revolution," 30
and racial inequality, 18, 24, 71, 73,
74, 83
Jim Crow laws, 20, 24, 140

Kelley, Florence, 156
Key, V. O., 6, 200–4
significance to Greenstone, 205–9
Kohl, Lawrence, 106
Korematsu decision, 17

Laissez-faire policies, 15, 134, 153
of Radical Republicans, 122
Laski, Harold, 15
"Liberal consensus"; *see* Hartz, Louis
Liberal oscillationism theory, 40

Liberalism; *see also* Constitutive
liberalism; Development;
Humanist liberalism; Reform
liberalism
as a boundary condition, 115
as a convenient label, 10
importance of analysis of term
users, 13
and "new liberalism," 15–16
stable principles and changing
exclusions, 47
vs. racial and gender politics, 116
vulnerability of advances to
reversals, 32, 34
Liberty, 98
Lincoln, Abraham, 24, 98, 100
Lind, Michael, 12, 18
Lippmann, Walter, 153
Lochner v. *New York*, 181, 193
"Lock-in" concept, 36–37
Logan, Adella Hunt, 147

McConnell, Grant, 199–200, 201
McDuffie, George, 70, 75, 77
McHenry, Henry D., 127
MacIntyre, Alasdair, 11, 14
Madison, James, 15, 23
Mann, Horace, 65
Marshall, T.H., 162, 192
Marx, Eleanor, 162
Mill, John Stuart, 15, 16, 153
Morton, Dr. Samuel George, 102
Murphy, Justice Frank, 17
Murray, Charles, 17

National American Women Suffrage
Association (NAWSA), 147, 162,
166
Nicholes, Anna, 143
Nott, Josiah, 17, 19

Oakes, James, 68

Paine, Tom, 23, 25
Parsons, Elsie Clews, 155
"Path dependence" concept, 36–37
Patriarchy, and liberal theory, 21

Phyler v. *Doe*, 187, 189, 194, 195
Pocock, J.G.A., 1, 12
Political culture, as diverse social
    movements, 31, 33
Political participation, 60
Pratt, Senator Daniel D., 120
Progressive era
    and challenge to citizenship vision,
        140–41
    progressivism, 16
    stress on interdependence, 142
Progressives, historians and cyclical
    view, 1
Proslavery movement, 69, 78–88; *see
    also* Consequentialist proslavery
    arguments; Contextualist
    proslavery arguments;
    Deontological proslavery
    arguments
    consensus framework explanation,
        68
    and the Declaration of
        Independence, 70–71
    defense attempts as a liberal
        institution, 69
    feudal and paternalistic tendencies,
        67–68
Protestantism, and multiple political
    traditions, 23–24
"Public" as an analytically reviewed
    concept, 3, 48, 51–53, 58
Purman, William J., 120

Racism, 17
    and Hartz's liberal tradition, 2, 15
    more than an American slavery
        issue, 20
    and phylogenetic liberals, 126–27
Rational-choice theory, 53
Rawls, John, 16
    veil of ignorance device, 51
Reagan, Ronald, 168
Reciprocity, as criterion to measure
    what is public, 55–56
Reconstructionist era citizenship,
    116–17
    anticaste liberalism, 118–25

black republicanism, 132–36
    and humanist universalism, 120,
        121
    importance of land redistribution to
        the black public, 133–34
    phylogenic liberalism, 125–32
    Radical Republicans, 121, 124, 125
Reform liberalism, 1, 19, 172, 177,
    187–90, 191–92
Regime theory, 33–36
    vs. political development, 39
Representation
    as a matter of "best use," 61–64
    as the political form of access,
        48–50
    proportional, 49
    token, 49
    virtual, 64
Republican vs. liberal tradition of
    ideas, 1, 115–16, 176–77, 186,
    190
Rights, individual vs. equal, 50
Royce, Josiah, 153
Rush, Benjamin, 24
Rushton, J. Philippe, 17

Schattschneider, E. E., 36
Scientific naturalism, 178
Shain, Barry, 23
Situatied rationality, and American
    politics, 6
Skocpol, Theda, 33
Slavery, and liberalism, 4
Smith, J. Ambler, 127
Smith, Rogers
    and comparative egalitarianism, 45
    "isms" as human constructions, 2,
        11
    multiple traditions, 32, 44, 47, 65,
        68, 99–100, 114, 115–16, 136,
        138
Social ethic; *see* Citizenship
Socialism, marginalization of, 18, 20
Spencer, Herbert, 15
    and sex role differentiation, 148
Strong, Josiah, 26
Sunstein, Cass, 184

Taft, Jessie, 143, 154–55
Thomson, J. Arthur, 149
Tocqueville, A. de, 15, 44, 114, 199
Traditions
  in American history and politics,
    7–8, 27, 44–45
  double construction, 9–14
Trumball, Senator Lyman, 126
Truth, Sojourner, 135

Veblen, Thorstein, 140
Voter rationality theory, 201–2
  and switchers, 204

Wald, Lillian, 144

Ward, Lester, 148
Washington, Booker T., 109
Webb, Beatrice, 162
Wechsler, Herbert, 173
Welfare state; *see also* Feminists
  dependency in the narrative
    structure, 165
  dismantlement efforts, 41, 168
Wilson, Senator Henry, 120
Woman's Peace Party, 149
Wood, Gordon, 1

X., Malcolm, 9